DICKENS STUDIES ANNUAL
Essays on Victorian Fiction

DICKENS STUDIES ANNUAL

Essays on Victorian Fiction

EDITORS

Stanley Friedman
Edward Guiliano
Michael Timko

DICKENS STUDIES ANNUAL

Essays on Victorian Fiction

VOLUME
27

Edited by
Stanley Friedman, Edward Guiliano, and Michael Timko

AMS PRESS
NEW YORK

DICKENS STUDIES ANNUAL
ISSN 0084-9812

Dickens Studies Annual: Essays on Victorian Fiction is published in cooperation with Queens College and the Graduate Center, CUNY.

International Standard Book Number
Series: 0-404-18520-7
Vol. 27:0-404-18547-9

Dickens Studies Annual: Essays on Victorian Fiction welcomes essay and monograph-length contributions on Dickens as well as other Victorian novelists and on the history of aesthetics of Victorian fiction. All manuscripts should be double-spaced, including notes, which should be grouped at the end of the submission, and should be prepared according to the format used in this journal, which follows *The MLA Manual of Style.* An editorial decision can usually be reached more quickly if two copies are submitted. The preferred editions for citations from Dickens's works are the Clarendon and the Norton Critical when available, otherwise the Oxford Illustrated or the Penguin.

Please send submissions to the Editors, *Dickens Studies Annual,* Room 1522, Graduate School and University Center, City University of New York, 33 West 42nd Street, New York, N.Y. 10036; pleas send subscription inquiries to AMS Press, Inc., 56 East 13th Street, New York, N.Y. 10003.

Manufactured in the United States of America

Contents

List of Illustrations

Preface

As editors of *Dickens Studies Annual: Essays on Victorian Fiction,* we are always mindful that our foremost obligation is to Dickens himself and the other literary artists to whose writings and lives our pages are devoted. Next, we acknowledge our dependence on the scholars and critics who submit their manuscripts for our consideration. The novelists often were rewarded with fame and at least some financial compensation, while our contributors may at times gain professional prestige or academic advancement. But we are also deeply indebted to another group of benefactors whom we regard as performing *pro bono* work: the readers who generously donate their time and expertise to assessing submissions and frequently offer extremely valuable suggestions for strengthening these essays. Those who accept our invitations to evaluate manuscripts help us in our efforts to be receptive to extremely diverse—even conflicting—approaches. We are grateful for this essential assistance.

This volume contains a particularly extensive review essay, for which we thank Professor Trey Philpotts.

We also express our deep gratitude to the following administrators for making available to us financial and other resources: President Frances Degen Horowitz, Provost Geoffrey Marshall, PhD Program in English Executive Officer William P. Kelly, and Linda Sherwin, Assistant Program Officer, PhD Program in English, all of The Graduate School and University Center, CUNY; President Allen Lee Sessoms, Provost John A. Thorpe, Dean Raymond F. Erickson, and Department of English Chair Steven F. Kruger, all of Queens College, CUNY; and President Matthew Schure of New York Institute of Technology.

We acknowledge with pleasure the steady support and encouragement of Gabriel Hornstein, President of AMS Press. In addition we thank Jack Hopper, our resourceful and dependable editor at AMS Press, and we convey our appreciation to Trevor Packer, our energetic and efficient editorial assistant for this volume.

Notes on Contributors

H. M. DALESKI is Professor Emeritus of English at The Hebrew University, Jerusalem. He has published six works of criticism, including books on D. H. Lawrence, Charles Dickens, Joseph Conrad, and recently, Thomas Hardy.

SCOTT DRANSFIELD teaches English at Waynesburg College where he specializes in Victorian literature and culture. His recent work focuses on constructions of "social pathologies" in the writings of Charles Dickens, Thomas Carlyle, and Elizabeth Gaskell. He has also published work on the travels of Sir Richard Burton.

MARTINE HENNARD DUTHEIL holds an M.A. from the University of Sussex and a PhD from the University of Lausanne (Faculty Prize 1997). She has published articles on Defoe, Dickens, Nabokov, and Rushdie. She is currently working on postcolonial rewritings of *Robinson Crusoe.*

KENNETH J. FIELDING is Emeritus Professor of English Literature at the University of Edinburgh. He is joint senior editor of the Duke-Edinburgh edition of the *Carlyle Letters,* has edited Charles Dickens's *Letters,* and published critical books or essays mainly on Dickens and Carlyle.

PAULINE FELTCHER is Professor of English at Bucknell University and General Editor of the *Bucknell Review.* She is the author of *Gardens and Grim Ravines: The Language of Landscape in Victorian Poetry* (1983), and has published essays on Victorian and South African literature.

JOHN P. FRAZEE is currently Dean of the School of Arts and Professor of English at Adams State College in Colorado. He has previously published articles on Dickens and Orwell as well as Thackeray.

DAVID GARLOCK is an adjunct Assistant Professor in the Department of Modern Languages and Comparative Literature at Baruch College, the City University of New York. He is currently working on a book entitled "The Darwinian World of Thomas Hardy."

TATIANA M. HOLWAY is writing her dissertation on "Dickens and the Victorian Economic Imagination" at Columbia University.

MARY LENARD has taught at the University of Texas at Austin, Alma College, and the University of Wisconsin at Parkside, where she has pursued her interests in Victorian studies, women's literature, and computer-assisted teaching in the humanities. She has just completed *Preaching Pity: Sentimentality and Social Reform in Victorian Culture,* a book that investigates how the feminization of nineteenth-century reform discourse affected the work of major writers like Dickens and Gaskell.

DEBRA MORRIS received her PhD in English from the Pennsylvania State University. She is currently a lecturer in English at Louisiana State University.

TREY PHILPOTTS is an Assistant Professor of English at Arkansas Tech University. He is the Review Editor for *Dickens Quarterly* and has published several articles on Dickens. He is currently in the final stages of work on the *Companion to Little Dorrit.*

DAVID ROSEN is pursuing a doctorate in modern and Romantic poetry at Yale University.

ELIZABETH DALE SAMET, Assistant Professor of English at the United States Military Academy, earned her PhD from Yale University. She is currently working on a book about authority, allegiance, and competing models of military heroism in America from 1775 to 1865.

TIMOTHY A. SPURGIN is Associate Professor of English at Lawrence University in Appleton, Wisconsin. In addition to teaching courses on nineteenth-century British literature, he currently serves as Director of Freshman Studies, a multidisciplinary program for first-year students. His interests include the history and theory of biography, as well as the novels of Dickens.

KENNETH M. SROKA is Professor of English at Canisius College, Buffalo, New York, where he teaches courses in nineteenth-century literature, including a course on Dickens's novels. He has published essays on *Oliver Twist, Barnaby Rudge, David Copperfield, Our Mutual Friend,* and is currently completing a study of *The Old Curiousity Shop.*

ROBERT TRACY, Professor of English and of Celtic Studies at the University of California, Berkeley, is the author of *Trollope's Later Novels* (1978), *The*

Unappeasable Host: Studies in Irish Identities (1978), has edited Trollope's *The Way We Live Now* (1974), *The Macdermots of Ballycloran* (1989), and *Nina Balatka* and *Linda Tressel* (1991) and has translated *Kamen'* (as *Stone*) from the Russian of Osip Mendelstam.

Bacchus in Kersey: Dickens and the Classics

Pauline Fletcher

"The novel is by nature an anti-classical art form," writes Richard Jenkyns in his fine study of the Victorian obsession with ancient Greece (112); and, one might add, the novels of Dickens are most particularly anti-classical in form. Indeed, Jenkyns has little to say about Dickens and the classics, concentrating instead on George Eliot who surpasses all other novelists "in fervency of enthusiasm for the ancient world" (113). Dickens did not share that enthusiasm; nor did he have a tenth part of George Eliot's learning and formidable command of languages, both ancient and modern. What he did share with her was the sense of not belonging to that exclusive club of university-bred English gentlemen whose knowledge of Greek could be assumed. Nevertheless, a close reading of Dickens's novels reveals a surprising number of classical allusions. Such allusions most often constitute what Bakhtin describes as a "comic-parodic reprocessing" (301) of the language of a particular stratum of society, thus providing a "point where centrifugal as well as centripetal forces are brought to bear" (272). I take it for granted that discourse containing classical references would normally be considered the language of the dominant and official culture, and would therefore be one of the linguistic "forces that unite and centralize verbal-ideological thought" (271). A parodic inversion of such discourse would therefore tend towards decentralization. However, as I hope to show, Dickens's use of classical material changes and develops as his art matures and, perhaps more significantly, as his relationship to the dominant culture evolves. The tension between centrifugal and centripetal forces described by Bakhtin may reflect not merely the heteroglossia of the novel, but also the conflicts and tensions of the novelist. I shall try to demonstrate these tensions through an examination of Dickens's use of classical allusions, including references to mythological and historical figures, in several novels. Dickens's use of Latinate

Dickens Studies Annual, Volume 27, Copyright © 1998 by AMS Press, Inc. All rights reserved.

language, which would certainly be part of the discourse of the dominant culture, is a related topic, but it has received sufficient attention from other critics.[1] I shall therefore limit my analysis to examples of discourse that contain classical allusions, but before doing so it may be useful to examine a little more critically Dickens's attitude towards a classical education.

In general such an education is not held up as an ideal in his novels. Indeed, in *Dombey and Son* it is the subject of heavy satire. We are told that Miss Blimber "was dry and sandy with working in the graves of deceased languages" which she digs up "like a Ghoul" (143); at Doctor Blimber's every "description of Greek and Latin vegetable was got off the driest twigs of boys, under the frostiest circumstances" (141), and the effect of this education is to make the boys bitter and to reduce all literature to grammar (143). In his next novel, *David Copperfield,* Dickens does adopt a more favorable attitude towards a classical education, presenting Dr. Strong and his Academy in a very favorable light. The Academy offers a classical curriculum and the Doctor is "a serious scholar and lexicographer" (Jenkyns 112). But just how seriously are we expected to take Dr. Strong's work as a lexicographer? We are given a comic view through David, who supposes Dr. Strong's interest in Greek roots "to be a botanical furor on [his] part" (205). The joke is not simply on David. Even more significant, perhaps, is the fact that we know that Dr. Strong's dictionary, like Mr. Dick's Memorial, will never be completed. Dr. Strong and Mr. Dick are deliberately paired off in the novel, two unworldly eccentrics whose moral sweetness is unquestioned, but whose life's work may be, in Dickens's view, of comparable worth to humanity. And the Doctor has paid for his classical learning: he is "rusty," and has "a lustreless eye" that reminds David of "a long-forgotten blind old horse who once used to . . . tumble over the graves" (196). As with Miss Blimber, classical learning and graves go together. Even David, as he becomes "great in Latin verses" (230) neglects the laces of his boots and is brought up short by a few blows from a vigorous and extremely proletarian young butcher. David's proficiency in Latin verses is a useless gentlemanly accomplishment. He has to teach himself shorthand to earn a living, and his later success as a novelist owes nothing to Greek roots or Latin verbs.

But Dickens remains ambivalent. Classical learning may be both useless and deadening, but it is still the mark of a gentleman, and Dickens was to send his own sons to Eton. He himself had won "a prize for Latin proficiency" at the Wellington House Academy (Kaplan 45). In later years, however, he was to describe the school as "a pernicious and abominable humbug"; its proprietor was "by far the most ignorant man I have ever had the pleasure to know" and "one of the worst-tempered men perhaps that ever lived" (Collins, *Dickens and Education* 12). The proprietor was immortalized as Mr. Creakle, who terrorized the boys of Salem House in *David Copperfield,* and Collins quotes

Matthew Arnold as saying that "Mr. Creakles's school . . . is the type of our ordinary middle class schools" (13).[2] Dickens may have despised Wellington House, but he seems to have been proud of his achievements in Latin, transferring that pride to David Copperfield, whose ability to "decline a Latin noun or adjective, or to conjugate a Latin verb" in the pawnbroker's ear (*Copperfield* 146), saves his self-esteem and ensures that he is still "the little gent" even during the harsh Murdstone and Grinby days (144). David later plays the gentleman towards Uriah Heep, offering to teach him Latin. Uriah refuses, "umbly" but also shrewdly, because there "are people enough to tread on me in my lowly state, without my doing outrage to their feelings by possessing learning. Learning ain't for me" (220).[3] The narrator's attitude here is delicately ambiguous. David comes across as patronizing, Uriah as grovelling, but as Simon Edwards has shown, Uriah's story closely parallels David's for much of the novel, and he may be seen as the hero's dark shadowself. To own classical learning as a birthright was one thing, but for a Charles Dickens or a Uriah Heep to parade or even attempt to attain classical learning was a dangerous mark of presumption. David Copperfield always knew that he was "really" a gentleman; Dickens was not so sure about himself.

In short, Dickens seems to have desired classical learning while simultaneously dismissing it as useless, even destructive. This was an attitude shared, in part at least, by George Eliot. She desired a classical education for herself and took great pains to acquire it, but the classics are wasted on Tom Tulliver and Fred Vincy, both of whom have to unlearn their expensive education and devote themselves to a more practical training. Many of George Eliot's lower- and middle-class characters also share her ambivalence. Knowledge of the classics undoubtedly confers status, but self-made men like Mr. Deane regard Latin as "a luxury much run upon by the higher classes, and not telling at all on the ship-owning department" (*Mill on the Floss* 213). A number of utilitarians and radicals also distrusted classical learning, but from a more informed perspective than Mr. Deane's. Herbert Spencer championed the Moderns against the Ancients and "evinced a particular dislike, almost a hatred, of anything Greek" (Jenkyns 277). The commissioners of an Inquiry into Grammar Schools (1868) reported that parents resented the time spent on the classics because they "were keen on money-making and pressed for a short, utilitarian education" (Jenkyns 278). The ranks of the anti-classicists were also joined by more thoughtful men like Huxley, who wanted more emphasis on the teaching of science, and by many non-conformists, who regarded ancient pagan literature as dangerously immoral. Dickens revealed his own dislike of utilitarian education and the new emphasis on science in *Hard Times,* but, as we have seen, he also had his reservations about the ancient languages. In part this is the typical attitude of the outsider, who affects contempt for the club that has excluded him. We would expect such an attitude in someone of Dickens's social background, although Pam Morris perhaps overstates the case when she claims that he "experienced the contradictions inherent in interpellation of margin to centre in extreme form: intense desire for narcissistic identification with social images of success and respectability, fused with a deep fear of personal lack, in turn stimulating an alienated, hostile perspective. on the object of desire" (10). In many of his novels Dickens did indeed take an outsider's revenge on the classics, although his hostility is almost always modified by humor or playful irreverence.

In *The Pickwick Papers,* for example, the comparatively few classical references are all satirical. Classical allusions in the mouth of Jingle, chief villain and con-man, are used to indicate his pretensions to gentility, but at the same time they do mark him as a man of some imagination, a poet who has, he claims, written an epic on the July Revolution: "Mars by day, Apollo by night,—bang the field-piece, twang the lyre" (11). Jingle is a word-smith, someone who, as his name suggests, plays with the small change of language; his telegraphic speech patterns, mental agility, and cryptic allusions leave the honest Pickwickians far behind:

> "I should be very happy to lend you a change of apparel for the purpose," said Mr Tracy Tupman, "but you are rather slim, and I am—"
> "Rather fat—grown up Bacchus—cut the leaves—dismounted from the tub, and adopted kersey, eh?—not double distilled, but double milled—ha! ha! pass the wine." (16)

Jingle may be a villain, but he gives Dickens the opportunity to allow his own imagination to work on a simple allusion to Bacchus, now transformed into a portly Victorian gentleman in a suit of kersey. It is not clear what the tub might be, but I suggest the following possibilities: a tub for the treading of grapes; a wine-press; the tub-shaped chariot of Bacchus; a confusion with the tub of Diogenes, here blending with Dionysus. It really doesn't matter whether it is all or none of the above; Dickens, through Jingle, is having irreverent fun with the classics, enjoying what Garrett Stewart aptly terms "the sheer verbal gymnastics of words on vacation from the chore of meaning" (14). Moreover, he demonstrates that the dry and dusty classical learning of Dr. Blimber can be transformed through the superior gifts of the rank outsider, Jingle/Dickens, into high-spirited carnival. Jingle's use of classical allusions simultaneously parodies upper-class speech and acts as a rebuke to the dull-witted, middle-class literalism of Mr. Tracy Tupman. As a speech act it is flagrantly narcissistic and non-communicative, denying any pretence of "orientation toward the listener" and his "specific conceptual horizon" (Bakhtin 282). Though Jingle refuses to enter into a dialogic relationship with Mr. Tracy Tupman, a listener outside the text is implied: the educated reader. But Jingle does not speak as one gentleman to another; he enters the dialogue as a guerrilla fighter and "breaks through the alien conceptual horizon of the listener, constructs his own utterance on alien territory, against his, the listener's, apperceptive background" (Bakhtin 282). In appropriating the classics in order to subvert them, Dickens, through Jingle, participates in what Bakhtin calls the "decentralizing, centrifugal forces" that shaped novelistic form; Jingle gives us the "heteroglossia of the clown . . . ridiculing all 'languages' and dialects," speaking from a place where there is "no language-center at all, where there [is] to be found a lively play with the 'languages' of poets, scholars, . . . where all 'languages' [are] masks and where no language [can] claim to be an authentic, incontestable face" (273). At the same time, Jingle is a parody of the "gentleman" who might use classical allusions to define his status and also as linguistic terrorism directed at his "inferiors." One might compare this to Henry Fielding's condemnation of Cenodoxus, who "talks of the classics before the Ladies; and of *Greek* Criticisms among fine Gentlemen. What is this less than an Insult on the Company, over whom he thus affects a Superiority, and whose time he sacrifices to his Vanity?" (*Essay* 143). The important difference is that whereas Cenodoxus may be a boor, his social status is not in question. Jingle's origins, on the other hand are murky; he is not presented as a member of the upper classes who is merely behaving badly, but rather as the outsider whose clever mimicry is itself a mockery of gentlemanly arrogance.

A more morally attractive version of the con-man may be found in Dick Swiveller of *The Old Curiosity Shop*. He too is a "poet," given to spontaneous rhyming couplets, and he too has classical connections. He is described as the "Perpetual Grand Master of the Glorious Apollers," a "convivial circle" (103). His appropriation of the classics may be comical, but it is not pretentious. Dick Swiveller lays no claim to gentility. He is a man of imagination, transforming Greek gods into drinking companions, just as he transforms a poor kitchen maid into a Marchioness and cheap gin and water into rosy wine. Dickens had a soft spot for such clever con-men, allowing both Jingle and Swiveller to be redeemed in the end.

But while quasi-poets may be redeemed, those who are merely pompous are ridiculed. In *Pickwick*, Dickens enjoys poking fun at the inflated rhetoric of small-town orators; thus, the "little man" of Dingley Dell:

> "Every gentleman who hears me, is probably acquainted with the reply made by an individual, who—to use an ordinary figure of speech—'hung out' in a tub, to the emperor Alexander:—'If I were not Diogenes,' said he, 'I would be Alexander.' I can well imagine these gentlemen to say, 'If I were not Dumkins I would be Luffey.' " (94)

In his opening phrase the speaker makes a direct claim to be speaking to "gentlemen," and by implication claims that status for himself. His speech presumably excludes those who are not gentlemen, and who will therefore not really "hear" him; nor will they understand the references to Diogenes' tub, and indeed the qualifier "probably" indicates a further principle of exclusion: not all "gentlemen" will be acquainted with the reply of Diogenes. The "little man" further exalts himself by the chummy condescension of his "ordinary figure of speech—'hung out' in a tub." All this culminates deliciously in the banality of Dumkins and Luffey.

Small-town pretension is also satirized in the person of Mrs. Leo Hunter of Eatanswill, who has set up as a collector of celebrities. She invites Pickwick and his friends to a fancy-dress-breakfast, where she appears as Minerva. Mrs. Pott, carrying a lyre and wearing "a white satin gown with gold spangles," (196) represents Apollo, and "was heard to chirp, faintly forth, something which courtesy interpreted into a song, which was all very classical" (204). In such examples of the satirical usage of classical allusion, Dickens is working very much in the tradition of Fielding, who undermines the pretensions of those who "have robbed classical tradition of its meaning by separating its form from its content, thus reminding readers who could evaluate their flawed quotations that the classical tradition was often meaningless in the modern world" (Mace 85). However, it must be stressed that the classics are much more peripheral to Dickens than they were to Fielding. Dickens lacked the depth of classical education that Fielding had acquired at Eton and Leyden University; Fielding might indeed have regarded "his work as a continuation of the classical tradition begun by Homer and continued by Aristotle, Cicero, Virgil, and Horace" (Mace 127). No such claim could be made for Dickens, nor would he have made it for himself.

Satire in *Pickwick* remains fairly good-humored; we are merely asked to laugh at the Dingley Dellers and at Mrs. Pott in gold spangles as Apollo. But when we move on to *Martin Chuzzlewit* the satire becomes more vicious. Dickens sees America as a land of false rhetoric and posturing, and we are not expected to find Mrs. Hominy, the objectionable American literary lady, amusing. Mrs. Hominy, wears a "classical cap," is referred to as "the mother of the modern Gracchi," and carries herself with "a stateliness of deportment" which is "quite the Last Scene from Coriolanus" (541–42). Dickens's satire has darkened and we have passed from a festive parody of the Greek pantheon to a world of Roman militarism and politics, with Mrs. Hominy as Volumnia prepared to sacrifice all human feeling to the blind patriotism that Dickens found so distasteful in America. A similar ideological message is buried in the ironic name, Cicero, of the ex-slave who is befriended by Mark Tapley. We know that Dickens was disgusted by American slavery, and the name acts as a reminder of what America, land of Liberty, the republic of Dicken's own idealistic imagination, should have been. Stewart sees the name as totally inappropriate and bestowed by those "who are slaves to their own rhetoric'' (17). This may be so, but the irony seems to me to be double-edged. Given Mark Tapley's positive reaction to Cicero, the slave might be seen as the only true philosopher in this society. However, his philosophy is expressed not through inflated pseudo-classical rhetoric, but through what he has suffered, to which the marks on his body bear silent testimony. He apparently tells Mark Tapley his story, but the text contains only his silence. In the land of false rhetoric, the true philosopher withholds speech.

A common characteristic of all the examples I have discussed so far is that the classical references come through the words or actions of the characters. Even the satirical ''quite the Last Scene from Coriolanus'' is attributed to a ''shrill boy'' (548) in the audience and is not given to us as an authorial comment. Dickens seems to want, in these earlier novels, to hold himself aloof from the classicizing tendency that he satirizes as a part of lower-class or provincial attempts to attain ''gentlemanly'' status. Nor does he allow the characters for whom he wants our approval to mouth classicisms. Pickwick himself does compare the idyllic countryside to the city, where there is ''nothing redolent of Pan but pan-tiles'' (82), but this is a private thought and Pickwick never uses classical allusions in order to impress others with his learning. And only once in *Pickwick* does the narrator risk a classical allusion, telling us that Mr Pickwick ''sprang like an ardent warrior from his tent-bedstead'' (82). On one level this is, of course, a piece of comic deflation, with Pickwick as Achilles, but the comparison does not work to Pickwick's disadvantage, largely because he would have no thought of projecting himself as a Greek hero. His naive honesty remains untouched by the reference, which works on the positive side to project the energy and innocent enthusiasm with which he confronts the freshness of country sights and sounds in the early morning. Moreover, there is a level on which Pickwick, like a latter-day Don Quixote, really is a warrior on the side of virtue and innocent romance.

Dickens as narrator uses another Homeric reference in *Martin Chuzzlewit*, but this one is less kindly though it too describes a character's wakening moments:

> It was morning; and the beautiful Aurora, of whom so much hath been written, said, and sung, did, with her rosy fingers, nip and tweak Miss Pecksniff's nose. It was the frolicsome custom of the Goddess, in her intercourse with the fair Cherry, so to do; or in more prosaic phrase, the tip of that feature in the sweet girl's countenance was always very red at breakfast-time.   (85)

For Homer the rosy fingers of Dawn always bring freshness and beauty, but the Pecksniff world denies such qualities and the goddess is as mean-spirited as the misnamed Charity herself. Dickens here is taking pains to make the classical reference work hard as satire; indeed, one might say that the satire and the sarcasm of such phrases as ''sweet girl'' are rather too obvious and heavy-handed. Dickens as narrator is not quite sure enough of himself to toss off a classical reference casually, as a "gentleman" might, although, as we have seen, he does allow his clever tricksters and pseudo-gentlemen, like Jingle, to use the classics more subtly and imaginatively.

After finishing *Martin Chuzzlewit,* Dickens decided to take an extended holiday. In July of 1844 he set off in high spirits, with a large entourage of family and servants, for a year in Italy. A by-product of this year must have been an enhanced sense of his own social status. With the blacking-warehouse days far behind him, and even partly exorcized by the writing of *David Copperfield,* Dickens now embarked on the equivalent of the Grand Tour. He purchased a "Magnificent Carriage" (Kaplan 170), travelled in style, rented various Italian palaces, and generally lived like an English milord. Before leaving he drew up an inventory of the books in his library, which included translations of Ovid, Plutarch, and Greek tragedies, but almost nothing else relating to ancient Greece and Rome (*Letters* 711). The catalogue of his library at the time of his death reveals a number of additions, including histories of Rome by Thomas Arnold and Goldsmith, and Macaulay's *Lays of Ancient Rome* (Stonehouse). It is likely that Dickens's interest in the ancient world was stimulated by his year in Italy, to which he returned for a second visit in 1853. We know from his letters just how much the Roman ruins impressed him: "All the ancient part of Rome is wonderful and impressive in the extreme, far beyond the possibility of exaggeration" (*Letters* 268).

His sense of the grandeur of vanished Rome, however, did not exactly drive him into the arms of the classicists. *Dombey and Son,* written after his first trip to Italy, shows, as we have seen, that his attitude to the learning of dead languages was extremely negative. Nevertheless, there is a marked development in the way in which he handles classical allusions in this novel. The most obvious change is that the narrator no longer distances himself from the classics by placing classical references in the mouths of disreputable or pretentious characters. Apart from the chapters on Dr. Blimber's school, almost all classical allusions come through the narrative voice. Only two are attributed to characters in the novel: Miss Tox is allowed the wit to describe the lugubrious Mrs. Wickam as "a daughter of Momus" (96), a minor Greek god who was always complaining; Major Bagstock, hearing of the bankruptcy of his erstwhile friend Dombey, distances himself by declaring that he is totally disillusioned with humanity and ready to "have a tub in Pall Mall tomorrow, to show his contempt for mankind!" (814). Neither of these characters is particularly sympathetic, but their use of the classics is casual and informed.

Major Bagstock's pretentious self-designation as Diogenes, however, acts as a reminder that there is another Diogenes in the novel. This is "the rough and gruff" dog befriended by little Paul before he dies and given to Florence by the devoted if ridiculous Mr. Toots (253). Diogenes is "a blundering, ill-favoured, clumsy, bullet-headed dog," and as suspicious of mankind as his namesake, since he is "continually acting on a wrong idea that there was an enemy in the neighbourhood" (323). Dickens is surely playing off the fact that Diogenes the Cynic reportedly "called himself the 'Dog,' and held up the life of animals as a model for mankind" (Copleston, 141). Diogenes the dog does become such a model when he is transformed from cynic to devotee by Florence, who suggests that they should " 'love each other" as she caresses his shaggy head. The story of Diogenes merges with that of Beauty and the Beast, foreshadowing the larger theme of redemption in the novel. Dickens adds another twist after telling us how the dog "put his nose up to her face and swore fidelity": "Diogenes the man did not speak plainer to Alexander the Great than Diogenes the Dog spoke to Florence. He subscribed to the offer of his little mistress cheerfully, and devoted himself to her service" (253). It is surely indicative of a new sense of ease with the classics that Dickens does not feel it necessary to remind the reader that, according to Plutarch, Diogenes' retort to Alexander's offer of help was to request that he "stand a little out of my sun" ("Alexander," 259). The softening of the dog may point to the ultimate softening of Mr. Dombey, but Major Bagstock's identification with the Cynic acts as a reminder that not everyone is a candidate for the redeeming powers of love.

Not all of the narrator's classical allusions in *Dombey* resonate thematically through the novel; a number of them seem to have been included merely because they are comically inappropriate, as for example when Captain Cuttle, surrounded by a sea of soapy water, beams on Florence "like a new description of Triton" (330); or when, during the alterations to Dombey House, "a whole Olympus of plumbers and glaziers was reclining in various attitudes, on the skylight" (405). This last is almost certainly an irreverent allusion to the Elgin Marbles, whose gods and heroes are democratized and humanized by Dickens. Perhaps they needed to be democratized. Jenkyns states that "Grecian sculpture easily became a visible symbol of social or cultural pretentiousness," and that "people easily came to associate museums with Greek sculpture, and Greek sculpture with culture at its most 'museumified' " (137,138). Dickens certainly takes the marbles out of the museum.

With his more relaxed attitude towards classical knowledge, Dickens sometimes drops references quite casually among the clutter of daily life. Thus, the wheeled chair of the Honourable Mrs. Skewton is transformed into the stuff of legend, while itself transforming the legend into the mundane:

Withers, the wan page, slept out of the house immediately under the tiles at a neighbouring milk-shop; and the wheeled chair, which was the stone of that young Sisyphus, passed the night in a shed belonging to the same dairy, where new-laid eggs were produced by the poultry connected with the establishment, who roosted on a broken donkey-cart, persuaded, to all appearance, that it grew there, and was a species of tree. (292)

Another seemingly playful reference has more relevance than might at first appear: the wooden Midshipman, indifferent to Walter's departure, is compared to "Archimedes at the taking of Syracuse" (258), indifferent to his own imminent destruction. The comic inappropriateness of the comparison masks its warning of impending disaster for Walter. Dickens issues a more obvious warning when Walter boards his ship. He becomes "the lawful prize" of "a dirty Cyclops of the Captain's acquaintance, who, with his one eye, had made the Captain out some mile and a half off, and had been exchanging unintelligible roars with him ever since" (269). This is high-spirited comedy, but it casts Walter as the patient Odysseus who will have to endure shipwreck and misery before returning home. Dickens clearly knows the details of the Cyclops episode in Homer, but he handles it with unpedantic freedom, turning the roars of the angry Cyclops who is trying to sink the ship that he hears "some mile and a half off" into roars of supplication for a customer. And this Cyclops, unlike Homer's, will suffer shipwreck along with his Odysseus.

In both of these examples Dickens cavalierly transforms the qualities belonging to a classical character, or displaces them onto another referent. An even more bizarre example of such displacement is the transformation of Caius Marius, exiled Roman general, into the bankruptcy broker who takes possession of Sol's furniture. The broker is a man of "an easy temper—for that class of Caius Marius who sits upon the ruins of other people's Carthages, can keep up his spirits well enough" (115). The point of the comparison is not obvious, since Plutarch, who was almost certainly Dickens's source, tells us that Caius Marius, far from being a man of "an easy temper," was "incapable of controlling his passions" ("Caius Marius," 11). The exiled Marius, seeking to take refuge in Libya, is forbidden to land; at first speechless with "grief and indignation. . . . Marius then groaned aloud and said: 'Tell him that you have seen Caius Marius sitting as a fugitive among the ruins of Carthage' " (49). Ironically, Dickens uses the memorable and tragic words of Marius to describe a man who benefits from the losses of others; the anguish is separated from the words and transferred to the dispossessed Sol. And lest we accuse him of being ignorant of the character or circumstances of Marius, he is careful to include the phrase "that class of Caius Marius." The point, surely, is that it is a class invented by Dickens, who uses Plutarch's striking words for his own satirical purposes.

A similar freedom with classical allusion is shown in *Our Mutual Friend* when Dickens describes a fashionable wedding at which "the bride's aunt . . . a widowed female of a Medusa sort, in a stony cap, [is] glaring petrifaction at her fellow-creatures'' (120). The "stony cap," already suggestive of a deliberate blending of the Medusa and her victims, becomes an "impenetrable cap" a little later, and her snorts of contempt become the "snorting armour of the stony aunt" from which "all weapons rebound powerless" (121). The aunt is simultaneously Medusa, the victims she turns to stone, and Perseus, whose own "impenetrable cap" acquired from Hermes, protects him against the Medusa. Ordinarily, a reference to Medusa might be counted among the ready small-change of the general public, and, in *Dombey* Dickens's allusions to the Medusa operate on this level of common currency: Edith Dombey is "a beautiful Medusa" (651), and the blank walls of the Dombey house look down upon Florence "with a vacant stare, as if they had a Gorgon-like mind to stare her youth and beauty into stone" (320). Dickens's playful adaptations of the Medusa legend in *Our Mutual Friend,* his move from straightforward metaphor to the imaginative license and freedom of metonymy, point to a growing sense of confidence in his use of classical allusion. This confidence even allows him a touch of self-parody. A particularly arcane classical reference in *Our Mutual Friend* is described with mock pride by the narrator as "a neat point from the classics" (245).

Only the omniscient narrator is allowed such stylistic flourishes. When he turns to first-person narrative in that most autobiographical of novels, *David Copperfield,* Dickens does not allow his narrator to quote (or misquote) the classics. As we have already seen, he allows David his moment of class triumph over Uriah Heep in the matter of knowledge of Latin, but the triumph is uneasy and Uriah is permitted to hint at David's snobbery. Dickens was to atone for that snobbery in *Great Expectations* with another first-person narrator who lays no claim to classical learning. Nor would it have been appropriate in *Bleak House* for Esther to use classical allusions in her first-person narrative, although Dickens does permit her one very simple reference when she remarks to Ada "half-jestingly, half-seriously," that Richard "needed to have Fortunatus's purse, he made so light of money" (242). Richard is also half-jesting and half-serious when he refers to Esther as "Minerva" (233). In an earlier novel such references would have been satirical; here they add a little depth and dignity to Esther's character. Even though when Richard calls her Minerva he is expressing irritation at her wisdom and common sense, the name gives her more consequence than affectionate but somewhat patronising nicknames like "Dame Durden," "Mother Hubbard," or "little old woman" used elsewhere (112–14). Richard's eight years of public school, during which he learnt "to make Latin verses of several sorts" (168), has fitted him for nothing, but it does allow him to drop the occasional classical allusion with gentlemanly carelessness.

A new rhetorical element in *Bleak House* is the use of an extended classical reference as ironic commentary on the action, or to foreshadow future developments. The figure of "Allegory, in Roman helmet and celestial linen" (130), on the painted ceiling of Mr. Tulkinghorn's apartment, is introduced early on as a comic touch, and perhaps represents Dickens's reaction to an excess of painted ceilings in Italy, particularly in the sumptuous Palazzo Peschiere where the Dickens family lived for several months. His description of the fictional painting is characteristically irreverent: the figure "sprawls among balustrades and pillars, flowers, clouds, and big-legged boys, and makes the head ache—as would seem to be Allegory's object always" (130). There is surely more than a touch of Dickens's own frustrated and somewhat philistinish attempts to extract meaning from florid neoclassical murals, and we must ask what this has to do with Tulkinghorn. But the narrator keeps returning to the figure of Allegory, which conveys multiple and shifting messages to the reader. At one stage this somewhat multicultural Roman points "with the arm of Samson," directing our attention to the disguised Lady Dedlock as she hurries past the house (222); later, rather than being a symbol of omniscience, it will find its eyes blinded by "as much dust . . . as the law—or Mr. Tulkinghorn, one of its trustiest representatives—may scatter, on occasion, in the eyes of the laity" (305). However, it is Tulkinghorn whose eyes are blinded on the night of the murder, and who fails to detect any "new significance in the Roman's hand" (662). That hand, of course, will point at his dead body, causing others to shriek and flee in horror. The meaning of Allegory becomes plain at last: "For many years, the persistent Roman has been pointing, with no particular meaning, from that ceiling" (664), but now at last the gesture has acquired significance.

Dickens's treatment of this recurring motif certainly has many playful, comic, and merely irreverent elements, but as the novel develops the figure of Allegory moves further and further from its classical origins. It becomes a symbolic representation of the narrator himself, directing the reader's attention towards people and events. It also becomes a metaphor for the kind of novel Dickens is writing, one that will finally reveal its meaning and demonstrate that its multitudinous world of seemingly insignificant people and irrelevant details does after all, have pattern and significance. Finally, the pointing finger of the Roman on the ceiling becomes identified with the forefinger of Mr. Bucket, the detective. Like that other legal figure, Jaggers, Bucket has a formidable finger that conveys information, secrecy or the threat of imminent destruction. That finger guides the detective through a maze of clues, just as the Roman's finger guided the reader, and as Mr. Bucket closes in on his quarry "he and the Roman will be alone together, comparing forefingers" (712). The Roman, Mr. Bucket, and the narrator therefore converge, at least in terms of their narrative function.

In *Hard Times* Dickens uses another extended classical reference, that of Mrs. Sparsit's "Coriolanian style of nose" (43), but here it is used purely for comic and satirical purposes. The nose is always Roman, but undergoes various bizarre transformations: it suggests "a hawk engaged upon the eyes of a tough little bird" (105); when its owner is keeping a sharp lookout, her eyes become lighthouses, her Roman nose a "bold rock" (192); finally, caught in a thunderstorm as she is spying on Louisa, Mrs. Sparsit is transformed into "a classical ruin" (237).

A more significant development in *Hard Times,* however, is the association of the circus people with classical imagery. Whereas Mrs. Sparsit was stern, Roman, and like the objectionable Mrs. Homing of *Martin Chuzzlewit,* associated with Volumnia, the circus people are associated with the Greeks and Greek mythology. One of the circus mothers "alone in a Greek chariot, drove six in hand into every town they came to" (35). The fact that the chariot is driven by one of the mothers transforms it from a war machine into a triumphant demonstration of the skills of the circus women, who, in spite of their irregular "domestic arrangements," and lack of education, are gentle, childish, and incapable of "any kind of sharp practice" (35). This circus procession was almost certainly inspired by a similar event that greatly amused Dickens in Rome, where he saw "six or eight Roman chariots: each with a beautiful lady in extremely short petticoats" advertizing the arrival of the equestrian Company from Paris *(Letters* 226). It is surely significant that the Roman chariots become Greek in *Hard Times,* and that they are associated with people who have a childlike innocence coupled with a pagan unconcern for bourgeois respectability. Victorian Hellenists consistently associated the Greeks with the childhood of Western civilization, an attitude deriving originally from Winckelmann, and it is interesting to see Dickens, who was for the most part untouched by enthusiasm for all things Greek, adopting this idyllic view of the Greeks as part of an attack on modern utilitarianism.[4] Evangelicalism may also be under attack here. "Most often when representing the Greeks as childlike, a British writer was simply regarding them as exemplifying human virtues and normal healthy impulses that were repressed in an evangelical Christian culture" (Turner 41). Dickens makes it clear that the ladies driving the Greek chariots do indeed enjoy a "pagan" freedom from constraint, indulging in behavior that Mrs. Grundy (or the Gradgrinds) would have condemned.[5]

The circus folk are to be found at the Pegasus's Arms, a public-house in the meanest part of Coketown. Behind "the dingy little bar" of the public-house there is a representation of the winged horse "with real gauze let in for wings, golden stars stuck on all over him, and his ethereal harness made of red silk" (28). Superficially this Pegasus might seem to be in the same category as the hilariously inappropriate Mrs. Pott in *Pickwick,* masquerading as Apollo with spangled dress and lyre. But Dickens's satirical thrust is quite different in *Hard Times*. Mrs. Pott was an object of ridicule, and her Apollo costume marked her pretentiousness. In *Hard Times* the satire is not directed against the public-house, but against the Coketown establishment that relegates the arts to a marginal and despised place. Moreover, the winged horse in the bar is a fitting symbol of the art of the circus itself, simultaneously tawdry and yet magical, able to transform Bitzer's graminivorous quadruped into a mythical creature. The "real gauze" and "red silk" carry a note of childlike wonder at the power of illusion. Greek myth is here used to signify the redemptive power of imagination, and is set against the Coriolanian sternness of Mrs. Sparsit, or the utilitarianism of the Gradgrind party, who "wanted assistance in cutting the throats of the Graces" (124). The anti-classicism of the Gradgrind party extends only to what it considers frivolous: art, the imagination, the Graces. Gradgrindery rejoices in Roman sternness and duty; it is, however, in favor of Greek roots, to the confusion of Mrs. Gradgrind, who tells Louisa to "Go and be somethingological directly" (17); it also prefers latinate terms to plain Anglo Saxon words. As Barry Thatcher has pointed out, at the time Dickens was publishing *Hard Times* in *Household Words,* he was also participating in a debate on the nature of language between the Benthamites and Richard Trench. Dickens published articles entitled "Saxon English" and "Calling Bad Names," both of which advocated the use of plain Anglo-Saxon words rather than the "fancy Greek and Latin" vocabulary favored by the Benthamites (Thatcher 22). In *Hard Times* Dickens is therefore rejecting one form of the classicizing tendency, but simultaneously redeeming another form in his use of playful classical allusions. "Romans," who talk about graminivorous quadrupeds and have Coriolanian noses are set against "Greeks," who live under the sign of the winged horse; or, one might say, Apollo is set against Dionysus in the pitting of utilitarian Reason against the subversive forces of the Imagination.

The redemptive power of classical myth is also hinted at in Dickens's last completed novel, *Our Mutual Friend,* in the strangely titled chapter "Mercury Prompting" (268). Mercury is normally taken as referring to the villainous money-lender, Fledgeby, and *The Companion to* "Our Mutual Friend" has the following note on the chapter heading: "Mercury was the Roman god of merchants: the name is linked with the root *merx* ('merchandise') and *mercari* ('to deal, trade'). In Roman art Mercury is represented with a purse in his hand" (Cotsell 152). Such an interpretation would certainly fit Fledgeby, whose mean-spirited dealings dominate the chapter. However, I should like to propose a completely different reading. Like most of the classical deities, Mercury/Hermes has various characteristics and functions, and in his role as Hermes Psychopompus, he was responsible for conducting the souls of the dead to the Underworld. Dickens would have been familiar with this function from Ovid and also from Homer, where Hermes is Messenger of the gods and conductor of souls rather than the patron of thieves and swindlers. Moreover, in *Bleak House* the footmen who conduct souls through the dismal passages of the Dedlock mansion are consistently referred to as Mercuries. It is therefore entirely possible that "Mercury Prompting" refers, not to Fledgeby, but to Jenny Wren, the doll's dressmaker, whose strange prompting to Riah closes the chapter:

> As he mounted, the call or song began to sound in his ears again, and, looking above, he saw the face of the little creature looking down out of a Glory of her long bright radiant hair, and musically repeating to him, like a vision: "Come up and be dead! Come up and be dead!" (282)

A Hermes function for Jenny Wren, while not immediately obvious, is in keeping with other aspects of her role in the novel. This function might be hinted at in the scene where she escorts her "bad child" to the grave, and she is also in some sense a messenger from the gods, with her visions of children "in long bright slanting rows" (239), and her imaginary flowers and birds. Even more suggestive might be the role she plays in bringing Eugene Wrayburn back from the grave, like a Hermes escorting Euridice back from the Underworld. She alone understands Eugene's unspoken desires and acts as "an interpreter between this sentient world and the insensible man" (739). Jenny has, as Stewart says, "a 'secret power' that brings her once again into contact with that other world on whose border Eugene is now wandering" (218).

The identification of the crippled Jenny Wren with the swift-footed Hermes might seem preposterous, but Jenny lives by transformations and inversions, turning scraps of waste into beautiful gowns for her society dolls, and her drunken father into her own naughty child. Similarly, the idyll enacted by Jenny, Lizzie Hexam, and Riah takes place in a "garden" on the roof of Pubsey & Co., amidst a "few boxes of humble flowers and evergreens . . . and the encompassing wilderness of dowager old chimneys" (279). So here, the smoky roof-top becomes the Elysian Fields of the classical Underworld, but, by placing it above the "people who are alive, crying, and working, and calling to one another down in the close dark streets" (281), Jenny transforms it into the Christian Heaven above the Inferno of the city. Jenny, with the "Glory of her long bright radiant hair" is part Christian angel, part Hermes. In Jenny's world death is a state to be preferred to life; when you are "dead" you feel "so peaceful and so thankful!. . . . And such a chain has fallen from you, and such a strange good sorrowful happiness comes upon you!" (281). In this respect she transforms the classical presence of death in the pastoral idyll (Et in Arcadia ego), into the triumph of death over a life of suffering, thus christianizing the afterlife. In classical literature, the Underworld is never to be preferred to the upper world.

Pam Morris comments shrewdly on Jenny's "transformative discourse [which] is always inclusive, inviting others into the playful arena of the imagination" (136). However, Morris does not see the particular transformation offered by the roof-top as positive, referring to "the falsifying sentimentality of her religious rhapsodies and her siren song 'Come up and be dead' " (138). Hillis Miller, on the other hand, sees the "rooftop of Pubsey and Co. . . . [as] a place from which the various possibilities of life in the novel may be clearly seen," and states categorically that "No passage in *Our Mutual Friend* is of greater importance. These sentences are a kind of focal center around which the rest of the novel organizes itself and becomes comprehensible" (314). If this is so, then we can assume that Jenny in some sense speaks for Dickens, and the sentimentality noted by Morris might, according to Bakhtin, indicate the authorial presence. Commenting on heteroglossia in the English comic novel, Bakhtin writes:

> This usually parodic stylization of generic professional and other strata of language is sometimes interrupted by the direct authorial word (usually as an expression of pathos, of Sentimental or idyllic sensibility), which directly embodies (without any refracting) semantic and axiological intentions of the author.   (301)

As we have seen, Dickens's use of classical motifs is almost always comic and parodic. Here, although elements of parody remain, the slide into pathos, sentiment, and the idyllic marks Jenny's discourse as an embodiment of authorial "intention," albeit refracted rather than direct.

In whatever manner we interpret "Mercury Prompting," as a rhetorical device it must be seen as marking Dickens's own final transformation from outsider to accepted member of the club. So comfortable is he with the classical allusion that he allows it to float free above the chapter, leaving the reader to determine its referent and significance. A neat point from the classics, indeed! And if, as I have suggested, we take Mercury to be a reference to Jenny Wren, the allusion marks not only the willingness of the narrator/ author to take ownership of the classics, but also his willingness to associate the classics with a character who, in some sense, must be seen as embodying authorial intentions. In *Pickwick,* as we saw, only disreputable or pretentious outsiders were associated with the classics, while the solidly bourgeois, "good" Mr. Pickwick remained free of any such taint, as did the narrator himself. What is remarkable is that in the course of his journey from margin to center, Dickens, far from leaving the "outsider" behind, has taken that figure with him. Ultimate outsiders such as the circus folk of *Hard Times* and the crippled doll's dressmaker now embody morally positive aspects of the novels, and they do so partly through their associations with the classics.

The "center" that such figures help to define is not the comfortable bourgeois world of the Pickwickians or Mr. Brownlow. Nor is it the "individualistic middle-class retreat" most often associated with Dickens's use of the pastoral (Bodenheimer 117). It is an alternative world of imaginative license, subtle subversions, compassion, and extraordinary inclusiveness. Jenny Wren's rooftop world, in spite of elements of cloying sentimentality, brings together gentile and Jew, grimy city and pastoral Arcadia, life and death, classical Underworld and Christian Heaven.[6] It is an Arcadia populated by outcasts from modern industrial society, and although, like all Arcadias, it provides a refuge from that society, it does so not through the privilege of class, but only through the transforming power of the imagination. Moreover, Jenny Wren's transformative imagination includes the suffering multitudes in the streets below her haven, for whom she speaks through the authority of her own twisted body and life of arduous poverty. Classical allusion is used here in the service of Dickens's moral, and essentially humanistic, vision.

Frank Turner claims that "during much of the nineteenth and well into the twentieth century the critical and moral tradition of humanism provided the primary channel through which the civilization of ancient Greece became transformed into a useful past for a large portion of the educated British public" (15). He traces this humanistic tradition from its sixteenth-century roots through such figures as "Milton, Swift, Pope, Johnson, Reynolds, Burke, Coleridge, Newman, Arnold, Eliot, and Leavis" (15). Dickens would be an odd addition to such an intellectual and highly educated group, but it might not be too much to claim that at certain points his practice touches their theory. He does not preach Arnoldian sermons on the virtues of Hellenism but, like Arnold, he does invoke the Greeks "to oppose commercialism, excessive religious zeal . . . philosophical mechanism" and utilitarianism (Turner 21). He does so, however, through the anarchistic play of an exuberant imagination that transforms tawdry inn signs, circus ladies, and rooftop "gardens" into mythical symbols. It is a process that Arnold, in theory at least, found reprehensible. Hellenism, according to Arnold, might help to cure us of "the great vice of our intellect, manifesting itself in our incredible vagaries in literature, in art, in religion, in morals; namely that it is *fantastic*, and wants *sanity*"; reading the ancients, he continues, will help to cure us of "our caprice and eccentricity" (*On the Classical Tradition* 17). We may be thankful that Dickens had not read very widely in the ancients, or that his imagination was powerful enough to absorb what he did read without destroying his capricious and eccentric gift for the fantastic.

In other respects, too, Dickens occupies a very marginal position in relation to Victorian Hellenism. He borrows from Homer, but shows no knowledge of or interest in the debates that raged over the authorship of the Homeric poems or the relationship between Homer and Hebrew scripture; he does not invoke Athens as the fountainhead of democracy, nor does he show any interest in Greek philosophy, even though he owned a copy of Grote's *Plato, and the Other Companions of Socrates.* He transforms Bacchus into a besuited Victorian gentleman for comic and satiric purposes, but he does not seek to transform Socrates into a Liberal Anglican or a Victorian Rationalist, "the founder of natural religion, the upholder of a universal moral law, and the advocate of a moderate inductive view of philosophy and morality resembling Francis Bacon's" (Turner 270).[7] Dickens plundered the classics with a fine recklessness for whatever suited his fancy, and his major sources are "stories": the stories found in such writers as Homer, Vergil, Ovid, Plutarch, and the dramatists. Most of these he read in translation, although, as Ackroyd points out, he did consult Vergil in the original (1095).

One cannot claim that Dickens took more than a passing interest in the great debates provoked by the Hellenistic revival; similarly, it would be a mistake to claim that the classics had as much significance for him as for such novelists as Fielding, Eliot, and Hardy. He does work within the same comic tradition as Fielding, but, as we have seen, never claims the same degree of familiarity with the classics as Fielding. There is nothing in Dickens to compare with Fielding's meditation on "the Serious in Writing" in *Tom Jones,* for example, with its quotations from Latin authors.[8] Nor does Dickens use Greek tragedy as a frame of reference for the tragedy of ordinary life, as both Eliot and Hardy do.[9]

Dickens's most serious use of a classical reference may indeed be, as I have suggested, the reference to Jenny Wren as Mercury, and even that has a playful, comic element. English novelists were all keenly aware of the huge gap between the mundane elements of modern life and the heroic actions of ancient epic and drama; all of them exploit that incongruity and many of them comment directly on it. Dickens never felt that he had the authority to philosophize about the classical tradition, but his lack of confidence in his own learning saved him from sententiousness or pedantry.[10] The classics existed for Dickens not so much for their own sake or as objects of veneration to be emulated, but as material for his free-wheeling imagination to use as it pleased. He knew what Yeats discovered only late in life: that the ancient myths were rooted in the ordinary and the sordid, and that we can only make real use of them by lying down "where all the ladders start/In the foul rag-and-bone shop of the heart" (*Poems* 392). Dickens always wrote from the heart rather than the intellect, and everything he encountered (rags, bones, and stray classical allusions) was just so much grist in the powerful mill of his imagination.

NOTES

1. See for example, Garret Stewart, *Dickens and the Trials of Imagination,* and Robert Golding, *Idiolects in Dickens.*
2. In an age when schooling was still completely unregulated, anyone could open an "Academy." Such establishments might offer instruction in Latin, thus catering to the ambition of the new middle classes, or they might be little better than Dotheboys Hall, the dumping ground for unwanted children in *Nicholas Nickleby.* Class distinctions existed between Latin and Greek. Middle-class establishments like Wellington House offered Latin, but almost certainly not Greek, which would be taught at such schools as Eton and Harrow. Greek remained the "stamp that authenticated culture and class" (Jenkyns 63). Knowledge of Greek was essential for admission to both Oxford and Cambridge, and the "examinations for the Home Civil Service, the Indian Civil Service, and the Royal Military Academy afforded considerable advantage to students who could score well in Greek," so that "a familiarity with Greek culture [was] characteristic of a large portion of the British political elite" (Turner 5). Girls' schools in general offered neither Latin nor Greek, substituting modern languages such as French and German, and tuition in the arts. Lower still on the social scale were schools for the children of the poor, including the Dame Schools such as that run by Mr. Wopsle's great-aunt in *Great Expectations.*
3. Uriah's rejection of David's offer demonstrates a keen appreciation of the attitudes held by some of his "betters." Many members of the ruling classes feared the consequences of educating the poor, producing evidence to support their contention that "education and not ignorance caused crime" (Brantlinger 68). Dickens may have shared some of their misgivings, since he creates in Uriah a brilliant example of education in the service of criminality. However, he also shared the hope of liberal reformers that education could save pauper children from a life of crime, and he devoted considerable energy to the establishment of the Ragged Schools. See Philip Collins, "Dickens and the Ragged Schools"; also Collins, *Dickens and Education.* Such schools, of course, did not teach the classics; they were heavily evangelical in flavor, stressing "religious and moral instruction," and "teaching the students not to steal seems to have been the first order of business" (Brantlinger 73).
4. In this respect Dickens anticipates Matthew Arnold, who, in *Culture and Anarchy* (1869), was to appeal to his version of Hellenism as an antidote to philistinism, non-conformism, and utilitarianism. In almost every other respect, however, Dickens, with his cheerful philistinism, would stand as a contrast to Arnold.
5. At the same time, it must be stated that while Dickens is happy to champion the Greeks against Mrs. Grundy, he would surely not have endorsed the further license in favor of the "love that dare not speak its name" claimed by later Hellenists such as Wilde and Symons. See Jenkyns 280–293 for a discussion of this topic.
6. In a fascinating article on Dickens's use of the pastoral, David Wilkes argues not only for classical influences on Dickens, but also for the transformation of Fagin

into a neopastoral shepherd who "herds, refreshes, and instructs his flock of pickpockets" (59). Jenny Wren may also be seen as a neopastoral shepherd, although her moral orientation is, of course, very different from Fagin's.

7. Turner gives a very full and informed discussion of the aspects of Hellenism I have touched upon here. Not surprisingly, he does not mention Dickens.

8. *Tom Jones,* Bk.V, Ch. 1. Other prefatory essays in *Tom Jones* make similar appeals to the classics, as, for example, Bk. II, Ch. 1, in which Fielding places himself in relation to other "historians" and claims that he is the "founder of a new province of writing" (88). George Eliot is perhaps the true successor to Fielding in her use of the classics for philosophical or moral commentary.

9. See Jenkyns' excellent chapter on George Eliot and the classics. See also Kramer's book on Hardy. It is significant that one of Hardy's most powerful tragedies concerns Jude's attempt to gain entrance into the exclusive club of the ancient university of Christminster through a formidable process of self-education in the classics.

10. George Eliot was to accuse herself of "pedantry" for quoting two lines of Greek verse in an early short story. However, as Jenkyns points out, she continued to quote Greek, and what she really regretted seems to have been the fact that the *"Quarterly Review* pounced on a couple of mistakes in her accents" (Jenkyns 114).

WORKS CITED

Ackroyd, Peter. *Dickens.* New York: HarperCollins, 1990

Arnold, Matthew. *On the Classical Tradition.* Ed. R.H. Super. Ann Arbor: U of Michigan, 1960.

Bakhtin, Mikhail. "Discourse in the Novel." *The Dialogic Imagination.* Trans. Caryl Emerson and Michael Holquist. Austin: U. of Texas P, 1981.

Bodenheimer, Rosemarie. *The Politics of Story in Victorian Social Fiction.* Ithaca: Cornell UP, 1988.

Brantlinger, Patrick. "How Oliver Twist Learned to Read, and What He Read." *Culture and Education in Victorian England.* Ed. Patrick Scott and Pauline Fletcher. *Bucknell Review* 34, no. 2 (1990); 59–81.

Collins, Philip. *Dickens and Education.* London: Macmillan, 1964.

————. "Dickens and the Ragged Schools." *Dickensian* 55 (1959): 94–109.

Copleston, S.J., Frederick. *A History of Philosophy, Vol. 1: Greece and Rome, Part 1.* New York: Doubleday, 1962.

Cotsell, Michael. *A Companion to* Our Mutual Friend. London: Allen and Unwin, 1986.

Dickens, Charles. *Bleak House.* Oxford Illustrated Dickens. London: Oxford UP, 1948; rpt. 1970.

———. *David Copperfield.* Ed. Jerome H. Buckley. New York & London: Norton, 1990.

———. *Dombey and Son.* Oxford Illustrated Dickens. London: Oxford UP, 1950; rpt. 1968.

——— *Great Expectations.* Ed. Margaret Cardwell. Oxford: Clarendon, 1993.

———. *Hard Times.* New Oxford Illustrated Dickens. London: Oxford UP, 1955.; rpt. 1959.

———. *The Letters of Charles Dickens.* Ed. Kathleen Tillotson. Vol. IV. Oxford: Clarendon, 1977.

———. *Martin Chuzzlewit.* Oxford Illustrated Dickens. London: Oxford UP, 1951; rpt. 1968.

———. *The Old Curiosity Shop.* Oxford Illustrated Dickens. London: Oxford UP, 1951; rpt, 1957.

———. *Our Mutual Friend.* Oxford Illustrated Dickens. London: Oxford UP, 1952; rpt. 1967.

———. *The Pickwick Papers.* New Oxford Illustrated Dickens. London: Oxford UP, 1948; rpt. 1952.

Edwards, Simon. "David Copperfield: The Decomposing Self." *The Centennial Review,* 29 (1983): 328–53.

Eliot, George. *The Mill on the Floss.* London: Dent, 1966.

Fielding, Henry. "An Essay on Conversation." *Miscellanies* Vol. I. Ed. Henry Knight Miller. Oxford: Oxford U P (1972): 129–52.

———. *The History of Tom Jones.* Ed. R. P. C. Mutter. Harmondsworth: Penguin, 1966.

Golding, Robert. *Idiolects in Dickens.* New York: St. Martin's Press, 1985.

Jenkyns, Richard. *The Victorians and Ancient Greece.* Cambridge, Mass: Harvard U P, 1980.

Kaplan, Fred. *Dickens: A Biography.* 1988. New York: Avon, 1990.

Kramer, Dale. *Thomas Hardy: The Forms of Tragedy.* Detroit: Wayne State U P, 1975.

Mace, Nancy A. *Henry Fielding's Novels and the Classical Tradition.* Newark: U of Delaware P, 1996.

Miller, J. Hillis. *Charles Dickens: The World of His Novels.* Cambridge, Mass: Harvard U P, 1958; rpt. 1970.

Morris, Pam. *Dickens's Class Consciousness: A Marginal View.* New York: St. Martin's P, 1991.

Plutarch. "Alexander." *Plutarch's Lives VII.* Trans. Bernadotte Perrin. London: Heinemann, 1919.

————. "Caius Marius." *Fall of the Roman Republic.* Trans. Rex Warner. London: Penguin, 1958.

Stewart, Garrett. *Dickens and the Trials of Imagination.* Cambridge, Mass: Harvard UP, 1974.

Stonehouse, J.H. ed. *Catalogues of the Libraries of Charles Dickens and William Thackeray.* London: Piccadilly Fountain, 1935.

Thatcher, Barry. "Dickens' Bow to the Language Theory Debate." *Dickens Studies Annual* 23 (1994): 17–47.

Turner, Frank M. *The Greek Heritage in Victorian Britain.* New Haven: Yale UP, 1981.

Wilkes, David. "Dickens, Bakhtin, and the Neopastoral Shepherd in *Oliver Twist.*" *Dickens Studies Annual* 24 (1996): 59–79.

Yeats, W.B. *The Collected Poems.* London: Macmillan, 1961.

Imaginary Capital: The Shape of the Victorian Economy and the Shaping of Dickens's Career

Tatiana M. Holway

" 'Money is the word' " (690), remarks a character in *Bleak House* (1852–53)—a phrase readily transposed in any account of Dickens's career: "The word is money." Language was, of course, notoriously a mode of economic action for Dickens, who was preoccupied with "the Whole Duty of Man in a commercial country" (*Little Dorrit*, 136) and determined to extract every shilling from each novel's circulation. " 'Money is the word,' " however: this bears not so much on the economics of literature as it does on the language of the economy—that is, on the increasing textuality of the Victorian market, where written language was becoming the primary means of exchange. " 'Money is the word' " suggests, then, the relation about which Jean-Joseph Goux theorizes broadly: the "isomorph[ic]" identity of language and money, their structural "coherence," which is "organic, rather than accidental" (110), and therefore historical. Hence, when Dickens wrote " 'Money is the word,' " he was making a particular cultural observation about the development of capitalism in the mid-Victorian period, one that had been emerging since the earlier decades of the century, when he was a young writer setting out to make his word some money.

He began to do so with his third novel, *Nicholas Nickleby* (1838–39), which was tied to the production and circulation of *The Pickwick Papers* (1836–37), his first. As implicated in the economy as anything Dickens wrote, *Nicholas Nickleby* calls attention through its marketing to the precarious system of inscription emerging in the market of the 1820s and 1830s. In that novel, Dickens also initiated a critique of the practical and ethical contradictions of capitalism—contradictions that nonetheless shaped his early career. While the critical project of *Nicholas Nickleby* remained limited, Dickens completed

Dickens Studies Annual, Volume 27, Copyright © 1998 by AMS Press, Inc. All rights reserved.

it twenty years later in *Little Dorrit* (1855–57), which systematically examines the history of capitalism in the intervening years. Written when Dickens had become a well-capitalized institution himself, this later novel not only made him more money than any previous work, but also focused directly on the mid-century institutionalization of the word as money, even as it posed the dilemma of distinguishing between literary and economic representation. In Dickens, then, we find, in historically specific ways, how "the economic complicity of literature is integrally connected to the discursive complexity of economics" (Heinzelman, 9).

The "discursive complexity of economics" itself has a complex history in nineteenth-century England—a history that can be summarized as an escalation in the circulation of increasingly abstract and arbitrary monetary forms that contributed to both the expansion and the frequent dislocation of the economy.[1] Throughout much of the century, the gold standard prevailed, serving as the "solid ground" (Mill, 4:79) not only of value, but also of representation: it was the "real" basis for the inscription of "nominal" values. Thus, while any kind of paper currency was suspect in the beginning of the century, Victorians came to regard Bank of England notes as legitimate economic security because of their immediate convertibility, as representations of the exchange value of gold, to gold itself. Nevertheless, the circulation of other credit instruments consistently surpassed that of Bank of England notes, and for all the monolithic materiality of industrial England, by the 1850s and 1860s, its financial infrastructure had taken the form of a "City of Unlimited Paper" (Hollingshead). The economy had become "symbolic" in the sense that Goux defines it, organized around, and through, a "complex linkage and diacritical discrimination" (Goux, 49) of monetary forms that existed on, and were exchanged along, a representational continuum, from the symbolic association of Bank of England notes to gold, to the more attenuated and abstruse relations of credit to capital and of credit and capital to stock issues, or "scrip," as they were tellingly called. The increasing gaps in representation in this "symbolic order" (Goux, 49) are also the increasing gaps in time on which potentially more profitable exchanges depend and through which capitalist expansion occurs; they are the gaps where contingencies intervene, the gaps of speculation.[2] The symbolic economy of mid-century England was, then, a speculative economy, and its development bears out Kurt Heinzelman's observation that "What the movements of the economy reflect is nothing less than the shape of our imagination" (7).

Those economic movements were erratic, especially in the early decades of the century, when speculative activities contributed to severe fluctuations of the market, as well as to its growth, and they continued to be regularly erratic throughout the Victorian period, with "manias" and "panics" recurring in decennial intervals. The experience of these eruptions of contingency and irrationality conflicted directly with capitalist ideology, with its insistence on the determinacy of exchange, the rationality of homoeconomicus, and the inevitable "progress" of the economy. Insofar as political economists and moralists sought a cause for speculative crises in the laissez-faire climate of Victorian England, they found it not in the institutions of capitalism, but in the imagination of individuals, whose imprudence in "gambling" on the Stock Exchange—in surrendering present, known assets to contingencies in the hope of uncertain future gains—was the manifestation of a mental delusion—a capitulation to illusions of desire projected onto paper inscriptions with fluctuating nominal values at best and certainly no "solid ground" of representation. Speculators were, in effect, the consumers of economic fictions—of "mere" language that appeared to be deracinated from any basis in reality, but that nevertheless radically and repeatedly disrupted economy and society.

Dickens's emergence as a popular novelist coincided with the emergence of this speculative economy, and the conflicts between industrial modes of production and newer financial practices informed the imaginative and material production of his works. Indeed, to call his novels "works" is already to begin to engage in some of the kinds of ideological ironies and practical problems into which he plunged. Dickens himself thought of his imaginative writing as middle-class capitalist labor: he assumed the principle that his efforts should be rewarded with money (Patten, 10), and he embraced the capitalist ethos, with its privileging of prudence, rationality, and above all "energy of will" in the business of getting ahead (Welsh, 75). As Forster remarked of his later, and lucrative, commitment to arduous reading engagements, Dickens's "task . . . self-imposed, was to make the most money in the shortest time without any regard to the physical labour undergone" (bk. 8, ch. 7), an observation equally applicable to his earlier career: in three years, he wrote three serialized novels, sometimes simultaneously, and committed himself to two more; published numerous sketches and republished them in two volumes; composed one play; edited a monthly journal; and contributed prefaces and notes to a number of other works. In spite of his popular and commercial success, it was not until the late 1840s that Dickens began to profit from the enlarging market for his work, but, exacting in "punctuality, order, diligence" (Welsh, 75) and obsessed with saving, he did accumulate money "penny by penny" (Patten, 235)—and eventually accumulate quite a lot.

Dickens, from this point of view, appears as a proto-Smilesean paragon of the gospel of labor and self-help, and the discipline he imposed on his imaginative work is directly related to the publishing innovations his work initiated. The serialization of the English novel, begun with *The Pickwick Papers,* involved precisely the routinization of creative energy by capitalist means of production. As N. N. Feltes has argued, the transformation of the "monthly something" envisioned by Dickens and his publishers, Chapman and Hall, into a "commodity text" not only employed industrial techniques, but also interpellated capitalist ideology in their form: accessible to and purchasable by a mass audience and developed in ample detail, each part of the serial projected the effect of plenitude, while the publication of discrete monthly installments that became integrated over time reinforced notions of "progress" (8–10). Contingencies and coincidences appearing in each part promised to become rationalized within a larger pattern of significance, and even in "novels so chance-ridden" as Dickens's, according to George Levine, "chance serves the purpose not of disorder, but of meaning" (137). Indeed, he goes on to claim, "narrative makes chance impossible" (138).

Perhaps. But it is also true that "chance" made the Dickensian novel possible—that the early efforts of this model of capitalist virtue, who prudently abstained from risking his money on the Stock Exchange, were at the same time speculative ventures. For if *Pickwick* was an outcome of determinate means of production and replicated the rationale of capitalism, its serialization, as well as Dickens's early successes, were also the consequence of "a series of accidents, perhaps more accurately, contingent opportunities" (333), as Robert Patten points out, and foregrounded the essential precariousness of the rapidly expanding market. The novel that generated a "Bozmania" was also, in the moral economy of Victorian England, a "reckless speculation" on the part of Chapman and Hall, who were risking capital on a project barely conceived in a volatile publishing market, and a "hazard" for fortune on the part of Dickens, for whom manuscripts, like "scrip," represented only an anticipation of money. Moreover, while Dickens's early readers were immersed in tangible commodities, not ephemeral shares, they were nevertheless speculating first when they purchased and then when they consumed the new author's twenty-part serials, the ultimate "value" of which would not be realized for well over a year. Even when the initial gamble of *Pickwick* was paying off for the public who were smitten by Boz and the publishers who were cashing in on his growing reputation, the business of writing remained risky for Dickens. Throughout the 1840s, although he gained an increasing share of the profits from his novels, these were consistently tied to paying off past debts to Chapman and Hall, who repeatedly advanced money to Dickens—a proceeding contemporaries who emphasized the "probity" and "prudence" of "abstain[ing] from risking in *any* speculation" would certainly have condemned as *"rash"* (Mill, 4:78; his emph.).

Dickens's early novels were, therefore, "imaginary capital" in the fullest sense of the phrase, and they not only exploited the imaginative potentialities of the market, but also expressed the emerging conditions of finance capitalism formally, in their prose. Radically new, this prose was capable of a "constant, rapid, and virtually limitless multiplication of effects and forms in new inventions and configurations," as Steven Marcus puts it—capable of precisely the seeming self-generation and versatile proliferation of "scrip." Looking back on the "new and spectacular event" of *Pickwick,* Marcus deliberately borrows from the language of economic historians when he claims that it "is the timely equivalent in written novelistic prose of the take-off into sustained growth," and when he claims further that "in *Pickwick Papers* the English novel becomes as it were airborne" (*Representations,* 224), he echoes Dickens's contemporaries assessment of the writer whose "genius" had "risen like a rocket" and created a "Bozmania" (q. in Collins, 10).

Back on earth, where Dickens's novels were published and distributed as commodity texts, they further helped to stimulate the expanding market, principally through the innovation of a supplement sewn into the covers of the monthly numbers, which became known as the "Dickens Advertiser."[3] Advertising all manner of commodities, it also promoted Dickens's forthcoming serials and new editions. Indeed, commodities and Dickens rapidly became intertwined in a process that might be as readily regarded as the Dickensification of commodities as the commodification of Dickens—a metamorphosis that also acquired the features of speculation, as the circulation of *Nicholas Nickleby,* with its attendant paraphernalia, illustrates particularly well.

Thus, while reprints of Dickens's portrait were offered for sale through the *Nickleby* Advertiser, "Readers of *Nickleby*" were assailed with the virtues of (among many other things) "Intense Diamine Ink": asking whether "the freedom and fluency with which the author gives expression to the most intense feelings" may be a result of "something in *The Ink* he uses," the ad promised that "Its luxuriant colour will prompt the richest train of ideas, and its softness and fluidity facilitate their expression" (no. 17). Assuring prolixity, a "puff" such as this was no different in principle from the prospectuses that promoted share offerings by promising profit by association with other successful share-issuing ventures—at which point the materiality of the economy appears to dissolve into textuality, as Dickens himself was well aware. In *Nicholas Nickleby,* he offered up the "United Metropolitan Improved Hot Muffin and Crumpet Baking and Punctual Delivery Company" (10) as a parody of the notorious verbosity of contemporary "bubble" ventures. " 'Why the very name will get the shares up to a premium in ten days' " (10), one promoter gloats. A swindle, the "United" is no more than a prospectus, its advertisement of "capital, five millions, in five hundred thousand shares of ten pounds each" notwithstanding (10). Noting that the "sums" are "duly set forth in fat black figures of considerable size" (11), Dickens points to the economic credibility that (spurious) scriptural *presentation* could (falsely) confer. But for all of its deflationary humor, Dickens's *representation* of deceptive speculative language could not forestall the efforts of plagiarists to profit from his novels and soaring reputation.

Since copyright laws were inadequate to protect Dickens's work from piracy early in his career, he was especially vulnerable during the "Boz-mania" to the "popular imitativeness" of speculators (Mackay, 88), who were in this instance literary hacks. As soon as the first number of *Nicholas Nickleby* had begun to appear, "Bos" began to publish *Nickelas Nickelbery*.[4] There, the "United Metropolitan" became "The New London Limited Hot-Baked Floury Potato Conveyance and Delivery Company"—Dickens's representation of the fictional, fraudulent language of speculation now itself becoming subject to another false permutation. We seem to have entered directly into a thoroughly self-referential, self-perpetuating sphere, and Dickens's subsequent efforts to extricate his work from it only extended it further. Having recourse only to advertisement, Dickens issued the "*Nickleby* Proclamation," in which he asserted the exclusive authority and authenticity of the work of "the only true Boz" as opposed to the "cheap and wretched imitations" that "impose on the credulous." Written in pseudo-legalistic form, however, the "Proclamation" was itself a "puff," and it could, of course, be readily imitated or deflated, as "Bos" proceeded to do in *Nickelas Nickelbery*.

It is hardly surprising, then, that *Nicholas Nickleby* should be overtly concerned with speculation. Plagiarism aside, the production, promotion, and circulation of this novel suggest a tendency toward an increasing interpenetration of the economy with fictions and fiction with economic forms. But whereas the marketing of *Nicholas Nickleby* as a commodity calls attention to the contingencies of representation in the market itself, the text focuses on the market's contingencies per se, and in representing economic growth as continually erratic and unpredictable and capitalist enterprise as speculative and irrational, it provides a vision of early Victorian culture which foregrounds the conditions contemporary ideology sought to suppress.

This oppositional perspective appears boldly from the very beginning of the novel, where the cover of the monthly installments depicts the goddess Fortune and the full title, *The Life and Adventures of Nicholas Nickleby, containing a Faithful Account of the Fortunes, Misfortunes, Uprisings, Downfallings, and Complete Career of the Nickleby Family,* not only refers to the lives of the Nicklebys, but also represents the experience of the urban middle classes during the earlier Victorian period, as well as presciently delineating the course of nineteenth-century economic history as a whole. Moreover, the novel is set in 1825–26, during the first modern economic crisis, and one that was "so devastating, dangerous, and alarming in the public mind" that it became "part of national folklore" (Russell, 48)—"folklore," that is, of the gratifyingly receding past, which Dickens, in 1838, just after the recurrence of another such crisis, makes disturbingly present. And emphatically so, for in the first chapter, which "Introduces All the Rest," the "game of Speculation" propels all that ensues. It is Nicholas's father's loss of his fortune when a "mania prevailed" and a "bubble burst" (5) that sends the hero into the world to seek his fortune.

" 'The world is before me, after all' " (144), Nicholas announces, and his ambivalence is well-founded, for the capitalist world the novel engages in from the beginning appears to divide into two opposing camps, represented by Nicholas's father and his uncle, Ralph. Insofar as the brothers are figures for, respectively, the irrationality and improvidence of "rash speculation" and the rationality and prudence of disciplined enterprise, Dickens appears to reproduce, yet again, the conventional opposition within the Victorian moral economy.[5] But the fact that the two men are brothers already suggests the critical direction the narrative will take: "There is nothing like money" (3), says Ralph, and his speculating brother, "look[ing] about for the means of repairing his capital" (4), concurs. A family resemblance thus emerges as these "different" brothers look to the same end—to profit, the rationale of capitalism per se. Morally dubious, if not irrational, this motive was suppressed in the capitalist ethos, which concentrated instead on making the kinds of ethical distinctions in conduct that the two men appear to represent. But even these distinctions fade, as Dickens shows that the brothers' conduct does not differ in principle and that the conduct the capitalist ethos values is based on a shaky foundation.

Thus, when Nicholas's father speculates, he joins in a "game" in which "the players see little or nothing of their cards" and in which "gains *may* be great—and so may losses" (5)—and either way the outcome depends not on reason and will, but on the arbitrary motions of Fortune. Predictably, he loses. If this speculator exemplifies those who were "relying in no inconsiderable degree on chance for the improvement of their means" (1), Ralph appears initially to represent the opposite: avoiding "mere abstract speculations" (3), obsessed with "t[elling] the chances" (341), he chooses instead the security of usury. With his "love of saving" (441) reinforced by the cautious principle that "there was no getting money in once it was out" (470), his capital predictably grows. But his "thirst for gain" (441) overrides his knowledge that contingencies necessarily intervene in exchange: he "invests" all his capital and, predictably, loses it. In contradistinction to contemporary wisdom, then, Dickens emphasizes that the market does not lend itself to "rational calculation" (Mill, 4:74), and while he may be open to the charge that he merely exploits the ambiguity of chance, engineering risks in the plot to create an opportunity for critique, he also goes further in his ideological opposition by questioning the most valued asset of the capitalist ethos, prudence itself.[6]

Ralph, the self-styled " 'man of activity and prudence' " (25) serves this subversion. Although he is an unscrupulous usurer, a miserly villain, he is also "the capitalist" (3), as Dickens repeatedly calls him, or the representative "man of business" (6), as Ralph also thinks of himself. As such, he embodies the complementary and conventional characteristics of selfishness and misanthropy, but Ralph, who "affected to consider himself a type of all humanity . . . and, choosing to imagine that all mankind were cast in the same mould, hated them" (567), is driven by masochism as well. Indeed, his self-hatred derives from the very ethic he values, from the energetic self-denial he practices in his economic self-interest—from prudence, which brings him to his unprofitable end. For, when Ralph's schemes fail, he commits a violent suicide, the ultimately self-negating act of self-control and a logical extension of the irrational principles according to which he has lived. Furthermore, its melodrama notwithstanding, Ralph's demise subsequent to his losses recapitulates his brother's, subsequent to his, in the beginning of the novel. There, the insolvent speculator had headed for bed with a "languidly beating heart," sunk "exhausted on his pillow," lost his mind, and expired (5), his passive suicide providing a fitting conclusion to the willed will-lessness which the nonaction of speculation entails. Thus, through the deaths that frame the narrative of capitalist opportunity, through the antithetical brothers' similar "careers," Dickens suggests that the world which was " 'before' " Nicholas is " 'after all' " closed.

This critique of capitalism, however, poses a dilemma for Dickens. For *Nicholas Nickleby* is also from the outset a bildungsroman: a narrative that engages its impoverished hero in the business of acquiring economic status and social identity, this narrative engages in the business of shaping his "Life and Adventures" into a "progress"—a "progress" that conflicts with the erratic paradigm set forth in the full title of the novel. Nor can the project of the bildungsroman be sustained where Dickens has shown Nicholas to have no acceptable choices for conduct in the world. And the "solution" to this dilemma at the end of the novel, through the miraculous intervention of the benevolent Cheeryble Brothers, who give the inexperienced Nicholas a ridiculously high-paying job, is no solution: it involves an impossible retreat from the harsh conditions of the market—their counting house is tucked away in "a quiet, little-frequented, retired spot" (468)—and, simultaneously, a reinscription in the ameliorating ideology of capitalism—their unaccountable intercession looks very much like the providential work of the "invisible hand." Thus, in articulating—that is, giving expression and form to—the contradictions of capitalist culture, Dickens ran the risk of replicating them;

as the title promises, *Nicholas Nickleby* provides a "Faithful Account" of the economic experience of the earlier decades of the Victorian period, but the novel is also finally uncritically "faithful" to the ideological shaping of that experience.

Limited as it was in its realization in this early novel, the satirical aim of showing "the world, which is so very credulous in what it professes to be true" and "most incredulous in what it professes to be imaginary" (*NN*, pref.), that the novel can provide a "Faithful Account" of "reality" remained Dickens's goal. Although he always privileged "fancy" (*LD*, pref.), in preface after preface he insisted on the factual basis of his representations—that they were "pictures of an existing reality" *(NN)*, "precisely from the life" *(MC)*, "substantially true" *(BH)*. Claiming that his fictions were credible, he claimed, in effect, that, like Bank of England notes, they "should strike conviction at once" ("Review," 426) and legitimately so, because like those notes, his novels were "representatives of weightier value" ("Old Lady," 130) and derived their moral authority from a "solid ground." Ruskin made the analogy explicit when he argued that "The reader expects wisdom from a book as the owner of a bank note expects it to be transferrable for gold" (Shell, *Economy*, 135). This "realism," in short, modeled itself on an ideal monetary economy;[7] conversely, but similarly, political economists looked to aesthetics when they defined credit: "Credit, having a legitimate origin, is like the image in a mirror, existent only when representing a tangible reality; if of spurious birth, it is an ignis fatuus leading astray the unwary" (Langton, 4).

By this definition, however, no media of exchange would circulate except Bank of England notes, and that was hardly the case. Although the gold standard remained fixed, and although, under the circumstances, "money—in the form of precious metals—remain[ed] the foundation from which the credit system, by its very nature c[ould] never detach itself'" (Marx, 3:606), the credit system expanded considerably in the 1840s and 1850s through a proliferation of forms that bore an increasingly attenuated relationship to capital and yet were considered "indispensable for rendering the whole capital of the country productive" (Mill, 3:529) and responsible for the mid-century "bound in national prosperity" (Bagehot, 9:124). An abstract and problematic prosperity, though, since the value accruing from the "extension of the unreal basis of circulation" (Mills, 19) appeared to be merely nominal: not only does "credit . . . divorce the name entirely from what it is supposed to represent" (Shell, *Money*, 109), but also it places into question the representational claims per se of any economic inscriptions. The development of the symbolic economy thus required that an alternative but still "legitimate origin" for truth and value be found. Through a series of elaborate rationalizations, "character" supplanted capital[8] and justified its lack.

The very abstractness of credit made this possible. As a " 'force,' " an " 'imponderable,' " and even a " 'faith' " (Langton, 4), credit appeared to leave the materialism of capitalism behind. Dispensing with the limitations of cash, credit also dispense with its stigma: "confidence" was exchanged rather than money. "Credit is a thing of moral essence" (Mills, 19), political economists insisted, and its extensive circulation thus marked "a great progress" (Bagehot, 9:389) in the moral economy. Where the media of exchange represented not capital but (putative) character, "A man" could "deriv[e] an income from his credibility . . . and from the confidence reposed in him" (9:324), Bagehot argued, and the profits homoeconomicus thereby accrued could be tallied to his further reputation: "credit," Bagehot claimed, was synonymous with " 'respectability' " (9:324). Thus, the "imprudence" of engaging in "*any* speculation" had become the "probity which . . . is really . . . a conspicuous feature in the English character" and "has enabled us to aid our enterprises by a vast and elaborate system of credit" (Bagehot, 10:53). In effect the means for concealing the motive of capitalist enterprise had been institutionalized, and moralized, within capitalism itself. Of course, where "Our hard capital is clothed in that soft webwork of confidence and opinion; on a sudden it may be stripped bare" (Bagehot, 10:54) when crisis develops and hard cash comes into demand. But even as "Panic, the most rigorous of realists" (Mills, 19) periodically exacted its dues and exposed the "hollowness" of England's "apparent prosperity" (Evans, 1), it did not take ideology to account. On the contrary, in the "elaborate commercial civilisation" where "we have coined credit itself into a currency" (Bagehot, 10:67)—and, not incidentally, increased the "contingent opportunities" for profitable exchange—"honesty and veracity" had come to look like "the very soul of commerce" (Sargant, 428).

Ironically, then, the political economists and moralists who could censure the circulation of "fictitious capital" (Spencer, 140) had nevertheless found profit in fiction by (nominally) appropriating the "higher" moral values it was said to represent and to inculcate, in opposition to the debased, materialist "values" of commerce. Indeed, Dickens (of all writers) had been "credited with halting 'the decline which the influx of wealth, and the prevalence of commercial ideas, might otherwise have a tendency to produce" (Poovey, 103) in the earlier part of his career. Not so in the later part, though, when, beginning with *Bleak House,* his value with critics depreciated as they claimed that he took imaginative liberties in his novels and that they therefore no longer exemplified the gold standard of "realism." Thus, one critic asserted that because the "materials" of *Bleak House* were not "true" or "suggestive allegorically," no proper value could accrue from the exchange between Dickens and his readers. He had over-extended his credit:

The plot is invariably his great difficulty; and, like other gentlemen similarly circumstanced, he strives, by every artifice at least, to hide them, for the sake of his credit. He wants the reader to trust him. He has the art of exciting the most lively expectations; he has the art of sustaining them. Renewal upon renewal he obtains for those literary bills, during the progress of the story's existence; and, when it dies, there are no assets found to pay half-a-crown in twenty shillings.   (q. in Collins, 281)

Failing to realize the speculative interest he had aroused through his ''fail[ure] in the construction of the plot,'' Dickens had, of course, failed to meet the critic's conventional expectations of narrative in general and Dickensian narrative in particular. But as Jonathan Arac remarks, ''In realism, the imagination is always at a crisis, passing judgment on the inadequacy of old forms for the urgencies of the moment'' (*Commissioned Spirits,* 65): ''reality'' always outstrips literary convention, and so in order for the novel to remain true to the standard of ''realism'' epitomized by Bank of England notes, it must find new modes of representation that will yield a ''Faithful Account.'' This problem continually prompted Dickens's further literary innovations and, beginning with *Bleak House,* put his critical reputation at risk.

His readership, however, grew even more at this time, and while his accounts with critics appeared to be overdrawn, his bank account, unlike that of the nation as a whole, was quite flush. Not only was the sale of *Bleak House* considerably greater than that of any previous serial, but also this novel ''inaugurated a sustained increase in Dickens's circulation'' (Patten, 216)—in his popularity and his profitability, as ''the reputation earned by any of his novels seemed to work on the next'' (Patten, 207). Even reviewers who took Dickens to task admitted in the 1850s that ''His name is . . . a 'Household Word' '' (q. in Collins, 382); circulating ''universal[ly]'' (q. in Collins, 383), not unlike a Bank of England note, it had come to represent a sure investment for his readers, as well as for his publishers (not to mention the innumerable organizations and individuals who continued to seek to profit from the credibility the use of his name would confer). Thus, Dickens's publishers suggested that he serialize the novel that would become *Hard Times* (1854) in order to improve the languishing sales of *Household Words,* which it did. For, as the *Economist* wrote, ''The works of Dickens . . . are [as] sure to be sold and read as the bread which is baked is sure to be sold and eaten'' (q. in Patten, 236). By the 1850s, then, the ''United Metropolitan Improved Hot Muffin,'' etc., had gained weight; the Dickens venture in imaginary capital had become an establishment producing sure profits from a known commodity; Dickens had acquired a ''capital name'' (*Letters,* 7:613).

This is the phrase he used in 1855 when describing the title of his new serial, ''Nobody's Fault,'' and although he eventually (and significantly) changed it to *Little Dorrit,* the phrase continues to reverberate ironically and resoundingly throughout the novel and the culture it represents. For *Little Dorrit* is centrally about credit,[9] which signifies the absence of capital in relation to any name; it is about exchange conducted in name alone and about the essential social and economic "hollowness" that the circulation of credit conceals; and it is about what Dickens regards as the absolute debasement of value and negation of truth that the universal exchange of this currency entails. In *Little Dorrit,* then, Dickens returns to the aim of *Nicholas Nickleby* of demonstrating that "the world, which is so very credulous in what it professes to be true" and "most incredulous in what it professes to be imaginary," credits the wrong professions—in this case, the rhetoric of political economists and the discourse of credit. But insofar as he also calls attention to the "coining" of this medium of exchange through the equivocal nature of language itself, he also jeopardizes the project of realism and the credibility of a novel with a "capital name."

The credibility of economic credit, however, can easily be dispensed with: "credit" is simply a misnomer; it is "debt" by a more decorous name. The standard mid-century definition of "the party who borrows" as the one who "obtains credit" (McCulloch, 70) makes this substitution tacitly, for it makes no mention that "the party who borrows" goes into debt. The consequences of this verbal sleight of hand are profound. For where Parliament could argue that " 'Credit must be, or commerce cannot be, and without it, no civilization,' " and that " 'All transactions have a claim to credit, from the milk score or the newspaper bill to the State loan' " (q. in Dunlop, 26), not only was an entire culture based on and sustained through the circulation of a figure of speech—metonymy, literally "name-change"—but also the lack that the language of credit conceals became a right and a virtue. The inhabitants of Bleeding Heart Yard in *Little Dorrit* certainly express these "noble sentiments" as they patronize Mrs. Plornish's grocery, "exclusively confining themselves to owing," though they do provide her with an " 'excellent connexion.' " " 'The business is very steady indeed,' " says Mrs. Plornish; " 'The only thing that stands in the way . . . is the Credit.' " This "large stumbling-block in Mrs. Plornish's trade" (575) is hardly limited to Bleeding Heart Yard, for as political economists noted, "it is contended that half the business of the country is really carried on by its [credit's] means." When this contention was translated as "What all such statements really amount to is, that a large proportion of those engaged in industrial occupations do not employ their own capital merely, but also that of others" (McCulloch, 73), what this situation "really amounts to" begins to emerge: a vast appropriation of "social capital" and its concentration in the hands of individual bankers and "creditors." Credit, then, is not only debt rendered respectable, but also a socially sanctioned form of fraud and theft,[10] justified—that is, obscured—by a "name-change" and perpetuated by and through the linguistic medium that constitutes socio-economic exchange—by and through the dis-course of credit.

These complex observations inform Dickens's representation of Merdle, the shady financier and a focal point of the novel, who "was in everything good, from banking to building. He was in Parliament, of course. He was in the City, necessarily. He was Chairman of this, Trustee of that, President of the other" (246–7), and, crucially, "chief projector establisher, and manager" of "the wonderful Bank . . . the latest of the many Merdle wonders" (558) and the sort of establishment that "lives on its credit" and profits from "belie[f]" (Bagehot, 9:394). Merdle's "credit," however, depends on the willful suspension of disbelief, for the eventual "revelation," subsequent to his suicide, that Merdle's earlier mysterious "complaint" "had been simply, Forgery and Robbery" (710) has been obvious all along, where Bar, Bishop, Treasury, the Circumlocution Office, and all of Society have Merdle "habitu-ally in their view" (556) and where the mute Merdle habitually and expres-sively stands "with his hands crossed under his uneasy coat-cuffs, clasping his wrists as if he were taking himself into custody" (394). But where "Soci-ety and he had so much to do with one another in all things else, that it is hard to imagine his complaint . . . being solely his own affair" (254), there is "a tacit agreement" that any questions regarding his "credit"—its own—"must be stifled" (556).

It is in Society's best interest, then, that the inflationary rhetoric that accom-panies Merdle be sustained and that his name be circulated ever more widely. In the upper tiers of government, the Barnacles pay "homage" to Merdle and thus "bolstered . . . the wonderful Bank and all the wonderful undertak-ings went on and went up" (570), while "Down in Bleeding Heart Yard, . . . as lively an interest was taken in this paragon of men as on the Stock Exchange" (571). Arthur Clennam, who "observed anew, that wherever he went, he saw, or heard, or touched, the celebrated name of Merdle" (585), observes, in effect, that the name of Merdle is coextensive with space, as it is with time: " 'The name of Merdle is the name of the age' " (484). It has become the universal medium of exchange, and its comprehensive circulation in *Little Dorrit* is indicative of the totalizing discourse of credit in the mid-Victorian period.[11]

This discourse, a textual *"concatenation"* (Goux, 48; his emph.) which organized the attenuated and comprehensive configurations of exchange into "that web-work of confidence and opinion," had paradoxically become more binding than the "cash-nexus." Conducted through language slipping along a representational continuum, with metonymy stretching toward metalepsis, the expansive circulation of credit in the 1850s was also centralized, in the manner of synechdoche, in the institutions of the City. The "City" thus stood for the economy as a whole, exerting a centrifugal attraction for far-flung capital and credit and dispersing these centripetally in ever wider spheres of circulation. The versatile medium of language had expanded the horizons of exchange in time and space, but for all of its latitude, credit was, and is, a "dimension of constraint" (51), as Jean Baudrillard observes, and as Dickens emphasized: "credit" is only a nominal transformation of the reality of "debt," and debt shackles the present and the future to the past and places volition under distraint. " 'I have no will' " (20), says Arthur Clennam, the middle-aged hero of this mid-century novel, in which the defunct Marshalsea Debtors' Prison provides a fitting image for the mid-Victorian world—an image at one end of "the great carceral continuum, which . . . extends without interruption from the smallest coercions to the longest penal detention" (Foucault, 303). At the other end, stands the Circumlocution Office, which has forced Clennam's partner and alter-ego, the industrious Daniel Doyce, to take his invention abroad through its institutionalization of the rule of "How Not To Do It" (104) in a proliferation of forms and formalities that absorb "all the business of the country" (106). These two institutions of the novel "neatly epitomis[e]" (57) each other, and credit, a totalizing system of free-floating signs and rigid coercion, subtends both—and not only in *Little Dorrit*. For, where the discourse of credit is coterminous with the money-market, and the money market, as contemporaries observed, "like the principle of life, is everywhere" (Lalor, 68), this discourse has become, in "reality," a carceral totality.

Its exposure as such is central to the "realist" project of *Little Dorrit*. Indeed, Dickens appears to have been very deliberate in this "deliberately pondered" (Butt, 2) novel to shape the narrative to coincide with the structure and circulation of this discourse, for the "economy" of *Little Dorrit*—from its conception, to its organization and narrative development, to its specific system of tropes—is not simply analogous to, but identical with the economy as a whole.

"People to meet and part as travellers do, and the future connexion between them" should "be worked out as in life," Dickens noted in the number plans; "Try this uncertainty and this not putting of them together, as a new means of interest," he added. "Indicate and carry through this intention" (no. 1). Thus, all the characters are "thrown together by chance" (23), but through the "destined interweaving of their stories" (100) in the "bad design" (pref.) Merdle epitomizes, they find themselves literally and figuratively incarcerated. Bound within such a determinate world, the characters in *Little Dorrit* are also situated within a larger nineteenth-century development Ian Hacking terms "the taming of chance"[12] in which the efforts of statisticians to understand the speculative crises precipitated by the expansion of the credit system had a decisive role. For when they looked back on the recurrence of "mania" and "panic" since 1825 and "discovered" that they "occur periodically, and in accordance with natural law" (Williams, 49), they could assert that "The philosophy of this matter recognises as little of Fate as it does of Chance" (Mills, 38)—quite an intellectual "progress," in which crises are inevitable and can be charged to "Nobody's Fault." Precisely these rationalizations provide the rationale for the "progress" of the narrative toward the universal speculation in Merdle, the failure of the "wonderful Bank," and the ensuing crisis in *Little Dorrit,* through which Dickens represents the crisis that occurred in the money market while the novel was being serialized (December 1855–June 1857).

That crisis had, in fact, been triggered by the revelation of fraud in a number of wonderful Banks and their subsequent failure. "Panic" then exposed the "deep-rooted system of fictitious credit" that "had so thoroughly expanded through all branches of business" (Evans, *History,* 30) and "drawn[n] its nutriments from . . . underneath our whole social fabric" (Spencer, 146), and this led, of course, to a great deal of moralizing about "the decline and fall of mercantile morality throughout the civilized world" (Evans, *Facts,* 5), which, of course, problematized the notion that "as civilization advances, credit advances" (Bagehot, 9:324). An elaborate ideological calculus came to the rescue, though, in the argument that the distinguishing feature of "the advanced and highly organized" society of England was "the evolution of something that stands for a *social self-consciousness*" ("credit," no doubt) and that "to this is chiefly ascribable the impression that commercial malpractices are increasing" (Spencer, 141). Fraud, in effect, had become a sign of moral "progress" and a cause for self-congratulation.

Topically charged with the events of 1856–57,[13] *Little Dorrit* radically criticizes the ideology that found in the credit crisis ways to "bolster" its credit. Defending "the preposterous fancy that a bad design will sometimes claim to be a good . . . design" by the "curious coincidence" between the individuals and concerns implicated in the scandals of 1856–57 and "that extravagant conception Mr. Merdle" and his "laudable enterprises" in the novel (pref.), Dickens asserts that his critical "realism" is factually based. But he also reinforces his opposition to contemporary ideology through narrative strategies that undo "progress" precisely because they mimic the structure of credit. Thus, even as recent events in the money market inform *Little Dorrit,* the novel is set in 1826,[14] during the crisis that "Introduce[d] All the Rest." In returning to the period of *Nicholas Nickleby*—to the emergence of the speculative economy and the explosion of "contingent opportunities"—Dickens not only again foregrounds the irreducible (and inadmissable) chanciness of exchange, but also negates both "progress" and its "cause" as the conflation of the past with the present brings history to a standstill and recapitulates the way that "credit" constrains time.

Moreover, while the narrative of *Little Dorrit* cannot entirely halt the narrative process which is history, its shaping of the economic developments between 1826 and 1856 does directly negate the conventional history of capitalism in that period. Thus, with its parody of a residual agrarian capitalism through the heavily mediated economic relations of the suburban Patriarch to the income-producing urban "estate" of Bleeding Heart Yard; with its figuration of the decline of mercantile capitalism through the literal fall of the House of Clennam; with its critical commentary on the marginalization of industrialization through the forced emigration of Doyce; and with its ironic representation of Merdle as "the shining light of the time" (513) and the apotheosis of capitalism in the credit system, *Little Dorrit*'s history is both inclusive and subversive. In this history, furthermore, the progressive scheme that nominally defines the division of the novel into two books, "Poverty" and "Riches," is reversed in a pattern of "gain and loss" which organizes the "general economy of the novel," an economy "that ensures that anything taken will be taken away" (Nunokawa, 8–9); as Mr. Plornish "growled, in his philosophical but not lucid manner . . . there was ups, you see, and there was downs" (731).

Those "ups and downs," finally, are generated in the novel by the figures of speech that literally generate and circulate credit. The "ups" derive from both metonymy, through which, again, credit is "coined" and exchanged—thus Merdle's "daily occupation of causing the British name to be more and more respected in all parts of the globe"—and synechdoche, through which, again, its circulation is centralized—thus the globe's "appreciation of world-wide commercial enterprise and gigantic combination of skill and capital" focused on Merdle's name (394). The "downs" also derive from these tropes, from synechdoche, through which the circulation of credit contracts as "Panic" develops—when Merdle's "complaint" becomes public, "the night air" in the City is "laden with a heavy muttering of the name of Merdle, coupled with every form of execration" (710)—and from metonymy, as the effects of "Panic" spread outward, along the linkages of exchange—"The Inquest was over, the letter was public, the Bank was broken, the other model structures had taken fire and turned to smoke" and there "was nothing but ruin" (711).

Through this mimetic correspondence between the "pattern" the novelist "weave[s]" (pref.) and the discourse of credit, *Little Dorrit* demystifies the "web-work" in which Victorian culture was enmeshed. But insofar as the novel calls attention to credit as a totalizing discourse, it is of course fully entangled in this language that is "everywhere" and everywhere corrupting. Indeed, Dickens points to language itself as both the source and the symptom of the "moral disease" that sweeps through the novel. As "the name of Merdle" is "deposited on every lip, and carried into every ear" (571), speculations in his name "spread with the rapidity and malignity of the Plague"

(571)—"the metonymic malady par excellence" (Arac, *Commissioned Spirits,* 181), the malady that Dickens's spreads metonymically through the novel. "The poison is communicable" (571), and it is communicated through language—and, more specifically, through the written language that links credit and the novel directly.[15] Thus, the pupils in Bleeding Heart Yard, who "had been sent the copy, 'Merdle, Millions' " (575), had been set to write the text that constitutes credit and the novel, to produce the form in which both circulate, as ink on paper, "ink" itself being associated with *infecere,* to stain, to taint, to infect (Arac, *Commissioned Spirits,* 131) and circulating, we recall, in association with Dickens's name.

Under the circumstances, Little Dorrit's assertion, " 'We can always go back to the plain truth' " (497), sounds wistful at best,[16] and Dickens's depiction of her as an angel of truth and the locus of value in the novel hardly seems plausible. That may be the point[17]—to challenge the faith of the world, which "is so very incredulous in what it professes to be imaginary," to believe the linguistic fiat by which Dickens creates her; after all, "the world, which is so very credulous in what it professes to be true," believes in the fiat currency of credit. The figurative "vanishing point" (733) of the novel, Little Dorrit provides the corrective perspective on Merdle, its literal "vanishing point." But the references to her as " 'the best of all . . . riches' " (418) do not so much affirm her value as call attention to the equivocal nature of language, and where the angel of truth is also the angel of death,[18] her promise of apocalyptic revelation is also incommensurate with any claim to credible representation. The "solid ground" of realism vanishes through her, as it does through Merdle. Indeed, with the "realism" of *Little Dorrit* tied to the representation of the misrepresentation that constitutes the discourse of credit, this "realism" seems to have floated free of any "solid ground" whatsoever. Paradoxically, then, Dickens's investment in the gold standard of representation has rendered "realism" bankrupt.

While Dickens cannot resolve this crisis through Little Dorrit herself, through the "pattern" he "weave[s]" between Little Dorrit's name and Merdle's, the "nominal" coincides with the "real" in one instance to affirm—albeit marginally—the possibility of truthful representation. Thus, in contrast to Merdle's name, which epitomizes the way that "credit . . . divorces the name entirely from what it is supposed to represent," Little Dorrit's name literally materializes when Flora Finching calls the unfinished dress Little Dorrit had been sewing for her "Little Dorrit" (417). Here, " 'Investments *is* the word' " (581, my emph.), unequivocally, as it is not when Pancks insists that "Investments is the word' " for speculations in Merdle's name. For, whereas Merdle's self-incarcerating stance with "his hands crossed under his uneasy coat-cuff" points precisely to the disjunction between the nominal attribution and the real situation, Little Dorrit's investment of her labor in this dress suggests that Flora does not in fact take a "liberty" (416) "with that strangest of denominations" (417). Exemplifying the gold standard of representation, "Little Dorrit" thus secures the credibility of "realism," and "laid by for a keepsake, just as it is" (417), the unfinished dress becomes a token not of an obsolete mode of representation, but of a "pattern'" for the novelist to take up and "weave" again. For the time being, though, "Little Dorrit," rather than Little Dorrit herself, serves as the "solid ground" for *Little Dorrit's* claim to a " 'capital name.' "

NOTES

1. See Court (100ff., 175ff.) and Checkland (13ff., 50–51, 189–212) for details. Marx analyzes these developments thoroughly (see esp. 3:39lff.). Cf. Goux's summary of this history as a "passage from fetish to symbol to sign" (49).
2. Marx points to the fundamentally speculative nature of exchange (1:113).
3. Wicke discusses the Advertiser in relation to Dickens' novels and contemporary promotional practices in detail.
4. The ensuing account of plagiarism is based on Slater's (xxvi–xxxii).
5. Marcus, along with other critics, has noted the way that this opposition persists in Dickens' conception of virtually every character in the novel (*Dickens,* 95ff.).
6. Cf. Weber (17, 53).
7. Vernon also notes that "the conventions of paper money and the conventions of realistic fiction constitute a code collectively shared" (96 & passim).
8. Cf. Arac's discussion of the production of the Victorian conception of "character" and his allusion to both economic reasons for and economic expressions of its privileged position ("Hamlet," esp. 84, 86, 93).
9. Although many critics have focused on social "respectability" (e.g., Lund), none, as far as I know, has considered the its economic "synonym," in relation to *Little Dorrit.* Holoch's remarks concerning the novel's exposure of the use of "the language of abstract cultural values to justify economically motivated social practices" (346) comes the closest.
10. "Social capital" is Marx's term for credit, and he makes these points about its appropriation explicitly (3:438–39).
11. Cf. Childers' discussion of "progress" as the totalizing discourse of the mid-Victorian period and of *Little Dorrit.*
12. My remarks on statistical political economy follow the argument Hacking lays out concerning the self-justifying premises and operations of statistics generally (15ff.).
13. See Butt, Russell (ch. 6), and Weiss (ch. 8) for detailed accounts of the scandals in the City during the 1850s.
14. As Russell notes (131), Dickens establishes this date explicitly (in bk 1, ch. 18).
15. Shell, *Money* (7).

16. Cf. Carlisle's argument that *"Little Dorrit* is an inquiry into the moral status of fiction" (195) which ultimately concludes that "Like Little Dorrit herself, [fiction] cannot tell the whole truth" (211).
17. Raymond Williams argues thus about "the act of faith" Dickens's "miracle" requires (224).
18. Welsh, 182.

WORKS CITED

Arac, Jonathan. *Commissioned Spirits: The Shaping of Social Motion in Dickens, Carlyle, Melville, and Hawthorne.* New York: Columbia UP, 1989.

——. "Hamlet, *Little Dorrit,* and the History of Character." In *Critical Conditions: Regarding the Historical Moment.* Michael Hays, ed. Minneapolis: U of Minnesota P, 1992.

Bagehot, Walter. *The Collected Works of Walter Bagehot.* Norman St John-Stevas, ed. 13 vols. Aylesbury, Bucks: Hazell Watson and Viney, Ltd., 1965–78.

Baudrillard, Jean. "Consumer Society." In *Selected Writings.* Mark Poster, ed. Stanford: Stanford UP, 1988.

Butt, John. "The Topicality of *Little Dorrit.*" *University of Toronto Quarterly* 29 (1959):1–10.

Carlisle, Janice M. *"Little Dorrit*: Necessary Fictions." *Studies in the Novel* 7, 2 (Summer 1975):195–214.

Checkland, S. G. *The Rise of Industrial Society in England, 1815–1885.* London: Longmans, 1964.

Childers, Joseph. "History, Totality, and Opposition: The New Historicism and *Little Dorrit.*" *Dickens Quarterly* 6, 4 (December 1989):150–57.

Collins, Philip. *Dickens: The Critical Heritage.* London: Routledge and Kegan Paul, 1971.

Court, W. H. B. *A Concise Economic History of Britain from 1750 to Recent Times.* Cambridge: Cambridge UP, 1954.

Dickens, Charles. *Nicholas Nickleby, Martin Chuzzlewit, Bleak House, Little Dorrit. The Oxford Illustrated Dickens.* New York: Oxford UP, 1989.

——. "The Old Lady in Threadneedle Street." In *Charles Dickens' Uncollected Writings from Household Words, 1850–1859,* vol. 1. Harry Stone, ed. Bloomington: Indiana UP, 1968.

Dunlop, C. R. B. "Debtors and Creditors in Dickens' Fiction." *Dickens Studies Annual* 19 (1990):25–47.

Evans, D. Morier. *Facts, Failures, and Frauds: Revelations Financial, Mercantile, Criminal.* London: Groombridge and Sons, 1859.

————. *The History of the Commercial Crisis, 1857–58, and the Stock Exchange Panic of 1859.* London: Groombridge and Sons, 1859.

Feltes, N. N. *Modes of Production of Victorian Novels.* Chicago: U of Chicago P, 1986.

Forster, John. *The Life of Charles Dickens.* New York: Doubleday, 1928.

Foucault, Michel. *Discipline and Punish: The Birth of the Prison.* Alan Sheridan trans. New York: Random House, 1979.

Goux, Jean-Joseph. *Symbolic Economies after Marx and Freud.* Jennifer Curtiss Gage, trans. Ithaca: Cornell UP, 1990.

Hacking, Ian. *The Taming of Chance.* Cambridge: Cambridge UP, 1990.

Heinzelman, Kurt. *The Economics of the Imagination.* Amherst: U of Massachusetts P, 1980.

Hollingshead, John. "The City of Unlimited Paper." *Household Words* 17 (19 December 1857).

Holoch, George. "Consciousness and Society in *Little Dorrit.*" *Victorian Studies* 21 (Spring 1978):335–51.

Langton, William. "Observations on a Table Showing the Balance of Account Between the Mercantile Public and the Bank of England, from 1844 to 1857, Inclusive." Rev. 1876. *Transactions of the Manchester Statistical Society, 1857–58.* Salford: J. Roberts, 1876.

Lalor, John. *Money and Morals: A Book for the Times.* London: John Chapman, 1852.

Levine, George. *Darwin and the Novelists: Patterns of Science in Victorian Fiction.* Chicago: U of Chicago P, 1991.

Lund, Roger D. "Genteel Fictions: Caricature and Satirical Design in *Little Dorrit.*" *Dickens Studies Annual* 10 (1981):45–66.

McCulloch, J. R. *The Principles of Political Economy, with Some Inquiries Respecting Their Application.* 5th ed. Edinburgh: Adam and Charles Black, 1864.

Mackay, Charles. *Extraordinary Popular Delusions and the Madness of Crowds* (1841). New York: Crown, 1980.

Marcus, Steven. *Dickens from Pickwick to Dombey.* New York: Norton, 1865.

————. *Representations: Essays on Literature and Society.* New York: Columbia UP, 1990.

Marx, Karl. *Capital,* Frederick Engels, ed. Vol. 1, New York: International Publishers, 1967. Vol. 3, Moscow: Progress Publishers, 1966.

Mill, John Stuart. *The Collected Works of John Stuart Mill.* J. M. Robson, ed. Toronto: University of Toronto Press, 1967.

Mills, John. "On Credit Cycles and the Origin of Commercial Panics." *Transactions of the Manchester Statistical Society, 1867–68.* Manchester: J. Roberts, 1968.

Nunokawa, Jeff. *The Afterlife of Property: Domestic Security and the Victorian Novel.* Princeton: Princeton UP, 1994.

Patten, Robert L. *Charles Dickens and His Publishers.* Oxford: Clarendon, 1978.

Poovey, Mary. *Uneven Developments: The Ideological Work of Gender in Mid-Victorian England.* Chicago: U of Chicago P, 1988.

Russell, Norman. *The Novelist and Mammon: Literary Responses to the World of Commerce in the Nineteenth Century.* Oxford: Clarendon, 1986.

Sargant, William Lucas. *The Science of Social Opulence.* London: Simpkin, Marshall & Co., 1856.

Shell, Marc. *The Economy of Literature.* Baltimore: Johns Hopkins UP, 1978.

———. *Money, Language, and Thought: Literary & Philosophical Economies from the Medieval to the Modern Era.* Berkeley: U of California P, 1982.

Slater, Michael. "The Composition and Monthly Publication of *Nicholas Nickleby.*" In *Nicholas Nickleby* facs. ed. Philadelphia: U of Pennsylvania P, 1982.

Spencer, Herbert. "The Morals of Trade" (1859). In *Essays Scientific, Political, and Speculative,* vol. 3. New York: D. Appleton and Company, 1892.

Storey, Graham, Kathleen Tillotson, and Angus Easson, eds. *The Letters of Charles Dickens.* Vol. 7, 1853–55. Oxford: Clarendon, 1993.

Vernon, John. *Money & Fiction: Literary Realism in the Nineteenth and Early Twentieth Centuries.* Ithaca: Cornell UP, 1984.

Weber, Max. *The Protestant Ethic and the Spirit of Capitalism.* Talcott Parsons, trans. Scribner's, 1958.

Welsh, Alexander. *The City of Dickens.* Cambridge: Harvard UP, 1986.

Wicke, Jennifer. *Advertising Fictions: Literature, Advertisement, and Social Reading.* New York: Columbia UP, 1988.

Williams, Raymond. "Social Criticism in *Little Dorrit.*" *Critical Quarterly* 6 (1964):217–29.

Williams, T. H. "Observations on Money, Credit, and Panics." *Transactions of the Manchester Statistical Society, 1857–58.* Manchester: J. Roberts, 1858.

Wills, W. H. "Review of a Popular Publication." *Household Words* 1 (27 July 1850).

"Mr. Popular Sentiment": Dickens and the Gender Politics of Sentimentalism and Social Reform Literature

Mary Lenard

The career of Charles Dickens is a crucial site for investigating the gender politics of sentimentalism and social reform because in order to be effective as a social reform writer who opposed the masculinized discourses of Utilitarianism and laissez-faire capitalism, Dickens used the same feminized language of emotion and sentiment that the Victorian reading public associated with women writers. When, for example, he said in an 1854 article opposing the ideas of political economy that "into the relations between employers and employed . . . there must enter something of feeling and sentiment" ("On Strike" 553), Dickens echoed cultural agents like the following extract from an 1853 review in the *Gentlemen's Magazine:* "our literature and our morals require more and more for their basis a sound increasing knowledge and sympathy between all orders of men . . . [which] women can especially forward" ("Lady Novelists of Great Britain" 24). Statements like the one in this review, however, identified women, with their "naturally" more emotional and sympathetic perspective, as ideal social reform writers, and the Victorian reading public seems to have concurred with this identification, as feminist critic Christine Krueger has pointed out: "By 1850 the tradition of the woman preacher as the writer of the social narrative had been thoroughly integrated into Victorian culture. Women were expected to place their literary talents in the service of social reform" (231).

As Krueger suggests, these cultural expectations affected women writers, because while on one hand they were given a powerful political voice through their social reform writing, this writing was limited in both tone and subject matter. But Dickens's own position as a male writer trying to work within this feminized discourse was also fraught with difficulty, both within the

Victorian period and in his critical history since. Like Charlotte Elizabeth Tonna, Dickens used fiction to advocate the creation of moral consciousness; he played the role of the "good spirit who would take the house-tops off . . . and show a Christian people . . . pale phantoms rising from the scenes of our too-long neglect" *(Dombey and Son* 738).[1] Sentimentalist social reform discourse, with its use of Christian preaching and pathetic scenes of physical and emotional suffering, was clearly one of the most effective methods that he used to fulfill that design. The "exaggerated forms" of Dickens's characters—such as the crossing-sweeper Jo in *Bleak House* and Betty Higden in *Our Mutual Friend*—enabled his readers to see and feel the urban poor, even as Tonna's readers saw and felt the workers in the textile mills (Collins, *Critical Heritage* 524). In other words, Dickens's fiction often had the same moralistic sense of social purpose, and reliance on pathos and emotionalism, that his audience normally associated with women writers. If we lay out some key Victorian cultural assumptions in a series of binaries that have been suggested by Nancy Armstrong, Jane Tompkins, and other feminist critics, it is possible to see that Dickens fits in the right-hand column of all of the binary pairs except, conspicuously, the first:

male	female
intellect/mind	emotion/heart
objectivity	sympathy
abstract	personalized
financial/physical power	spiritual/moral power
realistic/objective	sentimental

Although these binaries essentialize gender, they are crucial for any discussion of social reform literature, which depends on such commonly-held cultural values, generalizations though they may be, for its cultural work. In addition, I think that feminist critics have already demonstrated the cultural significance of these binaries for the production and reception of women's writing in the nineteenth century. What I want to do is demonstrate their cultural significance for the production and reception of Dickens's writing: first by revealing Dickens as a male sentimentalist, and second by exploring the implications of this uneasy position.

One of Dickens's earliest novels, *Oliver Twist,* clearly shows Dickens deliberately using sentimentalist conventions and assumptions, especially those about gender. The novel was the first that Dickens himself planned from beginning to end, since the original idea of *Pickwick Papers* had come from its publishers, Chapman and Hall. He wrote that he had "thrown his whole heart and soul'' (*Letters,* vol. 1, 227) into it and it is evident that the criticism of the 1834 New Poor Law was a key element in his design from the very beginning.[2] Following the classic theories of economists, the law discouraged freeloaders by making workhouse life deliberately less attractive than private employment. Inmates were kept on a sparse diet, denied outdoor exercise, received poor medical care, and married couples were separated so that they could not produce children to further burden the parish. The Utilitarians who originated and supported the law probably intended for it to be more humanely enforced, and resented what they saw as a cheap emotional attack based on ignorance—an accusation that established Dickens's feminized cultural position. Dickens's opposition constructed him as a well-meaning, but basically ignorant, individual who was too easily moved by pathos and was misleading society by his sentimental and hysterical rhetoric.

Harriet Martineau, a well-known public defender of political economy, made this somewhat restrained comment on the subject in her *Autobiography,* deploring Dickens's ''vigorous erroneousness about matters of science, as shown in *Oliver Twist* about the new poor-law . . . there are many who wish that he [Dickens] would abstain from a set of difficult subjects, on which all true sentiment must be underlain by a sort of knowledge which he has not. The more fervent and inexhaustible his kindliness (and it is fervent and inexhaustible,) the more important it is that it should be well-informed . . . '' (*Autobiography,* vol. 2, 62).[3] This critique responds to Dickens's own use of the feminized cultural values of sentimentalist social reform discourse in *Oliver Twist.* The way that Dickens connects evil and cruelty with a cold and ruthlessly self-serving Utilitarian ''philosophy'' sets up two entirely opposed value systems in the novel, a ''masculine'' Utilitarian value system and a feminine one based on sentimental morality. In addition, although the novel heavily favors the sentimental value system as the only available option in opposition to the Utilitarian values represented by the New Poor Law and Fagin's gang, it also betrays Dickens's discomfort with the gender binaries that classify these value systems. This discomfort, I believe, is emblematic of Dickens own vexed position as a male sentimentalist.

The ''good'' characters in *Oliver Twist,* such as Mr. Brownlow and the Maylies, are explicitly shown to base their actions on altruistic impulses that derive from sympathetic feelings, and these characters are feminized as a result. The sight of Oliver recovering from his illness in chapter 12, for example, moves Mr. Brownlow to stereotypically sentimental tears: ''Mr. Brownlow's heart, being large enough for any six ordinary old gentlemen of humane disposition, forced a supply of tears into his eyes, by some hydraulic process which we are not sufficiently philosophical to be in a condition to explain'' (129–30). The sarcasm in this passage places Brownlow's display of feeling in explicit opposition to the ''philosophical'' (Utilitarian) failure to account for feeling; his tears are the outward signs of a "heart" that is somehow outside the understanding of masculine discourses like philosophy or science. Brownlow's actions in this scene in fact echo those of a specific woman, his old housekeeper Mrs. Bedwin, who begins "to cry most violently" because of her "considerable delight at seeing him [Oliver] so much better" (128).[4] Oliver's other benefactors, the Maylies, are also prone to these displays of feeling, which are endorsed and even added to by the novel's narrative commentary, especially in the scenes of Rose Maylie's illness and near escape from death.

In fact, it is in the treatment of death that this novel, and Dickens's other novels, are at their most sentimental. As Jane Tompkins has pointed out in her analysis of Harriet Beecher Stowe's *Uncle Tom's Cabin,* sentimentalist death scenes are of supreme cultural importance because they use commonly held religious beliefs in order to judge the injustices of the world by a higher, heavenly standard. When Stowe's Little Eva, passing from life into death, exclaims "O love!—joy!   peace!" (Stowe 257), she "testifies to the reality of the life to come" (Tompkins 129) and to all that that entails. According to the system of eschatological Christian beliefs that guides the sentimentalist vision, the earthly world is subject to a higher order, and the deaths of characters like Little Dick in *Oliver Twist* and Jo in *Bleak House* serve to remind both the other characters and the audience of that order.[5] When Oliver says good-bye to Dick before traveling to London, for example, Dick already prefigures his own death not only in order to arouse audience sympathy, but to remind the audience that what is present in his heavenly vision is *not* present in his earthly life: " 'I heard the doctor say I was dying,' replied the child with a faint smile, . . . 'I know the doctor must be right, Oliver, because I dream so much of Heaven, and Angels, and kind faces that I never see when I am awake' " (96).

These sentimental religious values, which characterize so much of Dickens's fiction, have been summarily dismissed by critics because they have been interpreted as "repositories of clichés from which to draw to evoke automatic reactions for certain kinds of novelistic occasions, such as the child's deathbed or the exaltation of the heroine's virtues" (Larson 6). The "cliché" of the child's deathbed, however, is one of the many aspects of Dickens' work that can be better understood in the context of sentimentalist discourse. The weepy, sentimentalist understanding of death, as embodied by Little Dick and other scenes in *Oliver Twist,* is a crucial part of the sentimental value system that Dickens proposes in opposition to a "masculine," self-serving Utilitarianism which attempts to crush sympathy and sentiment in the name of "philosophical" self-interest.

The values of the "evil" characters, both the parish officials who exploit and mistreat Oliver in the beginning of the novel and the members of the criminal underworld represented by Fagin and his gang, are based on these "masculine," self-serving theories of Utilitarian political economy. In *Oliver Twist,* Dickens portrays the Poor Law's wrongs as directly resulting from its "philosophy" of emotionless practicality. For example, he calls Mrs. Mann, the woman who runs the branch-workhouse where Oliver spends his early childhood, a "very great experimental philosopher" because acting on her "accurate perception of what was good for herself" she "appropriated the greater part of the weekly stipend for her own use" (48). Similarly, the respectable members of the parish poor relief board are "sage, deep, philosophical men" because "they established the rule, that all poor people should have the alternative . . . of being starved by a gradual process in the house, or by a quick one out of it" (55). Moreover, in order to reinforce what he believes is the evil nature of this Utilitarian philosophy, Dickens also tries to rip off its mask of respectability by describing the behavior of Fagin's gang of criminals in terms of "philosophy." When the Artful Dodger and Charley Bates allow the innocent Oliver to be arrested for their crime in chapter 13, for example, they show a "laudable and becoming regard for themselves" that "corroborate[s] and confirm[s] the little code of laws which certain profound and sound-judging philosophers have laid down as the mainsprings of all Nature's deeds and actions" (132).

Neither Mrs. Mann nor the board members show sympathetic feelings towards Oliver, or towards anyone else for that matter, unless it is their practical interest to do so. The same goes for the parish beadle, Mr. Bumble, who only shows emotion when expedient (such as when he courts the well-left widow, Mrs. Corney) and believes that everyone else he encounters is equally insincere. When Oliver shows "horror and fear, too palpable to be mistaken" at the prospect of being indentured to a brutal chimney sweep and pleads for a magistrate's mercy, Bumble calls him an "artful and designing orphan" (65–66). And, although the respectable Mr. Bumble would be horrified at the very idea, Fagin and the other criminals reveal an attitude towards emotion similar to his, in the scene where Fagin and Bill Sikes rehearse Nancy for her mission to recover Oliver from the police after his arrest for pick-pocketing:

> "Oh, my . . . poor, dear, sweet, innocent little brother!" exclaimed Miss Nancy, bursting into tears, and wringing the little basket and the street-door key in an agony of distress. "What has become of him!". . . . Having uttered these words in a most lamentable and heartbroken tone to the immeasurable delight of her hearers, Miss Nancy paused, winked to the company, nodded smilingly round, and disappeared.   (139–40)

Bumble, Fagin, and their ilk tend to see emotions, especially sympathetic emotions such as affection and grief, as strategies to be simulated in pursuit of ruthlessly businesslike goals. So much so, in fact, that they fail to recognize real feeling when it presents itself to them. For example, when Bumble cannot see Oliver's fear and horror in the passage cited earlier, Fagin also fails to recognize Nancy's growing sympathy for Oliver. When she first intercedes to protect the boy, he compliments her acting "more clever than ever tonight. Ha! ha! my dear, you are acting beautifully" and is unpleasantly surprised by the reality of her "strong passions," which increasingly ally her with the forces of good in the novel (166).

Dickens's narration explicitly associates these feelings with Nancy's femininity—"[t]here is something about a roused woman . . . which few men like to provoke" (166)—and this association suggests that, in the value system of Oliver Twist, there is something essentially feminine about Nancy's growing sympathy for Oliver, signified by her passionate emotional reactions, and her inability to stand seeing him mistreated. Fagin himself identifies Nancy's more sympathetic attitude towards Oliver as something in the nature of an occupational hazard: "It's the worst of having to do with women . . . but they're clever, and we can't get on, in our line, without 'em" (167). In addition, Dickens's naming of the baby-farming Mrs. Mann demonstrates how he aligns feminine feelings with goodness: since Mrs. Mann's actions are self-serving and reasonable, rather than altruistic and emotional, Dickens claims that she is, in effect, a man.[6]

This connection of goodness with feminized displays of feeling, accounts for Dickens's "mawkish" (Wilson 20) and sentimental treatment of the good characters. Conversely, what marks the evil characters in this novel is their failure to respond to occasions for sentimentality, like deathbeds, with the "change of heart" that is just as crucial to Dickens as it is to any other sentimentalist writer. Mr. Bumble and Mrs. Mann, for example, completely fail to appreciate the suffering of Little Dick: when Dick says that he will be "glad to die" and go to heaven, the two react with disbelief and cynicism—"I never see [sic] such a hard-hearted little wretch!" (173). Under the lens of a sentimentalist discourse of social reform, the sentimentality that most critics have seen as a flaw therefore reveals itself as an important aspect of the novel's design because in Dickens's construction of things, positive social values are consistently linked with feminized displays of genuine emotion. This construction links Dickens with a sentimentalist cultural discourse primarily associated with feminized social values and with women writers.

The central figure of this novel, however, is not a woman but a boy—a boy, moreover, who continually exhibits "feminine" displays of feeling such as weeping, heart palpitating, and fainting because, as Dickens tells us early in the novel, "Oliver, instead of possessing too little feeling, possessed rather too much" (72). This sentimental quality of "too much feeling" ensures Oliver's salvation, in one scene after another in the novel. Even in the beginning, Oliver escapes from indenture to the brutal chimney sweep by the open display of emotion before the magistrate that is looked on so suspiciously by Mr. Bumble, "He [Oliver] trembled violently, and burst into tears" (66). When first rescued from Fagin's gang by the intervention of Mr. Brownlow, Oliver (quite unintentionally) convinces Mr. Brownlow and Mrs. Bedwin of his sensitivity and essential goodness with the way that he shows his strong emotions: he faints at the sight of the portrait of a dead woman who strongly resembles him (his mother, as it later turns out), and cries when he starts to tell Mr. Brownlow his life story. It is Oliver's "appearance and manner" (149) which arouse the sympathies of Brownlow and Mrs. Bedwin, and the same holds true later in the novel when Rose and Mrs. Maylie are moved by Oliver's attempts to "say . . . in a few tearful words, how deeply he felt the goodness of the two sweet ladies" (284–85). In the moral world of this novel, it seems to be better to have too much feeling than to have too little.

One cannot help noting, however, that it is this same quality of "too much feeling" that sets Oliver up to be a victim in one incident after another—at the hands of Mr. Bumble, Noah Claypole, the Artful Dodger, Fagin, and Bill Sikes. Moreover, Oliver is not the only one of Dickens's many heroes to have "too much feeling." Compare Oliver, for example, to the young David Copperfield, who is given the girlish nickname "Daisy" by Steerforth. The "femininity" of Dickens's heroes was also noted by some astute contemporary readers of Dickens, such as Margaret Oliphant, who noted that "[t]heir [the heroes'] courage is of the order of courage which belongs to women" (Oliphant 451). These incidents seem to signify the instability of the gender binaries embedded in the Victorian domestic ideology, because if physical displays of emotion, and more highly developed moral sensibilities were to be associated mainly with women, as the domestic ideology dictated, then what becomes of the male sentimentalist? In fact, Oliver Twist's situation may be in many ways emblematic of Dickens's own dilemma as a male writer uneasily aligned with a feminized, sentimentalist social reform discourse.

I contend that Dickens's "cross-dressing"—the disjunction between Dickens's own gender and the "gender" of his fiction—has, in many ways, shaped both his work and its critical reception over the years. On one hand, Dickens's admirers, such as Queen Victoria, praised the author's "large loving mind and . . . strongest sympathy with the poorer classes," domesticized feminine virtues which made his death "a great loss" (Collins, *Critical Heritage* 502).[7] On the other hand, many critics also agreed with Thomas Carlyle's assessment that, like a woman (or, more accurately, like the nineteenth-century idea of the domesticized woman), Dickens based his ideas about social issues on his emotional reactions and was simply incapable of grappling intellectually with complex social problems—which meant that he was not taken seriously as an artist or a social critic.[8] Intellectuals, both in the nineteenth century and later, came to look down on Dickens's lack of formal education and his engagement with popular culture; he was considered by George Henry Lewes to be "completely outside philosophy, science, and the higher literature" (*Collins, Dickens: Interviews and Recollections* 26) and by Fitzjames Stephen, to be "utterly destitute of any kind of solid acquirements" (Stephen 9).[9] The identification of "Mr. Popular Sentiment" (as Anthony Trollope labeled Dickens in his 1855 novel, *The Warden*) with sentiment and sympathy, and with popular culture, aligned him with nineteenth-century cultural construc-tions of femininity; indeed, Fitzjames Stephen said that Dickens's "melodra-matic and sentimental stock-in trade" was well suited to "a feminine, irritable, noisy mind, which is always clamouring and shrieking for guidance" (Stephen 9).[10]

This wide divergence in response can be partially explained by shifts in critical values that occurred in the nineteenth century, as Romantic idealism gave way to Realism and then to Aestheticism. In the eighteen-thirties and forties, Lord Jeffrey, the "hanging judge" of literary critics during the Ro-mantic period, wept openly on reading Dickens's famous deathbed scenes in *The Old Curiosity Shop* and *Dombey and Son,* and his Christmas Books, but by the eighteen-sixties and seventies critics like Lewes and Stephen were openly disparaging Dickens's sentimentality even though his popularity with the reading public remained relatively unaffected.[11]

In an 1899 critical study *The Development of the English Novel,* the Yale scholar, Wilbur Cross, theorized that:

> The effect of Dickens's pathos has, in the lapse of a half-century, undergone change; it seems to be of a fanciful world far removed from the actual. It no longer moves to tears, but awakens rather a pleasing aesthetic emotion, because of its poetic qualities, most completely manifest in the marvellous description of Paul Dombey's death. . . . The time comes when both the public and the critic express their want of sympathy with all premeditated emotion by calling it sentimentalism. Against the current offhand condemnation of Dickens's senti-mentalism history, however, will surely protest . . .   (186)

The contrast between the comments of Lord Jeffrey and Cross effectively demonstrates the critical turn away from sentimentalism. By the eighteen-nineties, Cross, in response to famous dismissals like Oscar Wilde's (however ironically intended) statement that "one must have a heart of stone to read the death of Little Nell without laughing" (Ellman 469), had to present an apologia for Dickens's use of pathos. Finally, in an age dominated by New Criticism, it was probably no accident that Dickens, "the thorn in the flesh [of] the formalist" (Edgar 122), reached the nadir of his critical reputation. Pelham Edgar's 1934 "systematic study of the structural evolution of the English novel" is a good example of the typical formalist/structuralist dis-missal of Dickens. Dickens, according to Edgar, was "one of the anomalies of literature who would seem to have produced a great result by defective means'' and was a ''standing menace to the academic critic'' (117).[12] Edgar chiefly disliked Dickens's sensationalism, including his sentimentality, and the moralizing commentary, which was the result of Dickens's unfortunate ''view that the novel was an instrument of social regeneration'' (123).

Most importantly, however, all of these critical assessments implicitly show how Dickens was aligned with the ''feminine'' side of the gender binaries, both before and after the shift in critical values. The alignment had advantages, as Dickens was celebrated for his ''goodness'' and ''kindly feelings,''[13] but it also hindered his capacity to be taken seriously as an intellectual or an artist, even during his lifetime. This dilemma, I believe, provides valuable insights into Dickens's career as a novelist and social reformer and his relationships with his female colleagues. Dickens's novels contain many elements in common with sentimentalist discourse: his use of pathos, his narrative ''preachiness,'' the way that he alluded to commonly-held religious beliefs in order to support his views. Moreover, Dickens publicly supported many causes in common with crusading women reformers like Tonna: causes such as factory reform, poor relief, the reclamation of prostitutes, etc. Even while he favored these causes, however, Dickens continually distanced himself from female social reform writers like Frances Trollope and Harriet Beecher Stowe by claiming artistic superiority over them, and, for good measure, he then went on to satirize female social reformers in caricatures such as Mrs. Jellyby and Mrs. Pardiggle in *Bleak House.*

At two different points in his career, Dickens privately accused women writers of plagiarizing his ideas and fictional techniques, usually in snide ''asides'' written in letters to friends. These episodes may have been signs of Dickens's efforts to fight the Victorian cultural imperatives that placed him in a feminized cultural space due to his use of feminized, sentimentalist techniques to call his audience's attention to social problems. The plagiarism episodes suggest, specifically, that Dickens sued the legitimizing argument of artistic originality in order to claim himself as the ''owner'' of that cultural space and thereby exclude the female social reform writers who shared it with him by discrediting them.

In 1839, early in Dickens's career, Frances Trollope's novel, *Michael Armstrong, Factory Boy,* was published serially by Henry Colburn and advertised in the March, 1839 number of *Nicholas Nickleby* as ''printed and embellished uniformly with the 'Pickwick Papers,' 'Nicholas Nickleby,' &c'' *(Letters,* vol. 1, 506).[14] This advertisement implied that Mrs. Trollope's novel was of the same type—in both senses of the word—as Dickens's novels, and set up comparisons between them which irritated him immensely. Although Dickens protested that the comparisons between *Michael Armstrong* and his own works did not bother him, telling his informant Samuel Laman Blanchard on

February 9, 1839 that "[i]f Mrs. Trollope were even to adopt Ticholas Tick-
leby[15] as . . . a better sounding name than Michael Armstrong, I don't think
it would cost me a wink of sleep, or impair my appetite in the smallest
degree" *(Letters,* vol. 1, 507), his reaction to the advertisement shows to
the contrary.

On February 8, 1839, the day that Dickens saw the advertisement for
Michael Armstrong, sent to him by Blanchard, he wrote in his diary:

> Letter from Blanchard in the evening, inclosing another from Colburn relative
> to the Trollope advertisement, and its doubtfully honest or respectable imitation
> of Nickleby, which it seems was "unintentional'—of course. Colburn himself
> called late at night but I was not visible. If they hurt anybody it will be them-
> selves most likely—not me.[16]   *(Letters,* vol. 1, 640)

This entry is unusual, for most of Dickens's diary entries during this period
simply record appointments, and are extremely brief, even perfunctory, and
usually do not mention dealings with other writers. Dickens was upset enough,
obviously, to alienate Colburn by refusing to see him—an impolitic and risky
move for a young writer, even one as famous as Dickens already was—and
the tone for the whole entry is rather sullen and defensive. Dickens's two
letters to Blanchard also carry much the same tone, particularly when he
stoops to insulting the Trollopes personally, "I will express no further opinion
of Mrs. Trollope, than that I think *Mr.* Trollope must have been an old dog
and chosen his wife from the same species" *(Letters,* vol. 1, 507), a remark
that was even more inappropriate when made to someone like Blanchard,
who was not a very close friend of Dickens's.

It is true that this whole episode took place at a time when Dickens was
particularly sensitive to the issue of copyright, and his concerns in this area
are well documented. Greatly offended and upset by cheap imitations of
Pickwick Papers and *Oliver Twist* that had appeared in print and on stage
even before the novels were finished running, Dickens tried to protect *Nicholas Nickleby* by publishing a public statement as a separate pamphlet and
newspaper advertisement claiming to be the "only true and lawful **Boz,**" and
condemning "those dishonest dullards . . . [who] . . . impose on the unwary
and credulous by producing cheap and wretched imitations of our delectable
Works" (Slater xxix–xxx).[17] Concerns about plagiarism are also brought up,
briefly, but conspicuously and awkwardly, within *Nicholas Nickleby* itself,
showing that the whole subject of plagiarism was very much on Dickens's
mind.[18]

Compared to egregious imitators like one unknown author who, under the
pseudonym "Bos," produced an *Oliver Twiss* and, in spite of Dickens's
efforts with the public statement, a *Nicholas Nickelbery,* Frances Trollope
was not guilty of plagiarism or anything even close.[19] Since *Michael Armstrong* was not a direct imitation of one of Dickens's works, his ire towards

her seems exaggerated and misplaced. There is no way to know what was in Dickens's mind at that time, of course, but the most important question is: what elements of *Michael Armstrong* (besides the physical appearance of the type) would set up comparisons between it and Dickens's works, especially *Oliver Twist* and *Nicholas Nickleby?* *Michael Armstrong* was intended as a passionate denunciation of the factory system: the bound edition's preface announces that "it was her [Trollope's] intention . . . to drag into the light of day, and place before the eyes of Englishmen, the hideous mass of injustice and suffering to which thousands of infant labourers are subjected, who toil in our monster spinning mills" *(Michael Armstrong* iii). Accompanied by Auguste Hervieu's engravings, her detailed and graphic descriptions of suffering are powerful weapons against child labor. Using material from her own observations in Manchester and that gleaned from reliable sources, Trollope tried to "awaken the national conscience on behalf of the factory children" (Heineman 172) with harrowing scenes of dangerous working conditions, much like Dickens would try in *Nicholas Nickleby* to awaken sympathies for the hapless child victims of the Yorkshire schools. And, as we have seen, Dickens used similar sentimentalist techniques in *Oliver Twist* as an attack on the New Poor Law, and, moreover, he may have planned to write a similar novel in support of factory reform and child labor laws.

Evidence suggests that not only were *Michael Armstrong's* sentimentalist techniques similar to Dickens's, but that its subject matter (factory reform) impinged on literary territory that Dickens had already marked out for himself. Obviously responding to statements in Colburn's letter, shown to him by Blanchard, Dickens made the following statement to Blanchard, in a letter dated February 9, 1839 (the day after the diary entry), about the proposed subject matter of his yet unwritten next novel, *Barnaby Rudge*:

> That gentleman [Colburn] is quite right in supposing that Barnaby Rudge has nothing to do with factories, or negroes—white, black, or parti-colored. It is a tale of the riots of Eighty, before factories flourished as they did thirty years afterwards, and containing—or intended to contain—no allusion to cotton lords, cotton slaves, or anything that is cotton.   *(Letters,* vol. 1, 507)[20]

I deduce that Colburn had defended Mrs. Trollope by arguing that *Michael Armstrong's* subject matter had not been treated by Dickens, in past or even in projected, novels. Dickens's seeming contempt for the subject matter of factory reform—seen in his extravagantly flippant dismissal of "negroes—black, white, or parti-colored" and "cotton lords, cotton slaves, or anything that is cotton"[21]—was not in evidence a few months earlier, when he went to Manchester in November of 1838.[22]

Immediately after his visit, Dickens wrote a very different kind of letter to an acquaintance who was distantly connected to the reforming politician and nobleman, Lord Ashley, proposing another trip to Manchester, and asking for letters of introduction from Lord Ashley:

> With that nobleman's most benevolent and excellent exertions, and with the evidence which he was the means of bringing forward, I am well acquainted. . . . [W]hat I have seen has disgusted and astonished me beyond all measure. I mean to strike the heaviest blow in my power for these unfortunate creatures,[23] but whether I shall do so in "Nickleby," or wait some other opportunity, I have not yet determined. . . . Will you make known to Lord Ashley (confidentially) my intentions on this subject, and my earnest desire to avail myself . . . of his kind assistance?   *(Letters* 483–84)

In spite of these apparently serious intentions, Dickens was to write no novel addressing factory issues until much later in *Hard Times* (1854). What happened right after he wrote this letter in 1838 was, of course, that Frances Trollope went to Manchester in February of 1839, armed with several letters of introduction to radical reform leaders, and used this visual evidence, together with that gleaned from the *Memoir of Robert Blincoe* (1828),[24] Lord Ashley, the Parliamentary Blue Books,[25] and other sources, to produce *Michael Armstrong* in monthly parts beginning in February, 1839. In December of the same year, Charlotte Elizabeth Tonna began to serialize *Helen Fleetwood* in *The Christian Lady's Magazine*. Both of these works became so identified with the factory controversy that any contribution by Dickens would probably have seemed superfluous.

Some contemporary reviewers saw *Michael Armstrong* as an imitation of *Oliver Twist* and *Nicholas Nickleby* because of its focus on exploited children, even though neither one of Dickens's novels has anything to do with the factories that Frances Trollope explores in her novel. One June, 1839 reviewer wrote:

> Boz, like Byron, has his imitators; since the increasing demand for the *Nickleby* article, Boz, not being protected by patent like Mackintosh [the inventor of waterproof cloth], has been pirated; cuckoos lay their eggs in his nest; countless are the Factory-Boys which Mrs. Trollope has turned loose.   (Ford 90)

Frances Trollope's biographer, Helen Heineman, argues, on the other hand, that it was Trollope who "boldly led the way in making fiction the 'medium of interpretation' for a new age, and the novel with a purpose rapidly became a common and then a dominant type as the 1840's progressed" (171).[26] The real issue, however, is not who "invented" sentimentalist social reform discourse, if it can even be said to have been invented at all.

My own conclusion is that sentimentalist social reform discourse was too broad, and the product of too many commonly-held cultural values, to be claimed as the intellectual property of any one author. This discourse, as I have argued, came from the intersection of two major cultural factors: the breakdown of the moral economy, which resulted from the new material conditions of the industrial era, and the hardening of a domestic ideology that gave women a specifically affective function within those material conditions. The consequence of this cultural "intersection" was that social reform discourse, with its task of using sentiment to create sympathy for exploited and oppressed groups, was increasingly seen as the province of women writers.

This feminization resulted in a kind of critical depreciation that affected Dickens's own critical reputation—as is evidenced by critical comments ranging from Fitzjames Stephens's acid statement that Dickens as a politician was (or appealed to) "a feminine, irritable, and noisy mind" (9),[27] to another milder, but still devastating, remark in an 1858 review by Richard Holt Hutton:

> Indeed, the type of Dickens' genius, in many respects, feminine. Like most women's genius, it is founded on the delicate powers of perception alone. . . . There is no intellectual background to his pictures; and in this respect, he resembles the numerous authoresses of modern English fiction.[28] (Hutton 469)

Although the reception of Dickens's works was inevitably entangled in the same gender binaries that affected women writers, he still did his best to fight for his status as an artist by consistently declaring himself an original and women writers the imitators and usurpers. In 1852, for example, Dickens, also attacked the American novelist, Harriet Beecher Stowe, in a private letter. Publicly, Dickens lauded Stowe's anti-slavery novel *Uncle Tom's Cabin,* calling it in an 1853 speech during Stowe's visit to England "a noble book with a noble purpose" *(Speeches* 165). In 1852, however, he had confided to a friend that he thought Mrs. Stowe had "appropriated" material from his own work" (Knight 43):

> She (I mean Mrs. Stowe) is a leetle unscrupulous in the appropriatin' way, I seem to see a writer with whom I am very intimate (and whom nobody can possibly admire more than myself) peeping often through the thinness of the paper. Further I descry the ghost of Mary Barton . . . but in spite of this, I consider the book a fine one . . . and worthy of its reputation.   (Knight 44)[29]

Since Stowe herself had told Dickens that he had inspired her work, his conclusions are perhaps understandable,[30] but more importantly, the act of declaring himself the original and Stowe the imitator shows Dickens's attempt to fight the discursive categories being constructed by cultural agents like the *Gentleman's Magazine* review that I quoted in the beginning of this article, which designated social morality in literature as a specifically female task, and made sentimentalist social reform discourse a feminized discourse. By arguing that he was the source of this discourse, Dickens tried to deny its gender classification and its depreciation; if he, a male writer, had originated it, then it could not be a feminine discourse.[31]

Another method that Dickens may have used to distance himself from female social reformers like Charlotte Elizabeth Tonna is his devastating satire of them, namely in the novel *Bleak House*. Many readers, both contemporary reviewers and later critics, have noted the acidity of Dickens's portrayals of the two 'meddling' female philanthropists, Mrs. Jellyby and Mrs. Pardiggle. As feminist critic Beth Tobin has noted, "Dickens' disdain for these women is so strong that his sarcastic, angry voice displaces Esther's usually diffident, modulated voice" (135). The first of these characters, Mrs. Jellyby, is so involved in her charitable activities (currently centered around a Christian mission to the African country of Borrioboola-Gha) that she ignores her own family and her own home. Her children are neglected to the point of abuse; the house is "not only very untidy, but very dirty" *(Bleak House* 85) and very poorly run. These deficiencies are particularly damning in the world of this novel, as "[i]n the emblematic qualities of the characters and of their 'connections' *Bleak House* is an interpretation of Victorian society" (Miller 13). Dickens uses the novel to portray a society that is on the verge of collapse, due to generations of neglect and misuse. This neglect is symbolized by many characters and institutions in the novel, the Court of Chancery, Mr. Turveydrop, and Mr. Skimpole among them, and the fact that Dickens includes Mrs. Jellyby (and for that matter, Mrs. Pardiggle as well) among these represents a serious attack on the activities of charitable women.

According to Dickens, the problem with Mrs. Jellyby is that not only do her activities injure her husband, children, and home, but they are ultimately futile and self-serving because they are not based on Mrs. Jellyby's genuine feeling for the causes she supports. Indeed, Dickens implies that the actual cause itself does not matter to Mrs. Jellyby, since "[s]he has devoted herself to an extensive variety of public subjects at various times, and is at present (until something else attracts her) devoted to the subject of Africa . . . " *(Bleak House* 82). When the Africa project becomes a failure due to "the King of Borrioboola wanting to sell everybody . . . for Rum (933), Mrs. Jellyby turns her attention to women's rights, which Dickens implies is yet another futile and worthless project, "involving even more correspondence than the old one" (933).

Mrs. Pardiggle represents another variation on this theme: her innumerable visits to the cottages of the poor accomplish nothing except to annoy and harass them, in the process making her neglected children "absolutely ferocious with discontent" (151). In sum, *Bleak House* seems to contain nothing but contempt for the "rapacious benevolence" (150) of "the Women of England, the Daughters of Britain, the Sisters of all the Cardinal Virtues

separately, the Females of America, the Ladies of a hundred denominations''
(150). Dickens contrasts the activities of these businesslike female philanthropists in the novel against the quiet, self-sacrificing, self-effacing, domesticized
charity of the heroine, Esther Summerson. Esther's charitable activities are
not public and institutionalized but spontaneous, private, and always the result
of personal sympathy for those afflicted.[32]

In this manner, as Beth Tobin has suggested, Dickens represents a subversion of the more activist model of female charity that is part of what I have
labeled as sentimentalist social reform discourse:

> Whereas Hannah More locates in the public sphere a space in which her heroine
> can exercise her ''female benevolent power,'' Dickens limits his heroine to the
> domestic sphere. . . . Dickens refuses to bestow his approbation on any woman
> who extends her realm of influence beyond these boundaries. (Tobin 146–47)

At the same time, Dickens's portrayal of Esther derives in many ways from
the feminized, sentimentalist idea that true charity comes from the heart, but
his version of sentimentalism limits Esther's activities to the domestic sphere:
in her case, what Charlotte Elizabeth Tonna called the ''talent of female
influence'' does not extend very far.[33]

Tobin also argues that ''Esther's 'circle of duty' sounds a retreat for women
into the domestic sphere and a retirement from public activity and from
participating in institutional solutions to social ills'' (147). She does not
attempt to explain Dickens's motives for sounding this retreat, and it is of
course impossible for us to divine the deep-seated psychological reasons that
lie behind Dickens's portrayals of his women characters. It is important to
point out, however, that Dickens was himself involved with many of the same
causes as these ''meddling'' female social reformers, and probably had his
own fingers in more charitable pies than Mrs. Jellyby herself.[34] In fact, one
of Dickens's sharpest critics, Harriet Martineau, pointed out that ''the names
of Dickens and Jellyby are joined in a firm as humanity-mongers in the minds
of his [Dickens's] readers'' (''The Factory Controversy'' 45). In addition,
Dickens enjoyed a close personal friendship with at least one ''meddling''
woman philanthropist, Angela Burdett-Coutts, and worked closely with her
on some of her charities, namely Urania Cottage, a home she established for
the reclamation of prostitutes. Dickens also publicly expressed admiration
for many female social reform writers, regardless of what he might have said
or thought about them privately. How, then, can we explain these inconsistencies on Dickens' part?

Part of the problem was that, as historian F. M. Prochaska has suggested,
''the view of woman's mission was influx in the nineteenth century'' (1).
On one hand, the ''separate spheres'' philosophy allowed, even encouraged,

women towards charitable work: "Free from the cut and thrust of commercial life and thought to be more sensitive to personal relations, women were increasingly called upon to be agents of social improvement" (Prochaska 7). Therefore, Charlotte Elizabeth Tonna's idea of "the talent of female influence" was a natural outgrowth of a domestic ideology that assigned women the affective functions of society (Tonna "Politics"). On the other hand, there was disagreement about the extent to which women could go in exerting this influence without being thought "unwomanly," as Dickens's satire in *Bleak House* shows. In many ways, the "talent of female influence" could become a trap in which women "willingly reinforced the stereotypes of women as the more compassionate, self-sacrificing sex" because the "claims of women to moral authority and greater social recognition depended on public belief in their special and essential qualities" (Prochaska 8).

My main focus in this article, however, is the extent to which Dickens himself was caught up in the cultural expectations set up by Victorian gender binaries. I have demonstrated that many of Dickens's central themes and literary techniques—his use of illness and other forms of physical suffering to arouse feelings of pathos in his audience, his allusions to commonly-held religious beliefs, his understanding of death, even his construction of himself as a preacher who taught his audience their social duties—all mark Dickens as a part of a feminized, sentimentalist discourse of social reform. Even Dickens's later novels, which have traditionally been seen as more mature, complex, dark, and less sentimental, display many of these same characteristics.[35] Indeed, *Bleak House* itself, in spite of its satire of women reformers, still makes use of their sentimentalist conventions. Dickens's condemnations of English society in the novel are rhetorical blasts worthy of Charlotte Elizabeth Tonna herself, since they threaten divine retribution for society's tolerance of social ills, and his heart-wrenching descriptions of the poor and downtrodden in the novel have a great deal more in common with Tonna, and other women writers like her, than they do with any of Dickens's male contemporaries, or, for that matter, any of his male precursors.

An understanding of the feminized nature of nineteenth-century sentimentalism, therefore, is clearly crucial for Dickens critics: it is a "missing piece" that explains much about his fiction that has not yet been properly understood. In his 1987 book *Sacred Tears,* Dickens scholar Fred Kaplan advanced the idea that Dickens's sentimentality derived directly from eighteenth-century moral philosophy, especially as it was exhibited in novelists like Fielding, Goldsmith, and Richardson, whom Dickens certainly read. This connection between Victorian sentimentality and the eighteenth century is valuable because the idea that social benevolence had to come from the heart rather than the head was, in many ways, a carry-over from the eighteenth-century "cult of sensibility." Feminist scholars like Janet Todd and Nancy Armstrong have since noted that the sentimental virtues of benevolence and compassion were increasingly gendered as feminine in the late eighteenth century and the nineteenth century. This growing cultural identification of women, with their culturally designated attributes of "religious sensibility and social pity" (Prochaska 7), as ideal charity workers and social reform writers was clearly a key part of the culture in which Dickens was working.

My reading of Dickens shows, however, that such a gendered discourse could be separate from the biological gender of the writer. How did Victorian society receive a male writer, who, in many respects, wrote like a woman? As I have demonstrated, Dickens's reception was mixed. Although he was the darling of the Victorian middle class, and indisputably the most popular of all the Victorian novelists, both male and female, he was still labeled by many of the serious thinkers of his day as "a feminine, irritable, and noisy mind" (Stephen 9). In an age where men were supposed to be men and women were supposed to be women, this was clearly an uncomfortable position to be in, and may in part explain, although of course not excuse, Dickens's sometimes unreasonable attitude towards his female colleagues. Most importantly, his problems as a male sentimentalist indicate firstly, that sentimentalism was an ideological and aesthetic system to which both Dickens and his female colleagues had access during the Victorian period; secondly, that the decline of sentimentalism had a negative impact not only on the women writers, but also on Dickens. In the final analysis, however, Dickens's juggernaut-like popularity, fueled by his use of the nineteenth-century version of Public Relations (such as his public-reading tours), enabled his critical reputation to overcome these critical vicissitudes more successfully than the women writers.[36] While many sentimentalist women writers simply disappeared from literary history (Charlotte Elizabeth Tonna, Frances Trollope, Camilla Toulmin, Caroline Norton) and others who were too important to ignore, like Elizabeth Barrett Browning and Elizabeth Gaskell, were pushed aside, Dickens's popularity and success, his prominence in nineteenth-century literature, made him impossible to ignore or push aside.

NOTES

I would like to thank Peter Lang Publishing for permission to print this article, which reproduces some material from my forthcoming book *Preaching Pity: Sentimentality and Social Reform in Victorian Culture*.
1. Tonna was the editor of the influential *Christian Lady's Magazine* from 1834 to 1846 and *The Protestant Annual* from 1841 to 1846, and author of several fictional works, including an anti-slavery novel, *The System* (1827), an indictment of the

factory system, *Helen Fleetwood* (1839–40), an exposure of the abuses of women and child laborers in *The Wrongs of Woman* (1843–44), and the anonymous, nonfictional *Perils of the Nation* (1843).

2. In a letter to his friend Thomas Beard the Saturday before the publication of the *Bentley's Miscellany* containing the opening installment of *Oliver Twist,* Dickens called it "my glance at the new poor Law Bill" *(Letters,* vol. 1, 231).

3. In an 1855 pamphlet, "The Factory Controversy: A Warning Against Meddling Legislation," (written around the same time as her *Autobiography)* Martineau again attacked the interventionist views of Dickens and other humanitarians as "the pseudo-philanthropy which is one of the disgraces of our times" (95). She also criticized Dickens specifically, as having "acted the part of sentimental philanthropist in *Oliver Twist"* (95) and demanded that Dickens's audience "require from him some soundness of principle and some depth of knowledge . . . " (96).

4. Like Dickens, Mrs. Bedwin also asserts the "normality" of these emotional tears, assuring Oliver that "I'm only having a good cry . . . and I'm quite comfortable" (128).

5. Many of Dickens's other novels make use of the sentimentalist understanding of death, especially (but not limited to) the deaths of children: to name a few, the deaths of Little Nell in *The Old Curiosity Shop,* Little Paul Dombey in *Dombey and Son,* Smike in *Nicholas Nickleby,* William and Frederick Dorrit in *Little Dorrit,* and baby Johnny in *Our Mutual Friend.* The sentimentalist value system also informs that quintessentially Dickensian text, *A Christmas Carol,* since it is, finally, Scrooge's encounters with the possible death of Tiny Tim, and with his own death in the person of the Spirit of Christmas Yet To Come, that lead to his becoming a more generous and sympathetic individual.

6. I would like to thank my colleague, Holly McSpadden, for bringing Mrs. Mann's name to my attention.

7. In his funeral sermon for Dickens, Dean Arthur Stanley also celebrated Dickens's efforts to create connections between social classes:

> By him that veil was rent asunder which parts the various classes of society. Through his genius the rich man . . . was made to see and feel the presence of the Lazarus at his gate. The unhappy inmates of the workhouse, the neglected children in the dens and caves of our great cities . . . far from the observation of men . . . had been, it may be sometimes, in exaggerated forms, made to stand and speak before those who hardly dreamed of their existence.
> (Collins, *Critical Heritage* 524)

Stanley's construction of Dickens credits Dickens's fiction with creating affective bonds between classes and assigns Dickens the role of preacher—a role held in common with women writers like Charlotte Elizabeth Tonna who, in the words of Christine Krueger, were thought to be the "evangelists of reconciliation" (157).

8. Carlyle saw Dickens as a "good little fellow" with one of the most "cheery, innocent natures he had ever encountered," but thought that Dickens' "theory of life was entirely wrong" because it was too "soft and accommodating" (Collins, *Dickens: Interviews and Recollections* 63).

9. I agree with Harold Orel *(Victorian Literary Critics,* 1984) that Lewes, unlike Fitzjames Stephen, did not consider himself one of the critics who wrote about Dickens with "mingled irritation and contempt" (Lewes 99), and he did concede Dickens's "glorious energy of imagination" (Lewes 97). In the final analysis, however, Lewes' assessment of Dickens in "Dickens in Relation to Criticism" *(The Fortnightly Review,* 1872) is more about Dickens's deficiences than it is his strengths. I cannot disagree with George Ford's immortal characterization of Lewes' attitude towards Dickens:

> His [Lewes'] expression throughout his essay is as if a bad smell had penetrated into his library. He has gone out to the kitchen to find out what the help have been eating with such enthusiasm, and he has brought back a plateful to his desk for examination and analysis. His own sniff of disapproval is unrelieved, though he does take pains to explain why the kitchen help are under the illusion that the dish is tasty.   (Ford 151)

10. Stephen's use of the indefinite article makes it unclear whether he meant to accuse Dickens himself or Dickens' reading public of having "a feminine, irritable, and noisy mind"; either way, however, the statement links Dickens with femininity in a far from complimentary manner.

11. In a letter to Dickens responding to *The Chimes* (1844), Jeffreys wrote:

> Blessings on your kind heart, my dearest Dickens, for *that,* after all, is your great talisman, and the gift for which you will be not only most loved, but longest remembered. Your kind and courageous advocacy of the rights of the poor . . . have done more to soothe desponding worth—to waken sleeping (almost dead) humanities—and to shame even selfish brutality, than all the other writings of the age, and make it, and all that are to come after, your debtors.
>
> You understand from this . . . that the music of your chimes [has] reached me, and resounded through my heart, and that I thank you with all that is left of it.
>
> . . . but I could not *reserve* my tears for your third part. From the meeting with Will on the street, they flowed and ebbed at your bidding; and I know you will forgive me for saying that my interest in the story began there.
>   (Cockburn 390–1)

12. In contrast to Dickens, Edgar argued that "[George] Eliot and Hardy hold secure rank as thinkers" (151).

13. These words are taken from Lord Jeffrey's letter complimenting Dickens on *A Christmas Carol,* Dec. 8, 1843 (Cockburn 380–81). It is interesting to note that both Cross and Edgar, while noting Dickens's formal defects, still express admiration for his "finer qualities" of heart (Edgar 117).

14. Later known only as the mother of novelist Anthony Trollope, Frances Trollope was in 1839 a well known writer in her own right, already celebrated for *The Vicar of Wrexhill,* and a travel memoir, *Domestic Manners of the Americans.* Deciding to write a novel "on the condition of the factory hands" in 1839,

she became one of the first of the so-called "Condition of England" novelists, anticipating Elizabeth Gaskell, Disraeli, Kingsley, and as will be seen, Dickens himself.

15. Dickens at this time had just finished running *Oliver Twist* in *Bentley's Miscellany,* was writing *Nicholas Nickleby* serially for Chapman and Hall, and had seen the advertisement for *Michael Armstrong* in the March monthly number of *Nicholas Nickleby.*

16. Samuel Laman Blanchard was the editor of a newspaper, the *True Sun*; Colburn was a publisher, the former partner and now rival of *Oliver Twist's* publisher, Richard Bentley.

17. See Michael Slater's monograph on "The Composition and Monthly Publication of *Nicholas Nickleby*" (*Nicholas Nickleby* vii-1xxii).

18. In the August, 1838 number, the corrupt MP, Mr. Gregsbury, says that he would never support a bill "giving poor grubbing devils of authors a right to their own property" (*Nicholas Nickleby* 149).

19. *Michael Armstrong's* focus on the industrial North makes it distinctly different from either *Oliver Twist* or *Nicholas Nickleby* because neither of Dickens' novels deals with child labor in factories; in addition, there are no direct references to Dickens in Trollope's novel (such as similar names, etc.; finally, the plots are only generally [good and evil characters fighting over the fate of a poor boy] not specifically similar.)

20. In the discourse surrounding factory reform, workers were often compared to negro slaves, an issue which Catherine Gallagher discusses thoroughly in *The Industrial Reformation of English Fiction.*

21. I take "parti-colored" to mean exactly that—black and white in zebra stripes or in spots—not to refer to racially mixed people. Sarcasm is also evident in Dickens's use of "anything that *is* cotton," rather than "anything that has to do with cotton."

22. The previous month, in *Fraser's* magazine, a notice had appeared that invited Dickens to turn to factory reform as his next subject:

> No one who reads his papers can doubt the excellence of his [Dickens's] disposition. The very choice of his later subjects [the Poor Law, the Yorkshire schools] proves his desire to do good. . . . But there is a public crime more vast than either of these, and capable, from its peculiar character, of being put down, in whole or in part by legislative enactment. I mean, the *working little boys and girls to death in the factories.* . . . In these matters . . . Mr. Dickens might, without diverging into the thorny path of politics, be of incalculable service to his fellowmen.   ("Loose Thoughts" 500)

23. Here, Dickens refers to Lord Ashley's July Speech revealing the nightmarish working conditions for child laborers in factories.

24. This work, written by John Brown, was the autobiography of a mill worker, and gave harrowing accounts of his existence as a parish orphan exploited by the factory system. The *Memoir* has been reprinted in *The Slaughterhouse of Mammon,* a 1992 anthology of Victorian social-protest literature.

25. Reports on the effects of the Industrial Revolution, especially the Sadler Committee's report on children's employment of 1832.
26. Heineman makes this argument for Trollope's pre-eminence even at the expense of Charlotte Elizabeth Tonna, who, Heineman believes, "emphasized the wickedness of the workers" at the expense of the "intolerable [working] conditions" (172). Since Tonna's novel provided extensive descriptions of poor living and working conditions, especially of children, in explicit support of the Ten Hours Bill, this criticism seems overstated.
27. Fitzjames Stephen made two other comments in the same article, "Mr. Dickens as a Politician," that obliquely associated Dickens with femininity: "As there are reproaches which can be uttered by no one but a woman or a child, there are accusations which can only be conveyed through a novel" (9), and "But just as a foolish gossip in a country-town, who says what she pleases . . . a popular novelist may produce more disaffection and discontent than a whole army of pamphleteers and public orators . . . " (9).
28. George Henry Lewes's comments that "Thought is strangely absent from his [Dickens'] works" and "Compared with that of Fielding or Thackeray, his [Dickens's] was merely an *animal* intelligence, i.e., restricted to perceptions" in his 1872 essay "Dickens in Relation to Criticism" also echo Hutton's reasoning (Lewes, 104–05).
29. Both H. L. Knight and Harry Stone argue that the veiled reference seems to be to Dickens himself, and *Mary Barton* is of course a reference to the novel of the same name by Elizabeth Gaskell.
30. Stowe sent a copy of *Uncle Tom's Cabin* to Dickens, inscribing it to "the first writer in our day who turned the attention of the high to the joys and sorrows of the lowly. . . . If I may hope to do only something like the same for a class equally ignored and despised by the fastidious and refined in my country, I shall be happy" *(Letters* vol. 6 716).
31. Dickens, however, probably was unaware of Stowe's connections with another author who could more justly than himself lay claim to Stowe. In 1844, several years before writing *Uncle Tom's Cabin,* Stowe edited an American edition of Charlotte Elizabeth Tonna's works. In an introductory essay written for that edition, Stowe explicitly compared Tonna and Dickens, claiming that Tonna's social reform fiction was more practical and effective than Dickens's: "[t]his lady's [Tonna's] portrayals of factory life are just illustrations of what such delineations ought to be . . . " *(Works* 3). Stowe's acquaintance of Tonna's work clearly put her in full possession of another tradition that encompassed Dickens's narrow conception of his own work; Stowe was influenced by Dickens's use of sentiment, but was also influenced by the more overtly religious Tonna, and this indicates the presence of a larger, feminized, cultural discourse that encompassed both Dickens and Tonna.
32. For example, Esther's kindness to the Jellyby children, her visits to the brickmakers' cottage, and her taking in the crossing-sweeper, Jo, when he is ill all conform to this model.
33. In an 1834 "Politics" column for her *Christian Ladies Magazine,* Tonna carefully restrained the woman's influence to the home, in accordance with the domestic

ideology, but she constructed this domestic role in a way that included, even demanded, the "high responsibility" of moral activism.

> Can we write for CHRISTIAN LADIES, and be guiltless, if we neglect to enforce upon them their high responsibility, in the use of that mighty talent, female influence?... It is when his [man's] home becomes the abode of gentle sympathy and intellectual companionship, and spiritual communion, that man begins to feel that he has somewhat worth fencing around.... And thus ... does the talent of female influence form the basis of even all commercial intercourse among the nations of the earth.
> *(Christian Lady's Magazine* vol. 1, 249–50)

34. See Norris Pope's *Dickens and Charity* (1978) for a detailed account of Dickens's charitable activities, which included the Ragged School movement, sanitary reform, and poor relief.
35. My sense is that this critical concentration on Dickens's later fiction is part of a formalist attempt to resuscitate Dickens's reputation by arguing that his later novels "grow out" of the sentimentalist flaws of the earlier novels and become darker and more psychologically complex. See, for example, F.R. and Q.D. Leavis's study of *Dickens the Novelist,* which does not discuss any of Dickens' novels before *Dombey and Son* (1844–46).
36. By "PR" I mean that as a man, Dickens had a greater capacity to become a public figure, because he was able to have his image distributed, make public appearances, and give public reading tours—all of which a woman writer would not have been able to do without risking being thought unladylike.

WORKS CITED

Armstrong, Nancy. *Desire and Domestic Fiction.* New York: Oxford UP, 1987.

Cockburn, Lord. *Life of Lord Jeffrey With a Selection from His Correspondence.* Vols. I–II. Edinburgh, 1852.

Collins, Philip, ed. *Dickens: the Critical Heritage.* New York: Barnes and Noble, 1971.

———, ed. *Dickens: Interviews and Recollections.* 2 vols. London: Macmillan, 1981.

Cross, Wilbur. *The Development of the English Novel.* London: Macmillan, 1899.

Dickens, Charles. *Bleak House.* Ed. Norman Page. London: Penguin, 1971.

———. *Dombey and Son.* Ed. Peter Fairclough. London: Penguin, 1970.

———. *Letters of Charles Dickens.* vols. 1–10. eds. Madeleine House and Graham Storey, et al. Oxford: Clarendon P, 1965–88.

————. *Oliver Twist*. Ed. Peter Fairclough. London: Penguin, 1966.

————. "On Strike." *Household Words* 11 February, 1854, 553–59.

————. *Speeches*. ed. K. J. Fielding. Oxford: Clarendon P, 1960.

Edgar, Pelham. *The Art of the Novel from 1700 to the Present Time*. New York: MacMillan, 1934.

Ellman, Richard. *Oscar Wilde*. New York: Knopf, 1988.

Ford, George H. *Dickens and His Readers: Aspects of Novel Criticism Since 1856*. Princeton: Princeton U P, 1955.

Ford, Richard. Rev. of *Oliver Twist*, by Charles Dickens. *Quarterly Review* 64 (1839): 83–102.

Heineman, Helen. *Mrs. Trollope: the Triumphant Feminine in the Nineteenth Century*. Athens: Ohio U P 1979.

Hutton, Richard Holt. "Novels by the Authoress of John Halifax." *North British Review* 29 (1858): 466–81.

Kaplan, Fred. *Sacred Tears: Sentimentality in Victorian Literature*. Princeton: Princeton UP, 1987.

Knight, H. L. "Dickens and Mrs. Stowe." *Dickens Studies Annual* 5 (1976): 43–58.

Krueger, Christine. *The Reader's Repentance*. Chicago: U of Chicago P, 1992.

"The Lady Novelists of Great Britain." *Gentleman's Magazine* 40 (1853): 18–25.

Larson, Janet. *Dickens and The Broken Scripture*. Athens: The U of Georgia P, 1985.

Lewes, George Henry. *Literary Criticism of George Henry Lewes*. Ed. Alice R. Kaminsky. Lincoln: U of Nebraska P, 1964.

Martineau, Harriet. *Autobiography*. 2 vols. ed. Maria Weston Chapman. Boston: Houghton Mifflin, 1877.

————. *The Factory Controversy: A Warning Against Meddling Legislation*. Manchester, 1855.

————. *Selected Letters*. ed. Valerie Sanders. Oxford: Clarendon P, 1990.

Miller, J. Hillis. Introduction. *Bleak House*. By Charles Dickens. New York: Penguin, 1971.

Oliphant, Margaret. "Charles Dickens." *Blackwood's Edinburgh Magazine* 77 (1855): 451–66.

Orel, Harold. *Victorian Literary Critics*. New York: St. Martin's, 1984.

Pope, Norris. *Dickens and Charity.* New York: Columbia U P, 1978.

Prochaska, F. M. *Women and Philanthropy in Nineteenth-Century England.* Oxford: Clarendon P, 1980.

Slater, Michael. "The Composition and Monthly Publication of Nicholas Nickleby." *The Life and Adventures of Nicholas Nickleby.* ed. Michael Slater. Philadelphia: U of Pennsylvania P, 1982.

Stephen, Fitzjames. "Mr. Dickens as a Politician." *Saturday Review of Politics, Literature, Science, and Art.* 3. (1857): 8–9.

Stowe, Harriet Beecher. *Uncle Tom's Cabin.* New York: W. W. Norton and Co., 1994.

———. Introduction. *The Works of Charlotte Elizabeth.* By Charlotte Elizabeth Tonna. New York: M.W. Dodd, 1844.

Tobin, Beth. *Superintending the Poor.* New Haven: Yale U P, 1993.

Todd, Janet. *Sensibility: An Introduction.* London: Methuen, 1986.

Tompkins, Jane. *Sensational Designs.* New York: Oxford U P, 1985.

Tonna, Charlotte Elizabeth. "Politics." *Christian Lady's Magazine* March, 1834.

Trollope, Frances. *The Life and Adventures of Michael Armstrong, the Factory Boy.* London: Henry Colburn, 1840.

Wilson, Angus. Introduction. *Oliver Twist.* By Charles Dickens. London: Penguin, 1966.

Reading the Gordon Riots in 1841: Social Violence and Moral Management in *Barnaby Rudge*

Scott Dransfield

Charles Dickens's *Barnaby Rudge,* a tale of the Gordon "No Popery" Riots of 1780, begins with a curious passage foreshadowing the violence that erupts upon the scene five years from the starting point of the novel. In a manner that evokes Carlyle's *French Revolution,* Dickens writes:

> There are times when, the elements being in unusual commotion, those who are bent on daring enterprises, or agitated by great thoughts, whether of good or evil, feel a mysterious sympathy with the tumult of nature, and are roused into corresponding violence. . . . Men, self-possessed before, have given a sudden loose to passions they could no longer control. The demons of wrath and despair have striven to emulate those who ride the whirlwind and direct the storm; and man, lashed into madness with the roaring winds and boiling waters, has become for the time as wild and merciless as the elements themselves.
> (17)[1]

Dickens sees in social violence a type of human pathology that transcends politics and enters a more naturalistic realm. While social violence is seen to be prompted by political agitation, or "daring enterprises," the pathology really stems from an individual's loss of self-possessed reason and from the consequent loosing of dangerous "passions." In the process, an individual becomes "morally insane," lacking that entirely moral function of putting a rein on one's natural propensity toward madness and criminality.

Dickens constructs his historical novel of the Gordon Riots of 1780 and the events leading up to them as one of the times he writes of in the above passage.[2] He believes that a written history of the riots may serve a didactic purpose: that "those shameful tumults, while they reflect indelible disgrace upon the time in which they occurred . . . teach a good lesson'' (xxiv). Dickens explains in his Preface that this lesson demonstrates the evils of religious intolerance; yet the novel clearly illustrates a more pressing lesson: the vital need to regulate society's pathologies. As insanity and the act of social revolt maintain a close connection through the novel—even besides the fact that Barnaby, Hugh, and Dennis, the three leaders of the mob, are discernibly insane—the main source of social revolt is established not necessarily in the political agitations of Lord Gordon, but in a pathological social body.[3] This body, made up of ''the very scum and refuse of London, whose growth was fostered by bad criminal laws, bad prison regulations, and the worst conceivable police'' (374), is presented as requiring special attention by a reformed government to treat the pathologies and regulate the behavior that are a part of this body.

Many critics have argued persuasively concerning the novel's topicality relating to its representation of the lower classes, especially in light of the social disturbances that shook the industrial regions of England between 1836 and 1841, making the novel ''almost journalistically apt'' (Butt and Tillotson 82). That *Barnaby Rudge* had much to say in regard to Chartist demonstrations and threats of working-class violence has been critically and historically well established.[4] Yet another element of the novel's topicality has been relatively overlooked: its representations of insanity and criminality and the social context from which they emerge. Critics have written that one of the problems in *Barnaby Rudge* is its lack of resolution; that the predicament of social violence is never brought under any satisfactory control, but only ends, in Steven Marcus's words, in ''exhaustion, defeat, or death'' (204). As Marcus further writes, ''nowhere in *Barnaby Rudge* do we find anything that genuinely suggests reconciliation; nowhere is an understanding arrived at; nowhere are reciprocal concessions brought about. Contradictions in authority are neither resolved nor appeased'' (204). The problem of authority is especially tricky in this regard, since most representations of paternal authority in the novel are found to be corrupt or ineffective. On the other hand, a closer look at how representations of insanity and the social body function in the novel will show that a resolution is strongly implied. In short, these various representations imply their own cure, one that emphasizes ''treatment'' and ''management.'' But the mechanisms of ''treatment'' and ''management'' are not merely terms reflecting reforms in psychiatric practice; they also take root in a ''liberal mode of government,''[5] or in a kind of reformed, administrative governance to replace the old, one that sought humane, morally correct ways for regulating society's pathologies.

I

Barnaby Rudge was written and published at a time in which the conception and administration of insanity was in significant transition. From the vantage point of nineteenth-century liberal progress, the novel portrays the past—the late eighteenth century—as a socially unenlightened period. Even besides Dickens's tirade over the "bad criminal laws, bad prison regulations, and the worst conceivable police" that he saw to be characteristic of the period, the novel portrays several "dangerous" characters whose unregulated actions escalate to the point of social crisis as a result of their victimization by corrupt father figures and, perhaps of more consequence, simply because they are on the loose in the first place. As they are shown to have no genuine guardians over them, these characters, and the countless others who join them in the riots, present the real social menace in the novel. An important aspect of Dickens's reading of the eighteenth century in *Barnaby Rudge,* therefore, concerns a generalized understanding of insanity, of the care (or lack thereof) for the insane, and of the social consequences of such.

The first and perhaps most significant distinction to make regarding the treatment of madness during the period Dickens represents is the position insanity held in relation to society. Whereas nineteenth-century "social medicine" sought to rehabilitate, reform, and nurture the insane back to social health and accountability under the guidance of expert practitioners, the mad of the eighteenth century were generally denied the proper category of "human," and took on quite literally an animalistic existence. Reduced to such terms, and seen to be essentially incurable, the insane were given care designed merely to tame the wild, not in the sense of improving the functional capabilities of the subject, but "as one might domesticate and thus render predictable the behavior of a wild beast" (Scull 57). The overriding principle was physically to restrain the subject. Furthermore, as care for the insane had not yet achieved the professional status and the more bureaucratic administration that defined mid-nineteenth-century practice, lunatics most often remained at home or even roamed at large, while "a few were sent to Bethlem, or delivered as pauper lunatics to private madhouses or to the new public asylums in great towns" (Porter 119). Because the public asylum was still a very new feature and, to many, did not present itself as an option in providing care for the insane, the figure of the madman in public space was a more common, if not accepted, spectacle. Altogether, the madman was an alien in society and, at the same time, merely one of many public nuisances.

The turn of the century brought about a number of changes in the understanding of insanity and for a number of reasons,[6] the most significant of which concerns the belief in its curability. An essential element of liberal progress, the drive to provide remedies for the insane took root in new ideas concerning the social nature of the "disease" of madness, as well as in ideas about social order and public well being.[7] No longer seen as mere "animality," insanity became connected with a variety of moral and behavioral causes stemming mostly from ideas about the effects of environment. As a social disease, in other words, the unruliness and violence associated with insanity came to be seen as originating not in a lack of "humanity" in the subject, but in deviant behavioral patterns brought about by a number of causes, by a lack of training or education, for example, or by uncontrollable emotions such as melancholy, rage, or a strong propensity to sensuality. And, as a general rule, they were discerned entirely through a largely middle-class sense of social "equilibrium" and order.[8]

In order to transform the insane, this new treatment and its rationales, known widely as "moral management," emphasized the priority of establishing mental health through fostering an "internalization of control" in the subject.[9] Rather than controlling the insane through external, physical measures applied directly upon the body of the subject, moral treatment sought to provide the subject with a "gentle," yet disciplined, program that would stimulate the moral faculties, or "soul," of the patient, leading to a recovery of characteristics thought to define proper forms of life within the social order. This could only be achieved through a reformed and professionalized therapy practiced within the guarded confines of a closely monitored environment. Further, as the insane began to be identified as bearing a potential for recovery, which could only emerge in an individual through this kind of treatment, the project of reforming the insane became more administrative in method. No longer was it adequate simply to physically restrain lunatics through purely restrictive methods; in fact, the "traditional" methods of dealing with the insane began to be outwardly shunned. What was now required was a "moral management": an enterprise that was established in the asylum.

Besides being noted for the abandonment of the exclusive use of physical restraints, the methods of certain nineteenth-century reformed asylums sought most of all to develop "self command" in the inmates. Samuel Tuke, a pioneer in English lunacy reform, insisted on this, asserting that "most insane persons, have a considerable degree of self command; and . . . the employment and cultivation of this remaining power, is found to be attended with the most salutary effects" (139–40). In order to develop this "remaining power," patients were introduced to a "morally rigorous" lifestyle, including a good dose of exercise, work, and otherwise productive activity. Along with an internalization of moral self-control, this regime also sought to build "esteem" in the subject, an important aspect of moral management. Meanwhile, the government of inmates was replaced by an internal organization resembling the discipline of family life. Good behavior was motivated out of what Tuke admittedly calls "fear," but "it is not allowed to be excited, beyond that degree which naturally arises from the necessary regulations of the family" (141). Those who exercised authority among the inmates in the asylum naturally took on a kind of patriarchal authority, inspiring both esteem and obedience. John Conolly was described in his role of superintendent of the Hanwell Asylum by one of his contemporaries as "a father among his children, speaking a word of comfort to one, cheering another, and exercising a kindly and humane influence over all" (Wynter 108).[10]

By mid-century, moral management thus sought to domesticate insanity in a very literal and conventional sense. No longer an unruly element of society at large, the insane were tended in asylums that provided a home away from home, and their recovery was presided over by a professional foster father who monitored behavior and provided a means for patients to reassert their moral faculties. This kind of administrative care offered much to the vision of Victorian social reforms and added to a general sense of pride in "progress" and "humanitarianism."

Moral management and other "humanitarian" reforms in the care of the insane was also a project that attracted the interests of Charles Dickens. Although he did not formally address topics concerning insanity until the early 1850s, when he published a series of articles in *Household Words,* written by himself and others, praising and advocating reforms in care for the insane,[11] Dickens's interest in these matters at the time of his composing *Barnaby Rudge* is quite clear. First, and perhaps most importantly, Dickens made several visits in the spring of 1841 to both Coldbath Fields and Tothill Fields, two prisons based on the principles of the "silent system,"[12] in order to examine two petty criminals with "ricketty intellects" *(Letters* 2:273) and, no doubt, to help him form the characters in his novel. One of these convicts, known with some public notoriety as "The Boy Jones," (and a likely model for Dickens's Barnaby), was arrested in Buckingham Palace "while eating cold meat from the Palace larder," claiming that his only intent for entering the Palace "was to hear the conversation of her Majesty and Prince Albert, in order to write a book" *(Letters* 2:246n). Dickens responded to these visits with characteristic sympathy, and after each, sent money and clothes for the inmates who were soon to be released. He also approved of the "humane and wise government" of the prisons by the superintendents, who viewed the "imbecile" prisoners differently than the rest. In these cases, Dickens asserts the inappropriateness of the prison for confinement of lunatics and applauds special, "humane" attention given toward the reform of these inmates.

In fact, he came to believe, like John Conolly and other practitioners of moral management, that moral and humane care could actually improve the subject's ability for self-government, and that by following a regime of moral and domestic rigor, the unrestrained and dangerous behavior in insanity (like that which would lead a young insane man to break into Buckingham Palace) could be controlled without resorting to methods that appalled Dickens and many other middle-class liberals. Following a proper treatment of the "disease" of madness not only attended to the needs of the insane with humanity, but it also was believed to inhibit the insane tendencies toward public outbursts of violence and unruliness. This understanding was obviously fresh in Dickens's mind during the composition of *Barnaby Rudge,* and it left a strong impression that remained with him following the publication of the novel.

Directly after the completion of *Barnaby Rudge,* Dickens embarked on his trip to America, the experiences of which he recorded in *American Notes* (1842). Upon his landing in Boston, his first item of interest appears to have been the city's many "public institutions and charities," which he considered "as nearly perfect, as the most considerate wisdom, benevolence, and humanity, can make them" (28); and he wasted no time making visits to hospitals and asylums, as well as houses of correction. In his visit to the State Hospital for the Insane, Dickens finds that the institution is "admirably conducted on those enlightened principles of conciliation and kindness, which twenty years ago would have been worse than heretical, and which have been acted upon with so much success in our own pauper Asylum at Hanwell" (45). Not only does he demonstrate a familiarity with the Hanwell Asylum and John Conolly's pioneering reforms, but he is also aware of the progress in lunacy reform and frequently criticizes the past for its abuses. He makes particular note of the peaceful manner in which the insane carry on in the Boston asylum, contrasting their behavior to the assumed violence of madness:

> Every patient in this asylum sits down to dinner every day with a knife and fork; and in the midst of them sits the gentleman, whose manner of dealing with his charges, I have just described. At every meal, moral influence alone restrains the more violent among them from cutting the throats of the rest; but the effect of that influence is reduced to an absolute certainty, and is found, even as a means of restraint, to say nothing of it as a means of cure, a hundred times more efficacious than all the straitwaistcoats, fetters, and handcuffs, that ignorance, prejudice, and cruelty have manufactured since the creation of the world. (47)

In the presence of a gathering of insane subjects, a setting supposed to be beset with violence and disorder, Dickens identifies an "absolute certainty" in the rule of "moral influence." This influence comes from the benevolent father figure dining with "his charges" and from the domestic atmosphere itself. Dickens sees this as "a hundred times more efficacious" clearly because "restraint" is placed within the subjects, within their minds and "souls." Their behavior, in other words, is governed by restraints they have internalized, rather than by restraints placed on their bodies. On the other hand, he condemns by contrast the practice of bodily restraint, seeing it as inhumane and cruel and belonging to a benighted, ignorant past.

Dickens's mindset here reveals an important aspect of his social vision to the same extent that it reveals his opinions on lunacy reform. While he finds authoritative abuses repugnant (a theme that resounds through much of his fiction) and condemns them openly, he seeks at the same time a moral certainty and an agent of "benevolence" to maintain a sense of social order and restraint by controlling subjects through "moral" means.[13] In *Barnaby Rudge,* this agent is the one thing needful to control the violent pathologies that drive the riots (besides the presence of Gabriel Varden, who clearly embodies both moral restraint and benevolence, but who is also overwhelmed by the magnitude of the mob). The type of social control sought for in the novel controls the violence and reduces the actions of insane people to "absolute certainty" through its domestic and moral nurture. Because the violence in *Barnaby Rudge* is represented as aimless and insane, led by the sociopath Hugh and the moral idiot Barnaby, both of whom have no political stake in the riots and are shown to be victims of abuse and domestic fracture, the novel suggests the appropriate cure through these representations. Dickens's praise of "moral influence," its effects and its discourse, can thus be seen as a subtext to the dark, insane, violent world of *Barnaby Rudge.*

II

Critics have argued that in several respects *Barnaby Rudge* is a novel about the public consequences of private abuses, that disorder and violence in the public realm are "merely logical extensions of perverted ideas in domestic government" (Rice, "A *Vade Mecum*" 91). This is certainly a plausible way to see the novel. The problematic intersecting of private and public realms is a common feature in Dickens's fiction, and *Barnaby Rudge* especially probes this relationship, showing how elements in private family lives enter the scene of public crisis. The structure of the narrative is in fact built on this progression, as the first half of the book is preoccupied with the portrayal of five families and their problems, interrupted by a five-year break in the narrative. After this break, the Gordon Riots dominate the narrative and we then see private lives taking part in, and even generating to an extent, the public crisis. Implied in this is a cause/effect relationship: private situations involving abusive fathers and broken homes contribute to the public violence that erupts in the latter half of the novel.

Yet I believe much more is at stake. Given the fact that the characters who do the real work of the Gordon Riots are not simply derelicts (or even religious extremists as would be suggested by the nature of the uprising) but are indeed insane, the problem they present must be seen in a scope greater than private family life. Because insanity becomes a matter for "social medicine," even when the cause originates in the private realm (as it was thought to), the insane require a special governing agency in order to regulate social equilibrium. In sum, the narrative does not simply imply the bad social effects of broken families, it points to a portion of the social body that should be made more "administrable."[14]

What the novel attacks, then, is not just bad "domestic government," but bad social government. In this regard, Dickens finds himself at odds with the divisive hierarchies he associates with a more traditional, generally Tory, paternalism. He scorns the aristocratic pretensions and power abuses of the likes of Sir John Chester, who shows indifference and neglect toward those "beneath" him. Power abuses like these are in fact at their worst when their governance is weak, arbitrary, provincial, or misdirected. Indeed, Dickens shares Carlyle's spiteful attitude towards "a Governing Class who do not govern, nor understand in the least that they are bound or expected to govern" (Carlyle 10:150); but he also sees their method of governance to be lacking. "More concerned with administration than with politics proper" (House 182), Dickens shares with the "bureaucratic elite" of his day a new vision of social order carried out through specialized institutions to implement correct and timely interventions into the social body. Thus, in all his characterizations of abusive families and sociopathic victims, he suggests an underlying hope in a "benevolence" practiced at various places through the larger social realm to make up for those less than adequate families. Likewise, the treatment of the insane, which was becoming in Dickens's day more a matter of social administration than of private concern, established in its practice, perhaps more than anything, the importance of the moralizing influence of family relations and duties.

Barnaby Rudge, a novel about social fracture, thus begins with a domestic scene whose very inadequacy suggests the need for a larger practice of "domesticity" to pervade the social domain and to make up for what is lacking within private boundaries. Of course, this is just what eighteenth-century London lacked. Bad or neglectful social government forms a mirror image of bad domestic government in the novel, generally taking the form of a corrupt paternalism; and bad domestic government is a spawning ground for a multitude of pathologies.

John Willet is perhaps the most scrutinized figure of corrupt paternalism in the novel. More than a tyrant father, he is also the proprietor of the Maypole Inn, which is portrayed in the novel "not just as a vital center of man's civilized life but as a symbolic representation of civilization itself" (Magnet 52). As such, the place Mr. Willet inhabits and rules suggests his dominance in the society of the 1780s. But the Maypole Inn equally represents a view of the pastoral past, a view evoked in the "Merrie England" of Mr. Pickwick and Sam Weller. This particular representation is quite ironic because of the presence of Mr. Willet and his brutal authoritarianism. While the inn seems almost to burst with abundance and good cheer, it also possesses the seeds of its own destruction in Willet's complacent, status quo attitude that accepts the selfish reign of unjust authority. This corrupt, tyrannous authority produces an ineffectual domesticity, ruining the vital, "humanizing" influences of "home." As it turns out, in the wake of the violence, the old inn becomes a target of plunder for the crazed mob—certainly a climactic scene in the novel that I will discuss later.

Leading up to this, the Maypole is primarily the site of a struggle between the father and his capable son, Joseph Willet, whose attempts to voice his opinion or speak at all are immediately thwarted by the elder's constant "Silence, sir!" Mr. Willet denies Joe the natural right to be his own person, and Joe's life is forced entirely within his father's shadow because of his father's absurd and extreme belief in absolute hierarchy: "there an't any boys left—that there isn't such a thing as a boy—that there's nothing now between a male baby and a man—and that all the boys went out with his blessed Majesty King George the Second" (9). As a twenty-year-old baby, forced to defer absolutely to his father, Joe receives no parental esteem (a vital element in moral management), which produces significant inner turmoil. That Joe is an oppressed son is clear enough; what is important about his oppression, about his being denied his right to individuality, comes in the form of his desperate violent outburst toward the close of the first part of the novel. After an especially insulting episode with his father as Sir John Chester takes leave of the Maypole, Joe is taunted by one of his father's cronies and finally cracks.

> Crowding into one moment the vexation and the wrath of years, Joe started up,. overturned the table, fell upon his long enemy [Mr. Cobb], pummeled him with all his might and main, and finished by driving him with surprising swiftness against a heap of spittoons in one corner; plunging into which, head foremost, with a tremendous crash, he lay at full length among the ruins, stunned and motionless. (231)

This is in many ways a very satisfying moment and one that the reader almost expects. When Joe's insurrection does finally come, there is no question as to the reason Joe acts this way or whether he is justified. The novel clearly projects Mr. Willet as one who exercises over his son an unreasonable form of restraint, and his attempts in confining his son to his "place" backfire on him. At the same time, Mr. Willet's form of "government" neglects the nurturing role meant to foster esteem, self-government, and moral control in a person; besides his continual attempt to restrain his son, Mr. Willet never enters meaningfully into his son's life. As a result, Joe's violence, obviously directed toward his father, is uncontrollable and frightening, even to himself, and Mr. Willet is essentially helpless against it.

The episode of Mr. Willet and his son enacts the predicament of revolt on a miniature scale. In the face of intolerable injustice, Joe can only lash out at those who have kept him in his place. But rather than being driven to insanity (besides the moment he plunges headlong into a Carlylean "berserkir rage" [Carlyle 29:140]), Joe leaves his home and joins the British forces bound for America. As he certainly represents a character well endowed with moral accountability (in spite of the abuse he suffers), he finds a morally acceptable alternative to revolt, fully aware of the impossibility of continuing to live under his father's government.

Because Joe moves on, and conveniently absents himself from the narrative, he escapes further victimization by the corrupt authority and perverted paternalism of his father. Those who remain behind under the same conditions suggested by the Maypole drama eventually become swept up in the riots—in particular, the two madmen and eventual ringleaders of the riotous mob, the savage, Hugh, and the idiot, Barnaby. Although these two characters are neither institutionalized (an accurate reflection of the lack of centralized, professional care in the eighteenth century) nor suffer under the practice of physical restraint, they are both subject to the neglectful attitudes and lack of care about which Dickens reacts so indignantly. Further, and perhaps more importantly, the pathologies they both suffer (which are obviously different in nature but alike in effect) are presented as direct consequences of their own broken families—broken due to the sins of their fathers. All the same, we see in these two characters not so much the suffering of individual abuses as the seeds of social crisis when, later in the novel, their neglected and unregulated pathologies become the destructive drive behind the mob.

Hugh, the savage and "untamed" hostler of the Maypole Inn, endures a similar treatment (or lack thereof) to that which marked the inhumane and "backward" treatment of madmen in earlier days. Although he does not exhibit the level of "idiocy" that Barnaby does, he nonetheless assumes the category of insanity and is identified among the other characters as lacking human characteristics, having, as John Willet claims, "no more imagination than Barnaby has" (86). Willet, who clearly exercises his paternal authority in a "backward," abusive, and provincial manner, explains to his cohorts, who take alarm at Hugh's "savage" manner, that "he's more at his ease among horses than men. I look upon him as a animal himself." Willet reasons that this is the appropriate way to see Hugh, since his faculties "was never drawed out of him when he was a boy." He thus categorizes Hugh and treats him in a manner he sees fitting: "that chap that can't read nor write, and has never had much to do with anything but animals, and has never lived in any way but like the animals he has lived among, is a animal. And . . . is to be treated accordingly" (87). Willet perceives Hugh "in immediate relation to his animality" and sees an animalistic treatment as appropriate for him (Foucault, *Madness* 74). As he explains later to Mr. Chester, "if he has any soul at all, sir, it must be such a very small one that it doesn't signify what he does or doesn't in that way" (97). What Mr. Willet seems to be explaining is Hugh's moral unaccountability, and, thus, his lack of humanity, which puts him on the same level as animals. Of course, Willet's "misunderstandings" and his abusive treatment unwittingly contribute to Hugh's becoming an awesome conductor of social anomie and violence later in the novel. In fact, right before the riots, even Mr. Willet, "by a species of inspiration," begins to think it "just barely possible that he was something of a dangerous character, and that it might be advisable to get rid of him one of these days" (258).

Of course, there are many suggested reasons for Hugh's fallen state. Rather than suffering from a congenital defect, like Barnaby, Hugh is living evidence of a sociopathic condition arising directly out of fractured domesticity and harsh authoritarianism. One aspect of Hugh's character is clear throughout the novel: even though he represents the most threatening figure as the riots escalate, the novel also establishes him as the most victimized figure as well. Mr. Willet continues:

> that chap, whose mother was hung when he was a little boy, along with six others, for passing bad notes—and it's a blessed thing to think how many people are hung in batches every six weeks for that, and such like offences, as showing how wide awake our government is—that chap was then turned loose.   (87)

Willet's attitude, no doubt meant to provoke anger in the reader, speaks on behalf of a corrupt paternalism associated with the past, a paternalism which creates the pathologies most feared later in the story.

Mr. Willet is not unique in this aspect. Just as Willet represents the kind of abusive social treatment Hugh is exposed to, his counterpart emerges briefly but quite conspicuously in an episode involving Barnaby and his mother as they are forced to flee from their humble country home. As they travel, they come upon the great house of a country gentleman and are admitted so that Barnaby may show his raven, Grip. Immediately they are looked upon suspiciously by the "genuine John Bull." He is especially suspicious of Barnaby's condition, asking "how long hast thou been an idiot?" Unable to respond, Barnaby defers to his mother, who informs the man, "From his birth." The gentleman then responds with disbelief, claiming, "it's an excuse not to work. There's nothing like flogging to cure that disorder. I'd make a difference in him in ten minutes, I'll be bound" (357). Like Mr. Willet, the "genuine John Bull" gentleman, who also goes by such titles as "a country gentleman of the true school" and " a fine old country gentleman," actually represents the staunch Tory paternalist, clinging to England's outworn aristocratic institutions, who sees "flogging" and other forceful practices exercised upon the body as appropriate means of social control.

While Barnaby is not shown to suffer from the same degree of domestic neglect as Hugh and is blessed with the constant companionship of his mother (although her grasp on Barnaby is somewhat ineffectual), his condition is still associated directly with corrupt domesticity, as he was born with his mental blight on the very night that his father committed murder. Although he is constructed clearly upon the innocent "idiot boy" type, the picture of him includes a frightening aspect because of his moral oblivion. Our first glimpse of Barnaby is noteworthy: "Startling as his aspect was, the features were good, and there was something even plaintive in his wan and haggard aspect. But, the absence of the soul is far more terrible in a living man than in a dead one; and in this unfortunate being its noblest powers were wanting" (28). Barnaby's "lack of soul," which condition can be blamed for his eventual participation in the crimes of the riots, constantly reflects the sins of his father. Mr. Rudge maintains an ominous presence throughout the novel, as if he alone were the source of madness, and Barnaby seems vaguely aware of the presence of his father in his own mind, as he says to Mr. Varden, "I dreamed just now that something—it was in the shape of a man—followed me—came softly after me—wouldn't let me be—but was always hiding and crouching, like a cat in dark corners, waiting till I should pass; when it crept out and came softly after me" (48). Whether this passage is read as a literal figuration of Mr. Rudge or as madness personified representing Barnaby's internal condition, it nevertheless identifies Barnaby as a victim of forces outside of himself.

Barnaby's mental blight, his "absence of soul," is thus both a sign and a product of his victimization, and the effect of this is a form of "moral insanity." Even in his innocence, Barnaby is utterly deprived of moral discernment. His involvement in the riots reveals a character who cannot detect anything morally or socially amiss in his actions or in the mob he is a part of. This is most clear in a passage where Barnaby stands guard for Hugh and Dennis taking rest in a stable after a night of rioting:

> the careful arrangement of his poor dress, and his erect and lofty bearing, showed how high a sense he had of the great importance of his trust, and how happy and how proud it made him. To Hugh and his companion who lay in a dark corner of the gloomy shed, he, and the sunlight, and the peaceful Sabbath sound to which he made response, seemed like a bright picture framed by the door, and set off by the stable's blackness. The whole formed such a contrast to themselves, as they lay wallowing, like some obscene animals, in their squalor and wickedness on the two heaps of straw, that for a few moments they looked on without speaking, and felt almost ashamed.   (398)

While Hugh and Dennis do in fact demonstrate a degree of moral feeling and conscience, Barnaby is devoid of it. As Steven Marcus suggests, Barnaby "is as much at home with [Hugh and Dennis] and the mob as he is with his mother and Varden" (193).

The destructive energy that both Barnaby and Hugh embody is a result of what they both lack (albeit in differing ways and degrees): moral reason. Barnaby's mental condition, traced to his guilty father, does not provide him with the capability to discern moral action, and his fractured domestic existence, one in which he and his mother constantly flee Mr. Rudge, leads him bewilderingly into the riots. Interestingly, as peace is later established throughout London and Barnaby escapes his death sentence, we read that as he "regained his old health and gaiety," he also became "more rational" (633), suggesting that through an improved environment and encircled about with friends and family, the insane may develop a measure of "soul," moral understanding, and control.

Hugh, on the other hand, who at the end speaks consciously of himself as "more brute than man," lacks what he does because of his victimization and complete deprivation of the cultivating influences of a proper domestic and moral authority. He acknowledges the effects of this deprivation before his execution, and even though he confesses his own guilt in the riots, he also identifies who is to blame, exclaiming,

> On that black tree, of which I am the ripened fruit, I do invoke the curse of all its victims, past, and present, and to come. On the head of that man, who, in his conscience, owns me for his son, I leave the wish that he may never sicken on his bed of down, but die a violent death as I do now, and have the night-wind for his only mourner.   (596)

Hugh's curse is not only on his guilty father, Mr. Chester (who is also a figure of corrupt paternalism and, of course, proves the truthfulness of Hugh's prophecy), but on the "black tree" that produces a victimized, and morally insane, class of people. In this way he alludes equally to the responsibilities within the family and to those that extend beyond the home. The abuse that follows when these responsibilities are not heeded, the novel suggests, produces the sociopathic tendencies that feed riots and social revolt.

Individually, then, *Barnaby Rudge* constructs pathologies on the domestic level that bear socially destructive potential; idiots and lunatics carry their own histories of mistreatment and, in their inarticulate way, cry out for the esteem and moral guidance meant to be engendered in the home. Deprived of this, their consequent moral insanity presents a detriment to society. When the picture is enlarged, however, the novel shows, like Carlyle's *Chartism*, the need for a larger mechanism to provide collective moral management: a scene where the "popular commotions and maddest bellowings" are heard by the "ear of wisdom" to cry out "Guide me, govern me! I am mad and miserable, and cannot guide myself" (29:157). As the novel progresses from the domestic narrative into the story of the riots, familiar faces become an element of the larger entity. If Dickens's picture of this entity suggests any-thing, it suggests a loosing of uncontrollable madness—a predicament that could be prevented through reformed social government.

III

To an extent, Dickens's 1841 reconstruction of the "shameful tumults" of the Gordon Riots appears to indicate a liberal attitude of progress: an insis-tence that an uprising like the 1780 riots should never occur in the more civilized times of Queen Victoria with its social and political reforms. David Craig briefly suggests this in relation both to *Barnaby Rudge* and *A Tale of Two Cities*, writing, "That Dickens . . . chose episodes more than half a cen-tury old for his exhibition of mob violence may suggest that he saw it as typically bygone, and it is true that early in both novels he emphasizes the backwardness of the later eighteenth century" (86). *Barnaby Rudge*, in its portrayals of harsh penal codes and public lust for executions (characterized in the hangman, Dennis), insensitive treatment of the insane, and a city ill equipped to deal with the outbreak (having "the worst conceivable police" [374]), certainly produces an indelible image of an unenlightened past. This reading has led some critics, like David Morse, to assert that "the real signifi-cance of *Barnaby Rudge* . . . was that [Dickens] finally acknowledged the futility both of the pastoral ideal and of any kind of appeal to the example of the past" (152).

While this view of the past is an important part of the vision of the novel, especially as it relates to the social treatment of the insane characters and the inept administration of public order, there is also much to indicate that *Bar-naby Rudge* imagines the "insane" impulses in the social body to be a trans-historical phenomenon—one that concerns certain problematic aspects of human nature—and not simply a product of various historical circumstances unique to the Gordon riots. The novel also suggests that, by their very nature, social uprisings have no significant political bearing. In other words, just as Carlyle identified the "disease" of revolution to be located in the "human condition itself" (Brantlinger 61), Dickens's novel envisions the violence and disorder to arise out of the more chronic and underlying problem of human pathologies rather than out of genuine political discontent. As the behavior that leads to mob activity is seen to emerge out of "mad" passions that, at their height, are associated with acts of nature ("man, lashed into madness with the roaring winds and boiling waters, has become for the time as wild and merciless as the elements themselves" [17]), the novel strongly suggests the persistence of a similar social vulnerability into Dickens's own day, a day obviously marked by numerous public disturbances of its own.[15]

In fact, many critics have asserted that the historical novel forms a direct response to Chartism and to the violence generated in the political protests of the late 30s. Butt and Tillotson point out that during the five years' delay between the novel's design and publication (1836–41), the subject matter would have increased in "topicality":

> The Poor Law riots, the Chartist risings at Devizes, Birmingham, and Sheffield, the mass meetings on Kersal Moor and Kennington Common, and most pointed of all, the Newport rising of 1839 with its attempt to release Chartist prisoners—all these . . . gave special point in 1841 to "a tale of the Riots of '80."
>
> (82)

Butt and Tillotson also point out, however, the "imperfections of the historical parallel," asserting that the author "was responding not to enlightened historical analysis, but to the average man's horror of looted chapels and distilleries, armed robbery in the streets, [and] prisons and mansions ablaze." Any reading of the novel will reveal this horror—at times fascination—evoked by scenes of a mob in its mad ravages, as if the mob itself were the great fact of the novel. But while these depictions of the mob seem, at points, to leap out of history, they remain fixed in a middle-class perception of working-class pathologies, particularly in the decades of Chartist and other working-class uprisings—pathologies that were understood to require the same attention as individual cases of insanity.

While Dickens himself sympathized with certain political aspects of Chartism, his position on the movement in general makes clear the real issue in *Barnaby Rudge.* Humphry House writes, "Dickens might have sided with the Chartists. . . . But two things prevented Dickens's accepting this position—his horror of 'the mob' and (what was closely allied with it) his belief in the infallible virtues of education" (179). We see a similar attitude in *Barnaby Rudge:* on the one hand, Dickens portrays several characters subjected to injustices, and he sympathizes with their plight for a more just existence; but on the other hand, when the crowds emerge, he can only wish for a better police force. This has to do with his perceptions of the character of the militant crowd, an uneducated character (i.e., lacking morality and discipline, or "morally insane") that demonstrated a seemingly inherent tendency toward madness, disorderliness, and destruction leading to self-destruction. As the novel constructs precisely this kind of mob, it would have implied much to Dickens's middle-class readers about the threat of "similar" militant crowds that were active during the composition and publication of the novel. Further, the mob is constructed essentially as an apolitical entity; it is driven not by any political rally, but by pathological impulses inherent in its nature. The construction of the mob as a pathological entity creates a type of "otherness" that can then be reinscribed into a middle-class political process featuring an active and interventionist moral management of the social body. This is what Dickens's history of the Gordon Riots anticipates. But as a history, it also forms an argument for the greater implementation of such social government in his own day. His descriptions of the social body in *Barnaby Rudge* confirm this.

The crowds depicted in the novel emerge out of the generally unseen region of the lower-class lanes and courts; the "vast throng" that assembles as the riots progress does not come into town with Gordon and his supporters, but is "composed for the most part of the very scum and refuse of London" (374). We see these mobs rioting among various places in the metropolis, but only once do we catch a glimpse of where the people constituting the mob come from. In a scene where Gordon's secretary, Gashford, seeks out Dennis and Hugh for a private meeting, he finds himself in the "undiscovered country" of the lower orders:

> Great heaps of ashes; stagnant pools, overgrown with rank grass and duckweed; broken turnstiles; and the upright posts of palings long since carried off for firewood, which menaced all heedless walkers with their jagged and rusty nails; were the leading features of the landscape . . . and would have suggested (if the houses had not done so, sufficiently, of themselves) how very poor the people were who lived in the crazy huts adjacent, and how fool-hardy it might prove for one who carried money, or wore decent clothes, to walk that way alone, unless by daylight. . . . The population dealt in bones, in rags, in broken glass, in old wheels, in birds, and dogs. These, in their several ways of stowage, filled the gardens; and shedding a perfume, not of the most delicious nature, in the air, filled it besides with yelps, and screams, and howling.   (334–34)

This brief but important description establishes a more complete setting in the novel: one that would have rung true to middle-class readers exposed to the many reports on the physical and moral condition of the working classes. The fact that these lanes produce the "scum and refuse" that become the mob in *Barnaby Rudge* follows the prevalent, largely middle-class notions that people living in run-down, overcrowded houses among filth and disorder concretely signified a "dangerous" class because of their being deprived of the humanizing effects of domestic economy and moral education.

Composed in 1841, a year during which Edwin Chadwick's monumental sanitary investigation among the laboring population was in full swing, the novel's picture of working-class depravity follow those of the more prominent "social investigators" who insisted on moral rationales for working-class rehabilitation.[16] Whether these investigators proposed enhancing opportunities for education or improving sanitary conditions, the working-class courts were consistently reported to produce moral and physical depravity, as Chadwick asserts:

The facts indicated will suffice to show the importance of the moral and political considerations, viz., that the noxious physical agencies depress the health and bodily condition of the population, and act as obstacles to education and to moral culture;. . . that they substitute, for a population that accumulates and preserves instruction and is steadily progressive, a population that is young, inexperienced, ignorant, credulous, irritable, passionate, and dangerous, having a perpetual tendency to moral as well as physical deterioration.   (268)

As the passage indicates, Chadwick's concern is over "populations" and their effect on the social order. Repeatedly throughout his report, he suggests serious consequences in the neglect of impoverished domestic conditions that give rise to such populations, and he even blames an incident of violence during the French Revolution of 1830 on such a neglected population (162–63). Likewise, Dickens's portrayal of the "scum and refuse" of London with their decrepit houses and dungheaps is a picture of a lost and neglected population, one that is in bad need of repair.

And in many ways the picture itself is a call for intervention. The scene is all too familiar and possesses the well-known signs—heaps of trash, stagnant water, reeking offal—that became small arguments in themselves in Chadwick's sanitary report. (And of course the 1848 Public Health Act proved the effectiveness of this method of argument.) But besides seeking sanitary legislation, Dickens and many other middle-class liberals insisted on a form of moral intervention. James Kay, another prominent investigator of social conditions and author of *The Moral and Physical Condition of the Working Classes* (1832), puts it thus: "Ere the moral and physical condition of the operative population can be much elevated, a system of national education so extensive and liberal as to supply the wants of the whole labouring population must be introduced" (93). A fundamental aspect of this project, Kay explains, is that the working classes "should be instructed in the nature of their domestic and social relations" (98). Understanding the private lives of the laboring population to lack this vital form of instruction, Kay identifies a tutelary role at the heart of social government. Put another way, teachers could provide "the cheapest police, and the surest sanitary process" (Stow v).

The depictions of working-class depravity we read of in *Barnaby Rudge* (along with everything associated with them) are contrasted, on the other hand, to the order and discipline represented by the locksmith Gabriel Varden. Although part of the working class, but clearly not of the "dangerous" type, Varden (after whom the novel was originally entitled) forms something of an ideal: a happy, productive worker with a morally educated conscience, living by the "still small voice" of duty:

No man who hammered on at a dull monotonous duty, could have brought such cheerful notes from steel and iron; none but a chirping, healthy, honest-hearted fellow, who made the best of everything, and felt kindly towards everybody, could have done it for an instant. . . . It was a perfect embodiment of the

still small voice. . . . There he stood working at his anvil, his face all radiant
with exercise and gladness, his sleeves turned up, his wig pushed off his shining
forehead—the easiest, freest, happiest man in all the world.   (307)

Varden provides the only sense of moral sensibility and healthy vitality in
the novel; although he lives and works in the midst of chaos and riot, and
has a rebellious apprentice to boot, he and his work represent steadiness and
moral fortitude, best seen in his refusal among the hostile crowds to open the
locks of Newgate. More importantly, Varden stands out against the rest of
the unruly class he is a part of because his "passions" are sufficiently restrained. He exemplies a disciplined subject who has internalized the means
of his own moral control through his industry, domestic rigor, and atten-
tiveness to the "still, small voice."

Varden distinguishes himself, in other words, by having what it takes—the
training and moral health—to resist the contagions and diseases of the social
body. His character forms a model for what the working classes may become
when "instructed in the nature of their domestic and social relationships."
Meanwhile, we read that the pathologies that begin with the "scum and
refuse of London" spread, and otherwise non-threatening people become
swept up into the "infectious madness" of revolt:

> Each tumult took shape and form from the circumstances of the moment; sober
> workmen, going home from their day's labour, were seen to cast down their
> baskets of tools and become rioters in an instant; mere boys on errands did the
> like. In a word, a moral plague ran through the city. The noise, and hurry, and
> excitement, had for hundreds and hundreds an attraction they had no firmness
> to resist. The contagion spread like a dread fever: an infectious madness, as
> yet not near its height, seized on new victims every hour, and society began to
> tremble at their ravings.   (403)

The character of the "militant crowd" in *Barnaby Rudge,* with all its
dangerous social consequences, is thus sharpened through its contrast to Varden, the morally managed subject. Lacking internalization of control, individuals making up the social body are mostly portrayed in the novel as having
no particular aim in the riots, let alone any worthy political aim. Along these
lines, Dickens's picture of Lord George Gordon tends to distance him from
his supposed supporters, "relieving him of full responsibility for the ensuing
chaos" (Rice, "Politics" 60). While the novel shows a good deal of the
responsibility for inciting the riots to fall upon the machinations of Gordon's
secretary, Gashford, and upon the sinister Sir John Chester, the violence and
destruction that follow emerge directly out of the apolitical and insane character of the mob—a character that is initially formed out of pathologies specifically symbolized in Barnaby's moral oblivion and Hugh's socipathic
impulses, and not out of any cause for Protestantism.

Barnaby's naive entrance into the riotous faction in fact plays out the social dangers of unmanaged pathologies. Lacking the moral sensibility to judge the nature of the crowd because of his idiocy, Barnaby unhesitatingly joins, thinking that involvement in the crowd is certain to benefit his mother and himself. His demurring mother, in the meantime, finds herself defenseless against Gordon and Gashford, who encourage Barnaby's participation. As Barnaby's mother objects, stating that her son "is not in his right senses," Gordon dismisses the idea, insisting that "we must not construe any trifling peculiarity into madness" (366). While Gordon's own motives are questionable from a moral (and mental) standpoint, Barnaby's enthusiasm and energy derive entirely from a deluded hope for personal gain.

On the other hand, Hugh voices his motives to John Chester, for whom he has done a variety of dirty work through the novel: "Give me a good scuffle; let me pay off old scores in a bold riot where there are men to stand by me; and then use me as you like—it don't matter much to me what the end is!" (305). Like Barnaby, Hugh does not become involved for a political purpose. Instead, his participation in the riots stems from a destructive energy that is shown to derive from his victimization. From the start, Hugh confuses the cause for the riots, perhaps purposefully, and Dennis the hangman follows along. As Dennis signs up Hugh in Gordon's faction, they proceed to salute each other:

> "No Popery, Brother!" cried the hangman.
> "No Property, brother!" responded Hugh.
> "Popery, Popery," said the secretary with his usual mildness.
> "It's all the same!" cried Dennis. "It's all right. Down with him, Muster
> Gashford. Down with everybody, down with everything!"   (288)

"Down with everything!" turns out to be the true rallying cry of the mob; even though the blue cockades are worn and the targets of the mob include conspicuous Catholics, Popish sympathizers, and Catholic chapels, the rioters' excesses are shown to reflect directly back upon their own pathologies.

Along with an appetite for destruction, the above passage further suggests an appetite for plunder.[17] The depiction of plunder at the Maypole Inn especially evokes an image of the mob as sociopathic menace, while the cultural and traditional "sanctity" of the inn is ravaged in a beastly fashion:

> Here is the bar—the bar that the boldest never entered without special invitation—the sanctuary, the mystery, the hallowed ground: here it was, crammed with men, clubs, sticks, torches, pistols; filled with a deafening noise, oaths, shouts, screams, hootings; changed all at once into a bear-garden, a mad-house, an infernal temple: men darting in and out, by door and window, smashing the glass, turning the taps, drinking liquor out of China punchbowls, sitting astride of casks, smoking private and personal pipes, . . . putting things in their pockets

which didn't belong to them, dividing [Willet's] own money before his own eyes, wantonly wasting, breaking, pulling down and tearing up. . . . More men still—more, more, more—swarming like insects: noise, smoke, light, darkness, frolic, anger, laughter, groans, plunder, fear, and ruin!   (414)

This scene, delivered in hysterical pitch and mesmerizing rhythm, captures the essence of the mob and its driving, amoral behavior. The novel indicates no political motive for the mob to strike the Maypole in particular, in fact, earlier in the novel the inn had been an important stopping place for Gordon, and its proprietor is earlier shown to embody the same political sentiments as the "No Popery" crusaders. The inn is instead conveniently knocked off as an easy spoil as the rioters are en route to work the greater destruction of the house of the Catholic (and enemy to Gashford and Chester) Geoffrey Haredale.[18]

The scene of the destruction of Haredale's mansion further develops the qualities of the mob as the rioters appear not only to plunder and burn the mansion, but also to let their aimless and destructive impulses become self-destructive as well. At this point the pathological crowd begins to consume itself:

If Bedlam gates had been flung wide open, there would not have issued forth such maniacs as the frenzy of that night had made. There were men there, who danced and trampled on the beds of flowers as though they trod down human enemies, and wrenched them from the stalks, like savages who twisted human necks. There were men who cast their lighted torches in the air, and suffered them to fall upon their heads and faces, blistering the skin with deep unseemly burns. There were men who rushed up to the fire, and paddled in it with their hands as if in water, and others who were restrained by force from plunging in, to gratify their deadly longing. On the skull of one drunken lad–not twenty, by his looks—who lay upon the ground with a bottle to his mouth, the lead from the roof came streaming down in a shower of liquid fire, white hot; melting his head like wax. When the scattered parties were collected, men—living yet, but singed as with hot irons—were plucked out of the cellars, and carried off upon the shoulders of others, who strove to wake them as they went along, with ribald jokes, and left them, dead, in the passages of hospitals. But of all the howling throng not one learnt mercy from, or sickened at, these sights; nor was the fierce, besotted, senseless rage of one man glutted.   (423–24)

The scene possesses imaginative power, even if its historical fidelity may be questioned. But this scene is most instrumental in arriving at Dickens's conclusion concerning the morally insane character of the mob. Certainly the most shocking depiction of the crowd, with its "deadly longing" and utter insensitivity, is in the fact that "not one learnt mercy from, or sickened at, these sights."

Barnaby Rudge spares nothing in depicting "these sights," and their rhetorical impact is obvious: they establish vivid grounds in pointing out the dangers in a pathological social body to the extent that readers sicken at the same sights that are shown to energize the insane mob. At these moments, politics, even history, is forgotten as the picture of social violence unfolds before the reader. As one of Dickens' contemporaries, Henry Crabb Robinson, remarked about the novel, "the picture of the riots . . . is excellent and has poetical truth whether it be historical or not" (102). The logic of such a statement of course reflects how the "poetical" treatment of a historical event (regardless of its accuracy) can bear relevance to a contemporary reader at the time the novel was published. In short, the "poetical truth" identified in the novel reflects an awareness of a social condition whose veracity was confirmed in certain events occurring in the late 1830s and '40s. As the rioting depicted in *Barnaby Rudge* forms the symptom of a deeper pathology, the crowds of people involved in the rioting are likewise shown to be not politically motivated, but, by definition, diseased. Along these same lines, the extent to which Dickens's readers saw concrete political parallels to the Chartist movement is not as important as the way groups of rioting people were identified. Whether or not the novel reveals Dickens's attitude toward Chartism is another matter; the real issue concerns the nature of the threat perceived and imagined by the middle class within the context of growing public disturbances in the wake of Chartist agitations.

IV

After the first real episode of violence in the novel, Dickens comments on the rioters: "Hot and drunken though they were, they had not yet broken all bounds and set all law and government at defiance. Something of their habitual deference to the authority erected by society for its own preservation yet remained among them" (387). This assumes the idea that social beings have, or should have, constructed within them a "habitual" form of restraint, a sense of deference to an authoritative code. When we strip this away, we are left with a dark part of our humanity that is inherently destructive of the aims of society. Dickens's remark is somewhat reminiscent of Burke, who, in his *Reflections on the Revolution in France,* writes that "government is a contrivance of human wisdom to provide for human wants. . . . Among these wants is to be reckoned the want . . . of a sufficient restraint upon their passions" (57). Both of these statements were written in historical accounts of social revolt, and both associate outbreaks of violence with a social body that loses contact with moral regularity. Burke argued that government was the proper agency for moral conditioning. In *Barnaby Rudge,* however, social government of 1780 is clearly ill-equipped to deal with the pathologies of a morally diseased class that displays a tendency to strip away that which restrains them.

The story of Barnaby and Hugh, and later of the mobs in general, suggests a rethinking of the "authority erected by society for its own preservation." This suggestion reflects, perhaps more than anything, an acute awareness of dangerous elements existing in society that were plainly abounding at the time Dickens was writing the novel. Because these dangers are perceived in the novel to be attached not to political discontent but to a more fundamental deviancy, the dangers must be controlled through more attention to the moral "health" of the social body. Promoting and maintaining moral health, and thus social order, can only be attended to through greater care and treatment. *Barnaby Rudge* envisions the governmental need to minister to the pathologies of the social body rather than to exert mere force in restraining the rabble.

While the novel says nothing about moral management or the treatment of the insane in themselves, it tells a story of broken homes, bad fathers, victims of domestic fracture, insanity, mob violence, uncontrollable passions, and social revolt (all this besides religious bigotry). These signs were all part of a larger discourse whose logic identified them as social pathologies needing rehabilitation through moral means. They were also signs reflecting the condition of the working classes in the 1830's and 40's. As these two sign systems converge in *Barnaby Rudge,* a cure is suggested by the signs themselves: reestablish domesticity, foster self-government in the subject, build esteem and discipline. Morally manage. Manage morally.

NOTES

1. All quotations from the novel are from the *Oxford Illustrated Dickens* (Oxford: Oxford UP, 1954).
2. The Gordon Riots, which spread through London for three days in June 1780, were provoked by Lord George Gordon's attempt to petition a repeal of the 1778 Catholic Relief Act. When repeal was not granted, crowds of largely lower-class people, apparently incited by Gordon and his followers, took to rioting and looting of Catholic churches. At the height of the conflict, acts of arson (including an attempt to burn down Newgate prison as well as a London distillery) were reported. For full accounts of the riots, see de Castro and Rudé.
3. The phrase, "social body," used extensively in nineteenth-century social discourse, brought together important ideas addressed to the challenge of the vast lower-class populations that congregated mostly in cities and industrial regions. Mary Poovey writes of the term thus:

> By 1776, the phrase *body politic* had begun to compete with another metaphor, the *great body of the people*. . . .By the early nineteenth century, both of these phrases were joined by the image of the social body, which was used in two different ways: it referred either to the poor in isolation from

the rest of the population or to British (or English) society as an organic whole. The ambiguity that this double usage produced was crucial . . . for it allowed social analysts to treat one segment of the population as a special problem at the same time that they could gesture toward the mutual interest that (theoretically) united all parts of the social whole. The phrase *social body* therefore promised full membership in a whole . . . to a part identified as needing both discipline and care.   (7–8)

Appropriate to this phrase also is the metaphor of "body," which allowed a knowledge of anatomy and health to operate on the population of the poor.

4. See, for example, studies by Patrick Brantlinger, John Butt and Kathleen Tillotson, Jack Lindsay, Steven Marcus, Gordon Spence, and Thomas Rice.

5. I borrow this term from Mitchell Dean, who uses it to point out a "disjunction between mode of government and political doctrine":

> Liberalism is usually presented as a doctrine concerned with the optimisation of the sphere of individual freedom and rights, and the preservation of this sphere against any arbitrary encroachment by the state. It thus posits a sphere of private autonomy which is opposed to a domain of public intervention. The term "liberal mode of government" does not so much deny as contextualise this opposition. In this regard, the term implies [that] . . . the private sphere, far from being inviolate, is already the effect of a multitude of state and other governmental interventions which loosely cohere around the objective of the promotion of a specific form of life.   (13)

As the insane presented a special challenge to the "promotion of a specific form of life," the discourse of mental health medicine incorporates much of the same reasoning that underlies a "liberal mode of government."

6. Both Michel Foucault and Robert Castel attribute this change to conditions not immediately associated with psychiatric medicine per se, but with new governmental arrangements and conceptions of a "political anatomy." Foucault especially speaks of an "epistemological rupture" through which the very definition of madness changed. He asserts that "for classicism, madness in its ultimate form is man in immediate relation to his animality . . . . it manifested the very fact that the madman was not a sick man." From this point, Foucault charts a gradual transition, leading to a time "when from an evolutionary perspective this presence of animality in madness would be considered as the sign—indeed, as the very essence—of disease" *(Madness* 74). The disease spoken of here is of a special type originating in what was seen as moral and social deviation—manifested in the "presence of animality"—and reflecting a pathology of "soul."

7. Robert Castel has pointed out that the initiative to develop remedies for insanity derive from the "challenge of madness" to the rise of the nineteenth-century "contractual society" following the French Revolution. He sums up the "otherness" of the madman and his challenge to the social order as follows:

> Unreasonable, he is not amenable to the law; irresponsible, he cannot be the object of punishment; incapable of working or "being useful," he does not

enter the regulated round of exchanges, that "free" circulation of goods and men for which the new bourgeois legality serves as the blueprint. A focus of disorder, more than ever he must be repressed, but according to a system of punishments different from that laid down by the legal codes for those who have wittingly transgressed against the laws.   *(Regulation* 12)

8. See Robert Castel, "Moral Management," for a detailed account of the relation between the development of ideas pertaining to mental health and prevailing nineteenth-century cultural and moral norms.

9. See Scull, 75. Scull's definition of an "internalization of control" as the primary method in moral management by which the subject's "moral status" was the means of operation can be seen closely aligned with Foucault's "history of the modern soul and of a new power to judge" *(Discipline and Punish* 23).

10. John Conolly, author of several important books including *an Inquiry Concerning the Indications of Insanity* (1830) and superintendent of the innovative Hanwell Asylum, was the leading professional in Victorian psychiatry. He is perhaps best known for introducing a kind of rehabilitation which controlled the patient's environment and guided his activity rather than enforcing the more traditional method of physical restraint. For a more full account of Conolly's career and influence on asylum reforms, see Scull, chapter seven ("John Conolly, A Victorian Psychiatric Career").

11. Two of Dickens' articles are particularly noteworthy: "A Curious Dance round a Curious Tree" and "Idiots," both reprinted in volume 2 of *Uncollected Writings from Household Words, 1850–1859,* Ed. Harry Stone (Bloomington: Indiana UP, 1968), 381–91, 489–99.

12. Philip Collins defines the "silent system," a penal reform that Dickens supported, as follows: "prisoners were allowed to work together, but under very strict supervision, for they were forbidden ever to speak, or otherwise communicate, with one another . . . it was healthier, more reformative, more deterrent, less cruel, less costly, and so on" (58–59).

13. Humphry House defines an important element of Dickens's belief in "benevolence" as follows:

An acute feeling for suffering of all forms, whether caused by poverty, sickness, cruelty (mental or physical) or injustice. The feeling becomes most acute when all these causes of suffering are combined in the sufferer, and there is somebody who has power to relieve them all.

He adds to this an "indignation against all anomalies, abuses, and inefficiency in social organizations which cause suffering of any kind" (46). *Oliver Twist* and *Nicholas Nickleby,* composed in the years leading up to *Barnaby Rudge,* provide good examples of authoritative abuses (the workhouse, Dotheboys Hall) as well as practitioners of moral benevolence (the Cheerybles, Mr. Brownlow).

14. See Castel, 163–71, for an account of the formation of an "administrable" domain in society, and of the role of psychiatry as a "political science."

15. David Craig argues that in several of Dickens's novels, including *Barnaby Rudge,* the "militant crowd" is presented as the "most problematic social phenomenon" (80).

16. Edwin Chadwick's *Report on the Sanitary Condition of the Labouring Population of Great Britain* (published 1842), which Mary Poovey has judged *"the* protocol for government reports," had an immense influence over the middle-class public's awareness of the relation between sanitation and the spread of disease and did much to prompt official action. In its minute descriptions of lower-class slums, it also provided a good deal of shock value to its many readers. Although the extent to which Dickens himself was involved in the "sanitation movement" is somewhat unclear, he did receive a copy of Chadwick's report and, in an 1842 letter to Henry Austin, confirmed that "I do concur with him in the great importance and interest of the subject" *(Letters* 3:330).

17. Apropos of this depiction of the mob, Brantlinger asserts that "plunder is the lure that moves many of the rioters, and this fact more than any other is meant to connect them with the Chartists" (84).

18. Of course, more has been read into the attack on the Maypole Inn. Steven Marcus, for example, sees the episode as the symbolic destruction of the corrupt authority represented by John Willet. Almost as a means of poetic justice, "the rioters break into the Maypole and wreck it, destroying all those precious objects which old John has thought of as proof of his unassailable power" (189).

WORKS CITED

Brantlinger, Patrick. *The Spirit of Reform: British Literature and Politics, 1832–1867.* Cambridge, Mass.: Harvard UP, 1977.

Butt, John and Kathleen Tillotson. *Dickens at Work.* London: Methuen, 1957.

Carlyle, Thomas. *Works.* Ed. H.D. Traill. Centenary Ed. 30 vols. London, 1896–1901.

Castel, Robert. "Moral Management: Mental Therapy and Social Control in the Nineteenth Century." In *Social Control and the State.* Ed. Stanley Cohen and Andrew Scull. New York: St. Martins, 1981.

———. *The Regulation of Madness: The Origins of Incarceration in France.* Trans. W.D. Halls. Berkeley: U of California P, 1988.

Chadwick, Edwin. *Report on the Sanitary Condition of the Labouring Population of Great Britain.* Ed. M. W. Flinn. Edinburgh: U of Edinburgh P, 1965.

Collins, Philip. *Dickens and Crime.* London: Macmillan, 1962.

Craig, David. "The Crowd in Dickens." In *The Changing World of Charles Dickens.* Ed. Robert Giddings. London: Vision P, 1983.

Dean, Mitchell. *The Constitution of Poverty: Toward a Genealogy of Liberal Governance.* London: Routledge, 1991.

de Castro, J. P. *The Gordon Riots.* London, 1926.

Dickens, Charles. *American Notes and Pictures From Italy.* Oxford Illus. Ed. Oxford: Oxford UP, 1957.

———. *Barnaby Rudge, A Tale of the Riots of 'Eighty.* Oxford Illus. Ed. Oxford: Oxford UP, 1957.

———. *Letters.* Eds. Madeline House and Graham Storey. Vol. 2. Pilgrim Edition. Oxford: Clarendon P, 1969.

———. *Uncollected Writings from Household Words, 1850–1859.* Ed. Harry Stone. Bloomington: Indiana UP, 1968.

Foucault, Michel. *Discipline and Punish: The Birth of the Prison.* Trans. Alan Sheridan. New York: Vintage, 1979.

———. *Madness and Civilization: A History of Insanity in the Age of Reason.* Trans. Richard Howard. New York: Pantheon, 1965.

House, Humphry. *The Dickens World.* 2nd Ed. London: Oxford UP, 1942.

Lindsay, Jack. "Barnaby Rudge." In *Dickens and the Twentieth Century.* Ed. John Gross and Gabriel Pearson. London: Routledge and Kegan Paul, 1962.

Magnet, Myron. *Dickens and the Social Order.* Philadelphia: U of Pennsylvania P, 1985.

Marcus, Steven. *Dickens: From Pickwick to Dombey.* New York: Basic Books, 1965.

Morse, David. *High Victorian Culture.* New York: New York UP, 1993.

Poovey, Mary. *Making a Social Body: British Cultural Formation 1830–1864.* Chicago: U of Chicago P, 1995.

Porter, Ray. *Mind-Forg'd Manacles: A History of Madness in England from the Restoration to the Regency.* Cambridge, Mass.: Harvard UP, 1987.

Rice, Thomas J. "Barnaby Rudge: A *Vade Mecum* for the Theme of Domestic Government in Dickens." *Dickens Studies Annual* 7 (1978): 81–102.

———. "The Politics of *Barnaby Rudge.*" In *The Changing World of Charles Dickens.* Ed. Robert Giddings. London: Vision P, 1983.

Rudé, George. *Paris and London in the Eighteenth Century: Studies in Popular Protest.* London: Collins, 1970.

Scull, Andrew. *Social Order/Mental Disorder: Anglo-American Psychiatry in Historical Perspective.* Berkeley: U of California P, 1989.

Spence, Gordon. "Introduction." In *Barnaby Rudge.* Ed. Spence. Harmondsworth: Penguin, 1973.

Stow, David. *The Training System, Moral Training School and Normal Seminary.* London, 1854.

Tuke, Samuel. *Description of the Retreat.* 1813. Rpt. London: Dawsons of Pall Mall, 1964.

Wynter, Andrew. *The Borderlands of Insanity.* London: Hardwicke, 1875.

Seasonal Offerings: Some Recurrent Features of the Christmas Books

H. M. Daleski

Alas, nothing in the Christmas Books has the direct, sustained force of the Christmas story of Paul Auster's that comes at the end of the film *Smoke,* a tale that contrives to evoke the Christmas spirit, memorably and movingly, though its two protagonists are involved in lies and deception and theft. Eminent contemporaries of Dickens, however, were extravagant in their praise of his Christmas tales. The formidable Lord Jeffrey, the former editor of the *Edinburgh Review,* the scourge of Wordsworth and Byron's "great literary anthropophagus," told Dickens he had done "more good, and not only fostered more kindly feelings, but prompted more positive acts of beneficence, by this little publication [i.e., *A Christmas Carol*], than can be traced to all the pulpits and confessionals in Christendom, since Christmas 1842" (Collins 147–48). With reference to the same work, Thackeray, who could wield a caustic pen, said: "Who can listen to objections regarding such a book as this? It seems to me a national benefit, and to every man or woman who reads it a personal kindness" (Collins 149). If we would perhaps be more restrained in our evaluation of the *Carol,* there is no question that it is by far the best of the Christmas tales. Thereafter it is steadily downhill all the way. This, however, was not—or not at once—the view of Victorian critics. *The Chimes* was also praised lavishly. A reviewer in *The Times* declared that "for power and eloquence" it was "one of the most remarkable of Mr Dickens's productions" (Collins 156). Not to be outdone, a reviewer in *The Economist* wrote that "the *Chimes* is . . . one of the most remarkable books of the day, and it will mark, if not form, an epoch in the thoughts, creeds, and minds of mankind" (Collins 167). *The Chimes,* indeed, reduced Macready, the great tragic actor, to tears, as Dickens wrote to his wife: "If you had seen Macready last night undisguisedly sobbing and crying on the sofa as I read, you would have felt, as I did, what a thing it is to have power" (Johnson 1:532).

Dickens Studies Annual, Volume 27, Copyright © 1998 by AMS Press, Inc. All rights reserved.

With the publication of *The Cricket on the Hearth,* however, the rot set in. *The Times* called it " a twaddling manifestation of silliness almost from the first page to the last . . . the babblings of genius in its premature dotage" (Collins 154). The same paper said that Dickens was responsible for "the deluge of trash" that glutted the Christmas book market, and labelled *The Battle of Life* "the very worst" of the lot, without "one spark of originality, of truth, of probability, of nature, of beauty" (Johnson 2:610). From 1847 on, the Christmas book market included the five Christmas books of Thackeray, who set out to rival Dickens but who also wrote considerably below par in these works. In a review of Thackeray's *The Kickleburys on the Rhine, The Times* contrived to attack Dickens as well as Thackeray with some notable, typically Victorian rhetoric:

> It has been customary, of late years, for the purveyors of amusing literature—the popular authors of the day—to put forth certain opuscules, denominated "Christmas Books," with the ostensible intention of swelling the tide of exhilaration, or other expansive emotions, incident upon the exodus of the old and the inauguration of the new year. . . . For the most part bearing the stamp of their origin in the vacuity of the writer's exchequer rather than in the fulness of his genius, they suggest by their feeble flavour the rinsings of a void brain after the more important concoctions of the expired year. . . . To our own, perhaps unphilosophical, taste the aspirations towards sentimental perfection of another popular author are infinitely preferable to these sardonic divings after the pearl of truth, whose lustre is eclipsed in the display of the diseased oyster.[1]

The "vacuity of the writer's exchequer" is a resounding way of referring to the potboiler provenance of such Christmas tales—or opuscules. Potboilers they may be, but Dickens's tales, if not Thackeray's, nonetheless have some arresting features, especially in respect of their organizing mechanisms. I propose to discuss some of these under separate heads.

1. Indoors and Out

Alexander Welsh has analyzed what he calls "the basic antithesis of home and the streets" in Dickens's work as a whole (160); in the Christmas Books the action constantly veers from one to the other. What characterizes home is its fire, and references to fires abound in all the tales. The fire in effect constitutes home, for when fuel is "heaped upon the fire" in the *Carol,* Fezziwig's warehouse is transformed, becoming "as snug, and warm, and dry, and bright a ball-room as you would desire to see upon a winter's night," the site, indeed, of "a domestic ball" (31, 32).[2] Even Scrooge's room undergoes "a surprising transformation" when "such a mighty blaze [goes] roaring up the chimney, as that dull petrification of a hearth [has] never known in Scrooge's time'' (39). In his peregrinations with the Ghost of Christmas Present, Scrooge takes note of ''the brightness of the roaring fires in kitchens, parlours, and all sorts of rooms'' and of a general ''piling up'' of fires ''half-chimney high'' (49). In *The Chimes* the bells ''[hang] there, in all weathers, with the wind and rain driving in upon them; facing only the outsides of all those houses; never getting any nearer to the blazing fires that [gleam] and [shine] upon the windows, or [come] puffing out of the chimney tops'' (85). *The Cricket on the Hearth* opens with ''the jolly blaze [uprising] and [falling], flashing and gleaming on the little Haymaker at the top of the Dutch clock'' in the Peerybingle home (160). In *The Battle of Life* ''a raging winter day'' in the Christmas season is said to be ''a day to make home doubly home. To give the chimney-corner new delights. To shed a ruddier glow upon the faces gathered round the hearth, and draw each fireside group into a closer and more social league, against the roaring elements without'' (279). *The Haunted Man* brings the Christmas Books to an end with Redlaw's Christmas dinner that is held ''in the old Hall, by no other light than that of a great fire'' (398).

In these tales fire and a fireside not only constitute home but are viewed as ''its heart and core,'' as is the case specifically with Redlaw's dwelling (318). Fire, indeed, takes on a quasi-religious significance, for in *The Battle of Life* it is said to be ''the Genius of the room'' (285). With a capital G for genius, it is not surprising that Home too is given upper-case status (143). And the idea of Home lends itself easily and naturally to that of a ''domestic Heaven'' (161). In his sense of home Dickens anticipates Ruskin, who, some twenty years later in ''Of Queens' Gardens,'' gave the definitive Victorian account of it in a much-quoted passage:

> This is the true nature of home—it is the place of Peace; the shelter, not only from all injury, but from all terror, doubt, and division. In so far as it is not this, it is not home; so far as the anxieties of the outer life penetrate into it . . . it ceases to be home; it is then only a part of that outer world which you have roofed over, and lighted fire in. But so far as it is a sacred place, a vestal temple, a temple of the hearth watched over by Household Gods, before whose faces none may come but those whom they can receive with love . . . so far it vindicates the name, and fulfils the praise of home. (85)

With home doubling as a sacred temple, it was appropriate that the chaste lady of its hearth should be dubbed an Angel in the House, the name Coventry Patmore gave her at about the same time as Ruskin's essay. There's no question that with the Christmas Books Dickens got into the angel act with a vengeance. In *The Chimes* Trotty Veck's daughter Meg is initially presented as an angel in training: her eyes have ''a clear, patient radiance, claiming kindred with that light which Heaven called into being'' (88). By the end of the tale she makes it: Trotty looks at her as she sits by the fire and it is "as if it were an Angel in his house" (151). In *The Battle of Life* both Grace and Marion make the fireside "bright and sacred" (268), and both duly qualify for angel status: Marion looks into her sister's face "as if it were the face of some bright angel" (258); and with the sun shining on Marion's own face, "she might have been a spirit visiting the earth upon some healing mission" (305). And in *The Haunted Man* Mr. William tells Milly she is "like an angel" (396). With so much cloying sentiment oozing in these tales, it's a relief to have Scrooge's niece around to liven things up a bit in her exchanges with her husband. It is true that she "[plays] well upon the harp" (53), but then she also has "a ripe little mouth, that seemed made to be kissed" (51).

Opposed to homes with their opulent fires and their angels, there are the streets. Although early in Stave Three of the *Carol* there are festive descriptions of people in the streets looking at shops, the streets in poor areas are not a pretty sight, as Scrooge discovers:

> The ways were foul and narrow; the shops and houses wretched; the people half-naked, drunken, slipshod, ugly. Alleys and archways, like so many cesspools, disgorged their offences of smell, and dirt, and life, upon the straggling streets; and the whole quarter reeked with crime, with filth, and misery.   (61)

The narrators are always much more passionate about the suffering of the poor than they are about the bliss of their angels. The alleys that are like reeking cesspools disgorge life as well as smells and dirt, as if the poor were so much sewage, the waste products of society. When the general picture of poverty in the streets narrows, it is a child who becomes the focus. The cosy image of the angel in the house is countered by the stark image of the abandoned child of the streets. This image is as powerful as anything in the Christmas Books, and figures prominently in the opening and closing tales in the volume. Out in the streets with the Ghost of Christmas Present, Scrooge is taken aback to see the Ghost doing some disgorging on its own account:

> "Forgive me if I am not justified in what I ask," said Scrooge, looking intently at the Spirit's robe, "but I see something strange, and not belonging to yourself, protruding from your skirts. Is it a foot or a claw?"
>
> "It might be a claw, for the flesh there is upon it," was the Spirit's sorrowful reply. "Look here."
>
> From the foldings of its robe, it brought two children; wretched, abject, frightful, hideous, miserable. They knelt down at its feet, and clung upon the outside of its garment.
>
> "Oh Man! look here. Look, look, down here!" exclaimed the Ghost.
>
> They were a boy and girl. Yellow, meagre, ragged, scowling, wolfish; but prostrate, too, in their humility. Where graceful youth should have filled their features out, and touched them with its freshest tints, a stale and shrivelled hand, like that of age, had pinched, and twisted them, and pulled them into

shreds. Where angels might have sat enthroned, devils lurked, and glared out menacing. No change, no degradation, no perversion of humanity, in any grade, through all the mysteries of wonderful creation, has monsters half so terrible and dread. (56)

The children who emerge from the Spirit's robe are so "strange" that the narrator is reduced to a piling up of adjectives in a vain attempt to describe them: "wretched, abject, frightful, hideous, miserable . . . yellow, meagre, ragged, scowling, wolfish, prostrate." But clearly they are so strange because in their emaciated condition they are not like children at all; rather, with their claw-like feet and wolfish expressions, they are like wild animals—or "monsters." The narrator insists the children might have been angelic—if, we may take it, they were clustered round a warm, homely fire and a loving mother; instead they are devilish. Street devils are here ranged against domestic angels. And like all devils, they are "menacing," in their destitution threatening eventually to undermine safe houses, if not bring them down. This presumably is the Doom that the Spirit sees written on the boy's brow—though it is as much a pity that he does not leave it to speak for itself, as it is that he takes to allegorizing the children as Ignorance and Want (57). His meaningful injunction comes earlier when he commands Scrooge to "look, look, down here!" It is as if one only has to see things as they are, to look them squarely in the face, to be compelled to do something about them. It is an assumption that underlies much of Dickens's art.

The apparitions of Ignorance and Want spawn the unnamed but flesh-and-blood boy of *The Haunted Man,* who is cast in the same mould as his predecessors. With Redlaw, the boy goes out "with his bare head and his naked feet into the winter night" (363). In the streets he "[cowers] and [trembles] with the cold, and [limps] on one little foot, while he [coils] the other round his leg to warm it." Redlaw then sees him "trail himself upon the dust and crawl within the shelter of the smallest arch, as if he were a rat" (365). In this instance too the animal imagery is insistent. He is "more like a young wild beast than a young child" (330); he rushes into Redlaw's room "like a wild-cat and [crouches] down in a corner" (336); he is "used, already, to be worried and hunted like a beast" (337); he bounds "at the table like some small animal of prey . . . hugging to his breast bread and meat, and his own rags" (338); from birth he has been "abandoned to a worse condition than the beasts" (378). For good measure he is said on different occasions to be "a baby savage, a young monster" (337), to have a "savage little hand," and to be a "baby-monster" (363).

The general Doom that the Ghost of Christmas Present invokes is given a habitation and a name by Redlaw's Phantom, as he points to the boy. The speech is the speech of the Phantom, but the voice is the voice of the novelist in his hortatory and prophetic mode:

"All within this desolate creature is barren wilderness. . . . Woe, tenfold, to the
nation that shall count its monsters such as this, lying here, by hundreds, and
by thousands! . . . There is not . . . one of these—not one—but shows a harvest
that mankind MUST REAP. From every seed of evil in this boy, a field of ruin
is grown that shall be gathered in, and gathered up, and sown again in many
places in the world, until regions are overspread with wickedness enough to
raise the waters of another Deluge."   (378)

The sort of harvest that will be reaped in England is predicated more concretely in *The Chimes,* when Will Fern, the poor laborer, is finally hounded
into a readiness to burn it:

"There'll be a fire to-night," he said. . . . "There'll be Fires this winter-time,
to light the dark nights, East, West, North, and South. When you see the distant
sky red, they'll be blazing. When you see the distant sky red, think of me no
more; or, if you do, remember what a Hell was lighted up inside of me, and
think you see its flames reflected in the clouds. . . . "   (147–48)

In the end it is not merely the streets that are set against homes with their
fires but fires in the fields—or streets. And the fires of Hell burn against those
of the domestic Heaven. At the same time, however, the hope is held out that
the boy, who is a wild animal, can be domesticated. When he first appears
on the scene, shivering on the Swidgers' doorstep, Milly at once takes him
in, dries him and feeds him, and (of course) puts him before the fire. "If it
ever felt a fire before," says Mr. William, "it's as much as ever it did; for
it's sitting in the old Lodge chimney, staring at ours as if its ravenous eyes
would never shut again" (330). At the end of the tale the reformed Redlaw
vows "to protect [the boy], teach him, and reclaim him" (397), but it is the
angel in the house who saves the day. The boy steadily "[keeps] by Milly,
and [begins] to love her" (398)—and so, presumably, is well and truly provided for.

2. Now You See It, Now You Don't

The dramatic formula of the Christmas Books is the imagination of disaster—and its recuperation. That is to say, it is the deliberate titillation of the
reader. At the outset of the volume, Scrooge's nephew defines Christmas as
a time "when men and women seem by one consent to open their shut-up
hearts freely, and to think of people below them as if they really were fellow-
passengers to the grave" (10). Christmas, then, is associated with death rather
than birth; and it would seem that Dickens believes that the evocation of
death or of catastrophes that imply fates equal to or worse than death is a
sure means of wringing hearts. But then such things should not be taken too
far at Christmas time, and so they are magically erased.

That the Ghost of Christmas Yet To Come should show Scrooge harrowing scenes connected with his death but that he should live happily ever after is fair enough. That is part of the treatment, and, together with the other visions afforded him, this serves to redeem him. The death of Tiny Tim, however, is another matter. For a start, the description of the grieving Cratchit family is bathetic in the extreme and is marked by some peculiar inversions. Instead of the head of the family comforting his young children in their grief, "the two young Cratchits [get] upon his knees and [lay], each child a little cheek, against his face, as if they said, 'Don't mind it, father. Don't be grieved!' " (67). When Bob thinks of Tiny Tim's grave, he suddenly breaks down, crying out, with considerable reiteration, "My little, little child! My little child!" but then when he goes upstairs into the death chamber and "[kisses] the little face," he as suddenly becomes "quite happy"—it being a moot point as to which of the two words is more inappropriate (67–68). They are matched, at any rate, by Bob's telling his wife that the sympathy of Scrooge's nephew, whom he has just met in the street, was "quite delightful." But then Bob's grasp of English is surprisingly uncertain: his response to his report of the sympathy that Scrooge's nephew expresses for his "good wife" is:

"By the bye, how he ever knew *that,* I don't know."
"Knew what, my dear?"
"Why, that you were a good wife," replied Bob.   (68)

In the midst of his grief, moreover, Bob very much has an eye to the main chance: Scrooge's nephew, whom previously he has "scarcely seen but once," has been so delightful that Bob declares, with grovelling optimism and quite out of the blue, that he "shouldn't be at all surprised . . . if he got Peter a better situation" (68). The scene ends, after some further reference to the little, little child, with Bob dropping the "quite" and intensifying his satisfaction: " 'I am very happy,' said little Bob. 'I am very happy.' " All that remains is for the narrator to add: "Spirit of Tiny Tim, thy childish essence was from God!" (69).

After having all the stops pulled out for us in this way, we are merely informed, in a subordinate clause and on the last page of the tale, that "to Tiny Tim, who did NOT die, [Scrooge] was a second father" (76). For sheer effrontery that simply takes the cake. But then Dickens is clearly intent on having his cake and eating it—a large Christmas cake.

The formula of disasters undone is employed in all the tales that follow, though "disasters" is too strong a word for what happens in *The Haunted Man,* where we are treated to no more than the spectacle of ordinarily good-hearted people becoming unfeeling and then being restored to themselves. In the other three tales, however, the advent of catastrophe of one sort or another is insisted on; and though the instances of this are straightforward enough, I propose briefly to rehearse them both because we tend to forget the details and the seriousness of the novelist's determination to play with our hearts.

In *The Chimes* Trotty Veck's is the first reported death, and before we can get over that, he is, through the agency of the Spirit of the Chimes, a witness to the calamities that befall those dear to him. Nine years have elapsed since we first me him and the other characters, time enough for the cultivation of general ruin. Will Fern, that fine "sunbrowned, sinewy, country-looking man" (110) who is driven to projected arson, is shown as worn and old and grey and bent after repeated jail sentences. Jail, for him, has been home (131–33). Lilian, the orphan, the child of Will's brother, is nine years old when she first appears with her "beautiful face" (112). Nine years later, in abject poverty, she gives way to "the dreadful thoughts that tempt [her] in [her] youth" (127) and takes to the streets. Opposed to the angel in the house, we now have the street-walker. Lilian thus succumbs to a fate worse than death, but is granted death too, and dies of "a broken heart" in Meg's arms (137). Meg's young man, Richard, a blacksmith, "a handsome, well-made, powerful youngster . . . with eyes that [sparkle] like the red-hot droppings from a furnace fire" (93), nine years later—having followed the advice of his elders and betters not to marry Meg—is "a slouching, moody, drunken sloven, wasted by intemperance and vice," a "spectacle of . . . deep degradation, of . . . abject hopelessness, of . . . a miserable downfall" (134). "In the hope of saving him," Meg finally marries him and has a child by him, but he still dies a miserable death (144–45). Meg then "[languishes] away, in dire and pining want" (146), and, with the baby in her arms, finally makes for the river, "that portal of Eternity," pausing a moment "on the brink before the dreadful plunge" (150).

Even a bare recital of these events indicates how melodramatic and conventional the narrative is. But this is nothing compared to its resolution. Trotty, we discover, is not dead, nine years have not passed, all the characters are happily as they were, the one change being the coming marriage of Meg and Richard—and the only problem has been the tripe that Trotty consumed for lunch. His tripe has earlier aroused the ire of Mr. Filer, who says, beautifully:

> "Taking into account the number of animals slaughtered yearly within the bills of mortality alone; and forming a low estimate of the quantity of tripe which the carcases of those animals, reasonably well butchered, would yield; I find that the waste on that amount of tripe, if boiled, would victual a garrison of five hundred for five months of thirty-one days each, and a February over. The Waste, the Waste!"   (94–95)

A lot of tripe we might add.

Some vestigial conscience nagging a great novelist would seem to have led him to produce emblems in and of inferior work. Tripe for *The Chimes*, for instance. And the blind girl and her father in *The Cricket on the Hearth*. Their relationship is one in which Caleb sustains a lifelong deception of his daughter, and this tale differs from both the *Carol* and *The Chimes* in that it evokes its disaster not by means of ghosts and spirits but through the narrator's wilful deception of the reader. This narrator is not only unreliable; he deliberately prevaricates.

The disaster in this instance has a purely matrimonial framework, seeming to present a faithless wife and a disillusioned and murderous husband. Dot has apparently committed the unforgivable sin for a woman presiding over the home fires; she has "blighted the hearth," as the Carrier says (210); and he is ready to kill the violator of his domestic peace. When he relents and thinks better of that, he is selflessly ready to break up his marriage, to "make her the best reparation in [his] power" and to "release her from [what he takes to be] the daily pain of an unequal marriage" (218). When all is over and everything is happily resolved, what strikes us is how artificial Dot's deception of her husband is. There seems to be no good reason why she could not have taken him into her confidence in the first place, for her explanation afterwards that he could not be relied on to keep a secret seems a little thin in the light of what follows. But her innocent deception of her husband pales into insignificance beside the narrator's treatment of the reader.

When the disguised Edward first reveals his true identity to Dot, her reaction is extreme. She cries out loudly, making "the room ring, like a glass vessel," and she stands "like one transfixed by terror and surprise" (177). When her husband asks her what is wrong, she falls "into a wild fit of laughter" and then weeps bitterly (178). Since we do not know the cause of her behavior, and it follows Tackleton's reference to his "wife that is to be" (177)—his, like Dot's being a union of January and May—our first vague suspicions are aroused. The scene ends with a mysterious "young figure of a man" repeating over and over "Married! and not to me!" (181). This is acceptable as far as Edward is concerned, but it can in no way excuse the narrator's thereupon launching his campaign of deception with a blatant apostrophe: "O Dot! O failing Dot! There is no place for [that young figure of a man] in all your husband's visions; why has its shadow fallen on his hearth?" (181).

Thereafter the narrator really begins to rub it in. When Bertha tells the bride-to-be that it wrings her heart to know she is to marry Tackleton, the narrator comments that it was well for them that Dot was present, "that beaming, useful, busy little Dot—for such she was, whatever faults she had, and however you may learn to hate her, in good time" (202). A little later, when Dot is waiting for her husband to return home, we are told she is "very restless. Not as good wives are, when listening for their husbands. No, no, no. It was another sort of restlessness from that" (204). When the Carrier finally sees Dot with Edward, no longer in disguise, the narrator climactically orates: "Oh Shadow on the Hearth! Oh truthful Cricket! Oh perfidious Wife!" (206). Not content with this, the narrator then proceeds from having made Dot the subject of his misleading commentary to turning her into the mere puppet of his designs: having heard the Carrier declare he will release her that day and return her to her parents' home, but knowing that the happily married Edward and May will arrive any minute, she is nevertheless made to say, "Will you bring [the Baby] sometimes, to see his father, Tilly . . . when I can't live here, and have gone to my old home?" (220). After Caleb confesses his deception to Bertha, she says, "It is my sight restored. . . . I have been blind, and now my eyes are open" (223). When our eyes are opened to the narrator's deceptions, there is nothing left to restore.

In *The Battle of Life* the ostensible disaster is again related to a supposedly faithless woman, and so to "the desolation of [her] home, and shipwreck of its dearest treasure" (277). In this tale, however, the deception of the reader is accomplished by means of ambiguous action rather than misleading commentary by the narrator. That is decidedly preferable, but the whole conception is so saccharine that it does not much matter. Once again disaster is waved aside, and each sister gets her man: Grace marries Alfred, and Marion marries Michael Warden—though the narrator, with a sudden pang of conscience, shrinks a little from actually detailing that second happy consummation and puts it down to information derived from Time. As for himself, he hardly knows, he says in the closing sentence of the tale, "what weight to give to [Time's] authority."

3. Ghosts, Phantoms, Spirits, etc.

There are honest-to-goodness ghosts in only two of the tales—*A Christmas Carol* and *The Haunted Man.* These ghosts cannot compare, for example, with Henry James's ghosts in *The Turn of the Screw* if we take the governess at her word, but they are real ghosts. In *The Chimes,* with its "dwarf phantoms, spirits, elfin creatures of the Bells" (120), which are ultimately altogether undone by Trotty's lunch of tripe, and in *The Cricket on the Hearth,* with its fairies and "potent spirits" of "the Cricket tribe" (183), we have manifestations of the subnatural rather than the supernatural. In *The Battle of Life* there is an interesting attempt, though it does not succeed, to substitute for Spirits the spirit of place.

I think we are adverted to the function of the supernatural in the *Carol* and *The Haunted Man* by the Author's Preface to the Christmas Books:

The narrow space within which it was necessary to confine these Christmas Stories, when they were originally published, rendered their construction a matter of some difficulty, and almost necessitated what is peculiar in their machinery.

The problem that Dickens faced within the limited confines of these tales was how to portray change. It is arguable whether any of us actually change in life, but we like to believe that such change is possible in literature. To that end, however, what is needed is the depiction of a process, a gradual process of change, and that takes time and space. Dickens showed what he could achieve with developing characters in his portrayal, for instance, of Pip in *Great Expectations,* or Eugene Wrayburn and Bella Harmon in *Our Mutual Friend.* But these are full-length works. The "narrow space" of the *Carol* and *The Haunted Man* necessitated the "peculiar machinery" of the supernatural because their theme is the transformation of their protagonists, overnight transformations, and the supernatural is the means of achieving such dramatic change. It does not seem to me, however, that Dickens takes his ghosts very seriously: at the end of the *Carol,* which gives us his most powerful ghosts, we are told that Scrooge had "no further intercourse with Spirits, but lived upon the Total Abstinence Principle, ever afterwards" (76). It's a good joke, but a risky one, for it quite dissipates the ghosts.

If we view the three Christmas ghosts in the *Carol* as mere machinery, it enables us to sidestep the supposed problem of Scrooge's transformation. Edmund Wilson was the first of modern critics to suggest that the change in Scrooge is unconvincing:

> Shall we ask what Scrooge would actually be like if we were to follow him beyond the frame of the story? Unquestionably he would relapse when the merriment was over—if not while it was still going on—into moroseness, vindictiveness, suspicion. (60)

As opposed to Wilson, Elliot Gilbert has argued that "sufficient emotional intensity is generated by the visits of the three Christmas Spirits to justify . . . the old man's conversion at the end, and to cause us temporarily to suspend our disbelief in the reality of the conversion"; and he maintains that the *Carol* is "the metaphysical study of a human being's quest for, and rediscovery of, his own innocence" (22, 24). I would like to suggest that such arguments, pro and con, are beside the point: Scrooge's transformation, like Redlaw's, is Dickens's donnée and the supernatural its means. We are tacitly invited to accept the one as we do the other, "without any irritable reaching after fact and reason."

The most interesting piece of supernatural business in *Christmas Books* is Scrooge's encounter with Marley's Ghost, which seems to me to be different in kind from his subsequent experiences with the three Christmas Ghosts. At the outset it is suggested that Marley, Scrooge's dead partner, is his double.

The firm is known as "Scrooge and Marley," and Scrooge never "[paints] out Old Marley's name." Sometimes customers "[call] Scrooge Scrooge, and sometimes Marley, but he [answers] to both names" (8). Scrooge lives "in chambers" which once belonged to Marley (14), and the two are explicitly said to be "two kindred spirits" (11). The doubling of the two men points to the significance of what follows, which would seem to pertain to the realm of the uncanny rather than that of the supernatural, the uncanny, in Tzvetan Todorov's terms, being distinguished from the supernatural by being susceptible of a natural explanation (25, 33).

It is the visit of Scrooge's nephew on Christmas Eve, which is also the anniversary of Marley's death, that precipitates Scrooge's uncanny experience. As noted earlier in another context, the nephew associates Christmas with thoughts of death, and this remark, together with the fact of the anniversary, may be taken to weigh on Scrooge. Old Marley may be "as dead as a door-nail" (7), but when Scrooge reaches home that evening, he sees "in the knocker . . . —not a knocker, but Marley's face." The face has "a dismal light about it, like a bad lobster in a dark cellar." (In passing, it may be noted how much more vivid Dickens's writing is in the *Carol* than in the other tales.) As Scrooge stares at the face, it is "a knocker again" (15). What Scrooge experiences is clearly an hallucination.

Once inside, Scrooge checks his rooms to make sure everything is all right, and then proceeds to "[lock] himself in; [double-locking] himself in, which [is] not his custom" (16). The symbolism is neat, evoking Scrooge's fear—and his attempt to protect himself by repressing it. The fear of course bursts out in the form of Marley's Ghost. Though the Ghost has ghostly appurtenances and the ghostly function of framing and announcing the visits of the three Christmas Ghosts, it figures as much as a projected double of Scrooge as a ghost, concretizing what is potential in him. Marley's chain of cash-boxes and ledgers and so on images the way he, like Scrooge, has been bound to the money-mills; and his tale particularizes the guilts of a mean counting-house life. Scrooge is horrified by Marley's Ghost, but also begins "to apply" his story to himself (20). The encounter forcefully demonstrates that the apparently immovable Scrooge is actually deeply fearful about the consequences of his way of life; and though he has hitherto succeeded in repressing his fear, once it breaks into consciousness, he is ready for what follows.

I should like to conclude by briefly considering a feature that, unlike those previously discussed, is not a mechanism. The Christmas Books, like the third of the ghosts Scrooge encounters, also show us "shadows of the things that have not happened, but will happen . . . '' (58). That is to say that the Christmas Books have their reverberations in other works of Dickens, and I should like to refer to a few of these.

One of the salient characteristics of the unredeemed Scrooge is his coldness:

> The cold within him froze his old features, nipped his pointed nose, shrivelled his cheek, stiffened his gait; made his eyes red, his thin lips blue; and spoke out shrewdly in his grating voice. A frosty rime was on his head, and on his eyebrows, and his wiry chin. He carried his own low temperature always about with him; he iced his office in the dog-days, and didn't thaw it one degree at Christmas. (8)

Coldness is one of the images by which Dombey, one of Dickens's earliest large characters, is evoked in *Dombey and Son,* a novel which followed shortly after the *Carol*:

> [Mr Dombey's] cold and distant nature had neither sought [a friend], nor found one. And now when that nature concentrated its whole force so strongly on a partial scheme of parental interest and ambition, it seemed as if its icy current . . . had thawed for but an instant to admit its burden, and then frozen with it into one unyielding block. (47)

Thereafter are references throughout to Dombey's coldness. At Paul's christening he assists in "making it so cold, that the young curate [smokes] at the mouth" as he reads (56); unmoved by the "cold collation" that chills his guests after the christening, he "might have been hung up for sale at a Russian fair as a specimen of a frozen gentleman" (57); he has a "frosty heart" (91); he is the "icy patron" of Mr. Carker (379); his characteristics reply to Mrs. Skewton, who inquires how he found "that delightfullest of cities, Paris," is: "It was cold" (500); and ice is said to be an "unnecessary article in Mr Dombey's banquets" (514–15).

Want and Ignorance, the children in the *Carol,* are memorably projected in the portrayal of Jo in *Bleak House,* though, unlike them, Jo is not devilish:

> Jo lives—that is to say, Jo has not yet died—in a ruinous place, known to the like of him by the name of Tom-all-Alone's. It is a black, dilapidated street, avoided by all decent people. . . . Whether [the property's] traditional title is a comprehensive name for a retreat cut off from honest company . . . perhaps nobody knows. Certainly, Jo don't know.
> "For *I* don't," says Jo, *"I* don't know nothink." (219–20)
> Homely filth begrimes him, homely parasites devour him, homely sores are in him, homely rags are on him: native ignorance, the growth of English soil and climate, sinks his immortal nature lower than the beasts that perish. (641)

The unnamed child in *The Haunted Man* is surely one of the anonymous children in a scene in *Little Dorrit:* in Covent Garden Little Dorrit sees "miserable children in rags" who are "like young rats, [slinking] and [hiding], [feeding] on offal, [huddling] together for warmth, and . . . hunted about." Then there follows this parenthetic apostrophe: "(look to the rats, young and old, all ye Barnacles, for before God they are eating away our foundations, and will bring the roofs on our heads" (166).

Finally, to end on a lighter note, Mr. Filer, with his exact calculation of the waste of tripe, is consanguineous to Mr. Gradgrind of *Hard Times*:

> Thomas Gradgrind, Sir. A man of realities. A man of facts and calculations. A man who proceeds upon the principle that two and two are four, and nothing over, and who is not to be talked into allowing for anything over. Thomas Gradgrind, Sir—peremptorily Thomas—Thomas Gradgrind. With a rule and a pair of scales, and the multiplication table always in his pocket, Sir, ready to weigh and measure any parcel of human nature, and tell you exactly what it comes to. It is a mere question of figures, a case of simple arithmetic.   (3)

These few passages point to the mystery of creative generation, a phenomenon that is as apparent in the work of other novelists as in that of Dickens. Virginia Woolf, for instance, in an early, immature novel, *Night and Day,* makes use of an elaborate lighthouse simile that encapsulates a major dimension of the lighthouse symbol that is central to a later, famous work. Similarly, D. H. Lawrence, in a minor novel, *The Lost Girl,* describes the tattoo of an eagle and a serpent on the shoulders and loins of a character in terms that anticipate his use of the plumed serpent symbol in the novel of that name years later. Moving in a mysterious way its wonders to perform, the creative imagination casts shadows ahead of itself, as it were. The Christmas Books, for all their deficiencies, may in a number of respects also be seen as leading to more significant work and so as an integral and formative part of Dickens's larger creative enterprise.

NOTES

1. Thackeray reprinted the review as part of the preface to the second edition of *The Kickleburys on the Rhine: The Christmas Books of Mr M. A. Titmarsh* (London, Smith, Elder, 1869).
2. References to the Christmas Books and to other texts of Dickens are to *The New Oxford Illustrated Dickens* (London: Oxford UP, 1948–58).

WORKS CITED

Collins, Philip, ed. *Dickens: The Critical Heritage.* London: Routledge and Kegan Paul, 1971.

Gilbert, Elliot. "The Ceremony of Innocence: Charles Dickens's *A Christmas Carol.*" *PMLA* 90 (Jan. 1975).

Johnson, Edgar. *Charles Dickens: His Tragedies and Triumph.* London: Gollancz, 1953.

Ruskin, John. *Sesame and Lillies.* New York: Chelsea House, 1983.

Todorov, Tsvetan. *The Fantastic: A Structural Approach to a Literary Genre.* Trans. Richard Howard. Cleveland: P of Case Western Reserve U.

Welsh, Alexander. *The City of Dickens.* Oxford: Clarendon, 1971.

Wilson, Edmund. "Dickens: The Two Scrooges," in *Eight Essays.* Garden City: Doubleday, 1954. (rpt. From *The Wound and the Bow.*)

"A Whimsical Kind of Masque": The Christmas Books and Victorian Spectacle

Robert Tracy

When Dickens collected his Christmas Books together in one volume, in September 1852, he wrote a brief preface explaining both his method and his intention in writing them. "My purpose," he tells us, "was, in a whimsical kind of masque which the good humour of the season justified, to awaken some loving and forbearing thoughts," in effect, to arouse in his readers a sense of community and therefore a disposition to charity. The necessary brevity of a Christmas book—at most, no longer than two numbers of a Dickens novel—forced him to avoid "great elaboration of detail in the working out of character within such limits, believing that it could not succeed." And finally, that necessary brevity—"The narrow space within which it was necessary to confine these Christmas Stories when they were originally published, rendered their construction a matter of some difficulty, and almost necessitated what is peculiar in their machinery" (*Christmas Books* 1: xxix).[1]

By describing his Christmas genre as "A whimsical kind of masque," Dickens clearly indicates his literary model for the kind of story, partly realistic, partly allegorical, that he was attempting to write—an indication reinforced by his reference to "machinery." The masque is a literary form that had long been out of fashion by Dickens's time, but he was ready to revive it in a new way. The masque was traditionally a theatrical performance combining text, elaborate costumes, music, dance, and spectacular stage effects, some of them dependent on rapid changes of scene. Masques derived in part from medieval morality plays, in part from the elaborate parades and processions of Renaissance courts on such great state occasions as royal progresses or royal weddings, and by Shakespeare's time had evolved into formal indoor performances staged at the Stuart court of James I. In royal

Dickens Studies Annual, Volume 27, Copyright © 1998 by AMS Press, Inc. All rights reserved.

processions and at the court, allegorical figures representing virtues, vices, abstract concepts such as sovereignty or virginity, or perhaps England or Scotland, appeared. At court masques these figures appeared on stage, dressed in extravagant costumes and framed in elaborate settings. Great lords and ladies, and even Anne of Denmark, James I's queen, performed in masques, some of them devised so that the queen herself was at once the subject of the allegory—as, say, the embodiment of womanly virtue—and the performer of that role. Stuart masques were always ultimately political allegories, celebrating the new dynasty, even though they seemed concerned primarily with abstract virtues. They were intended to make visible the excellence and power of the sovereign, who could banish vice or transform it into virtue, and so emphasized the good fortune of the state which enjoyed the rule of so excellent a sovereign (Riggs 119–21, 147–8, 150).

The masque's overt purpose was to celebrate, encourage, or inculcate virtue. Personified Virtues rebuked or routed personified Vices, then danced to celebrate their triumph. The best known masques, those by Ben Jonson, are usually if not invariably on this theme and take this form.

Only one masque, and that a severely truncated one, can be considered at all familiar to modern audiences: that "vanity of mine art" (*Tempest* 4.1.41) which Prospero stages for Ferdinand and Miranda after they have become betrothed, and Prospero has made Ferdinand solemnly promise not to sleep with Miranda until the wedding service has been performed. "The strongest oaths are straw/To th' fire i' the blood" (4.1.52–53), Prospero cynically remarks, and so he stages a masque featuring Iris, the messenger of the gods, Ceres, goddess of fruitfulness, Juno, goddess of chaste marriages—who appears only after she has been assured of the absence of Venus, goddess of lust and extra-marital experiment. The masque allegorically restates Prospero's demand that Ferdinand keep his hands off Miranda until their wedding night, and celebrates the couple's agreement to restrain themselves; a chorus of Nymphs and Reapers dance to suggest the rewards of sexual restraint. Prospero's masque, however, is very brief. He breaks it off abruptly to tend to other matters, especially Caliban's conspiracy. It is as if Shakespeare noted in passing the new vogue for the masque, as created by Jonson, showed that he too could create a masque if he chose to do so, then dismissed the form to return to the more interesting business of his own more psychologically developed plot and characters.

The important thing about the masque, as Dickens adapted the term, is that it is a literary form that both demonstrates and inculcates virtue; and that the demonstration of virtue is usually the method of inculcation. The Stuart courtier, watching a masque of sovereignty, sees the power and virtue of his master allegorically demonstrated, and is presumably strengthened in his loyalty. Ferdinand and Miranda glimpse the rewards of a chaste marriage, and are strengthened in their commitment to pre-marital restraint. Ebenezer Scrooge watches a triple masque about Christmas and charity, staged for him by the three Spirits. Before his eyes the Cratchits, and nephew Fred with his friends, enact that family unity which is associated with Christmas, while glimpses of miners and lighthouse keepers celebrating Christmas with mutual good cheer show him the feast's universal appeal as an occasion when people behave most generously towards one another. What Scrooge sees reforms him. He changes from an opponent of Christmas to a keeper of Christmas, or, more accurately, from a selfish man to a man of charity—the lesson Dickens wished to teach. It is clear that the story describes the awakening—or re-awakening—of social morality and fellow-feeling in Scrooge. He changes from being "secret, and self-contained, and solitary as an oyster" (46) to wishing " 'A merry Christmas to everybody! A happy New Year to all the world!' " (127). After his encounters with the Spirits he pats children on the head, questions beggars (131), joins his nephew Fred for Christmas dinner, and makes himself into a kind of fairy godfather to the Cratchit family. Re-read at Christmas, experienced as a radio or TV broadcast, even as an animated cartoon, the story can still create a temporary charitable euphoria, of the sort Robert Louis Stevenson described: "But oh, dear God [the Christmas books] are *good*—and I feel so good after them—I shall do good and lose no time—I want to go out and comfort someone—I *shall* give money. Oh, what a jolly thing it is for a man to have written books like these and just filled people's hearts with pity" (vii). According to Jane Carlyle, even the dyspeptic Carlyle, after reading *A Christmas Carol,* was "seized with a perfect *convulsion* of hospitality, and has actually insisted on *improvising two* dinner-parties with only a day between" (*Christmas Books* I:35).

Apart from their allegorical characters, their celebration of virtue, and their moral purpose, masques were known for their elaborate costumes and scenery, and for their ingenious devices or "machinery," which permitted spectacular stage effects. Ben Jonson's court masques were staged by the great architect Inigo Jones, who played a major role in their success, though Jonson, jealous for the written word, dismissed his contributions as mere "painting and carpentry" (Jonson, "Expostulation"). Jones delighted in the cloud machine, a kind of basket in which a god could be lowered from the heavens to endorse or affect the action. He gave English theater the proscenium arch, which distanced the audience from the stage action—Shakespeare's audience had surrounded the stage platform—and by separating them from the stage, let them spy on stage action from a distance, as invisible Scrooge spies on the Cratchits' Christmas dinner. Jones also introduced movable scenery, which made it possible to change the stage setting rapidly, and perspective scenery, which helped the audience to pretend to believe that a play's characters were not really in a theater, but rather in whatever setting they claimed to be: in a forest, a palace, a prison, aboard ship. Jonson objected to Jones's spectacular effects as usurping the roles of text and actors (Jonson, "Expostulation"; Rosenfeld 24). Jones can in fact be seen as a forerunner of Victorian staging methods, which gave spectacle precedence over everything else, even the texts of Shakespeare.

Dickens borrowed the term "machinery" from Fielding, who uses it in *Tom Jones* to describe methods of organizing a plot. Fielding, in turn, borrowed it from seventeenth-century critics, who also used the term to discuss plot devices—frequently the devices of Homer and the Greek tragic playwrights, who brought a god or goddess into human action to assist or destroy a character, a device we still call *deus ex machina*, the god from the machine, in Graeco-Roman theater an earlier version of the cloud machine. In the seventeenth: and eighteenth-century theater, machinery meant whatever technical devices were used for supernatural intrusions—for example, the ghost trap with a kind of elevator under it, by which King Hamlet's ghost, or Banquo's, could suddenly appear or disappear. It also came to denote any technical device which permitted an instantaneous change of scene without lowering the curtain.

Dickens's machinery allows the Spirits to transform reality in an instant, and even fly Scrooge out over the sea, so that he may witness Christmas revels: Bob Cratchit's house, Fred's house, the lighthouse, the graveyard. By supplying the Spirits with this ability to transport Scrooge rapidly from scene to scene, Dickens dramatizes the ease with which a novelist can instantaneously transfer characters and reader from one locale to another.

The nineteenth century was the great age of stage machinery, and at the same time an inglorious period in the annals of English drama. These two facts are not unrelated. A succession of great poets—Wordsworth, Coleridge, Shelley, Byron, Tennyson, Browning—all wrote plays which failed and have never been successfully revived. The great novelists of the period also failed as dramatists, though Dickens's works succeeded on the stage when adapted by theater hacks. The century shows no list of great or even memorable dramatists between Richard Sheridan, who ceased to write for the stage around 1780, and the advent of Shaw and Wilde in the eighteen-nineties. Plays were of course written and performed, often to great applause, in the intervening years, but only the specialist will recognize such playwrights as Tom Taylor, Leopold Lewis, F. C. Burnand, Tom Robertson, Dion Boucicault, or, apart from his novels, Charles Reade.

The century's technical developments in stage machinery, which involved heroic efforts to produce stage settings that were both realistic and, where relevant, historically and geographically accurate, seem to be closely related to the era's failure of dramatic achievement. In Dickens's lifetime, as theater became more and more capable of spectacular effects, spectacle became much more important than text or plot, and sometimes overwhelmed the actor. Victorian playbills often fail to mention the author of a play, but almost invariably they do list those responsible for the special effects, as well as the actors. The more difficult and complex those special effects were, the more spectacular the stage setting, the more exotic the locale depicted, then the more strenuously was the stage machinery advertised, usually with many exclamation points. When Mr. Crummles hires Nicholas Nickleby, he hires him both as actor and as a translator/adapter of French plays (whose authors did not have to be paid, another reason for the invisibility of the playwright in nineteenth-century London). Crummles impresses upon Nicholas the need to incorporate into the play such feeble devices for realistic action as the Crummles Company can muster: a washtub and a workable pump.

The great metropolitan theaters could offer a dazzling sequence of spectacles and special effects. A little before Dickens's time, Astley's Amphitheatre developed two dramatic forms, the equine drama and the aquatic drama. Equine drama featured real horses and usually presented at least one cavalry charge. Its most popular play was *Mazeppa,* adapted from Byron's poem, with Cossacks and a beautiful heroine riding bareback. As late as the eighteen-seventies, Ada Rehan was famous for her performances in *Mazeppa.* Out of the same tradition came Buffalo Bill's Wild West Show, which featured mounted Indians attacking a wagon train, and the successful intervention of the United States cavalry—as exciting to nineteenth-century audiences as the Apache attack on the stagecoach in John Ford's famous film. The aquatic drama could be even more spectacular. Astley's Amphitheatre could be flooded for re-enactments of Trafalgar or other naval battles. During the Napoleonic Wars, these were sometimes presented within a few weeks of the battles themselves.

The invention of the moving picture provided even greater opportunities for the realistic effects at which the nineteenth-century theater aimed. The decline of the spectacular theater at the beginning of the twentieth century is directly related to the greater opportunities for spectacle that film offered. Once the performance could take place out of doors, with real trees, clouds, streams, horses, ships, and locomotives, and then be presented to an audience seated in a theater, the stage ceased to compete in terms of spectacle. Even before the invention of the moving picture, dramatists had begun to offer social and psychological analysis for a new anti-melodramatic theater. Here Tom Robertson was a pioneer, with such plays as *Ours* (1866) and *Caste* (1867), domestic dramas produced in a comparatively realistic manner by the Bancrofts (Rowell 79–82). Ibsen, Chekhov, and Shaw would make the theater of spectacle obsolete.

Victorian theatrical spectacle was anti-literary in that it replaced language with special effects. It dazzled its audiences by bringing on stage authentic-looking mountain passes, seascapes, Pompeii during the eruption of Vesuvius.

Charles Kean was famous for his elaborate "archaeological" settings. When he staged *A Midsummer's Night's Dream* in 1856, an elaborate program told the audience what they were seeing. Theseus is Duke of Athens, a figure out of Greek mythology with a medieval crusader title, ruling a city containing some very English "rude mechanicals," Bully Bottom and his pals. Kean raised his curtain to reveal the Athens his audience would expect to see, Athens at the time of Pericles, with the Acropolis in the background, on it the Parthenon, Erechtheum, and other famous structures from the fifth century B.C. (Nagler 483–85). Elaborate sets like this were slow and difficult to shift, requiring battalions of stage hands. As a result, Shakespeare's texts were drastically cut to allow time for scene shifting. In Shakespeare's wonderfully flexible theater, the setting could change immediately, as when in *Antony and Cleopatra* a brief scene in Rome is followed by one in the mountains of Turkey, and that by another on a galley off the coast of Sicily—all done with words. Victorian directors were often the prisoners of the sets their audiences expected. *Hamlet* was played without Fortinbras until William Poel experimented with a bare Elizabethan stage in 1894 (Speaight 51–52, 57), and Shaw records his astonishment that the part was cast in Forbes-Robertson's 1897 production (Shaw 2:316). The revered Sir Henry Irving usually omitted Act V of *The Merchant of Venice,* partly because he wanted to end with his own moving performance of a victimized Shylock in the trial scene (Auerbach 226), but perhaps also because it would take too long to bring back on stage Portia's estate at Belmont, where the love stories find their resolution.

This commitment to spectacular scenery rather than text partly explains why the great nineteenth-century poets and novelists failed as playwrights. Their model was Shakespeare, and they were trying to write five-act Shakespearean dramas with multiple settings to be performed in a very different kind of theater. In a theater incapable of Shakespearean flexibility, their plays were not performed, or were drastically cut to make time for cumbersome changes of scenery. Tennyson's *Queen Mary* and *Becket* succeeded to some extent on the stage only because Irving subjected them to drastic pruning (Buckley 200, 207; Stoker 131, 144, 146-147, 148, 150).

The Victorian theater struggled with the tension between the playwright's wish to shift the action freely from place to place, with the freedom that Shakespeare, or, for that matter, the contemporary novelist enjoyed, and the audience's expectation that each setting would be realistically created on stage. The resulting compromise was usually a victory for the stage designer and his eagerness to provide spectacle. Here, for example, is the playbill for *No Thoroughfare,* the Christmas story which Dickens and Wilkie Collins wrote together for *All the Year Round* in 1867, and together dramatized for Dickens's friend Charles Fechter, the great French actor, who performed it successfully at Christmas 1867. The playbill, preserved in the Dickens House, London, begins by proclaiming

NEW SCENERY AND EFFECTS

APPOINTMENTS   MACHINERY

COSTUMES   GAS ARRANGEMENTS

Only after these devices have been listed does the playbill get to the play, and it does so in order to entice the playgoer with a long list of settings for the action, each one guaranteed to be shown on stage as realistically as possible. They range from familiar London settings, or versions of same, where the audience would be ready to spot inaccuracies, to the less familiar Swiss interiors and exteriors, and finally to exotic Alpine scenes:

Overture [Dickens's term]

London

October 1847

Scene: Exterior of the Hospital for Foundling Children

Scene: Interior of Same

Twelve Years Elapse

Act I

Scene: The Court Yard at Wilding and Sons, Wine Merchants

Scene: Cripple Corner, near Break-Neck Stairs

Act II

Scene: Obenreizer's Lodgings, Soho Square

Scene: A Room in Wilding's House

Scene: The Cellars at Cripple Corner

Act III

Scene: The Counting House at Cripple Corner

Scene: A Room at Cripple Corner

Scene: Obenreizer's Drawing-Room

Act IV

Scene: An Inn Room in Switzerland

Scene: Exterior of the Swiss Inn

Scene: The Pass in the Mountain

Act V

Scene: The Monastery of St. Bernard

The plot involves Obenreizer's attempts to kill Vendale, on one occasion by pushing him into an Alpine chasm, Vendale's miraculous escapes, and Obenreizer's own death in an avalanche—"I am racking my brains for a good death to that respectable gentleman," Dickens told Collins in October 1867 (D. to Collins, 9 October 1867). Dickens himself had pointed out to Collins the theatrical possibilities in their story, and divided it into an overture and five acts for publication in *All the Year Round*. He also entered enthusiastically into details of the machinery and special effects, insisting that "a drugging and attempted robbery in a Swiss inn be done with the sound of a waterfall in the background," adding, "it would enhance enormously 'the mystery and gloom' " (Johnson 2:1099). Dickens also advised when the play was produced in Paris as *L'Abime*.

Posters for the 1844 production of *The Chimes* as a Christmas pantomime suggest equally serious demands on the scenic painters' skills, though they were not asked to create the Alps on stage. *The Chimes* was presented with Dickens's "Especial Permission," and his name received top billing. The sets copied the illustrations in the printed book, and again it is the scene painters and the illustrators who take precedence over the writers who adapted the text for the stage:

> The scenery painted by Messrs. T. PITT and JOHNSTONE, FROM THE ORIGINAL Sketches of DANIEL MACLISE, R. A. CLARKSON STANFIELD, R. A. JOHN LEECH and RICHARD DOYLE. The Overture and music by J. H. TULLY. The Story Dramatised by MARK LEMON & GILBERT A. À BECKETT.

After a prologue by "a Spirit of the Chimes," Act 1, or "First Quarter," was simple enough, Trotty Veck's station at the foot of THE TOWER OF THE CHIMES. "Second Quarter" was more ambitious: Scene 1, Entrance Hall of Sir JOSEPH BOWLEY, Bart.; Scene 2, LIBRARY of Sir JOSEPH BOWLEY, Bart.; Scene 3, THE STREET; Scene 4, TROTTY'S ROOMS OVER THE STABLE. "Third Quarter" began with "Trotty's interview" in THE BELL TOWER OF THE CHIMES. THE GOBLIN SIGHT, followed by BOWLEY HALL (Scene 2) and THE GARRET OF THE SEMPSTRESS. In "Fourth Quarter" we have MRS. CHICKENSTALKER'S SHOP & PARLOR, followed by MEG'S HOME (Scene 2), THE RIVER (Scene 3), and, as "Scene the Last," THE NEW YEAR (Original playbill, Guildhall Museum, Rochester). Counting the prologue, this makes thirteen scene changes, with each scene attempting accuracy and most of them also copying the style of whichever illustrator had drawn that scene for the book. Dickens's adapters, and their scenic colleagues, were on the whole faithful to the book, but also eager to show their skill by the variety of settings they could provide.

The format of the Christmas Books specifically recalled the theatrical. Most of Dickens's novels were published with illustrations, usually two to a number. The Christmas Books are much more lavishly illustrated, so much so that the text sometimes seems subordinate to the illustrations—as nineteenth-century dramatic texts were subordinate to visual effects. In fact, some of Dickens's Christmas Books illustrators also designed stage settings for the London theaters. Dickens was willing to risk this subordination of text to picture partly to emphasize *seeing* as a moral theme—Scrooge, Trotty Veck, John Peerybingle must *see*—and partly to draw on the spectacular visual devices of the contemporary stage.

The invariable performances of each new Christmas Book or Christmas Story as a Christmas pantomime, starting with *A Christmas Carol,* recognized the close affinity between Dickens's imagination, especially when engaged with the often supernatural elements of the Christmas writings, and the conventions of the Victorian theater. As a novelist, Dickens had Shakespearean flexibility. He could change his scene instantly. In the Christmas Books and Stories, he often gives to Spirits or other supernatural agents the power to transport a character—Scrooge, for example—from one place to another instantly, or to transport a character into an imaginary future, as the Goblins of the Bells transport Trotty Veck. Something very similar occurs in Dickens's first Christmas story, that of the Sexton taken off by the Goblins, which Mr. Wardle tells in *Pickwick Papers.*

There is a resemblance between Scrooge's adventures and the conventions of the Christmas pantomime, which inherited, in adulterated form, some of the conventions of the court masque. Edwin Eigner has suggested that Scrooge and Bob Cratchit resemble traditional pantomime characters. Scrooge is Pantaloon, Cratchit is Clown (Eigner 1993, 182). The use of spectacle is another resemblance. Pantomimes were mostly spectacle, and particularly relied on the so-called transformation scene—also used in the regular theater—an instantaneous change of locale. One setting was replaced by another without lowering the curtain: a London street could suddenly become a forest glade, or Fairyland, or Robinson Crusoe's island. Cinderella's kitchen could become the Prince's ballroom. These mechanical transformations were usually presented as performed by magic: the Fairy Godmother waved her wand to transform both Cinderella and her setting, the Genie turned a hovel into a palace. Such literal transformations echoed the action of many pantomimes, the transformation of the principal character—Aladdin, Ali Baba—from rags to riches. For Dickens, I suggest, the pantomime's transformation scene had a moral rather than a socio-economic analog, the moral transformation of the principal character. In this sense, *A Christmas Carol* and some of its Christmas Book successors are extended transformation scenes. They reproduce in prose the transformation techniques of contemporary stagecraft. Their rapid and sometimes magical changes of scene, and the sudden dissolution of walls or other barriers to reveal what is passing within, imply that Scrooge's spirits have access to the most sophisticated machinery of the contemporary theater, and employ it to work a moral transformation, to make Scrooge a better man. If the Victorian theater often indulged itself with spectacle for spectacle's sake, Dickens was able to adapt one of its most spectacular effects, the instant change of scene, to assist him in effecting

Scrooge's change of heart in a single night. The Spirits waft Scrooge through time past, present, and future to show him himself as a schoolboy or as apprentice; to admit him to the Cratchit's Christmas dinner and the after-dinner games at nephew Fred's; and to show him his own deathbed and a world where he is not. Even more spectacularly, they take him on an aerial journey across Britain, presenting him with brief glimpses of lighthouse-keepers, miners, and sailors keeping Christmas as best they can. These are scenes very much in the style of nineteenth-century theater. After passing over crowded London streets, Scrooge finds himself,

> without a word of warning from the Ghost . . . upon a bleak and desert moor, where monstrous masses of rude stone were cast about, as though it were the burial-place of giants, . . . Down in the west the setting sun had left a streak of fiery red, which glared upon the desolation for an instant, like a sullen eye . . .
> (100).

After the Ghost has brought him "through the wall of mud and stone" to see four generations of a miner's family celebrating Christmas together, Scrooge is airborne again, this time to be carried out over the sea, to

> a dismal reef of sunken rocks, some league or so from shore, on which the waters chafed and dashed, the wild year through, [where] stood a solitary lighthouse. Great heaps of sea-weed clung to its base, and storm-birds . . . rose and fell about it, like the waves they skimmed   (101).

One can imagine how Clarkson Stanfield, who designed icebergs and an Arctic cavern for *The Frozen Deep,* or, for that matter, any contemporary scene painter, would have enjoyed meeting these challenges to his skill.

We know that when Dickens read *A Christmas Carol* in public, he omitted these scenes, and gradually cut his text until eventually nothing was left of Scrooge's early life but the Fezziwigs' ball. But when we read *A Christmas Carol* we are given, like Scrooge himself, the privilege of the pantomime spectator, to pass rapidly from one scene to another. Scrooge's pantomime, based partly upon his own life, begins as in a theater, when "the curtains of his bed were drawn aside" (67) and his familiar bedroom is transformed, first into the road to his old school, where he sees his schoolfellows heading home for Christmas. A second transformation reveals the school, and a third shows Scrooge, a lonely child, reading in a deserted classroom. Yet another dissolve shows

> a man, in foreign garments: wonderfully real and distinct to look at: . . . outside the window, with an axe stuck in his belt, and leading an ass laden with wood by the bridle.
> "Why, it's Ali Baba!" Scrooge exclaimed in ecstasy. "It's dear old honest Ali Baba! . . . One Christmas time, when yonder solitary child was left here all

alone, he *did* come . . . just like that, . . . And Valentine . . . and his wild brother, Orson; there they go! . . . And the Sultan's Groom turned upside-down by the Genii; there he is upon his head! Serve him right. I'm glad. What business had *he* to be married to the Princess!''   (72)

Scrooge recognizes Robinson Crusoe's parrot—" 'Green body and yellow tail, with a thing like a lettuce growing out of the top of his head; there he is!' '' He pictures fictional events so vividly that he even tries to intervene to save Friday from the cannibals: " 'There goes Friday, running for his life to the little creek. Halloa! Hoop! Halloo!' '' Scrooge enters as imaginatively into his reading as did the young Dickens, who knew every detail of Crusoe's island and the exact location of every book in Don Quixote's study (Dickens, *Selected Short Fiction* 219–20), or the young David Copperfield, who believed that Smollett's fictional characters had visited his native village (*David Copperfield* 106). It is worth recalling that Ali Baba and Robinson Crusoe were also favorite characters in Christmas pantomimes (Nicoll 5:639; 641; 742–44, 749–50).

Theater, like fiction, depends, as Coleridge long ago reminded us, upon the spectator's/reader's willingness to suspend disbelief, to pretend that the events enacted on stage or narrated in a fiction are real and true. Scrooge is capable of salvation because he is the ideal theatre-goer, and especially the ideal reader of Dickens. He is an absorbed spectator at the drama of his own life, which the Spirits stage for him; he is an absorbed reader of the text in which he is contained, right up until that moment when he reads his own name on the gravestone which ends his story, and asks the Third Spirit to " 'tell me I may sponge away the writing on this stone!' '' (126), that is, begs to be allowed to rewrite his story and provide it with a different ending. Having seen/read the ending of Tiny Tim's life, he rewrites that too, becoming ''a second father . . . to Tiny Tim, who did NOT die'' (133)—a line Dickens's audiences sometimes cheered (Dickens, *Sikes and Nancy* 31). When we remember that Dickens forced himself NOT to spare Little Nell, despite the pleadings of his readers, we recognize how Dickens gives to Scrooge the author's supreme power, that of deciding fates.

Dickens begins Scrooge's adventures, then, with a reminder of his lonely childhood Christmases, and with a reminder of how imagination fed on fiction to solace that loneliness. In doing so, he not only shares with Scrooge his own childhood favorites—as he would do with David Copperfield. He also suggests at once the saving powers of fiction as text and as performance, and hints at the method *A Christmas Carol* is to employ. Scrooge is to be shown fictions produced by the Spirits. He is to have his imaginative capacity reawakened, and is even to try and participate in those fictions to alter them, changing his own and Tiny Tim's already written fates, just as he tried to help

Friday escape from the cannibals. Scrooge's recalled ability to participate in the fictions he used to read helps him to react to the Spirit-engendered fiction, the drama about himself he is made to watch. The landscape of his childhood, shown him by Christmas Past, evokes a tear (70), he sobs to see his schoolfellows leaving for their Christmas holiday (71), and he moves from participation in Friday's pursuit "with a rapidity of transition very foreign to his usual character" to say "in pity for his former self, 'Poor boy!' and cried again" (73).

A Christmas Carol is a fiction about read or performed fiction, and fiction's moral effects. The Spirits are personifications of Dickens's own fiction-making powers—and of his delight in theatrical effects. "In the ghostly unrest of going to begin a new book my time is like one of the Spirits in Macbeth, and 'will not be commanded'—even by me" (Nonesuch *Letters* 2:640) he told Maria Winter in 1855, as he began work on *Little Dorrit.* He saw fiction as originating or accompanied by "ghostly unrest," and the reference to Macbeth's Spirits—who write Macbeth's script for him to follow, and, like Christmas Yet to Come, show him the ultimate results of his behavior—suggests Dickens's instinctive association of Spirits and the act of fiction. When the first Spirit draws the curtain of Scrooge's bed, Dickens tells the reader that Scrooge "found himself face to face with the unearthly visitor who drew them: as close to it *as I am now to you, and I am standing in spirit at your elbow*" (68; italics mine).

The Spirits of *A Christmas Carol* are in effect projections of the author, theatrical illusionists, literary artists, presenting a series of dramatic vignettes in the manner of Charles Dickens, pitiful or joyous vignettes which will work upon Scrooge, arousing his pity and so his potential for charity, or showing the pleasures of social revelry to arouse his suppressed instinct for engaging himself with other people—Dickens's basic social and moral aims as a writer. He hoped that his fictions would reform his readers by showing them misery and abuses to provoke them into charity. In *A Christmas Carol* he brings about Scrooge's reform, and shows us that that reform is brought about by exposure to scenes similar to those presented in Dickens's own novels.

The scenes presented by Christmas Past depict Scrooge's dreary solitary boyhood and happy young manhood. Scrooge is first the neglected Oliver Twist, or Smike at Dotheboys Hall—or Dickens at Warren's Blacking (Langton 174–78). He is rescued unexpectedly, as Oliver is rescued by Mr. Brownlow, or Smike by Nicholas Nickleby. His father has undergone an abrupt change of heart, foreshadowing the change Scrooge himself is to undergo. Fan has been sent to restore him to family and Christmas cheer. " 'Father is so much kinder than he used to be, that home's like Heaven!' " Fan tells him. " 'I have come to bring you home. . . . And you're to be a man! . . . and are never to come back here; but first, we're to be together all the Christmas long, and have the merriest time in all the world' " (73–74).

The Fezziwigs' ball is a scene of cheerful abundance, like Mr. Wardle's Christmas revels at Dingley Dell. Scrooge seems to have reached a Dickensian Good Place. But then he alters the story by turning miser and losing Belle, who releases him from their engagement as an act of charity, " 'With a full heart, for the love of him you once were' " (80).

Christmas Present introduces a new story, from which Scrooge is essentially absent, by depicting Christmas with the Cratchits, at nephew Fred's, and among hard-living miners and sailors. The cheery closeness of the Cratchits is darkened by the pathos of Tiny Tim—who even sings "a song, about a lost child travelling in the snow" (Wordsworth's "Lucy Gray"?) in "a plaintive little voice" (99). In writing *The Old Curiosity Shop,* Dickens had learned how powerful the foreshadowing of a child's death could be, with its mixture of suspense and doom. Like the anxious readers of *The Old Curiosity Shop,* Scrooge senses Tiny Tim's impending death, hopes it will not happen, and urges the Spirit to " 'say he will be spared' " (97), to alter the story's predictable ending, as readers' letters urged Dickens to spare Little Nell.

With his eagerness to believe that what he reads/sees is real, Scrooge is every novelist's ideal reader, every dramatist's ideal audience. Reading *Robinson Crusoe* he threw himself into the action. Shown the Fezziwigs' ball, "His heart and soul were in the scene" (78). At nephew Fred's, though only an invisible spectator, he tries to participate in the party games:

> they all played, and so did Scrooge; for wholly forgetting in the interest he had in what was going on, that his voice made no sound in their ears, he sometimes came out with his guess quite loud, and very often guessed right too. (105)

"Dead: to begin with" (45) like Marley, Scrooge is alive to end with. The Spirits, despite their chronological identities, have dissolved chronological time, " 'have done it all in one night. They can do anything they like' " (128). Scrooge has altered his own story and Tiny Tim's, changed the texts that spelled out their fates, even assumed the author's right to name his characters: Tim will presumably cease to be "Tiny."

In altering the text, Scrooge has altered himself. He is in effect converted by reading/watching the first four (of five) staves/scenes of *A Christmas Carol,* in which the Spirits/author employ Dickens's favorite techniques for scene-setting and dialogue, his love of the grotesque, his habit of contrasting comic exuberance with sentimental pathos, and so employ as well the devices of contemporary theatrical spectacle. Scrooge is the first reader or viewer of *A Christmas Carol* after Dickens himself, who told Charles Mackay, "I was very much affected by the little Book myself; in various ways, as I wrote it" (19 December 1843; Pilgrim *Letters* 3:610). Scrooge responds to his immersion in the Dickens world by yielding to its combination of sentiment, comedy, and pathos, to amend his life by rewriting his story, writing himself back into the story of future Christmases, from which Christmas Yet To Come had excised him. Tiny Tim does not die like Little Nell, Scrooge does not perish miserably like Fagin and Quilp. Instead he makes himself the hero of the story, if not self-authored, at least self-revised.

Dickens imagines Scrooge. Scrooge then imagines the Spirits. The Spirits imagine and dramatize an abbreviated but characteristic Dickens text, which draws on previous writings from *Sketches by Boz* to *The Old Curiosity Shop,* and even anticipates further work: Old Joe and his rag and bone shop (114–17) reappear as Krook's shop in *Bleak House,* and Nemo's lonely grave is Scrooge's. More importantly, by showing Scrooge his own miserable and isolated childhood, the Spirits move beyond the pitiful child-victims of *Oliver Twist, Nicholas Nickleby,* and *The Old Curiosity Shop.* Scrooge is the first Dickensian child-victim to grow up, and so participate in that retroactive experience of the past which is the basis especially of *David Copperfield* and *Great Expectations,* novels in which the narrator narrates himself, imagines himself as protagonist of the story he is telling, simultaneously creating a past or child self and showing how that past self still survives, to shape the maturer self who narrates the story. David and Pip write as adults remembering childhood, but we experience their childhoods as immediate and contemporary. Like the Spirits, they can abolish the logical/chronological categories of past and present. Then is always now. Their imaginative engagement with their earlier selves recreates those past selves, as the Spirits—whether ghostly visitants or Scrooge's dreaming, story-telling mind—recreate Scrooge's earlier selves. David's process of narrative recollection—presumably the writing of *David Copperfield,* which is also the writing of David Copperfield—heightens his adult happiness, with Agnes and their family, by re-enacting his childhood solitude and misery. Agnes evokes "the sorrowful, distant music" (*David Copperfield* 912) of his past; sure of her at last, "Long miles of road . . . opened out before my mind; and, toiling on, I saw a ragged way-worn boy, forsaken and neglected, who should come to call even the heart now beating against mine, his own" (*David Copperfield* 62:937). Scrooge's narrative recollections are reversed, but similar: the imagined revelries at the Fezziwigs', the Cratchits', and at Fred's contrast with and heighten his solitude. Pip's recollection is a confession, through which he comes to recognize his selfishness and false values and so reform himself by recollection, the process the Spirits organize into a narrative for Scrooge. Scrooge has in effect been helped to objectify and re-experience his life as a dramatized story in pictures, as a series of tableaux, as David and Pip objectify and re-experience their lives in written narrative. The processes are similar, as they were for Dickens, who told George Henry Lewes "that every word said by his characters was distinctly *heard* by him." "When, in the midst of this trouble and pain, I sit down to my book, some beneficent power shows it all to me, and tempts me to be interested," Dickens insisted; "and I don't invent it—really do not—*but see it,* and write it down" (Forster 2:339–40). Like David, Pip, and the Haunted Man, the hero of the last Christmas book, Scrooge learns the salutary power of sad memories, their power to reform and bring joy. He combines David's self-pity with Pip's self-scrutiny.

In the Christmas Books, Dickens brings forward that "beneficent power" which made him SEE his characters and their adventures. The Ghosts of Christmas Past, Present, and Future are manifestations of that power. So is Trotty Veck's grim vision of what will happen if Richard and Margaret listen to Cute's narrative of their probable future, and do not marry. Caleb, in *The Cricket on the Hearth,* has created a whole fictional world which the Blind Girl sees. In the same story, the Cricket becomes a Fairy, a change very much in the pantomime tradition, and puts on for John Peerybingle a show "as in a Glass or Picture" (2:91), featuring troops of fairies in a kind of ballet celebrating Dot's virtues. Caleb even anticipates Tchaikovsky by proposing to turn the disguised Edward into a nutcracker (*Christmas Books* 2:46).

In *A Christmas Carol* the Spirits put on a show which is partly based on Scrooge's memories. Dickens concludes the Christmas Books with another reminder that memory can be redemptive. The Ghost renders Redlaw, the protagonist of *The Haunted Man,* incapable of Scrooge's redemptive process by tempting him to relinquish memory and therefore the possibility of redemption—which Dickens defines as fellow-feeling, sympathy, on which philanthropy depends. *The Chimes* partly reverses the method of *A Christmas Carol* by omitting a salutary past to show instead an alternative if imaginary future. *The Haunted Man* partly reverses *A Christmas Carol* by initially abolishing the inevitable mixture of good and bad memories which creates a personality. Redlaw is saved only when he does gain access to the puppet show of memory, and he marks his salvation by reviving an even more remote past when he hosts a traditional Christmas feast in the College's long abandoned Great Hall.

I have suggested that the spectacular effects so cherished in the Victorian theater anticipated the even more spectacular effects attainable in films. Scrooge's visual encounters with his own childhood and youth resemble the Victorian transformation effect, itself an anticipation of the film director's device of the flashback. Most drama is linear. *Hamlet,* for example, does not show us episodes from the Prince's youth, or Old Hamlet's battle with the "sledded Polacks." Shakespeare uses the clumsy device of the dumb-show to depict Old Hamlet's murder. There are no flashbacks in Ibsen or Chekhov except verbal ones, when a character describes a memory. Eugene O'Neill's *Long Day's Journey into Night* is, in a sense, entirely a flashback, but in form it brings us through a day in the life of the Tyrone family linearly, from morning to night. The past is evoked within the present, as when Mary Tyrone, drugged with laudanum, enters carrying her wedding dress to talk of her convent days and her courtship. A specific change of scene, so that the stage setting suddenly becomes somewhere else, was a technique often employed in Victorian theater. A notable example is Sir Henry Irving's famous scene in *The Bells,* when Irving, playing Matthias, and the audience together see the Polish Jew he long ago robbed and murdered, driving in a sleigh through the snowy landscape where the crime took place (Booth 160–61; Hartnoll, illustration 203). But the flashback is a staple of film. In Oliver Stone's *Nixon* (1995), where the audience is expected to know how the story comes out, how Nixon will rise and fall, the use of the flashback is classic. In a nonvisual way the recent past can be heard, as Nixon, like Beckett's Krapp, sits listening to tape recordings of earlier conversations. But a more remote past can be *seen,* when Nixon—and the audience—see episodes from his childhood and youth, as did Scrooge and Dickens's readers. Nixon's childhood is not photographed in color, like the rest of the film, but in black and white, a device that persuades us that we are looking at—or into—the past. Both *A Christmas Carol* and *Nixon* make the protagonist at times a spectator of his own earlier life, a passive but absorbed witness of events that have shaped the present where he watches them. Stone's cinematographic flashbacks give us, and Nixon, glimpses of another, very different film, which might be called *The Nixon Saga,* the story of a poor young man raised in a stern moral tradition, and how he heroically achieves the presidency while retaining his moral values. These fragments of a film about moral education and moral integrity play ironically against the compromised Nixon of history, and of the complete film Stone has made. In the same way, Scrooge sees in his earlier self that other, better Scrooge who will emerge after his encounters with the three Spirits—indeed, begins to emerge when he sees his old school and schoolmates. Unlike Stone's Nixon, Scrooge is obviously the kind of man who weeps at sentimental drama, an easy audience for the performance the Spirits put on for him. The technical difference lies in Dickens's literal and moral use of Victorian theatrical devices, and especially the transformation scene, in which both the setting and the protagonist are transformed, in an admirable coalescence of form and meaning. The magic of the Spirits is the magic of the Victorian theater.

NOTES

1. All page references, unless otherwise specified, are to volume 1 of the Penguin edition of the Christmas Books.

WORKS CITED

Auerbach, Nina. *Ellen Terry, Player in her Time.* New York: Norton, 1987.

Booth, Michael R. *English Melodrama.* London: Herbert Jenkins, 1965.

Buckley, Jerome Hamilton. *Tennyson: the Growth of a Poet.* Cambridge, Mass: Harvard UP, 1960.

Butterworth, R. D. "*A Christmas Carol* and the Masque." *Studies in Short Fiction* 30 (1993), 63–69.

Dickens, Charles. *The Christmas Books.* Ed. Michael Slater. 2 volumes. Harmondsworth: Penguin, 1971.

———. *David Copperfield.* Ed. Trevor Blount. Harmondsworth: Penguin, 1973.

———. *Letters.* Ed. Walter Dexter. 3 volumes. London: Nonesuch, 1937–38.

———. *Letters* (Pilgrim edition). Ed. Madeline House and Graham Storey. In progress. Oxford: Oxford UP, 1965– .

———. *Selected Short Fiction.* Ed. Deborah A. Thomas. Harmondsworth: Penguin, 1976.

———. *Sikes and Nancy and Other Public Readings.* Ed. Philip Collins. Oxford: Oxford UP, 1983.

Eigner, Edwin M. *The Dickens Pantomime.* Berkeley: U of California P, 1989.

———. "On Becoming Pantaloon." *The Dickensian* 89 (1993), 177–83.

Forster, John. *The Life of Charles Dickens.* 1872–74. 2 volumes. London: Chapman and Hall, 1899.

Glancy, Ruth F. *Dickens's Christmas Books, Christmas Stories, and Other Short Fiction.* New York: Garland, 1985.

Hartnoll, Phyllis. *A Concise History of the Theatre.* New York: Scribner's, 1968.

Hunt, Hugh, Kenneth Richards, and John Russell Taylor. *The Revels History of Drama in English.* Volume 7:1880 to the Present Day. London: Methuen, 1978.

Jaffe, Audrey. "Spectacular Sympathy: Visuality and Ideology in Dickens's *A Christmas Carol.*" *PMLA* 109 (1994), 254–65.

Johnson, Edgar. *Charles Dickens: His Tragedy and Triumph.* New York: Simon and Schuster, 1952.

Jonson, Ben. "Expostulation with Inigo Jones." Reprinted in Nagler, 154–56.

Langton, Robert. *The Childhood and Youth of Charles Dickens.* London: Hutchinson, 1891.

Nagler, A. M. *A Source Book in Theatrical History.* 1952. Rpt. New York: Dover, 1959.

Nicoll, Allardyce. *A History of English Drama 1660–1900.* 5 volumes. Volume 5, *Late Nineteenth Century Drama.* Cambridge: Cambridge UP, 1962.

Odell, G. C. D. *Shakespeare from Betterton to Irving.* 2 vols. 1920. Rpt. New York: Benjamin Blom, 1963.

Orgel, Stephen. *The Jonsonian Masque.* Cambridge, Mass: Harvard UP, 1965.

Patterson, Arthur P. "Sponging the Stone: Transformation in *A Christmas Carol.*" *Dickens Quarterly* 11 (1994), 172–76.

Riggs, David. *Ben Jonson: a Life.* Cambridge, Mass: Harvard UP, 1989.

Rosenfeld, Sybil. *A Short History of Scene Design in Great Britain.* Oxford: Basil Blackwell, 1973.

Rowell, George. *The Victorian Theatre: a Survey.* Oxford: Clarendon, 1967.

Shaw, Bernard. *Dramatic Opinions and Essays.* 2 vols. 1907. Rpt. New York: Brentano's, 1928.

Speaight, Robert. *William Poel and the Elizabethan Revival.* Cambridge, Mass: Harvard UP, 1954.

Sprague, Arthur Colby. *Shakespeare and the Actors: the Stage Business in his Plays (1660–1905).* 1944. Rpt. New York: Russell and Russell, 1963.

Stoker, Bram. *Personal Reminiscences of Henry Irving.* London: Heinemann, 1907.

Stone, Oliver. *Nixon: An Oliver Stone Film.* Ed. Eric Hamburg. New York: Hyperion, 1996.

Thomas, Deborah A. *Dickens and the Short Story.* London: Batsford, 1982.

Tillotson, Kathleen. "The Middle Years from the *Carol* to *Copperfield.*" *Dickensian* 65 (1970), 1–19.

"When Constabulary Duty's To Be Done": Dickens and the Metropolitan Police

Elizabeth Dale Samet

In the tenth chapter of *Bleak House,* a John Doe (a literal "nobody" later identified as Esther Summerson's father) is reported dead of an opium overdose in a room over Krook's rag and bottle shop. Two law enforcement officials respond to the call: a metropolitan policeman and a parish beadle. By the time the latter arrives, however, the policeman has already examined the crime scene and stationed himself at the street door, "where he stands like a tower," intimidating a throng of inquisitive neighbors. The excitement initially caused by the discovery of the body is renewed by the entrance of the "feeble-minded" beadle, whom the crowd taunts with a song about "having boiled a boy" into soup for the workhouse. The policeman, too, explains the narrator, deems the beadle "an imbecile civilian, a remnant of the barbarous watchmen times; but gives him admission, as something that must be borne with until Government should abolish him." While this ridiculous and outmoded parochial functionary "flit[s] about" and "exasperat[es] the public" with his "general idiotcy," the efficient policeman, conspicuous in "shining hat . . . , inflexible great-coat, stout belt and bracelet," disperses the jeering crowd and "pursues his lounging way with a heavy tread; beating the palms of his white gloves one against the other, and stopping now and then, at a street-corner, to look casually for anything between a lost child and a murder" (194–96).[1]

Beadles typically receive rough treatment from Dickens—*Oliver Twist*'s odious Mr. Bumble comes readily to mind. Policemen, on the other hand, as Orwell once suggested, seem to be the "only officials whom Dickens handles with any kind of friendliness" (26). This amiability has been variously interpreted: Philip Collins refers to it as "boyish hero-worship" (206), while

Dickens Studies Annual, Volume 27, Copyright © 1998 by AMS Press, Inc. All rights reserved.

D. A. Miller reads it as a "notorious willingness to serve as a propagandist for the New Police" (74). Julian Symons argues that Dickens's depiction of competent policemen working to improve urban life did, in fact, play "a considerable part" in changing the public's initially antagonistic attitude toward the force (46).

The *bobby* was still a relative newcomer to the London scene when Dickens and collaborator W. H. Wills published their series of admiring police portraits in *Household Words* during the early 1850s.[2] Created in 1829, the centralized "Police of the Metropolis" effectively superseded both the idiosyncratic parish policing system and the independent thief-takers—most notably, Henry Fielding's Bow Street Runners—affiliated with the law courts. The philosophy behind the new force was *preventive policing,* and it was founded on the assumption that a centralized, highly visible, uniformed police presence would deter potential perpetrators (Smith 61). In language more familiar to the twentieth-century reader, the bobby was expected to walk "a beat, alert to anything . . . requir[ing] his attention in terms of assistance, order maintenance, or law enforcement." Free to conduct "reactive" investigations in response to citizen complaints, he was not authorized to undertake "proactive" measures like raids, stings, or undercover work (Sanders 13). Dickens is quite careful in *Household Words* to document how the police brass disseminated the concept of non-intervention to patrolmen: "Be sure and look sharp after flower-girls," one inspector announces during roll call in "The Metropolitan Protectives." "Offering flowers for sale is a pretence [sic]. The girls are either beggars or thieves; but you must exercise great caution. You must not interfere with them unless you actually hear them asking charity, or see them trying pockets, or engaged in actual theft."[3]

Mistrusting the Police Commissioners' assurances about non-invasive policing, however, many Londoners thought of the new force as, in practical terms, a network of government spies. Citizens registered complaints with the Home Office about being "followed or watched by policemen" (Lee 249). Dickens attempted to assuage such fears by investing the New Police with an aura of incorruptible professionalism that distinguished them not only from their erratic historical forbears, but also from the amateur sleuths of contemporary fiction. The typical policeman in *Household Words* is not abstruse and flamboyant like Poe's Dupin. He is, instead, steady, workmanlike, and predictable: the vigilant constable transporting a boy knocked down by a horse to the hospital, the unflappable desk-sergeant booking a drunk and disorderly, the unglamorous detective hiding for hours under a sofa to catch a thief red-handed. While Dickens's policemen often betray a sincere sympathy for the people they are ordered to roust from vacant buildings, or for the juvenile delinquents they apprehend, they do not have the luxury of, for instance, a Sherlock Holmes, occasionally to "play tricks with the law of

England." As an accountable public servant, the metropolitan policeman cannot absolve a repentant thief or allow a murderer to escape even if, like Holmes himself, he secretly believes: "Once or twice in my career I have . . . done more real harm by my discovery of the criminal than ever he had done by his crime."[4] As the *Household Words* vignette "A Detective Police Party" makes clear, the new breed of policeman does not make a habit, as did his Bow Street predecessor, "of consorting with thieves," and needlessly "jobbing and trading in mystery."[5] "Something to Drink," which appeared in *Household Words* in 1853, reveals that even the off-duty London policeman is not prone to excessive frivolity: "Joviality" at the policemen's pub "is the exception. Although a vast counter-trade is done, and a considerable parlor trade too, the customers are for the most part anxious and preoccupied. The policemen drink; but not jovially. They are too busy and too conscious of the responsibility of their position to be merry."[6]

But it is to the figure of the plainclothes detective, as opposed to the uniformed constable, whom *Household Words* devoted the greater publicity and enthusiasm. The addition of a division of detectives in 1842 had fueled existing outrage among Londoners about "spy police" because it seemed to undermine the theoretical concept of high-visibility, preventive policing. In "The Modern Science of Thief-Taking," Wills responds directly to such a perception by revealing that the Detective Police "of which we hear so much, consists of only forty-two individuals." As Phillip Thurmond Smith attests, this force was hardly capable of performing the more exhaustive surveillance achieved by continental agencies utilizing networks of civilian informants.[7] Moreover, as Dickens reports in the two-part "Detective Police Party," the detectives are morally irreproachable. They are all "respectable looking men . . . with nothing lounging or slinking in their manners. . . ." Intelligent and forthright, they "have all good eyes; and they all can, and . . . do, look full at whomsoever they speak to." While it is certainly true that a law-abiding citizen may not recognize a detective in the street, "a thief [always] knows an officer, and an officer . . . a thief" under any disguise.[8]

Household Words also helped to demystify the role of the Metropolitan Police, and to accentuate their salutary influence, by demonstrating that crime was being elevated to an art in the rapidly changing city. In "Innocence and Crime," a piece appearing in the same number as "A Detective Police Party," a provincial Englishman named Mr. Harcourt Brown comes to London and promptly loses himself "in a maze of squalid streets." Alternately abused, ignored, and followed by the passersby from whom he asks directions, Mr. Brown encounters a little girl beaten by her mother for, as she puts it, "shaking the doll." After scolding the girl for abusing her baby sibling, Mr. Brown is seized by an "impulse of benevolence," but when he reaches into his purse to give the child some money, he discovers that "every single thing he had in his pockets is gone":

He called to mind the man with the fixed smile on his hollow cadaverous cheek, and several other faces of men whom he had casually noticed in the course of the last half hour, thinking what a pity it was that something could not be done for them. He now began to think it was a very great pity that something had not *already* been done for them or with them, for they had certainly "done" him. Poor Mr. Brown!

Only much later, when, on a tour of Coldbath Fields Prison, Mr. Brown sees the same girl behind bars, does he learn that she had been punished for shaking not an actual baby, but a dummy commonly used to instruct pickpockets-in-training.[9] Under such circumstances, what citizen would not welcome the advent of the Detective Police, especially if, as Wills insists in "The Modern Science of Thief-Taking," his very "appearance upon any scene of operations is a bar to anything or anybody being 'done.' "This is an excellent characteristic of the Detectives," the article continues, "for they thus become as well a Preventive Police."[10]

Albert Hutter has argued that the detective became integral to both the Victorian city and its fictions as a decoder of the increasingly indecipherable nuances of the urban world. Detective policemen like the celebrated Charles Frederick Field did indeed "read," listen to, and translate the rapidly changing city for the benefit of defenseless citizens like Harcourt Brown (194–95). Dickens's famous sketch, "On Duty with Inspector Field," reveals the extent to which that city remained a mystery to the majority of its inhabitants. Upon entering a street full of "sickening smells . . . heaps of filth . . . [and] tumbling houses," while accompanying Field on his tour—which suggested many of the details for Snagsby and Bucket's visit to Tom-all-Alone's in *Bleak House*—Dickens demands: "How many people may there be in London, who, if we had brought them deviously and blindfold, to this street, fifty paces from the Station House, and within call of Saint Giles's church, would know it for a not remote part of the city in which their lives are passed?"[11]

A Detective Inspector "reckons up" not only geography, but physiognomy as well: "The eye," one of them informs Dickens and Wills, "is the greatest detector. We can tell in a crowd what a [suspect] is about by the expression of his eye." Under the policeman's gaze, criminals disperse "as if by magic." The detective's acuity, guiding "him into tracks quite invisible to other eyes," enables him to catch even those criminals who have left "not a trail or trace," and to solve even those crimes where "every clue seems cut off." But despite the fact that he confines his surveillance exclusively to the "criminal classes," the detective's civilian clothes, "Protean cleverness of disguise and capacity to counterfeit," nevertheless permit him to circulate through the Victorian metropolis with anonymous ease.[12] Like the inspector in Bentham's "Panopticon," the "fundamental advantage" of the plainclothes urban policeman is his "apparent omnipresence . . . combined with the extreme facility of his *real presence.*"[13]

Considering the detective's irregular hours, his disreputable acquaintances, and the ethical ambiguities posed by plainclothes policing, it is hardly surprising that the London public believed that this branch of the force was a network of spies. The editors of *Household Words* worked zealously to combat this image, particularly in a piece entitled "Spy Police," which is generally ignored in discussions of Dickens and the police. "We have already given some insight into the workings of the Detective Police system of London," it begins, "and have found that it is solely employed in bringing crime to justice. We have no political police, no police over opinion." The article goes on to contrast the London police with their continental counterparts, and it is here, in the characterizations of these continental agents and the civilian spies whom they recruit, that Foucault's historically dubious "indefinite world of . . . permanent, exhaustive omnipresent surveillance," with its "thousands of eyes posted everywhere," is anticipated (213–14). In England, the citizen can, while riding on a public train, declare "himself freely on the conduct of the powers that be, because he knows that even if his fellow-passenger be a Sergeant Myth or an Inspector Wield, no harm will come to him." However, once he crosses the Channel to Europe, where the "criminal police is very defective, the police of politics is all powerful," the Englishman is at the mercy of both the criminal and the policeman. In Paris, for instance,

> thirty thousand political malcontents were swept beyond the gates . . . in a single morning, before the rest of the people were up; and nobody was any the wiser till the masterly feat had been performed; but during the same month several single individuals were knocked down and robbed—some in broad day, others at dusk—yet neither of the robbers were taken.

Similarly, in Naples, the thief has nothing to fear, but the law-abiding citizen is in perpetual danger of being "dragged from his bed" and "plunged into the dungeons of the Vicaria" by a police commissary. Possessing at once the predatory instincts of the "night-bird" and the stealth of the "cat," the spectral commissary occupies his time by "stealing along under . . . dark shadows."

The article also warns that the Neapolitan Commissary is followed by a veritable army of civilian informants: "Their multitude, their ubiquity, their unwearied perseverance, their sharp sting make them worse than the whole insect tribe united, and infinitely more dangerous." Ordinary insects may be given the brush, and they will always betray "some warning signs of their approach—but the Police Spy is invisible and never out of hearing." In Paris or Naples, the article concludes, "the influence of the Police Spy System . . . has been such as to convert the whole nation into spies upon each other."[14]

In Foucauldian terms, these nations have effectively internalized the principle of supervision. In London, presumably, the detective "spies" so that the citizen does not have to. Dickens continues to justify the gaze of London's Metropolitan Police in *Household Words,* and to distinguish it from that of continental agencies, by defining it as an eye of *conscience,* rather than surveillance. The fieldwork of the policemen who "watch over the peace of the huge Babylon when she sleeps" provides them with an insight into urban problems which the "gentlemen" in the House of Commons, buried as they are beneath self-imposed mountains of "Red Tape," reject. "There is not one" member of parliament, Dickens writes in "The Metropolitan Protectives," who could not, in the space of a week, if he chose,

> acquire as dismal a knowledge of the Hell upon earth in which he lives . . . as this Inspector has—as we have—as no man can by possibility shut out, who will walk this town with open eyes observant of what is crying to God in the streets. . . . Do . . . none of them look into it . . . ? Do none of [them] care to . . . see with their eyes and hear with their ears . . . ?[15]

In this account of his overnight sojourns with Wills at various police stations throughout the city, Dickens exposes a number of socioeconomic factors—including poverty, child neglect, and the overcrowding resultant from urban developments like New Oxford Street—to be "at the very source of crime." These visits prompt him to reevaluate the force's celebrated theoretical strength, *prevention,* as its great pragmatic limitation. He manifests what Alexander Welsh has called an "authoritarian indignation" over the government's effective handcuffing of the police through an insistence on the "doctrine of non-interference." When Dickensian police fail, suggests Welsh, "it is only because there are not enough of them on the job, or because they are not empowered to punish offenders swiftly and directly" (City 47–48).

But there is also an important sense in which the police are, by training and propensity, wholly unsuited to cope with many of the city's problems. In a letter to Angela Burdett Coutts on the advisability of asking Inspector Field to help with the clearance of a fever-ridden slum, Dickens suggests that despite the detective's intimate knowledge of the neighborhood, his "habits of mind" might actually interfere with the project (*Letters* 6:573–74). The police commissioners rightly would have countered that it was not their job to provide social services and direct urban renewal. In "The Metropolitan Protectives," a policeman can and does *prevent* a destitute man from spending the night in the streets by giving him shelter in a station house casual ward; he can and does *prevent* a child from starving by removing it from its drunken mother and bringing it to the workhouse, but no matter how excellent the method or careful the administration, these reactions are no substitute in Dickens's opinion for the proactive "interposition of the State, as a measure of human policy, if not of human pity and accountability."[16]

The moral abdication of the member of parliament has shifted the distasteful responsibility for literally *shedding light* on the urban plague to the policeman, but he fails, ultimately, to administer a lasting remedy. In "On Duty with Inspector Field," there is a surfeit of police eyes, from the "shrewd" and "roving" eye of Field himself to the "glaring" or "flaming red" eye of the constable's lantern. Field now joins to his superhuman powers of observation an "outward show of not attending to anything in particular," while the constable who accompanies him demonstrates that he can see even "behind him without any effort." The apparent purpose of making the rounds of assorted lodging-houses, attics, cellars, and gambling dens is to account for the whereabouts of as many criminals as possible: "Wherever the [lantern's] turning lane of light becomes stationary for a moment, some sleeper appears at the end of it, submits himself to be scrutinized, and fades away into the darkness." However, as D. A. Miller notes, these criminal bed-checks do not really "curtail delinquency" or even "prevent [the slums] from continuing to serve as a refuge for those wanted by the police" (76–77). The only moment that seemingly recuperates Field's campaign of nocturnal harassment occurs when he donates "coffee money" to a roomful of starving families. By publicizing such a gesture, Dickens attempts, however awkwardly, once again to show that the act of *looking* in the metropolitan sphere constitutes a moral imperative as opposed to a spying prerogative.[17]

In 1853 Dickens exported the figure of the detective policeman from the episodic milieu of *Household Words* to the sustained plot of the novel. Miller proposes that the "out of control" detective story accelerated in *Bleak House* by numerous unofficial sleuths like Tulkinghorn, Krook, Guppy, and the Smallweed contingent "eventually asks to be arrested by the Detective Police" (72–73). There is, however, an important historical as well as a narratological significance to the introduction of the detective policeman into the novel. The questionable methods and uneven successes of Inspector Bucket compromise to a degree Dickens's earlier characterizations of the force. Furthermore, what Miller refers to as "Bucket's amoral professionalization" refocuses attention on the lingering and finally disabling paradox of preventive policing (90).[18]

In his correspondence Dickens is for the most part full of praise for Inspector Field's talents and discretion, but he does betray a marked resentment towards the policeman's evasiveness and "horrible sharpness" (*Letters* 573). This uneasiness about police ubiquity and omniscience spills over into the contemporaneous fiction of *Bleak House*. Bucket's lynx-like furtiveness and habitual lurking and lounging ally him more closely to the continental commissary portrayed in "Spy Police," than to the "bustling," good-humored Inspectors of "A Detective Police Party." The first time Bucket (magically) materializes in the novel, it is to vex not a criminal, but the innocuous Mr. Snagsby:

Mr Snagsby is dismayed to see, standing with an attentive face between himself and the lawyer, at a little distance from the table, a person . . . who was not there when he himself came in, and has not since entered by the door or by either of the windows. There is a press in the room, but its hinges have not creaked, nor has a step been audible upon the floor. Yet this third person stands there . . . a composed and quiet listener. . . . Except that he looks at Mr Snagsby as if he were going to take his portrait, there is nothing remarkable about him at first sight but his ghostly manner of appearing.

"Don't mind this gentleman," says Mr Tulkinghorn, in his quiet way, "This is only Mr Bucket." (361)

Over the course of the novel, the primary objects of Bucket's policing—Gridley, Mr. George, and Jo—never know *when* they *are* being watched, so they believe that they are being watched all the time. To Mr. George, Bucket is simply a "rum customer" (694), but to the homeless Jo, who is repeatedly told by both Bucket and a uniformed constable to "move on," he is a source of terror. When questioned by the well-meaning Dr. Woodcourt, Jo becomes excessively "apprehensive of being overheard" and "looks about him . . . lest the object of his distrust should be looking over, or hidden" nearby. "I dustn't name him," admits Jo, "Ah, but I don't know . . . .as he *don't* hear. . . . He's in all manner of places, all at wunst" (689–90).

Later in the novel, of course, we discover that instead of distributing "coffee money" like Inspector Field, Bucket has in fact offered bribe money to Harold Skimpole for information concerning Jo's whereabouts. The snitch excuses himself to Esther by insisting:

If it is blameable in Skimpole to take the note, it is blameable in Bucket to offer [it]. . . . Now, Skimpole wishes to think well of Bucket: Skimpole deems it essential, in its little place, to the general cohesion of things, that he *should* think well of Bucket. The State expressly asks him to trust to Bucket. And he does. And that's all he does! (886)[19]

In the end, it is perhaps less significant that Bucket recruits Harold Skimpole as a paid informant, than that Dickens should place the novel's most accurate, detailed, and impartial description of a detective's job in the mouth of this reprehensible parasite: "Skimpole reasons with himself that [Bucket] is a tamed lynx . . . a person of a peculiarly directed energy . . . who discovers our friends and enemies for us when they run away, recovers our property for us when we are robbed, avenges us comfortably when we are murdered" (886). The phrase "tamed lynx" is suggestive: Bucket embodies a powerful force that has been newly domesticated to serve society's ends, but he nevertheless retains a certain feral quality at odds with that civilization.

Although, as Skimpole informs Esther, the State asks us to trust Bucket, it is by no means clear, as Miller notes, that Bucket does his detecting on that State's behalf. He initially becomes involved in the story at the behest of Tulkinghorn, the novel's malevolent "high-priest of noble mysteries." Again, Dickens's correspondence provides an illustrative parallel. In a letter to Edward Bulwer Lytton, Dickens promises that he can prevent Lytton's estranged wife from making a scene at a theater by enlisting the discreet services of Inspector Field who, "in plain clothes, will remain in the Hall all night." Dickens rather smugly boasts: "Field is quite devoted to me. . . . Any of the Detective men will do anything for me" (*Letters* 377). In the novel, too, the detective initially serves the private interests of wealth and privilege. In order to ferret out Lady Dedlock's secret, Tulkinghorn manipulates the police; in order to keep that secret, Sir Leicester hires Bucket after the lawyer's death. Residing simultaneously at the novel's moral nadir and its geographic summit, Tulkinghorn lurks either in his upstairs law chambers in London, where the "high chimney-stacks telegraph family secrets to him" (718), or in his "turret chamber" at the Dedlock estate, where he paces the balcony "like a larger species of rook" (212–13). Like a continental policeman, Tulkinghorn is always, to Lady Dedlock's distress, "at hand. Haunting every place. No relief or security from him for a moment" (708). He is the Mrs. Sparsit to Honoria's Louisa Bounderby.

After Tulkinghorn is murdered by Lady Dedlock's maid Hortense, his literal town-and-country Panopticons are superseded by Bucket's metaphoric one. Before setting out on the novel's climactic pursuit of Lady Dedlock, Bucket—now able to work in an official capacity on this missing person case—"mounts a high tower in his mind."

> [He] looks out far and wide. Many solitary figures he perceives. . . . But the figure that he seeks is not among them. . . . Where is she? Living or dead, where is she? If, as he folds the handkerchief and carefully puts it up, it were able, with an enchanted power, to bring before him the place where she found it . . . would he descry her there? (824)

When Bucket ascends this mental tower, physical evidence like the handkerchief proves useless to him, and he becomes bogged down with a surplus of extraneous data. He cannot, in the language of a modern criminology textbook, extract the "information" from the "noise" (Sanders 27). When Bucket finally does pick up the scent at the brickmaker's cottage, he fails to account for the criminological "theory of transference," which states that "when two objects meet, some effect of that meeting can be established and verified at a later time. . . . In short every criminal or violent incident will result in the transfer of material or an alteration which may be matched to the object causing the change."[20] Bucket misses the "transference" of clothing between Lady Dedlock and Jenny, and he therefore follows the wrong woman. But before we pardon him for his ignorance of twentieth-century forensic principles, we should recall that he is duped by exactly the same ruse with which he had once attempted to deceive Jo. Early in the novel, we remember, Jo had recognized that the veiled figure of Hortense offered for his consideration, was *not* in fact the same woman he had led to Nemo's grave in the parish burying ground, not, in other words, the disguised Lady Dedlock (368–69). Bucket's lapse results, of course, in the belated discovery of Lady Dedlock's already lifeless figure outside the gates of that same burying ground; it can even be said that Bucket's relentless pursuit accelerates her demise.[21] The corpse serves as a reminder to him of Hortense's earlier taunt that he cannot restore honor to the living nor bring the dead back to life (799). Bucket's expert powers of surveillance and detection desert him precisely when he is finally given the opportunity to prevent something from being done.

With elegant symmetry, the two "deaths" of Lady Dedlock contain the imperative for detection in *Bleak House:* the onset of "the faintness of death" which follows her recognition of Hawdon's handwriting in chapter 2 announces to Tulkinghorn the concealment of a secret, while the discovery of her body "cold and dead," outside the gates of the burying ground in chapter 59, largely dispels the investigative impetus which for so long energizes the novel. Perhaps it is fitting that a novel characterized, in the words of J. Hillis Miller, by the singular "absence of moral relationship between people" should be thus catalyzed by crime and enervated by the objective "modern science" of detection (206). Bucket's rallying cry to Esther during their pursuit of Lady Dedlock is: "You know me, I'm Inspector Bucket, and you can trust me." Certainly, Esther can trust to Bucket's good intentions, but she cannot ignore the fact that he arrives too late to *prevent* the thing from being "done." Like the antiquated beadle whom he has put out of business, Bucket can do nothing save reconstruct the crime, or, in his own words, to reveal that "the whole bileing [sic] of people was mixed up in the same business and no other" (863). Todorov would argue that Bucket has precisely fulfilled his structural obligations to the detective story: characters in the story of an "investigation, do not act, they learn" (44). But it has become apparent by the end of *Bleak House* that, at least as far as Dickens is concerned, a pound of police prevention in the ever-changing metropolis is not worth an ounce of social cure.

NOTES

1. In his detailed discussion of Dickens's relationship with the police in the ninth chapter of *Dickens and Crime,* Philip Collins identifies this particular moment in

the text as the "apotheosis of the Bobbie" (3rd ed. [New York: St. Martin's, 1994], 203).

2. It is, of course, not always easy to determine the authorship of every piece appearing in the magazine. As a rule, however, the editorial enthusiasm for the police pervades *Household Words*. For a notable comic exception, see "Some Wild Ideas," *HW* 19.475 (1859). Edgar Johnson records that "Dickens maintained a dictatorial control over every detail" of the magazine, and that readers inevitably attributed "everything good" to him (*Charles Dickens* [1952; rev. and abr. New York: Penguin, 1980], 356–68).

3. *Household Words*, 3.57 (1851), 98.

4. Arthur Conan Doyle, "The Adventure of the Abbey Grange," *The Complete Novels and Stories*, vol. 1 (New York: Bantam, 1986), 895–96. Holmes also allows a culprit to go free in "The Adventure of the Blue Carbuncle."

5. "The Modern Science of Thief-Taking," *HW*, 1.18 (1850), 409. Collins argues that although Dickens may have exaggerated the evils of the Bow Street Runners, the author's claims about the professionalism of the force were borne out by the fact that the New Police's first major corruption scandal did not occur until the 1870s. Collins adds: "it was not only the glamour, excitement, and usefulness of the detective police that attracted him [Dickens], but also their belonging—as he saw it—to a superbly efficient organisation" (*Dickens and Crime* 199–200 and 216).

6. *HW*, 7.171 (1853), 430–31.

7. *HW*, 1.16 (1850), 368. *Policing Victorian London*, 61–62 and 70–71.

8. *HW*, 1.18 (1850), 409–10.

9. *HW*, 1.18 (1850), 431–32.

10. *HW*, 1.16 (1850), 370.

11. *HW*, 3.64 (1851), 265.

12. *HW*, 1.16 (1850), 368–71.

13. Jeremy Bentham, "Panopticon: or, the Inspection-House," in *Works*, ed. John Bowring, vol. 4 (Edinburgh, 1843), 45.

14. *HW*, 1.126 (1850), 611–14. The police forces of Berlin, Naples, Austria, and Russia are all reviled for their corruption and brutality by Dickens and other contributors to *Household Words*. See especially, "Chip: Justice is Satisfied," *HW*, 10.233 (1854), 84; "Justice at Naples," *HW*, 14.349 (1856), 457; and several installments of "A Journey Due North," *HW* 14.345 (1856), 375; 15.360 (1857), 148–49 and 151–52; and 15.361 (1857), 175 and 180.

15. *HW*, 3.57 (1851), 97–98.

16. *HW*, 3.57 (1851), 104.

17. *HW*, 3.64 (1851), 265–70.

18. For a discussion of the various holes in the theory of preventive policing, see *Policing Victorian London*, 70.

19. Collins claims that Dickens "exonerates" the constable who moves Jo along by making him appear reluctant to perform this unpleasant task. He somewhat less convincingly maintains that Bucket detects throughout the novel "without ever being meant to forfeit our approval" (*Dickens and Crime*, 204). Miller, on the other hand, acknowledges that there are in the novel "a number of reservations

about the nature and effects'' of the Detective Police's power. He argues, however, that the "momentary collaboration between Skimpole and Bucket . . . , an alliance of two species of moral indifference, throws no more discredit on the aesthete who delivers a dangerously ill child over to the police for no better reason than a bribe, than on the officer who extends the bribe for no better reason than to cover his client's prying.'' In the end, Miller writes, "the game function of detection thoroughly dominates whatever ethical ends it presumably serves'' in *Bleak House* (*Novel and the Police,* 94–95).

20. *Criminal Investigation* (Gaithersburg: International Association of Chiefs of Police, 1971), 12.

21. Welsh observes: "Lady Dedlock's suicide is obscured by the pursuit of Inspector Bucket and Esther that purposes to prevent suicide but helps to drive the woman to exhaustion'' ("Blackmail Studies in *Martin Chuzzlewit* and *Bleak House*," *Dickens Studies Annual,* 11 (1983), 32).

WORKS CITED

Bentham, Jeremy. *Works.* Vol. 4. Ed. John Bowring. Edinburgh, 1843. 11 vols.

Collins, Philip. *Dickens and Crime.* 3rd ed. New York: St. Martin's, 1994.

Criminal Investigation. Gaithersburg: International Association of Chiefs of Police, 1971.

Dickens, Charles. *Bleak House.* Ed. J. Hillis Miller. London: Penguin, 1921.

———. *Household Words.* London, 1850–59.

———. *The Letters.* Ed. Graham Storey, et al. Oxford: Clarendon, 1988.

Doyle, Arthur Conan. *The Complete Novels and Stories.* Vol. 1. New York: Bantam, 1986. 2 vols.

Foucault, Michel. *Discipline and Punish.* Tr. Alan Sheridan. New York: Vintage, 1979.

Hutter, Albert D. "Dreams, Transformations, and Literature: The Implications of Detective Fiction.'' *Victorian Studies* 19 (1975): 194–95.

Johnson, Edgar. *Charles Dickens.* 1952. Rev. and abr. ed. New York: Penguin, 1980.

Lee, W. L. Melville. *A History of Police in England.* 1901; rpt. Montclair, NJ: Patterson Smith, 1971.

Miller, D. A. *The Novel and the Police.* Berkeley: U of California P, 1988.

Miller, J. Hillis. *Charles Dickens: The World of His Novels.* Cambridge: Harvard UP, 1958.

Orwell, George. "Charles Dickens," in *Dickens, Dali, and Others. New York: Harcourt, 1946.*

Sanders, William B. *Detective Works.* New York: Macmillan, 1977.

Smith, Phillip Thurmond. *Policing Victorian London.* Westport: Greenwood, 1985.

Symons, Julian. *Bloody Murder.* Harmondsworth: Viking, 1972.

Todorov, Tzvetan. "The Typology of Detective Fiction," in *The Poetics of Prose,* tr. Richard Howard. Ithaca: Cornell UP.

Welsh, Alexander. "Blackmail Studies in *Martin Chuzzlewit* and *Bleak House." Dickens Studies Annual* 11 (1983):25–35.

———. *The City of Dickens.* Oxford: Clarendon, 1971.

A Tale of Two Gospels: Dickens and John

Kenneth M. Sroka

*They have never asked me what my religion is. They asked
me what my story was, and I told them.* Lizzie Hexam, in
Our Mutual Friend

In Charles Dickens's *A Tale of Two Cities* (1859), Sydney Carton goes to the
guillotine reciting the famous words from the Gospel according to St. John
echoed in the refrain from the burial service of The Book of Common Prayer:
"I am the Resurrection and the Life, saith the Lord: he that believeth in me,
though he were dead, yet shall he live: and whosoever liveth and believeth
in me shall never die" (*A Tale* bk. III, ch. 15; John 11.25–26). In John,
Christ's words come at the approximate midpoint of the book, just before he
raises Lazarus from the dead (an event recorded in the New Testament only
in John's gospel). *A Tale of Two Cities* generally echoes the Gospel of John
in its explicit concern with "resurrection"—Book I is entitled "Recalled to
Life," and several major and minor characters are "recalled" in various
ways from death, from Charles Darnay's triple escape from execution to the
spy Roger Cly's figurative resurrection after his "burial."[1]

The echoes of John's gospel in *A Tale of Two Cities,* however, go well
beyond Sydney Carton's climactic self-sacrifice and beyond the more obvious
instances of the resurrection theme. In effect, the many similarities between
A Tale of Two Cities and the Gospel of John suggest that the novel may be
a kind of secular complement to John's book in which Dickens resurrects the
past to celebrate a poetic faith in the mystery of the basic paradoxes of human
experience. The novel may very well be itself another Victorian "gospel,"
similar in its function to the writings of Thomas Carlyle, whose works likewise served in large part as a witness to human value when conventional
religious faith and the Bible seemed no longer adequate responses to mid-
Victorian spiritual crises.

Both Dickens and John write historical narratives. Much like Walter Scott, who set *Waverley* (1814) "Sixty Years Since," they write stories whose historical roots lie in events which occurred about seventy years previous to the time of the writing (1789–1794 for Dickens; about 30–33 A.D. for John). For both writers and their contemporaries the events are recent enough to still have a strong impact upon them and far enough in the past to increase the objective distance of the writers. As historians, Dickens and John recall events to life, order them, and thus fix for the reader what would otherwise inevitably, more blurrily, recede into the past if left unwritten.

Beyond their function as historical story-tellers and salvagers of the past, however, both writers serve mythic and moral ends for readers in all times. John's purpose is more explicitly religious: " . . . these ['signs' which Jesus worked] are written that ye might believe that Jesus is the Christ, the Son of God; and that believing ye might have life through his name" (20.31). The morality which John preaches is synonymous with the second of the great commandments, to love one's neighbor as oneself: "Greater love hath no man than this, that a man lay down his life for his friends" (15.13). Dickens's mythic and "moral" ends, however, lie more implicitly in his story's celebration of the paradox of good coming out of evil and conquering mortality.

On the individual level, Dickens's "faith" climaxes in Carton's death which gives life to the Darnays and earns him a namesake in their child and a sanctuary in their hearts "generations hence." On the public level, the faith in *A Tale* lies in the historical fact of the resurrection of Paris and the French nation from the "abyss" of the Revolution and the Terror. Both John and Dickens offer the reader a mythological basis for spiritual truth that may move the reader to "believe." By fixing the mystery of the human past, both writers illuminate the present for their readers and prophesize with confidence the equally mysterious human future.

Unlike John's good news, Dickens's "faith," which can generally be found in all his writings, is less orthodox and more secular. As Andrew Sanders so aptly puts it, "For Dickens the only knowledge of heaven is based on what is learned on earth" (xii). Personally, Dickens was a religious man in the broadest sense of the word: he believed in God, but belonged to no particular church. While he said of the New Testament that it was "the best book that ever was or will be known in the world," his religious sense was based largely, as Peter Ackroyd says, on "natural love and moral feeling . . . a faith established upon practical philanthropy and conventional morality" (505–07). Dickens's expression of "faith" in his novels is a celebration of human wonder, the existence of the divine in humankind. Raymond Williams describes the faith implicit in Dickens's fiction as the belief in the "inexplicable" existence of human "miracle":

It is easy to show that having defined a social condition as the cause of virtue and vice, Dickens then produces virtue, almost magically.... We may or may not believe in it, as social observation, but though it has the character of miracle it is the kind of miracle that happens: the flowering of love or energy which is inexplicable.... The inexplicable quality of the indestructible innocence, of the miraculously intervening goodness, on which Dickens so much depends and which has been casually written off as sentimentality is genuine *because* it is inexplicable.... To believe that a human spirit exists ... is an act of faith but an act of faith in ourselves. That this became more and more difficult for Dickens is not surprising, but to the end, under increasing pressure, it is what he is not only saying but making happen. (52–53)

Throughout his writing career, Dickens made his faith happen through his use of story to empower the reader, his use of words to order and to resurrect human experience as religion, history, and fiction.[2]

In *The Life of Our Lord* (written in 1849, and first published in 1934), Dickens retells the New Testament story for his children, turning himself into an evangelist of sorts by composing what might be called the "gospel according to Dickens." Some years later, when Dickens turns historian in *A Child's History of England* (1853), he covers the seventeenth through the nineteenth centuries in the last two pages, but without any reference to the French Revolution. Still later, *A Tale of Two Cities* retells elementary Christian truths and, focusing on the period from 1775 to 1793, recreates the significance of history for adults as those earlier works did for children. By 1859, Dickens had matured as a novelist and as an historical novelist as well. Whereas *Barnaby Rudge* (1841) reveals Dickens's debt to Scott (especially to his *Old Mortality* [1816]), *A Tale of Two Cities* reveals Dickens's own unique voice incorporating "religion" into historical fiction, creating a myth for his age in the year when, coincidentally, Darwin's *On the Origin of Species* seriously shook Victorian religious faith.

Of the four evangelists, John alone shows the same curiosity that Dickens has about the power of words and story. While Matthew, Mark, and Luke end their gospels with accounts of Christ's resurrection and ascension, John's epilogue focuses on writing, books, and the writer's role as a limited witness: "This is the disciple which testifieth of these things, and wrote these things: and we know that his testimony is true. And there are, also, many other things which Jesus did, the which, if they should be written I suppose that even the world itself could not contain the books that should be written" (21.24–25). John's gospel proclaims that the Word was made flesh (1.14), but both he and Dickens perform the more human feat of turning the flesh of those who people history into words, a creation act which celebrates the uncommonness of human life by resurrecting it for their readers. Dickens and John both use concentrated "story" to make sense out of the chaos of living. They blend story, religion, and history to create and defend the truth of myth for times of spiritual darkness, whenever those times may arise.[3]

The structures of the Gospel of John and *A Tale of Two Cities* and the image patterns used with them are remarkably similar. Chapter 1 of John and Book I of *A Tale* function as overtures for their respective works. Both begin with poetic prose riddles which tease the reader into paying attention to the importance of paradox and mystery in the narratives which are to follow. Both overtures then develop their initial paradoxes in the remainder of the works through a wealth of paradoxical images which reiterate the mystery—death and resurrection, tigers and lambs, doubles, and food. Echoing Genesis, the verbal worlds created by John and Dickens evolve over and over again from darkness and lifeless mud to light and a transfigured vitality. Through their rich narrative elaboration, both works prophetically demonstrate the powerful reality of love and selflessness as the only means for the individual and the human race to transcend mortality.[4]

The Gospel of John and *A Tale of Two Cities* share famous beginnings which echo each other. John begins, "In the beginning was the Word, and the Word was with God, and the Word was God," the start of a paradoxical and mysterious chapter. Chapter 1 equates and separates "God" and "the Word" and makes both synonymous with "life" and "light" in a created world (1.1–4) which is "dark" because it does not "comprehend" (1.5); that is, the world neither understands nor accepts God, Word, life, or light. The gospel progresses through a series of miracles by which light overcomes darkness, and vital faith succeeds inert ignorance. The miracles climax in the resurrection of Lazarus at the end of the first half (11) and the resurrection of Jesus at the end of the second half (20–21). The human witnesses to the miracles respond at first with expressions of doubt and a naive sense that only rational, literal explanations can enable them to grasp such mysteries: "How can a man be born when he is old?" (3.4); "How can this man give us his flesh to eat?" (6.52); "This is an hard saying; who can hear it?" (6.60). Only the faith of those who accept the wonders they have seen—and have read about—can bring the believer to light and life: "I am come a light into the world, that whosoever believeth on me should not abide in darkness" (12.46) and " . . . these [signs] are written, that ye might believe that Jesus is the Christ, the Son of God; and that believing ye might have life through his name" (20.31).

Like John, Dickens begins *A Tale of Two Cities* very paradoxically, "It was the best of times, it was the worst of times . . . ," in a chapter full of paradox and mystery. In Chapter 1, the "best" is also "worst"; past is also present; Paris is also London; and England is also France. Book I and the novel as a whole move from the lifelessness of darkness, secrecy, and mud to the vitality of light, understanding, and resurrection. The mail coach travels by night in "mist," "mire," and "mud" with three passengers "wrapped to the cheek-bones . . . and each was hidden under almost as many wrappers from the eyes of the mind, as from the eye of the body, of his two companions." An approaching horse and rider are "covered with mud from the hoofs of the horse to the hat of the man" (ch. 2). The memorable opening of chapter 3 reminds us of the "wonderful fact" that "every human creature is constituted to be that profound secret and mystery to every other" and equates the inscrutability of the living with partially read books, the depths of unfathomable waters, and the dead themselves. What begins, however, as darkness, lifeless, mud, and inscrutability evolves into light, new life, and new faith, generally through the rich imagery of Book I and specifically in the story of Jarvis Lorry's and Lucie Manette's "recalling" Dr. Alexander Manette to life.

Two direct references to miracles in John appear in book I of *A Tale*. A reference to "the lords of the State preserves of loaves and fishes" (ch. 1) recalls John's account of the feeding of five thousand (6.1–13), an event recounted in all four gospels (Mat., 14.13–21; Mark, 6.34.44; Luke, 9.12–17). Similarly, the description of Dover (ch. 4) reminds us not only of the supposed healing effects of bathing in mineral waters in fashionable British seaside towns, but also of John's report of the cures at the Pool of Bethsaida (5.1–9): "The air among the houses was of so strong a piscatory flavour that one might have supposed sick fish went up to be dipped in it, as sick people went down to be dipped in the sea." In John's more miraculous account, "an angel went down at a certain season into the pool, and troubled the waters: whosoever then first after the troubling of the water stepped in was made whole of whatsoever disease he had" (5.4). As parts of the overture, such echoings of miracles involving food and water hint at motifs developed throughout the rest of both books. But the more general stylistic resemblances of the paradoxical beginnings of John and *A Tale* are as important as such easily recognizable allusions. The complex text forces the reader to pay more attention to their mutual concern for complex truth and the inadequacy of the physical plane of experience to capture and explain it. In John, Pilate's oversimple question, "What is truth?" (18.38) is rightfully left unanswered. In *A Tale,* rulers in England and France foolishly believe they know all there is to know, that "things in general were settled forever." The "answers" offered in both works, however, deny such oversimplification in their verbal creation of a puzzling world of "signs"—words, riddles,miracles—the imaginative, linguistic basis for faith in inexplicable realities. For both John and Dickens, the greatest of these signs is "resurrection."

The miracles in both works climax in "resurrection." In John the raising of Lazarus is the culmination of a great series of miracles which begins with a relatively more simple kind of "mind reading" (Jesus tells Nathanael what he was thinking [1.47–48]). The miracles, which mark the progress of Jesus' growing popularity, escalate in wonder in the first half of the book—changing water to wine (2), multiplying loaves and fishes and walking on water (6), curing the sick (4-5) and the blind (9)-and end with the story of Jesus' "fall," his arrest, scourging, and crucifixion, followed by his own climactic resurrection story (20–21). Similar accounts of Jesus' miracles are found in the other three gospels (Matt., 8.14–17, 12.22–25; Mark, 1.23–34, 8.22–26; Luke, 4.33–41), and, similarly, each of the other three reports the resurrection of a child (Matt., 9.18–26; Mark, 5.35–43; Luke, 7.11–17). *A Tale,* however, multiplies the resurrection motif so central to John.

The multiple resurrections in *A Tale of Two Cities* are not without precedent in Dickens's writing. In *The Life of Our Lord,* Dickens recounts four resurrection stories—that of a little girl (ch. 3), a young man (ch. 4), Lazarus (ch. 8), and Jesus (ch. 11). Moreover, twice in *The Life of Our Lord* Dickens specifically singles out words he wishes his young audience to remember, namely, "miracle" and "parable": "I wish you would remember that word [miracle], because I shall use it again, and I should like you to know that it means something which is very wonderful . . . " (ch. 1); and "I wish you to remember that word [parable], as I shall soon have some more of these Parables to tell you about" (ch. 6). Again, as in John, *The Life of Our Lord* is organized around miracles and parables, the most repeated of which is "resurrection." The quadruple resurrections in *The Life of Our Lord* are multiplied again and again in *A Tale,* beginning as early as book I, "Recalled to Life."

Jarvis Lorry's task in the early part of book I is to reunite Dr. Alexander Manette with his daughter Lucie after his imprisonment in the Bastille for eighteen years. He must "dig someone out of a grave" who has been "buried alive," a "spectre" of a man he envisions as "worn and wasted . . . of sunken cheek, cadaverous colour, emaciated hands . . . prematurely white [haired]." Lorry sleepily dozes as he travels in the company of other "slumbering forms," and "in his fancy would dig, and dig, dig . . . to dig this wretched creature out. Got out at last, with earth hanging about his face and hair, he would suddenly fall away to dust" (ch. 3). As the chapter ends, Lorry rises from the death-like slumber of the night and sees the rising sun, the first of many such "dawnings" in the novel. Though it is November, the dawn reveals "a ridge of ploughed land, with a plough upon it" and "though the earth was cold and wet, the sky was clear, and the sun rose bright, placid, and beautiful." The chapter, titled "The Night Shadows," which began by equating the living with the dead and bemoaning the tomb-like secrecy of individuals and cities, ends with an elaborate image of daily resurrection, both human and natural, amidst a scene which blends winter, sowing, night, and day with Lorry's short prayer of amazement: "Gracious Creator of day! To be buried alive for eighteen years!"

The second half of book I (chs. 4–6) reiterates the progress of the first three chapters from darkness and death to light and resuscitation. In the French village of Saint Antoine, the fifth-story room and the stairwell access to it where Dr. Manette is being sheltered by the wine merchant, Ernest Defarge, are tomb-like: each room of the building "left its own heap of refuse on its own landing, besides flinging other refuse from its windows. The uncontrollable and hopeless mass of decomposition so engendered" pollutes the air and makes the atmosphere "almost insupportable." The stench surrounding the "dead" Manette's room reminds us of the reason for Martha's hesitation in removing the stone from her brother Lazarus' tomb: "Lord, by this time he stinketh: for he hath been dead four days" (John, 11.39). Manette is skeletal, warding off with a "transparent" hand the scanty ray of light entering his garret. Lorry and Defarge attempt to bring Manette out of his tomb slowly: "The task of recalling him from the vacancy into which he always sank . . . was like recalling some very weak person from a swoon, or . . . to stay the spirit of a fast-dying man" (ch. 5). Only Manette's daughter, Lucie, who until now has believed her father to be dead, can restore his mind and spirits enough to enable him to leave France, even though she feels it is only his ghost she will see: "I am going to see his Ghost! It will be his Ghost—not him!" (ch. 4).

Lucie restores her father to life by letting him gradually see in her the triple animating identity of wife, mother, and daughter. Her presence slowly reestablishes Manette's sense of his identity before his imprisonment and begins to make him whole again by allowing him to put aside the divisive "shoemaker" personality he has assumed in order to erase his pain. Seeing her golden hair and hearing her voice, Manette first mistakes Lucie for his wife, but realizes, "No, no, no; you are too young, too blooming." As a life-giving mother figure, "She held him closer round the neck, and rocked him on her breast like a child." The scene, which precedes Manette's eventual recognition of Lucie as his daughter, is a Dickensian *Pietà*—a mother holding her dead son who would soon rise again.[5] Manette calls Lucie, whose name means "light," "my gentle angel," and the narrator refers to her as a "spirit" standing beside him as he works at his shoemaking. Like the sun on lifeless clay, Lucie's love reinvigorates her corpse-like father: "His cold white head mingled with her radiant hair, which warmed and lighted it as though it were the light of Freedom shining on him" (ch. 6). As animating human spirit and light, Lucie actualizes for her father what Jesus expresses as his role for the human race: "I am the light of the world: he that followeth me shall not walk in darkness, but shall have the light of life" (John, 8.12).

The roles of all the characters here are by no means simple allegorical ones. "Doctor" Manette, "the buried man who had been dug out" (I, ch. 6), is both the risen healer (who will later recall Darnay to life) and a Lazarus figure himself raised by other healers. Lorry, Lucie, and even Defarge are all instrumental in raising Manette, although Defarge's favorite oath as they approach Manette's garret—''Long live the Devil'' (I, ch. 5)—suggests his divided allegiance and later betrayal of Manette and his family. Likewise, Lucie's already multiple role is further increased by her resemblance to the angels at Christ's tomb (John 20.12). Dickens complicates the resurrection story of John by not allowing us simply to make any one of the characters alone Christ-like. Instead, all of Dickens's human characters (including Sydney Carton later) share an uncommonness, a trace of wonder and miracle inherent in and by virtue of their humanity, which lies dormant and can be recalled in everyone.

The evolution from darkness and inertia to light and life in John and, as we have seen it thus far, in book I of A Tale is truly a ''sym-bolic'' progress, a ''throwing together'' of otherwise disparate lives and experiences. John and Dickens knit the fragmented strands of the public and private past together to shape events into meaningful wholes. In both of their works, however, there is also a contrary ''dia-bolic'' movement, a divisive ''throwing apart.'' The ''antagonists'' in John, the chief priests and Pharisees, are motivated by self-interest and see Jesus' rising popularity as a direct threat to their power: ''If we let him thus alone, all men will believe on him: and the Romans shall come and take away both our place and nation'' (11.48). As the miracles continue and the followers of Jesus increase, so too does the seriousness of opposition to him. Early in John the enemies of Jesus accuse him of being diabolical because he works miracles on the Sabbath: ''Thou hast a devil'' (7.20). The raising of Lazarus confirms them in their determination to have him killed: ''Then from that day forth they took counsel together for to put him to death'' (11.53). In A Tale the movement opposing the progress from darkness to light and lifelessness to resurrection is, similarly, a dia-bolic counter-movement toward ''extermination'' specifically personified in Madame Therese Defarge and in the representative French aristocrats, Monseigneur and Monsieur the Marquis.[6]

Madame Defarge as negative-historian, diabolic force, and vengeful, exterminating angel is Lucie Manette's foil. Lucie is angelic ''light,'' ''the golden thread,'' ''weaving the service of her happy influence through the tissue of all their lives'' (II, Ch. 21), the restorative center of the new family and community of friends in Soho (II, ch. 4). Madame Defarge, on the contrary, is the ''wife of Lucifer'' (III, ch. 14) and resembles Clotho, one of the classical Fates. She mechanically knits her register throughout the novel for the ultimate purpose of exterminating the persons recorded there. Later, when Ernest Defarge asks his wife where all the slaughter which has accompanied the Revolution must stop, she responds, ''At extermination,'' and her companion ''The Vengeance'' hails her as ''an Angel!'' (III, ch. 12). The "shrouds" which she so diligently knits are writs of execution demanding the dia-bolical tearing apart of human bodies at the guillotine. With her "sisters," The Vengeance and "La Guillotine" ("the figure of the sharp female" [III, ch. 4]), Madame Defarge is the center of an unholy trinity, Clotho to their Lachesis and Atropos. She spins the thread of human history only for its eventual callous, statistical reckoning and severance at the daily executions: "The second tumbril empties and moves on; the third comes up. Crash!—And the knitting-women, never faltering or pausing in their work, count Two" (III, ch. 15).

In her fervor to send "Lucie" and her innocent family to death, Madame Defarge is an unsympathetic opponent to "the light." In earlier parts of the novel, however, she wins the reader's sympathy as a victim of the specific injustices committed against her and her family by the Evremondes and as a member of the general suffering peasantry of pre-revolutionary France. Furthermore, her hatred of abusive, established authority makes her an ironic "Lucifer" who justifiably rebels against the "divine right" of the "lords" of France. Dickens's narrator captures the aristocratic hubris which fuels her hatred by rewriting a verse of Paul's First Epistle to the Corinthians: "For the earth is the Lord's, and the fulness thereof" (10.26) becomes "The earth and the fulness thereof are mine, saith Monseigneur" (II, ch. 7). The aristocrats, especially the villainous characters of Monseigneur and Monsieur the Marquis, move the reader to another of the book's paradoxes, an ironic, sympathetic alliance with Madame Defarge.

The French aristocracy is, for the most part, satirically depicted in the collective character of "Monseigneur" as a false divinity whose materially luxurious, self-indulgent life reflects "the leprosy of unreality" characteristic of "the angels of that sphere." His sycophantic worshippers are hollow men, "Unbelieving Philosophers," "Unbelieving Chemists," and followers of the latest spiritualist fads ("Convulsionists," seekers of the "Center of Truth"). They reduce morality and salvation to fashionable correctness: "All the company at the grand hotel of Monseigneur were perfectly dressed. If the Day of Judgment had only been ascertained to be a dress day, everybody there would have been eternally correct." After taking his chocolate with the help of four attendants, Monseigneur condescends to appear briefly among his devotees, then ascends "to the remote region of the Circumference of Truth," has himself shut up "in his sanctuary by the chocolate sprites, and was seen no more." Leaving the gathering at Monseigneur's, the carriage of Monsieur the Marquis, more particularly characterized as the uncle of Charles Darnay, strikes and kills a young child. Irritated at the interruption of his journey and echoing Madame Defarge's remedy to the nation's ills, the Marquis callously remarks, "I would ride over any of you very willingly, and exterminate you from the earth." Madame Defarge witnesses the accident and knits on "with the steadfastness of Fate" (II, 7).

Despite the villainy of the nobility, Madame Defarge loses our sympathy in her blood-lust which transforms her into a dia-bolical "fallen angel." Obsessed with revenge, she creates and uses a mysterious system of signs and symbols which opposes the "sym-bolic" because its disjunctive function denies life's miracle. She "creates characters" only in order to later destroy them. Even the fragmented style of her "characterization" reduces the person to parts and mimics the fate she plans for her victims, namely to be cut into pieces, decapitated. She portrays the spy, John Barsad, for example, as she enters him into her register, as an inventory of human parts: "Age about forty, height about five feet nine, black hair, generally rather handsome visage, complexion dark, thin long and sallow face, aquiline nose but not straight, having a peculiar inclination towards the left cheek which imparts a sinister expression!" (Book II, ch. 16). Madame Defarge's writing with her knitting needles is thus the antithesis of Dickens's sym-bolic knitting with his pen. Her diabolical record "recalls to death," whereas Dickens resurrects and exorcises an unpleasant past to purge cultural memory by recalling and facing its offensive characters and incidents. Both reap what they "sew": Madame Defarge's death leaves her knitting indecipherable in the hands of The Vengeance, while Dickens's handiwork remains read by millions.

Madame Defarge "writes" as the agent of the diabolical side of the revolution, represented by the insatiable guillotine, which literally dissects its victims, guilty as well as innocent. Although it is the ultimate instrument of Madame Defarge's "re-membering," the guillotine simply continues the grisly "dis-memberments" of the abusive authorities which preceded it, such as having one's hands cut off or tongue torn out with pincers (I, ch. 1) or drawing and quartering, in which the victim is "sliced before his own face," has his inside "taken out and burnt while he looks on," his head chopped off, and his torso "cut into quarters" (II, ch. 2). In substituting the guillotine for the Christian symbol of the Cross, Madame Defarge and the revolution choose a rite of extinction over resurrection and become, in their new idolatry, no better than the tyrants they have replaced: "It [the guillotine] was the sign of the regeneration of the human race. It superseded the Cross. Models of it were worn on breasts from which the Cross was discarded, and it was bowed down to and believed in where the Cross was denied" (III, ch. 4).

The human sacrifices required by both the worshippers of the guillotine and the followers of the Cross are often associated with animal imagery, specifically the tiger and the lamb in Dickens and the lamb in John. In *A Tale* the tiger and lamb are at times ambivalent images which spill over into each other, suggesting the mixed and paradoxical realities they ultimately symbolize. For instance, Madame Defarge, the peasant revolutionaries, and even the marquis to some extent are all "lambs," victims in varying degrees. They are also, however, explicitly associated with the ferocious beauty of "tigers." Dickens's tigers suggest the brutality of the Revolution, but their physical beauty implies the fascinating attraction of violent social upheaval. The more obvious "lambs" in *A Tale* include selfless characters like Lucie and Jarvis Lorry, but more particularly the image applies to those who risk or lose their lives for others, such as Miss Pross, Dr. Manette, Charles Darnay, and, of course, Sydney Carton. Overall, the tigers and lambs in Dickens suggest William Blake's famous poems, "The Tyger" and "The Lamb," in *Songs of Innocence and of Experience* (1795), published shortly after the Reign of Terror (1793–94), the setting for most of Book III of *A Tale*. Dickens's animal imagery echoes Blake's in its paradoxical yoking of experience and innocence, terror and attraction, slaughter and survival.

Like William Blake's "The Tyger," Dickens's tigers capture the duality of the Revolution in its "fearful symmetry," its paradoxical beauty and ferocity. They are thus fitting images for the mixed attraction and repulsion of the novel's revolutionaries and aristocrats. When, for example, starving peasants greedily lap up spilled wine from a cask broken in front of Ernest Defarge's shop, they acquire "a tigerish smear about the mouth" (I, ch. 5). The scene rouses our sympathy, but contains its opposite, less attractive image of the tigerish peasantry as well. It portends the repugnant image of a people "changed into wild beasts" (II, ch. 14), frenzied devils, wine-stained and blood-smeared, sharpening hatchets, knives, bayonets, and swords at the grindstone to murder prisoners (III, ch. 2), "a company of Samaritans" tending the wounded one moment and plunging anew into dreadful butchery the next (III, ch. 4). The rebels rightly dethrone the false divinities of Monseigneur and Monsieur the Marquis, but the subsequent brutal execution of the displaced nobility, including Louis XVI and Marie Antoinette (III, ch. 4), and the willingness to execute Charles Darnay decrease our sympathy for the mob and qualify our dislike of the nobility. The same crowd which bestows "fraternal embraces" upon Darnay when he is freed after his first trial in Paris, "would have rushed at him with the very same intensity, to rend him to pieces and strew him over the streets" had he been convicted (III, ch. 6).

Similarly, Madame Defarge, who might well be considered a "lamb" in her patient, underserved suffering, aptly compares her desire for overdue justice to a restrained tiger and a devil: "When the time comes, let loose a tiger and a devil; but wait for the time with the tiger and the devil chained—not shown—yet always ready" (II, ch. 16). Like the brutal mob, who transform themselves from lambs into tigers, she too loses the reader's sympathy as the tigress who, about to search Lucie's apartments, threatens to tear Miss Pross to pieces: "imbued from her childhood with a brooding sense of wrong, and an inveterate hatred of a class, opportunity had developed her into a tigress. She was absolutely without pity. If she had ever had the virtue in her, it had quite gone out of her . . . 'I will tear you to pieces, but I will have you from that door.' '' Though Miss Pross survives her struggle with Madame Defarge, she emerges from it looking as if she has been fighting with a wild beast: "marks of griping fingers were deep in her face, and her hair was torn, and her dress . . . was clutched and dragged a hundred ways" (III, ch. 14).

Monsieur the Marquis's tiger-likeness is, at first glance, an attractive comparison between noble manner and animal grace. A closer look, however, shows the metaphor to be more critical of the Marquis because it exposes the artificial splendor of his refined dress and conduct and suggests that he is "handsomely diabolic," more a half-human,half-animal monster: "Rustling about the room, his softly-slippered feet making no noise on the floor, he moved like a refined tiger: —looked like some enchanted marquis of the impenitently wicked sort, in story, whose periodical change into tiger form was either just going off, or just coming on." Shortly after this description, the Marquis further devolves from animal to stone when, lying murdered by Gaspard (the father of the child killed by the Marquis's carriage), he is reduced to the stillness of one of the stone faces of men and lions which surround his chateau: "the stone face . . . lay back on the pillow of Monsieur the Marquis. It was like a fine mask, suddenly startled, made angry, and petrified" (II, ch. 9). Though the Marquis's murder may be viewed as an instance of poetic justice, it also makes him a victim, the first of many to be slaughtered in the violence of the revolution.

The tiger imagery in A Tale captures the fearful symmetry of Blake's "tyger," but its emphasis seems to be more on ferocity than beauty. As part of the riddle of human nature which Dickens portrays, the tiger images emphasize that violence and blood lust are genuine parts of being human, attractive and inherent in us along with our innocence and capacity for good. Just as the potential for resurrection lies dormant in every soul, the fatal attraction to the very thing that can destroy it is equally real and part of its latent wonder: "In seasons of pestilence, some of us will have a secret attraction to the disease—a terrible passing inclination to die of it. And all of us have like wonders hidden in our breasts, only needing circumstances to evoke them" (III, ch. 6). Like the tigers in A Tale, the "lambs" in Dickens's novel and John's Gospel admit the paradox of loss and gain, but seem to complement the tiger imagery by stressing the renewal which sacrifice brings more than the loss it requires.

The images of the "lamb" in John appear at the beginning, middle, and end of the gospel. Early in the text, John the Baptist, who himself was to become a sacrificial lamb, twice refers to Jesus as "the Lamb of God" (1.29, 36), an image which calls to mind the Paschal Lamb, the Agnus Dei, a symbol of the resurrected Christ. At the end of the gospel, the risen Jesus instructs Peter three times, "Feed my lambs. . . . Feed my sheep" (21.15–17). The lambs in the beginning and end of the text suggest a triple equation among the lamb, Jesus, and his followers, making them all sharers in a divinity which demands sacrifice and promises resurrection. One function of the lamb image, then, is to remove the divisions among animal, human, and divine planes of reality, to join and elevate them in what is essentially a sym-bolic union. In the middle of the book, the lamb image is elaborated in the parable of "The Good Shepherd" (10.1–18) (found only in John) which presents yet another triple equation. Jesus identifies himself with the door to the sheepfold ("I am the door of the sheep" [10.7]), and with the shepherd ("I am the good shepherd" who "giveth his life for the sheep" [10.11, 14–15]). As before, the equation suggests the mysterious union of separate entities, a paradox the hearers cannot grasp: "This parable spake Jesus unto them: but they understood not what things they were which he spake unto them" (10.6). The earlier and later associations of the lamb with God and resurrection combined with the human lambs in the parable of the Good Shepherd symbol-ize John's concern with both theological as well as ethical values.

For the most part, Dickens's lambs, like John's, are loving, sacrificial "scape-sheep" whose suffering and/or death bring life to others. Miss Pross, Dr. Manette, and Charles Darnay all suffer varying degrees of loss, small "deaths," because of their self-sacrifice. They, in turn, are all recalled to life because of the literal death of Sydney Carton, the most famous of Dickens's sacrificial lambs. Carton's heroic death not only restores the novel's lambs to life, but also ensures the survival of his own name and memory. Ironically, in two instances Dickens's lamb imagery extends to some less than sympa-thetic characters, John Barsad and Roger Cly. Barsad and Cly, who are referred to as "black sheep" (III, ch. 9), are traitors, spies or "sheep" ("Sheep was a cant word of the time for a spy . . . " [III, ch. 8], in a novel that celebrates fidelity. Barsad worries as Carton is on his way to the guillo-tine, "Has he sacrificed me?" (III, ch. 15). Cly, a "friend and fellow-Sheep" of Barsad's, who "spoke of himself as pasturing in the country prisons" (III, ch. 8), turns up alive in Paris after his "funeral" in London where he was mistakenly believed to be "Dead as Mutton" (II, ch. 14). Barsad and Cly are ultimately slaughtered themselves on the guillotine and included among the revolution's victims, denied the resurrection enjoyed by Miss Pross, Dr. Manette, Charles Darnay, and Sydney Carton.

Miss Pross loses her hearing in risking her life for her mistress, Lucie Manette. She has served Lucie with "pure love and admiration" since Lucie was a child. Her devotion was "free from any mercenary taint," causing Mr. Lorry to station her "much nearer to the lower Angels" than many of the wealthy ladies who had accounts at Tellson's (II, ch. 6). Miss Pross's life of selfless service culminates in her fight with Madame Defarge, when she de-clares, "I am a Briton . . . I am desperate. I don't care an English Twopence for myself. I know that the longer I keep you here, the greater hope there is for my Ladybird'' (III, ch. 14). When Madame Defarge the tigress is slain by her own pistol, Miss Pross the lamb survives, but gains her victory at the loss of her hearing when the gun discharges.

As a young and innocent idealist, Dr. Manette is imprisoned for his attempt to bring the Evrémondes to justice, but his sacrifice paradoxically becomes the source of his power to later free Charles (himself as Evrémonde) from La Force: ''For the first time the Doctor felt, now, that his suffering was strength and power. For the first time he felt that in that sharp fire, he had slowly forged the iron which could break the prison door of his daughter's husband, and deliver him'' (III, ch. 4). Despite the mixed success he has at keeping Charles out of the Defarges' hands, Dr. Manette survives his sacrificial efforts, ''aged and bent, but otherwise restored, and faithful to all men in his healing office, and at peace'' (III, ch. 15).

Reversing Miss Pross's kindness of servant to mistress, Charles Darnay himself risks his life to come to the aid of his servant, Theophile Gabelle, and nearly loses his life twice as a result. His selflessness leads to his imprisonment, a symbolic death of his aristocratic roots and a descent into a hell peopled with the ghosts of fellow aristocrats: ''Charles Darnay seemed to stand in a company of the Dead. Ghosts all!'' Even Darnay's gaoler appears himself a dead man, who was ''so unwholesomely bloated, both in face and person, as to look like a man who had been drowned and filled with water.'' In his tomb-like cell the vermin on his cot remind him of his own impending condition: ''Now am I left, as if I were dead. . . . And there in these crawling creatures is the first condition of the body after death'' (III, ch. 1). Darnay is recalled to life, however, first through the efforts of Dr. Manette and, a second time, by Sydney Carton's heroically taking his place at the guillotine.

Sydney Carton is the most important of the lambs of the novel because his sacrificial death saves the lives of all the others, making him a ''good shepherd'' as well. His literal death, however, is preceded by a figurative death and resurrection similar to Charles Darnay's. Early in the novel, Carton is depicted as a dead man, a wastrel always more intoxicated than not, exiled from all the living. As he dines with Darnay after the trial in London, Carton tells him: ''I care for no man on earth, and no man on earth cares for me.''[7] When Darnay leaves, Carton remains at the table in a drunken stupor, ''asleep on his arms . . . and a long winding-sheet in the candle dripping down upon him'' (II, ch. 4). A brief sleep, followed by a night's work for Mr. Stryver, leads Carton again to a sad sleep on a ''pillow . . . wet with wasted tears,'' as the sun rises ''sadly, sadly . . . upon no sadder sight than the man of good abilities and good emotions, incapable of their directed exercise.'' Carton's zombie existence is like the overcast day he faces, ''a scene like a lifeless desert . . . a desert all around . . . the wilderness before him'' resembling his own "mirage of honourable ambition" (II, ch. 5). Unlike the Marquis, Carton evolves from his death-in-life condition to become human and then to survive even his own physical death. His evolution is the result of his selfless and unrequited love for Lucie Manette.

In a rare intimate conversation with Lucie, Carton confesses: "I am like one who died young. All my life might have been." Lucie asks, "Can I not recall you . . . to a better course?" but she has, in fact, already recalled him through her role as "light" and "golden thread." She ensures Carton's further progress by receiving his promise: to embrace "any sacrifice for you and for those dear to you." Lucie's "light" and the sun itself brighten Carton's dark world and kindle the light dormant within him.

On the day of his actual death, the sunrise illuminates a life so often "overshadowed" by the "cloud of caring for nothing," a "fatal darkness, [which] was very rarely pierced by the light within him" (II, ch. 13). On the previous evening, Carton walks in a night which seemed "as if Creation were delivered over to Death's dominion. But, the glorious sun, rising, seemed to strike those words, that burden of the night, straight and warm to his heart in its long bright rays. . . . [A] bridge of light appeared to span the air between him and the sun . . . " (III, ch. 9). Earlier in this chapter, Carton himself becomes such a "bridge of light" when, like St. Christopher, he carries a small child not over a river, but "across the street through the mud"; and, later in the novel, he performs a similar action by carrying Lucie to a coach after she faints in the courtroom at the sentencing of Darnay (III, ch. 11). Sydney Carton's figurative nocturnal death and his resurrection at dawn ends with his repetition of the words from John, "I am the resurrection and the life" (III, ch. 9), a prayer he later repeats on the scaffold.[8] Beyond its conventional meaning of faith and hope in a spiritual afterlife, Carton's prayer suggests the new human power the newly-resurrected Carton has to recall Darnay and the other lambs to life through his literal sacrificial death.

Like John's and Dickens's tigers and lambs, the "double" contributes another recurrent image of paradox to the gospel and the novel. Doubles suggest both an increase and diminishment, a "doubling" and a "halving": twins, for example, double a person, but the existence of the other calls attention to the incomplete halfness of each. As the simultaneously opposite and synonymous prefixes "sym" (along with, together) and "di" (twice, twofold, double) suggest in the concurrent "symbolic" and "diabolic" movements of both works, doubles can and do function paradoxically, doubly, further reinforcing the tone of riddle and mystery in both works. The doubles in John include an interesting repetition of John the Baptist in John the Evangelist and brief appearances by Thomas, the doubting apostle who is also called "the Twin." The doubles in *A Tale* are more elaborate than those in John, but both offer variations on their common, central theme of resurrection.

By writing his gospel, John the Evangelist doubles the witnessing function which he attributes to John the Baptist. What he says of the Baptist is also true of himself: "He was not that Light, but was sent to bear witness of that light" (1.8). Both are enlighteners and precursors of Christ; both are voices crying in the desert. Another double, Thomas the Twin, is ready to die with Jesus, who is in danger of being stoned when he returns to Bethany, the village of Lazarus. Thomas courageously volunteers, "Let us also go, that we may die with him" (11.16). When Jesus appears to his disciples after his resurrection, however, Thomas's faith slackens, and he refuses to believe unless he might touch Jesus' wounds. Eight days later, when Jesus appears again and invites Thomas to place his hand in his wounds and side, Thomas believes and acknowledges him as "My Lord and my God" Jesus' mild admonition to Thomas is a reminder of the insufficiency of the senses and the need for faith to transcend the physical: "because thou hast seen me, thou hast believed: blessed are they that have not seen, and yet have believed" (20.24–29).

The Johns in the gospel illustrate the comprehensive strength of their faith, both before Christ's coming in the Baptist's ministry of preaching and baptizing and after his physical departure in the Evangelist's written record. Their double faith contrasts to Thomas's, whose twin we never meet and whose faith is half-hearted in its reliance on physical evidence. The doubles in John thus complement each other and emphasize that knowledge of the Word depends more on word-signs than demonstrable proof as the links to the mysteries they signify.

Doubles abound in A Tale, which is, after all, about two cities. There are twins, look-alikes, split personalities, multiple persons with a single name and appearance, and single persons with multiple names or functions. The most obvious doubles in the novel are Sydney Carton and Charles Darnay, whose striking resemblance to each other saves Darnay's life twice. Darnay/ Evrémonde has two names, feels allegiance to two countries, and sees his mirror image in the glass above him at the Old Bailey, a mirror which has reflected the ghostly images of countless others who have stood before it: "Haunted in a most ghastly manner that abominable place would have been, if the glass could ever have rendered back its reflections" (II, ch. 2). Carton doubles too as a "John the Evangelist" figure in his "prophecy" at the end of the novel and as a "John the Baptist" figure in his associations with the "wilderness" and his eventual beheading. Following his dinner with Darnay, Carton reflects aloud, talking to his mirrored image as if to another (II, ch. 4). All these ghostly reflections are images of death and resurrection. They reiterate in detail what Dickens accomplishes in the novel generally by his recreating a verbal past which is vanished but remarkably like "the present period" (I, ch. 1).

Some of the novel's split-personalities win our sympathy, for example, Dr. Manette in his defensive regressions to his shoemaker self, or Mr. Lorry, who prides himself on being a mere man of business ("I have no feelings; I am a mere machine" [I, ch. 4]), while he is in fact Manette's dear friend. For many of the novel's doubles, however, more is less. The Evrémonde twins are doubly villainous, and even so relatively harmless a character as Jeremiah Cruncher is a less than attractive inspiration to his look-alike son, young Jerry, who wants to be a "resurrection man" like his father. John Barsad, we discover, is in reality Miss Pross's brother, Solomon. In bearing false witness at Charles Darnay's trial, as a forger, and as a spy for both England and France, he reveals his duplicitous character, which is also reflected in his face: "the patriot, Barsad, was a hired spy and traitor, an unblushing trafficker in blood, and one of the greatest scoundrels upon the earth since accursed Judas—which he certainly did look rather like"(II, ch. 3).[9]

The single name "Jacques" both multiplies and diminishes the insurgents. It connotes both the collective strength of the peasantry and the anonymity they assume as brutal members of the mob. Similarly, the contrary sympathy and fear which the peasantry arouses as sufferers like Christ in one instance and as beheaders, in contrast to John the Baptist, in another, are reflected in Dickens's depicting them as doubles for Christ in one instance and a reverse John the Baptist in another.

Shortly before the death of the Marquis, in a scene set near a country cemetery, the narrator describes a wooden crucifix with a sculpture of Christ that resembles its peasant sculptor: "At the steepest point of the hill there was a little burial-ground, with a Cross and a new large figure of Our Saviour on it; it was a poor figure in wood, done by some inexperienced rustic carver, but he had studied the figure from the life—his own life, maybe—for it was dreadfully spare and thin." Afterwards, a widowed peasant petitions the Marquis, as he passes the cemetery, for a memorial for her dead husband. When the Marquis indifferently asks, "Can I restore him to you?" she responds, "My petition is that a morsel of stone or wood, with my husband's name, may be placed over him to show where he lies. Otherwise, the place will be quickly forgotten . . . " (II, ch. 8). The Marquis, who had earlier mumbled his wish that the peasantry be exterminated, ignores the request and drives on.

The peasant wood-carver, ironically, has already created a fitting memorial for the woman's husband in the crucifix whose sculpted Christ resembles both the artist and the other nameless peasants it memorializes. The scene portrays Christ and the peasants as doubles, and contrasts the sculptor's humble power with the impotence of the Marquis to "restore" the dead. The peasant wood-carver's art, like Dickens's fiction, recalls the dead and keeps those who see it from forgetting. The mirror image of the peasantry as Christ complements and contrasts with their resemblance to John the Baptist.

Two of the gospels portray John the Baptist as an unkempt wanderer dressed in camel's hair and a leather loin-cloth, eating locusts and wild honey (Matthew, 3.4; Mark, 1.6). In John, Christ speaks of the Baptist as "a burning and a shining light" (5.35) before he refers to himself as the "light of the world" (8.12). The peasant double of John the Baptist in Dickens's novel resembles his New Testament counterpart in outward appearance: he is a "rough figure . . . shaggy-haired . . . of almost barbarian aspect . . . [clothed in] the rough medley dress of home-spun stuff and hairy skins of beasts." He does not, however, bear witness to the light of Christ, but to the destructive flames of burning châteaux set afire by rioters: "Presently the château began to make itself strangely visible by some light of its own, as though it were growing luminous." As the envoy of violence, he inspires the mender of roads who imagines men like him multiplied across the nation: "And when he lifted his eyes . . . he saw in his small fancy similar figures, stopped by no obstacle, tending to centres all over France" (II, ch. 23). The mender of roads, meanwhile, metamorphoses into the wood-sawyer who mimics the guillotine in his work as he menaces Lucie and her child: "See my saw! I call it my little Guillotine. La, la, la; la, la, la! And off his head comes!" (III, ch. 5) As a disciple of the peasant-Baptist, the wood-sawyer is the double and contrary of the wood-carver whose image of Christ resembles him so much.

The burning homes of the nobility are precursors of grislier lights to come when the insurgents hang the dismembered bodies of the dead from the city's lamp posts: "The time was to come, when the gaunt scarecrows of that region should have watched the lamplighter, in their idleness and hunger, so long, as to conceive the idea of improving on his method, and hauling up men by those ropes and pulleys, to flare upon the darkness of their condition" (I, ch. 5). One of the victims, Foulon, who feigns death but is discovered, is brought to the light: "he was hauled to the nearest street corner where one of the fatal lamps swung . . . twice he went aloft, and the rope broke, and they caught him shrieking; then, the rope was merciful, and held him, and his head was soon upon a pike, with grass enough in the mouth for all Sainte Antoine to dance at the sight of" (II, ch. 22).

The doubles in A Tale are like the echoes in the corner of Soho where Lucie and her family live: "The wonderful corner for echoes resounded with the echoes of footsteps coming and going, yet not a footstep was there" (II, ch. 6). Like the echoes, the many doubles in the novel—characters, incidents, allusions—develop the riddles evident in the novel's overture in book I. They are at once real and ghostly, present and past, repetitions and diminishments, paradoxical signs of the mystery of human experience, and examples of the verbal power Dickens uses to capture it. Patterns of food imagery in John and A Tale perform a similar function. In both, patterns of eating and being eaten are further images of the paradox of living.

In *The Power of Myth* Joseph Campbell explains the basic function of food as an image of living as an interdependency: "None of us would be here if we weren't forever eating. What you eat is always something that just a moment before was alive. This is the sacramental mystery of food and eating . . . I am food! I am an eater of food . . . But holding on to yourself and not letting yourself become food is the primary life-denying negative act" (217–18). Dickens's fiction celebrates food and meals in Campbell's sense as metaphors for social and spiritual communion as well as greed. His fictional feasts also contribute greatly to his reputation as a Christmas writer and place him in the larger tradition of New Comedy as well in its use of meals, money, and marriage as conventional signs of comic resolution. In his use of food and drink imagery, John too is very Dickensian and illustrates Campbell's point. More than the other three gospels, John's gospel offers a wealth of feasts, food, bread, fish, water, and wine. Four important instances of John's "food and drink" imagery include the Marriage Feast at Cana, the Samaritan woman at the well, Christ's discourse on the Eucharist, and Jesus' offering Judas bread at the Last Supper. The food images develop much like the miracles in his gospel, beginning as literal food and drink for the physical body and evolving into signs of spiritual nourishment, equated with Christ himself.

Jesus changes water to wine at Cana a bit reluctantly and only at his mother's request because his "hour is not yet come" (2.4). This, his first public miracle, prefigures his own marriage to his church and the eventual equation of water, wine, and blood as physical as well as spiritual lifegivers. In another instance, when his disciples leave to purchase food, Jesus asks the Samaritan woman to draw water for him at the well, but on this occasion he hints at a figurative, more satisfying drink: "Whosoever drinketh of this water will thirst again. But whosoever drinketh of the water that I shall give him shall never thirst; but . . . shall be in him a well of water springing up . . . " (4.10–25). When the disciples return and encourage Jesus to eat, he answers mysteriously, "I have meat to eat that ye know not of" (4.32).

Similarly, on a larger public scale, the feeding of five thousand with five barley loaves and two fishes, miraculous as it is, is more important as a preface to Jesus' lengthy discourse on the Eucharist as spiritual food: "Labour not for the meat which perisheth, but for that meat which endureth unto everlasting life, which the Son of man shall give unto you. . . . I am the bread of life: he that cometh to me shall never hunger; and he that believeth on me shall never thirst" (6.27–35). Jesus' equation of himself with the bread of life puzzles his hearers: "How can this man give us his flesh to eat?" (6.53) Still, he repeats that the meal of his body and blood will enable them to overcome death: "Whoso eateth my flesh, and drinketh my blood, hath eternal life; and I will raise him up at the last day" (6.54). In suggesting the power of "food" both to sustain physical life and to overcome mortality, John adds another rich image of resurrection to his gospel.

John's unique account of Judas' "communion" at the Last Supper suggests the reverse of Christ's offering himself as the bread of life. At the Last Supper, Jesus offers bread to Judas, even though Judas is his enemy: " 'one of you shall betray me. . . . He it is, to whom I shall give a sop, when I have dipped it.' And when he had dipped the sop, he gave it to Judas Iscariot, the son of Simon. And after the sop Satan entered into him" (13.21–27). Judas desecrates Christ's loving gift of "food." Remaining on the level of animal appetite, his eating the bread is a selfish act, a cannibalistic betrayal of Christ's love, signalled by a traitorous kiss, paid for with thirty pieces of silver, and climaxing in his suicide. Taking the earthly bread and rejecting Christ, Judas rejects selflessness, compassion, and communion, and yields to the diabolical which severs him from life. Dickens uses the same food imagery to portray the opposing changes in the roles of the peasants and Sydney Carton.

In *A Tale* the peasantry are eaten more than they themselves eat. There is little bread and the wine is thin. In contrast to the morning chocolate served by four strong men to Monseigneur (II, ch. 7), the scanty food supply on the French landscape reflects the starved, barren lives of the poor: "A beautiful landscape, with the corn bright in it, but not abundant. Patches of poor rye where corn should have been, patches of poor peas and beans, patches of most coarse vegetable substitutes for wheat. On inanimate nature, as on the men and women who cultivated it, a prevalent tendency towards an appearance of vegetating unwillingly—a dejected disposition to give up, and wither away." The poor who live in such a wilderness shred "poor onions and the like for supper . . . any such small yieldings of the earth that could be eaten," but pay so many taxes that "the wonder was, that there was any village left unswallowed" (II, ch. 8). Later, the hanging figure of the murderer of the Marquis over the town's fountain poisons the water: "How can the women and the children draw water . . . under that shadow!" (II, ch. 15). Lacking real food, the hungry peasant women feed on the hope for revenge in their knitting: "The mechanical work was a mechanical substitute for eating and drinking; the hands moved for the jaws and the digestive apparatus: if the bony fingers had been still, the stomachs would have been more famine-pinched" (II, ch. 16).

The scene of the broken wine cask in front of Ernest Defarge's shop reverses the peasants' role from prey to predators. They are depicted as brutal eaters, devourers of those who once fed off of them. Furthermore, the broken wine cask portends the spilling of blood on the new Cross of La Guillotine, whose victims were so much red wine for her "daily brought into light from the dark cellars of the loathsome prisons . . . to slake her devouring thirst" (III, ch. 5). The scene portrays a feeding frenzy, a ghoulish "communion" in which mud (a more fitting image for the dust-covered peasants than bread) and wine stand for body and blood: "There was no drainage to carry off the wine, and not only did it all get taken up, but so much mud got taken up along with it, that there might have been a scavenger in the street" (I, ch. 5). Subsequently, the once grimly sober peasantry are described as chronically "drunken patriots" (III, ch. 1) who feed grass to the severed head of Foulon (II, ch. 22).

Like John, Dickens combines and equates images of wine, human flesh (mud), and blood. When Gaspard scrawls the word "BLOOD" in wine on a wall, Defarge erases it "with a handful of mud" (I, ch. 5). The mixture of wine, mud, and blood suggests the humble but worthy poor and also their regression from humanity. Dancing the orgiastic Carmagnole, young maidens mince their delicate feet in a "slough of blood and dirt" (III, ch. 5). Ironically, the "ink" used by Dr. Manette to write his vengeful sentence of extermination for the Evrémonde family was made of "scrapings of soot and charcoal . . . mixed with blood" (III, ch. 10).

Once again, in moving from victims to victimizers, from the devoured to the devourers, the revolutionaries lose the reader's earlier sympathy. Sydney Carton, on the other hand, moves from "drinker" to "drink," from an alcoholic life to being himself yet another sip of wine for La Guillotine. When we first meet Sydney Carton, he smells of port wine and believes that the world "has no good in it for me—except wine like this" (II, ch. 4). Carton and Stryver share the "Bacchanalian propensities" common to their profession: "What the two drank together, between Hilary Term and Michaelmas, might have floated a king's ship" (II, ch. 5). On the night before he dies, however, Carton has a "last supper," but no strong drink, and on the previous night "he had dropped the brandy slowly down on Mr. Lorry's hearth like a man who had done with it" (III, ch. 12). In feeding the guillotine, Carton becomes the bread of life for the Darnays and wins his own immortality.

At his death Carton looks "sublime and prophetic," and Dickens allows him in a hypothetical utterance to speak prophetically after his death. In his surviving words Carton resembles both John the Baptist and John the Evangelist as well as Dickens himself. His last words to Lucie—"A life you love"—are remembered by Lucie's daughter and repeated to her grandchildren (III, ch. 11). And he lives on not only in Lucie's son, who is his namesake, but in the story of him told to Lucie's grandson (III, ch. 15). The prophecy of the book's ending recalls the beginning of book I with its "Spiritual revelations" of Mrs. Southcott and the Cock-lane ghost. The reader is brought full circle, like Mr. Lorry's view of his life: "As I draw closer and closer to the end, I travel in the circle, nearer and nearer to the beginning" (III, ch. 9). Divisions among future, past, and present dissolve in a symbolic eternal moment, phoenix-like.

A brief look at a minor character in *A Tale,* Jeremiah Cruncher, may provide a fitting conclusion for our discussion of the Gospel of John and *A Tale of Two Cities.* Jerry leads the double life of working as a messenger for Tellson's Bank by day and as a grave robber, a "resurrection man," by night. In a novel generally lacking in Dickensian humor, Jerry is not one of Dickens's more memorable comic characters, but his role partially and in an oddly humorous way reflects that of John and Dickens who are likewise "messengers" ("apostles") and "resurrection men." Jerry is a "fisherman," as John literally was before he became a disciple of Christ, when he became a figurative fisher of men. In his role of evangelist John recalls the dead to heal his readers, just as Jerry, less reputably, robs graves for medical experimentation. Jerry's name also reminds us of the prophet Jeremiah, who prophesized the destruction of Jerusalem, and his initials, "J.C.," suggest Jesus Christ who was thought to be the new Jeremiah, preaching love and not vengeance. John, Christ's "beloved disciple," preaches the gospel of love; Dickens elevates selflessness over vengeance and digs up the past to warn the present and foretell the future.[10]

The Gospel of John is one of the cornerstones of Christian faith, and *A Tale of Two Cities* echoes the spiritual function of John in its mythic dimension. As mirror images of each other, John's theology and Dickens's poetic prose are complementary guides for the human spirit, one with its eye on an other-worldly heaven, the other looking more to earth. If *A Tale* falls short of the greatest story ever told, it nevertheless remains one of the best stories ever written. To read it as a remarkable mythic re-vision of John as well is to include it rightfully among the works of great literature which Northrop Frye speaks of as "the range of articulate human imagination as it extends from the height of imaginative heaven to the depth of imaginative hell. Literature is a human apocalypse, man's revelation to man, and criticism is not a body of adjudications, but the awareness of that revelation, the last judgment of mankind." (105).

NOTES

1. I am most grateful to Diane Ward, a Canisius College student research assistant and an avid reader of British fiction, for her valuable help in the completion of this study. Thanks also to the undergraduates in my Dickens course, especially Paul Endres, for their interest and insight.
2. Andrew Sanders sees *A Tale of Two Cities* as an instance of Dickens's "meeting the despair occasioned by the horrors of the Victorian city with a hope for the continued awakening of the Christian conscience" (118). Sanders examines the

religious tone in five Dickens novels (*The Old Curiosity Shop, Dombey and Son, Bleak House, Our Mutual Friend,* and *The Mystery of Edwin Drood*), focussing on "the extent to which Dickens drew on his experience and on his faith in his treatment of death and resurrection in his work" (x). Dennis Walder likewise offers an excellent introduction to the religious dimensions of several of Dickens's novels, especially *Little Dorrit.* The "Introduction" describes "religion" in Dickens's works as his implicit expression of the "union of religious sentiment and humanitarian concern which was central for the Victorian conscience"(6).

3. For studies of John's literary skills, see Louis Boyer and R. Alan Culpepper. Janet L. Larson examines the complexity of Dickens's incorporation of Bible texts in *Oliver Twist, Dombey and Son, Bleak House, Little Dorrit,* and *Our Mutual Friend* and illustrates how his novels incorporate and revise Scripture in order to "conceive the new Mythus" (314). Jane Vogel meticulously traces the relationship between Dickens's works and the Bible, focussing on *David Copperfield* and *Great Expectations.* Vogel argues that Dickens was an "anti-formalist Christian bent on dramatizing those lost saving truths and spiritual directions that in his view Christianity alone reveals" (21). Chapter 2, "The Christian Dickens" is a valuable introduction to Dickens's understated and indirectly allusive use of the New Testament in both his fictional and non-fictional writings. While Vogel's study sees theology in Dickens's myth, my case is that Dickens uses theology as a vehicle *for* myth, not so much to direct the reader to the renewed practice of the code of Christian values of the New Testament as to incorporate the truths of John's Gospel into a new aesthetic vision which endorses but amplifies its biblical source.

4. William H. Marshall discusses the complexity of several image patterns in the novel (life-death antithesis, food, blood and wine) and rightly cautions the reader against the temptation to read *A Tale* allegorically: "They are essential to the full meaning of the novel, but because of their nature and function—they constitute a complex of symbolism rather than sheer allegory—the full meaning is indefinite, elusive, and uncertain" (45).

5. Lucie's role as "mother" to her dead and resurrected "son" is an exception to Dickens's usual depiction of King Lear-like fathers holding their Cordelias, what Leslie Fiedler (speaking of Little Nell) refers to as Dickens's "Protestant *Pietá*: the white-clad daughter, dying or dead, in the arms of the old man, tearful papa or grandfather" (264).

6. Mr. Stryver, always mindful of his own professional ambition, endorses extermination as a way of dealing with the rebels: "Among the talkers, was Stryver, of the King's Bench Bar, far on his way to state promotion, and, therefore loud on the theme: broaching to Monseigneur, his devices for blowing the people up and exterminating them from the face of the earth . . . (II, ch. 24).

7. Carton's remark resembles the comment by George Rouncewell in *Bleak House*, ch. 55, that when he enlisted in the army he was "making believe to think that I cared for nobody, no not I, and that nobody cared for me"; T. W. Hill in "Notes on *Bleak House*," *Dickensian* 40 (June 1944): 139, observes that George is here echoing a line from the song "The Miller of the Dee," found in Isaac Bickerstaffe's comedy *Love in a Village* (1762).

8. Vogel discusses Sydney Carton's night walk into the dawn in an illuminating passage: "Sydney Carton standing on a bridge of earth sees a mystic one of light spanning the air and linking the here and hereafter, the Two Cities of God. . . . And, in *TTC,* as one worthy Charles D., Charles Dickens, relates how another worthy Charles D., Charles Darnay, is delivered from death by the sublime self-sacrifice of a 'C' or Christ figure upon the 'Cross,' an act inspired by the love of Lucie, Light, and the recovery of a faith that looks past death ('I am the resurrection . . . '), and sealed in a world-redeeming sunrise in the Son of God, one begins to see with new eyes into the spirit, purpose, and art of 'C.D.' " (55, 76). Walder acknowledges the "systematic expression of Dickens' religious views" in *A Tale of Two Cities,* but finds Carton's final moments improbable and Dickens's purpose puzzling: "it is hard to know how far Dickens really holds the belief expressed at the end, or indeed, what it is, exactly, that he is trying to convey" (198).

9. Sanders refers to several characters (Manette, Jerry, Barsad, Carton) who lead double lives as examples of "how a wasted life can give way to one of worth" (204).

10. For further discussion of Jeremiah Cruncher's function in the resurrection theme of the novel, see Albert D. Hutter.

WORKS CITED

Ackroyd, Peter. *Dickens.* New York: HarperCollins, 1990.

The Holy Bible (King James Version). New York: Ivy Books, 1991.

Boyer, Louis. *The Fourth Gospel.* Westminster: Newman, 1964.

Campbell, Joseph. *The Power of Myth.* New York: Doubleday, 1988.

Culpepper, R. Alan. *Anatomy of the Fourth Gospel: A Study in Literary Design.* Philadelphia: Fortress, 1983.

Dickens, Charles. *A Child's History of England.* Oxford: Oxford U, 1958.

———. *The life of Our Lord.* Philadelphia: Westminster, 1934.

———. *A Tale of Two Cities.* Oxford: Oxford UP, 1949.

Fiedler, Leslie. *Love and Death in the American Novel.* New York: Dell, 1960.

Frye, Northrop. *The Educated Imagination.* Bloomington: Indiana UP, 1964.

Hutter, Albert D. "The Novelist as Resurrectionist: Dickens and the Dilemma of Death," *Dickens Studies Annual* 12 (1983): 1–39.

Larson, Janet L. *Dickens and the Broken Scripture.* Athens: The U of Georgia P, 1985.

Marshall, William H. "The Method of *A Tale of Two Cities*," in Charles E. Beckwith (ed.), *Twentieth Century Interpretations of A Tale of Two Cities*, Englewood Cliffs: Prentice-Hall, 1972, 44–51.

Sanders, Andrew. *Charles Dickens, Resurrectionist*. New York: St. Martin's 1982.

Vogel, Jane. *Allegory in Dickens*. University, Alabama: The U. of Alabama P, 1977.

Walder, Dennis. *Dickens and Religion*. London: George Allen & Unwin, 1981.

Williams, Raymond. *The English Novel from Dickens to Lawrence*. London: Hogarth P, 1984.

A Tale of Two Cities: Theology of Revolution

David Rosen

At the Royal George Hotel in Dover, Mr. Lorry encounters, for the second time in his life, the heroine of the novel.

> As his eyes rested on [her], a sudden vivid likeness passed before him, of a child whom he had held in his arms on the passage across that very Channel, one cold time, when the hail drifted heavily and the sea ran high. The likeness passed away, say, like a breath along the surface of the gaunt pier glass behind her, on the frame of which, a hospital procession of negro cupids, several headless and all cripples, were offering baskets of Dead Sea fruit to black divinities of the feminine gender—and he made his formal bow to Miss Manette. (52)[1]

The moment is epiphanic. Mr. Lorry is not alone in feeling the past's mysterious, even ghostly, influence on the present. The pier glass, which, taken by itself, might suggest simply an innkeeper's fondness for exotic decor, circumscribes Lucie in a particularly sinister manner. The "short, slight, pretty" Frenchwoman, with her "quantity of golden hair, [and] pair of blue eyes" (52), contrasts sharply with the deformed—threatening, perhaps—pagan figures behind her. For an instant, Dickens has raised his action to the level of myth; he has also expressed many of his novel's main concerns in microcosm. His analysis of the French revolution in *A Tale of Two Cities* operates primarily on two grounds—myth and metaphysics—and his critique of the insurgents is ultimately a religious one. The germs implicit in this passage proliferate in the succeeding narrative.

In *The Golden Bough,* first published some thirty years after *A Tale of Two Cities,* Sir James Frazer traces the genesis and morphology of ancient Mediterranean vegetation rites. As Frazer explains, Adonis, Attis, and Osiris were divine or semi-divine figures, whose violent deaths and miraculous

rebirths insured the harvest's seasonal decay and growth. Since the fertility
of the land was contingent on the well-being of these gods, a complex system
of rituals was introduced to insure their strength:

> Men now attributed the annual cycle of change primarily to corresponding
> changes in their deities, . . . and thought that by performing certain magical
> rites they could aid the god who was the principle of life, in his struggle with
> the opposing principle of death. They imagined that they could recruit his failing
> energies and even raise him from the dead.   (324)

Not surprisingly, these rituals typically involved the shedding of human blood,
as persons were sacrificed in stead of the god. The Greek cult of Dionysus
(the Roman Bacchus) was particularly colorful: like the Egyptian Osiris,
Dionysus was cut to pieces by his enemies, only to rise reborn from the earth.
His worshippers, often in a state of wild intoxication, would devour their
victim (in later years, a bull), after treating him to a similar demise. Frazer
discusses the myth of Pentheus, familiar from Euripides' *Bacchae*:

> The [legend of Pentheus' death] may be . . . [a distorted reminiscence] of a
> custom of sacrificing divine kings in the character of Dionysus and of dispersing
> the fragments of their broken bodies over the fields for the purpose of fertilizing
> them. It is probably no mere coincidence that Dionysus himself is said to have
> been torn to pieces at Thebes, the very place where according to the legend the
> same fate befell king Pentheus at the hands of the frenzied votaries of the vine-
> god.   (392)

Dickens, writing long before Frazer, seems to understand both the significance
and the enduring power of such rituals; in his hands, the French revolution
follows the pattern of pagan fertility rites.

The centuries of aristocratic rule have left France a wasteland. In the most
palpable, physical sense, the rapacity of the nobility has emptied the national
coffers, and left the countryside barren. The Parisian elite has the ''truly
noble idea, that the world was made for them. The text of [Monseigneur's
order runs] 'The earth and the fulness thereof are mine, saith Monseigneur' ''
(135). As a result, the provinces—and the Evrémonde estate in particular—are desolate:

> Patches of poor rye where corn should have been, patches of poor peas and
> beans, patches of most coarse vegetable substitutes for wheat. On inanimate
> nature, as on the men and women who cultivated it, a prevalent tendency
> towards an appearance of vegetating unwillingly—a dejected disposition to give
> up, and wither away.   (143–44)

The blight is also spiritual and psychological. By attempting a sort of timeless permanence, and thus denying biology, the aristocratic ethos runs counter to normal, fertile human instinct. Monseigneur's drawing room is a menagerie wherein "charming grandmammas of sixty [dress and sup] as at twenty," and "it [is] hard to find . . . one solitary wife, who, in her manners and appearance, [would own] to being a mother" (137). The life of peasants is also unfruitful. In perhaps the novel's cruellest scene, soldiers play upon a common taboo and allow an executed man's blood to run into a village well, knowing that the community will be obliterated: "He is hanged there forty feet high—and is left hanging, poisoning the water . . . It is frightful, messieurs. How can the women and children draw water!" (201).[1] Within a few years, the Evrémonde estate, formerly in decline, is empty:

> Far and wide lay a ruined country, yielding nothing but desolation. Every green leaf, every blade of grass and blade of grain, was as shrivelled and poor as the miserable people. Everything was bowed down, dejected, oppressed and broken. Habitations, fences, domesticated animals, men, women, children, and the soil that bore them—all worn out. . . . Monseigneur had squeezed and wrung it, . . . had made edifying spaces of barbarous and barren wilderness. (256–57)

Dickens comments, in an ironic aside, that the aristocracy is "a great means of regeneration" (153); in the most ghoulish and literal sense possible, he is right. Even in their less bloodthirsty moments, the revolutionaries resemble dionysian maenads. The unearthly dance Darnay observes as he enters the country—

> After long and lonely spurring over dreary roads, they would come to a cluster of poor cottages, not steeped in darkness, but all glittering with lights, and would find the people, in a ghostly manner in the dead of night, circling hand in hand round a shrivelled tree of Liberty, or all drawn up together singing a Liberty song   (278)

—expands later into the Carmagnole, a "dance of five thousand demons" (307). When the mob turns homicidal, its impulse is plainly cannibalistic, with its victims often torn limb from limb. Jacques Three, the most savage of Defarge's cohorts, is at Darnay's second trial a "life-thirsting, cannibal-looking, bloody-minded juror" (345). Later, he relishes the thought of Lucie's beheading: "Ogre that he was, he spoke like an epicure" (388).[3] After his first trial, Darnay is astonished by the affection of people who,

> carried by another current, would have rushed at him with the same intensity, to rend him to pieces and strew him over the streets   (314)

During the La Force massacres, the murderers' "hideous countenances [are] all bloody and sweaty, awry with howling, and all staring with beastly excitement and want of sleep. . . . Some women [hold] wine to their mouths that they might drink'' (291). The ''vortex'' of the insurgence, naturally enough, is a wine-shop.

The long sequence surrounding the death of Foulon brings the action closest to its primordial roots. As in Euripides' play, the most brutal Bacchantes are women. Dickens's paganism (starting with the Royal George pier-glass) is largely a matriarchal affair; here the reaction of the women to Foulon's discovery bears no trace of civilization (Gilbert 256):

> The drum was beating in the streets . . . and The Vengeance, uttering terrific shrieks, and flinging her arms about her head like all the forty Furies at once, was tearing from house to house, rousing the women. The men were terrible . . . but the women were a sight to chill the boldest. . . . They ran out with streaming hair, urging one another, and themselves, to madness with the wildest cries and actions. . . . With these cries, numbers of the women, lashed into blind frenzy, whirled about, striking and tearing at their own friends until they dropped into a passionate swoon, and were saved only by the men belonging to them from being trampled under foot.   (252)

At the height of the delirium, the women's deepest motive comes out:

> Give us the blood of Foulon, Give us the head of Foulon, Give us the heart of Foulon, Give us the body and soul of Foulon, *Rend Foulon to pieces, and dig him into the ground, so that the grass may grow from him.* (252, italics mine)

And so, he is dismembered, and his mouth stuffed with grass. As Dickens puts it, the Terror ''has set a great mark of blood upon the blessed garnering time of harvest'' (283).

Although pagan in origin, the revolutionaries' acts are disconcertingly close, formally, to Christian sacrament. As Frazer recognizes, both Christianity and vegetation cults commemorate, through the symbolic or literal consuming of flesh and drinking of blood, the sacrifice of a man-god whose death and resurrection have delivered the community (360, 481). Indeed, as the revolution progresses, its practices seem both to parallel and reverse those of Christianity. The first Parisian scene hints already at the confusion to come; the breaking of a wine-cask, at first a cause for celebration, gradually develops ominous, eucharistic overtones:

> Those who had been greedy with the staves of the cask, had acquired a tigerish smear about the mouth; and one tall joker so besmirched, . . . scrawled upon a wall with his finger dipped in muddy wine-lees—BLOOD. The time was to come, when that wine too would be spilled on the street-stones, and when the stain of it would be red upon many there.

The insurrection takes hold, and the two fluids become almost interchangeable. At the grindstone, ''what with dropping blood, and what with dropping wine, . . . [all the murderers'] wicked atmosphere seemed gore and fire" (291; Glancy 108–10). By the culmination of the novel, during the terror, the sacrament has been perversely realized. At the scaffold, human "wine" is miraculously transformed into blood; tumbrils "carry the day's wine to La Guillotine" (399). In a brilliant extended metaphor, Dickens compares the Conciergerie's basement to a wine cellar:

> The Condemned . . . gentle born and peasant born; all red wine for La Guillotine, all daily brought into the light from the dark cellars of the loathsome prisons, and carried to her through the street to slake her devouring thirst.
>
> (304)

The guillotine, as the official center of revolutionary ritual, is itself of course sanctified. First a "sharp female, newly born" (383), then "canonized" as the "Little Sainte Guillotine" (307), and finally a goddess, the "retributive instrument" (404) replaces the Cross as the symbol of, and means towards, national fruition.

> It was the sign of the regeneration of the human race. It superseded the Cross. Models of it were worn on breasts from which the Cross was discarded, and it was bowed down to and believed in where the Cross was denied.

Vegetation myths reach from the rebellion's faith, to annex the forms of Catholic worship (Glancy 117).

While the presence of these myths in the deep structure of Dickens's narrative is beyond dispute, the matter of how they got there is not. Dickens's education was not wide, and as seen, Frazer's revelations were, in 1859, three decades away.[4] All attempts to explain this phenomenon—a creative response to the depiction of blasphemy? a strong connection to peasant (or pagan) culture? pure coincidence? —must, with one exception, remain unsubstantiated. The only extant paper-trail, evident as early as the novel's preface, leads to "Mr. Carlyle's wonderful book" (29), *The French Revolution*. Dickens's reliance on Carlyle for facts and imagery has long been documented; an overwhelming amount of telling detail is transferred intact from one work to the other. Madame Defarge is a near relation to "brown-locked Demoiselle Théroigne" of the "haughty eye and serene fair countenance" (I. 204). Her husband probably corresponds to "Cholat the wine-merchant," who at the Bastille becomes "an impromptu canoneer" (I. 154–55).[5] The broad outlines of Dickens's mythic conception are clearly perceptible, furthermore, in the earlier book. Carlyle, too, recognizes in the revolution's most violent moments the replacement of Christianity by heathen matriarchy. While "sullen is the male heart, . . . vehement is the female, irrepressible" (I. 200); the women are "dancing Bacchantes" (I. 232), a "menadic host," possessed by "inarticulate frenzy" (I. 205). During the massacres at La Force, "the doomed man is . . . [conducted into] a howling sea; forth under an arch of wild sabres, axes and pikes; and sinks, hewn asunder'' (II. 152). A basis of the insurgence, Carlyle writes, ''seems to be the primitive one of Cannibalism: that *I* can devour *Thee*'' (I. 44). Civilization, he speculates, may simply be a ''wrappage, through which the savage nature . . . can still burst, infernal as ever'' (II. 328). He clearly perceives, finally, in the abolition of Christianity, the possible return to primitive devotion (Baumgarten 168–69). ''Man is a born idol-worshipper, *sight*-worshipper, so sensuous-imaginative is he; and also partakes much of the nature of an ape'' (II. 312). And yet, the depth and consistency of Dickens's portrait are hardly explained by Carlyle's history. While Carlyle hits upon ample and natural metaphors to describe savagery—Maenads, Bacchantes, Cannibalism—those metaphors are not unified into a single vision. That much of the *Tale*'s symbolic vocabulary has been drawn from *The French Revolution* is obvious; its synthesis, however, has not. The intuition that the French are following a particular, ritual, sacrificial pattern, a pattern that both departs from and parallels Christian custom, belongs, it would seem, to Dickens alone.[6] Whereas Dickens departs from fact, and portrays pre-revolutionary France as an infertile wasteland, Carlyle assures us that the harvest in 1789 was bountiful (Oddie 80). The connection, so explicit in the novel, between bloodshed and regeneration, is similarly absent from the *History*. The earlier work fails, finally, to include a strong thematic counter-example to balance the general destruction.

In *A Tale of Two Cities,* that counter-weight is provided by Sydney Carton. If the revolutionary cult has adopted blasphemously the forms of Catholic sacrament, Carton's life and death follow true Christian typology. Although Carton is obviously a double for Charles Darnay, he has even deeper, if less transparent, affinities to his moral opposite, Madame Defarge. Dickens plants minor details that bind the ''catechist'' (208) of revolution and its main sacrificial victim together. Besides similar biographies—the traumatic and formative death of a family member, their own violent, parallel deaths—they have similar talents. Both are distinguished by their retentive memories: Stryver's nickname for Carton is ''Memory'' (118). Carton explains to Darnay the full effect of his dissipation: ''The curse of these occasions is heavy on me, for I always remember them'' (236). In Paris, he recalls Barsad, whom he has not seen in seventeen years: ''You have a face to be remembered, and I remember faces well'' (327). Mr. Defarge, similarly, boasts of his wife's mnemonic capabilities: ''Jacques, . . . if madame my wife undertook to keep the register in her memory alone, she would not lose a word of it—not a syllable of it'' (202). Both also have the knack of seeming oblivious to their surroundings, while perceiving them minutely (Glancy 80). Just as Carton spends most of Darnay's first trial staring at the Old Bailey's ceiling, yet discerning his own facial similarity to the accused, and moving the narrator to comment, "this Carton took in more of the details of the scene than he appeared to take in" (107), so the hyper-observant Madame Defarge "knitted with nimble fingers and steady eyebrows, and saw nothing" (66). Dickens's technique of portraying ethical opposites as formally analogous bears fruit by novel's end.

The sequence of events immediately preceding (and following) Carton's death tells of spiritual conversion, and emulation of Christ (Hutter 20). Where he spends the first three quarters of the book in dissipation, as, interestingly, a young man of "Bacchanalian propensities" (116), his "fervent and inspiring" (374) behavior at the end, unlike that of the rabble, is *not* fueled by alcohol:

> For the first time in many years, he had no strong drink. Since last night he had taken nothing but a little light thin wine, and last night he had dropped the brandy slowly down on Mr. Lorry's hearth like a man who had done with it.
> (368)

As he wanders the streets, he contemplates his own demise in Jesus' words from John 11:

> I am the resurrection and the life, saith the Lord: he that believeth in me, though he were dead, yet shall live: and whosoever liveth and believeth in me, shall never die   (342)

—words that return to him on the scaffold. Shortly before execution, the seamstress comments, "[I should not] have been able to raise my thoughts to Him who was put to death, that we might have hope and comfort here today. I think you were sent to me by Heaven" (402). And indeed, though the guillotine is the profanest of crosses, Carton's death is a sort of crucifixion, occurring, like Jesus', at 3:00 in the afternoon. His final vision even promises a vague second coming: another Sydney Carton will return to this spot, as the "foremost of just judges" (404). Dickens sets the seal on Carton's conversion, at the very moment of death:

> The murmuring of many voices, the upturning of many faces, the pressing on of many footsteps in the outskirts of the crowd, so that it swells forward in a mass, like one great heave of water, all flashes away. Twenty-Three.

If the number seems random, one need only recall any Christian funeral:

> Yea, though I walk through the valley of the shadow of death, I will fear no evil; for thou *art* with me; thy rod and thy staff comfort me.   (Psalm 23:4)

Sydney Carton manifests the sacramental, sacrificial norm, from which revolutionary paganism has departed (Fielding 200).

This pattern of sacrifice and redemption is repeated, less dramatically, by several other characters. During the La Force massacres, Manette finds that his eighteen years of suffering have allowed him an odd power over the murderers. Miss Pross, who is as willing to give her life for Lucie as Carton is, suffers a similar destiny: her deafness is a variation on his death, and her description of the disaster prefigures his beheading. "There was first a great crash, and then a great stillness, and that stillness seems to be fixed and unchangeable, never to be broken . . . " (399). And of course, the novel is saturated with the theme of resurrection. As countless commentators have recognized, Manette, Darnay (twice), Cly and Foulon (ironically) and Jerry Cruncher (satirically) all resemble Carton in this fashion.

The difference between Carton's and Miss Pross's Christ-like sacrifices, and the bloodletting exacted by the revolution is a simple one: the former work, and the latter fails. Carton's death is an effective fertility-rite in the simplest way: he not only saves the lives of Darnay and Lucie, but allows them to have more children (Gilbert 263). The Terror, however, leaves France even more barren than before. Madame Defarge, dedicated to the "extermination" (369) of the entire Evrémonde family, is conspicuously childless. In a moment of high irony, Lucie begs her "as a wife and a mother, . . . [to] have pity on me and [not] exercise any power that you possess against my innocent husband. . . . Oh sister-woman, think of me. As a wife and mother!" At that moment, of course, Madame Defarge is contemplating the slaughter of Lucie's daughter. The post-revolutionary landscape is as blasted as ever—"impoverished fields that yielded no fruits of the earth, . . . diversified by the blackened remains of burnt houses"—and the concluding image of tumbrils cutting through the Paris mob, in a travesty of tillage, is profoundly pessimistic:

> As the sombre wheels of the six carts go round, they seem to plough up a long crooked furrow among the populace in the streets. Ridges of faces are thrown up to this side and to that, and the ploughs go steadily onward.   (400)

As a means, in the deep pagan sense, of regeneration, the revolution has failed. As foreshadowed at the Royal George Hotel, the revolutionaries have cultivated

> Dead Sea fruits, that tempt the eye,
> But turn to ashes on the lips.[7]

The failure of the revolution is, of course, ethical; the climactic comic-epic struggle between Madame Defarge and Miss Pross contrasts, in the plainest terms, Christian love and self-sacrifice with pagan blood-lust. As a means towards revitalization, mass murder is inevitably self-defeating: "It was in vain for Madame Defarge to struggle and strike; Miss Pross, with the vigorous

tenacity of love, always so much stronger than hate, clasped her tight . . . ''
(397). Dickens's analysis of the revolution's inadequacy is not confined to
ethics, however, but pursues the repercussions of myth to the level of metaphysics—specifically, to the questions of time, space, and causation.

Briefly, the book's metaphysic is Augustinian. That is, it maintains an
orthodox, Christian distinction between heaven and earth, the latter mutable,
flawed and historical, the former eternally perfect (Welsh 118, 147–48). No
Dickens novel keeps track of the passage of time quite so obsessively as *A
Tale of Two Cities.* 'Almost inconsequently, Madame Defarge's mad sister
rattles off the numbers on a clock (351), and Carton's party at the scaffold
numbers fifty-two, matching the cycle of weeks (Alter 21). The passing seasons are noted minutely, and provide a sort of *cantus firmus* to the action;
just as Darnay's departure for France, the beginning of his long decline, takes
place on the longest of days, June 21, 1792 (270), so Madame Defarge's
sister dies—spurring the great mechanism of revenge—on the darkest, December 21, 1757 (348). Even a whirling grindstone becomes the perfect metaphor for transience, "the great grindstone, Earth" (293). At the same time,
heaven is "an arch of unmoved and eternal lights" (81). No one is as aware
as Sydney Carton of the distinction between the two; at the guillotine, he
contemplates, with the seamstress, the hereafter:

> "Do you think . . . that it will seem long to me, while I wait for [my sister] in
> the better land where I trust both you and I will be mercifully sheltered?"
> "It cannot be, my child; there is no Time there, and no trouble there."
>
> (403)

By imposing an artificial mythic understanding of history onto national
affairs, the revolution effectively ruptures, in two ways, the dichotomy between secular and divine time. First, in the sheer, abrupt violence of their
revolt, the revolutionaries attempt to stop and restart history. On the one
hand, their course is apocalyptic: the mass sacrifice of an entire class, and
the destruction of its property, will definitively end an era. The burning of
the Evrémonde estate—and especially the four, pale burners—evokes the
Book of Revelation (Alter 18):

> Hail-clouds, rolling away, revealed bright bars and streaks of sky . . . East,
> West, North, and South, through the woods, four heavy-treading, unkempt fig-
> ures crushed the high grass and cracked the branches. . . . Four lights broke
> out. . . . Soon, from a score of the great windows, flames burst forth. . . . In the
> roaring and raging of the conflagration, a red-hot wind, driving straight from
> the infernal regions, seemed to be blowing the edifice away. (259–61)

On the other hand, the sansculottes endeavor to begin time afresh, as at the creation or the flood. Their efforts lead not to renewal, however, but to an odd, static *timelessness,* an unreal *suspension* of time:

> What private solicitude could rear itself against the deluge of the Year One of Liberty—the deluge rising from below, not falling from above, and with the windows Heaven shut, not opened! There was no pause, no pity, no peace, no interval of relenting rest, no measurement of time. Though days and nights circled as regularly as when time was young, and the evening and morning were the first day, other count of time there was none.   (301–02)

Metaphorically, they have turned France into a prison. In much of Dickens's fiction, the state of imprisonment—of lost autonomy—is depicted as one in which the forward motion of time has unnaturally been halted. Both Dorrit and Clennam, in *Little Dorrit,* lose their sense of duration while incarcerated (hallucinating a return to the Marshalsea, Dorrit's first act is to pawn his watch), and Manette is no different: he "loses" nine days after his daughter's wedding. In retrospect, his life seems "to have been stopped, like a clock, for so many years, and then set going again, with an energy that had lain dormant during the cessation of usefulness" (300). As he enters the country, Darnay perceives exactly what France has become.

> Not a mean village closed upon him, not a common barrier dropped across the road behind him, but he knew it to be another iron door in the series that was barred between him and England. The universal watchfulness so encompassed him, that if he had been taken in a net, or were being forwarded to his destination in a cage, he could not have felt his freedom more completely gone. . . . (275)

> While ingress into [Paris] . . . was easy enough, egress, even for the homeliest people, was very difficult.   (279)

In a self-defeating way, the stasis of France mimics heaven's permanence.

Second, since the revolutionary myth is an intensely narrative one, the uprising proceeds with a strong sense of providence, of fate: human endeavor falls into channels that have, in effect, been pre-determined. Deeds are realized rather than performed; both individual freedom and personal responsibility are strictly curtailed. If any figure in the novel believes herself an instrument in the hand of destiny, it is Madame Defarge. She is absolutely confident in the eventual fall of the nobility: "Vengeance and retribution require a long time; it is the rule" (207). She does not fear, even, being unable to take part in that fall: " 'Well,' said Defarge . . . 'We shall not see the triumph.' 'We shall have helped it,' returned Madame, 'Nothing that we do, is done in vain' " (208). Even after the bloodshed has begun, she looks forward to a further fulfillment, in the slaughter of the Evrémondes: [Defarge]

" 'At last it is come, my dear!' 'Eh well!' returned madame. 'Almost' " (256). Her most common gesture is grimly portentous: "[she pointed] her knitting-needle at little Lucie as if it were the finger of Fate" (296), and her very knitting evokes perhaps the Parcae and the Norns, the Greek and Norse spinners of doom: "[Madame Defarge] knitted on with the steadfastness of Fate" (143).[8] In the first chapter, Dickens evokes the road as a metaphor for life. Later, he populates it with figures representing destiny. By the penultimate chapter, Madame Defarge has become such an embodiment. Jerry Cruncher and Miss Pross prepare to leave Paris:

> Madame Defarge, taking her way through the streets, now drew nearer and nearer to the . . . lodging.
> And still Madame Defarge, pursuing her way through the streets, came nearer and nearer.
> Madame Defarge was drawing very near indeed.   (391–94)

In a situation so soaked with pre-destination, both free-will and accountability are somewhat trivialized. The irony of Madame Defarge's life is that she is committing at least as great a crime as the Evrémondes' by having Charles Darnay, whose deeds bear no relation to his punishment, who in fact has risked his life for her sake, executed.

The opposite view of individual enterprise is assumed, quite naturally, by Sydney Carton. If Madame Defarge sees everywhere the operations of fate, Carton is well aware of chance, and treats personal behavior as a series of educated wagers. This is especially the case as he nears his end, and his life, formerly aimless, acquires a sense of purpose. The novel is saturated with gambling, symbolic and otherwise: the French wine shops are populated by domino and dice players; Jerry Cruncher's term for the Common Era is "Anna Dominoes: apparently under the impression that the Christian era dated from the invention of a popular game, by a lady who bestowed her name on it" (85). Darnay, sentenced to death, has "drawn a prize in the lottery of Sainte Guillotine" (383). Most importantly, existence seems a card game, and people cards to be hazarded and lost. We might read the book's second paragraph—

> There was a king with a large jaw and a queen with a plain face, on the throne of England; there was a king with a large jaw and a queen with a fair face, on the throne of France   (35)

—or indeed encounter the "Joker" Gaspard, without batting an eyelash, but by book III, chapter 8, appropriately entitled "A Hand at Cards," the metaphor has become deadly earnest. Here Carton blackmails Barsad (and Cly), in order to save Darnay and his family. His opponent is untrustworthy, having both "[cheated] at dice, [living] by play" (98), and squandered his sister's possessions on speculation (126–27). As the title of the next chapter indicates, "the game is made." Unlike Madame Defarge, Carton is a figure of free agency, who makes his own destiny, and knows himself answerable (to put it mildly!) for his decisions. The number of prisoners executed at the end of the novel, 52, evokes not only the weeks of the year, but also a deck of cards—a brilliant metaphor for shared fortune, and a reminder of common mortality.

The novel justifies Carton's outlook, without quite slighting the question of destiny. In a letter written shortly after composing the *Tale,* Dickens suggests that fiction should aspire to imitate the workings of providence. Indeed, intimations of the divine will seem to permeate the text. (*Letters* [W. Collins] 3:124–25) Foulon's capture:

> At length the sun rose so high that it struck a kindly ray as of hope or protection, directly down upon the old prisoner's head. The favour was too much to bear; in an instant . . . St. Antoine had got him!   (253)

Individuals are entirely free in, and responsible for, their own actions—actions that yield necessary, providential consequences (Oddie 65–66). Beginning the final chapter, Dickens returns, for the last time, to the image of growth, to express this point:

> All the devouring and insatiate Monsters imagined since imagination could record itself, are fused in the one realisation, Guillotine. And yet, there is not in France a blade, a leaf, . . . which will grow to maturity under conditions more certain than those that have produced this horror. Crush humanity out of shape once more, under similar hammers, and it will twist itself into the same tortured forms. Sow the same seed of rapacious license and oppression over again, and it will surely yield the same fruit according to its kind.   (339)

And so, Carton, in his limited way, defeats the purpose of the revolution (to slaughter the Evrémondes), and is able to change the world for the better. In a book so concerned with injustice and judicial reform, it is important that the Darnay's unborn son shall engage successfully in that pursuit. Conversely, the revolution, in its hubris, has managed only to repeat the crimes of aristocracy, barbarism for barbarism (Kukich 67). Dickens's seemingly casual observation in book II chapter 8, that "the watching towers of Notre Dame, almost *equidistant from the two extremes,* could see . . . both [Monseigneur's rooms and St. Antoine]" (136, italics mine), proves prophetic; by the end, the insurgents and nobles have sinned equally. Perhaps no single incident better illustrates the novel's attitudes towards fatalism and autonomy than the culminating deaths of Madame Defarge and Sydney Carton. While the former, so confident of her destiny, dies, as it were, by mischance, the latter's end has an air of fulfillment. Dickens explains this ironic reversal in his correspondence with John Forster:

> I am not clear . . . respecting the canon of fiction which forbids the interposition of accident in such a case of Madame Defarge's death. Where accident is inseparable from the passion and action of the character, . . . it seems to me to become, as it were, an act of divine justice. [I oppose] her mean death, instead of a desperate one in the streets, which she wouldn't have minded, to the dignity of Carton's. Wrong or right, this was all design, and seemed to me to be in the fitness of things   (Letters 3:117)

Early into the book's composition, Dickens boasted to Forster, "I have got exactly the name for the story that is wanted; exactly what will fit the opening to a T. *A Tale of Two Cities*" (*Letters* 3:95) And yet, the title is only partly applicable to Paris and London. England, despite escaping revolution, is depicted as uncomfortably similar to France; indeed, if the novel's first paragraph signifies anything, it is that not much has changed in the succeeding seventy years. The English are as potentially "orgeish" as their counterparts across the channel:

> The form that was to be doomed [i.e., Darnay] to be so shamefully mangled, was the sight; the immortal creature that was to be so butchered and torn asunder, yielded the sensation. Whatever gloss the various spectators put upon the interest, . . . the interest was, at the root of it, Ogreish.   (93)

In action, similarly, the British mob yields little in mindless destructiveness to the Parisians:

> The crowd being under the necessity of providing . . . entertainment for itself . . . conceived the humor of impeaching casual passers-by . . . and wreaking vengeance on them. . . . Some score of inoffensive souls . . . were roughly hustled and maltreated. The transition to the sport of window-breaking, and thence to the plundering of public-houses, was easy and natural. At last . . . sundry summer-houses [were] pulled down, and some area railings pulled up, to arm the more belligerent spirits. . . . This was the usual progress of a mob.   (187–88)

If justice is suspended during the terror, the English over-extension of capital punishment is hardly preferable: the gallows "[took] today the life of an atrocious murderer, and to-morrow of a wretched pilferer who had robbed a farmer's boy of sixpence" (37). After Darnay is condemned in Paris, the narrator calls it an immolation "on the people's altar"—exactly the phrase he'd used at the Old Bailey: "[Barsad] had resolved to immolate the traitor . . . on the sacred altar of his country" (96). As a sign of differentiation, the title hardly applies to the French and English capitals.

Rather it draws on a familiar trope introduced by Augustine—a trope so familiar that the title can hardly *not* evoke it—the two cities of man and God (Welsh 57). The earthly sphere is an ethical one, and in this book, a Christian one, in which Biblical typology is fully operative; free agency is a gift and a responsibility. By introducing a counter-myth into their revolution, the French are guilty of all sorts of blasphemy, from the immorality of their bloodlust, through the open sacrilege of their co-opting Christian forms to express this immorality, to their arrogant, and ultimately stultifying attempt to collapse the dialectic between an historical world, and the eternal, providential heaven beyond.

NOTES

1. All page references to Charles Dickens. *A Tale of Two Cities,* ed. George Woodcock, London: Penguin, 1970.
2. Ewald Mengel discusses the blood Taboo in "The Poisoned Fountain: Dickens's Use of a Traditional Symbol in *A Tale of Two Cities,*" *Dickensian* 80, part 1 (Spring, 1984): 29. See also Frazer 227–30.
3. John Gross, "A Tale of Two Cities," *Dickens and the Twentieth Century,* ed. John Gross and Gabriel Pearson (Toronto: U of Toronto P, 1962) 193.
4. The details of Dickens' education are recounted in John Forster, *The Life of Charles Dickens,* ed. J. W. T. Ley (London: Cecil Palmer, 1928) Book I.
5. Michael Goldberg, *Carlyle and Dickens* (Athens: of Georgia P, 1972) 118–19. This book best enumerates the many details transferred from *The French Revolution* to *A Tale of Two Cities.*
6. Michael Timko, "Splendid Impressions and Picturesque Means: Dickens, Carlyle and *The French Revolution,*" *Dickens Studies Annual* 12 (1983): 181.
7. Thomas Moore, *Lalla Rookh,* pt. V.
8. See n-2, Mengel 28.

WORKS CITED

Alter, Robert. "The Demons of History in Dickens's *Tale,*" in *Charles Dickens's "A Tale of Two Cities": Modern Critical Interpretations,* ed. Harold Bloom. New York: Chelsea House, 1987.

Baumgarten, Murray. "Writing the Revolution." *Dickens Studies Annual* 12 (1983): 168–69.

Carlyle, Thomas. *The French Revolution.* London: Dent, 1980.

Dickens, Charles. *The Letters of Charles Dickens.* Ed. Walter Dexter. Bloomsbury: Nonesuch, 1938.

Fielding, Kenneth J. *Charles Dickens: A Critical Interpretation.* Boston: Houghton Mifflin, 1958.

Frazer, James. *The Golden Bough: A Study in Magic and Religion.* 1890; abr. ed., New York: Macmillan, 1934.

Gilbert, Elliot L. " 'To Awake from History': Carlyle, Thackeray, and *A Tale of Two Cities.*" *Dickens Studies Annual* 12 (1983).

Glancy, Ruth. *"A Tale of Two Cities": Dickens's Revolutionary Novel.* Boston: Twayne, 1991.

Hutter, Albert D. "The Novelist as Resurrectionist: Dickens and the Dilemma of Death." *Dickens Studies Annual* 12 (1983).

Kukich, John. "The Purity of Violence." In Bloom: see Alter.

Oddie, William. *Dickens and Carlyle: The Question of Influence.* London: Centenary P, 1972.

Welsh, Alexander. *The City of Dickens.* Cambridge: Harvard UP, 1968.

"It's Me Wot Has Done It!" Letters, Reviews, and *Great Expectations*

Timothy A. Spurgin

1.

In October of 1860, shortly after beginning work on *Great Expectations,* Dickens sent the first installment of the novel, along with a letter, to John Forster. In his letter, Dickens described the emerging story, noting its main features and commenting on its origins. "The book will be written in the first person throughout," he observed,

> and during these first three weekly numbers you will find the hero to be a boy-child, like David [Copperfield]. Then he will be an apprentice. You will not have to complain of the want of humor as in the *Tale of Two Cities.* I have made the opening, I hope, in its general effect exceedingly droll. I have put a child and a good-natured foolish man, in relations that seem to me very funny. Of course I have got in the pivot on which the story will turn too—and which indeed, as you remember, was the grotesque tragi-comic conception that first encouraged me. To be quite sure I had fallen into no unconscious repetitions, I read *David Copperfield* again the other day, and was affected by it to a degree you would hardly believe. (Forster 2:285)

First published by Forster in 1874, this letter has now been reprinted dozens of times, figuring into the work of scholars from Edgar Johnson and Ada Nisbet to Alexander Welsh and Anny Sadrin; and in almost every case, the letter has been used in exactly the same way: to prove that Dickens conceived of *Great Expectations* as an autobiographical work and thought of Pip as a surrogate for himself.[1]

It is no surprise, then, to find that the letter has been put to such uses by Dickens's two most recent biographers. For Fred Kaplan, the letter suggests that *Great Expectations* was to be "the ultimate reworking" of Dickens's life story (432): "From the start," Kaplan says, "he had no doubt that [the new book] would be autobiographical, and he soon reread *David Copperfield* in order to avoid unintentional repetition, 'affected by it to a degree you would hardly believe' " (432). For Peter Ackroyd, the letter shows that Pip was to be a version of the young Dickens:

> [*Great Expectations*] was to concern the adventures of a "boy-child, like David" but, in order to avoid any kind of unconscious repetition, "... I read *David Copperfield* again the other day, and was affected by it to a degree you would hardly believe ... " So did his past, inserted within the narrative of the earlier novel, still haunt him; even now as he was beginning the life of Pip, an anxious and guilt-ridden child, sensitive to the point of hysteria and altogether a very queer, small boy.   (884)

Having identified *Great Expectations* as an autobiographical novel, Kaplan and Ackroyd widen the scope of their arguments, linking the book not only to Dickens's boyhood traumas, but also to his midlife crises—and in particular to events such as the beginning of his relationship with Ellen Ternan and the break-up of his marriage to Catherine Dickens. Kaplan establishes these connections carefully, suggesting that Dickens responded to "one of the most painful, destructive periods of his life" (438) by "creat[ing] transmutations" of himself, his parents, and his loved ones (433–38). Ackroyd is much more dramatic, likening Dickens's recent experiences to a "fever which allow[ed] him to speak freely for the first time" (900). Yet in the end, both biographers arrive at the same conclusion, presenting *Great Expectations* as the result of a "fresh access of self-knowledge," one brought on by "the events of the last two years" (Ackroyd 900).

It is tempting to read *Great Expectations* as a product of Dickens's growing self-awareness, but little support for such a reading can be said to come from his letter to Forster. The letter does not announce or even suggest that *Great Expectations* is to be an autobiographical novel; it merely states that the story will be told in the first person by a male narrator. In fact, the letter serves less as a means of self-expression than as a vehicle for self-display and self-promotion. In writing to Forster, Dickens was not only confiding in his closest friend, but also communicating with his authorized biographer. He had been supplying Forster with material for well over a decade, and he must have known that Forster would want to save the letter for future reference. Indeed, he may well have expected Forster to paraphrase or quote from the letter—and may even have used the letter to guide Forster, dictating the terms in which his future biographer would describe the emergence of *Great Expectations*.[2]

The difficulties of dealing with letters have been most imaginatively engaged by Rosemarie Bodenheimer, whose *Real Life of Mary Ann Evans* begins with several intriguing generalizations about the letter's "cultural position on the boundary of public and private discourse" (8). Bodenheimer explains that because letters are "neither primarily private nor essentially public" (8), they should not be thought to offer direct access to an author's most deeply buried feelings: like novels themselves, she points out, letters are "acts of self-representation in writing" and thus may be taken, "to begin with, as fictions" (5). Bodenheimer comments on the curious status of published letters, noting that a "letter published in a collected correspondence becomes a new kind of object" (18), but she does not take up the case of letters written with an eye towards eventual publication, either in a collection or in a biography. In such cases, as I have tried to suggest, writers have good reason to think about the issue of self-representation, and good reason to wonder what will remain private and what will become public, since they know, despite pretenses to the contrary, that their letters are addressed to multiple audiences—addressed, that is, to a initial reader who is usually both confidant and collaborator, and then, through that person, to posterity itself.

What is Dickens telling *his* collaborator, then? What does he want Forster to see in *Great Expectations?* At the outset, his effort is simply to describe the emerging novel, to introduce the characters and hint at the nature of the plot. He also seems concerned, however, to identify *Great Expectations* as the work of a disciplined professional. His tone is flat, his syntax self-effacing ("The book will be written . . . "), and as he goes on, he is careful to qualify any expression of enthusiasm for his work: "I have made the opening, *I hope,* in its general effect exceedingly droll. I have put a child and a good-natured foolish man, in relations that *seem to me* very funny" (emphasis added). Eventually, those qualifications give way to direct expressions of confidence in his ability, and by the end of the letter he is boasting of his determination to avoid "unconscious repetitions" of *David Copperfield.* Yet even that boast appears to be part of a larger strategy, one designed to distinguish *Great Expectations* from his earlier books. Acknowledging complaints about the "want of humor" in *A Tale of Two Cities,* Dickens makes no less than four references to the humor, comedy, and drollery of his new book. At the same time, he implies that in returning to comedy—and to a first-person story about a "boy-child"—he is not simply falling back on tired old routines. He may link Pip to David, and he may confess to being "affected" by his rereading of *Copperfield,* but he does not want Forster to think that he is repeating himself. Indeed, he encourages Forster to view *Great Expectations* as sharply distinct from *Copperfield,* to notice that in developing the "grotesque tragi-comic conception that first encouraged [him]," he has offered a powerful demonstration of his capacity for continued growth and development as a writer. As if following a cue, Forster did go on to emphasize the differences between *Great Expectations* and *David Copperfield,* asserting that the contrast between the two books was a clear sign of Dickens's literary genius: "It may be doubted if Dickens could better have established his right to the front rank among novelists claimed for him," Forster wrote, "than by the ease and mastery with which, in these two books of *Copperfield* and *Great Expectations,* he kept perfectly distinct the two stories of a boy's childhood" (2:285).

To read Dickens's letter in this way is not to reject the work of Kaplan and Ackroyd or to deny that *Great Expectations* was informed by Dickens's experiences as a neglected child, impatient husband, and anxious middle-aged suitor. The novel contains several passages in which Dickens appears to reflect on his own "worthless conduct" and a few in which he seems ready to renounce his "wretched hankerings after money and gentility" (see *Great Expectations* 236, 321). Yet even as we acknowledge these points, we must also consider the possibility that Dickens's biographers have not yet exhausted their sources. Those sources—including Dickens's letters and contemporary reviews of his novels—will be the main focus of my attention, for although they are quoted and cited frequently, they are seldom subjected to detailed analysis.[3] My analysis will suggest that Dickens did indeed imagine *Great Expectations* as a comment on and revision of his own life story, and not only in the ways described by Kaplan and Ackroyd. In addition to reviewing his relationships with his parents, wife, children, and mistress, Dickens was rethinking his relations with his readers and critics, wondering how future generations would plot the story of his literary career. As he wrote the story of Pip, then, he was also writing what we might call the story of the story of Pip—the story of how *Great Expectations* came into being, of how the novel was begun and completed, and of how the enormous difficulties associated with its composition and publication were first acknowledged and then, triumphantly, overcome. This was a story that engaged Dickens's imagination fully, a story that he not only shared with Forster, but also told and retold himself. It both excited and inspired him, helping him to gather the strength he needed to turn *Great Expectations* into an assertion of his own literary greatness, a demonstration of the powers he had gained over a lifetime of reading and writing.

2.

Of course, Dickens never failed to throw himself into his writing or to applaud his own work—as Philip Collins once noted, he was capable of heaping praise upon his most "forgotten and forgettable" productions (348)—yet the letters surrounding *Great Expectations* amount to more than the usual heap of praises; and their compelling qualities, including their keen sense of drama, are related to the unusual circumstances out of which the book emerged. By the time he wrote his letter to Forster in October of 1860, Dickens had arrived at a kind of crisis point in his writing life: his character and his ability had been impugned, as had his medium and his audience. In addition, one of his most valuable literary properties, *All the Year Round,* a magazine that embodied his hopes for professional vindication and redemption, had been seriously damaged by the incompetence of others. In this crisis, however, Dickens was able to discover a rare opportunity, one that he seized with a vigor and enthusiasm unusual even for him. Thus, although it is surely important to acknowledge that Dickens always tried his best, always viewed his writing as both a struggle and a pleasure, and always—as Edgar Rosenberg once put it—filled his "autocritical report cards" with straight A-pluses (103), it is no less important to avoid flattening out our image of his career by suggesting that there can be no significant difference between his attitude towards *Great Expectations* and his attitude towards any other novel.

To understand why *Great Expectations* was especially important to Dickens, and to appreciate the challenges and opportunities he faced when writing the novel, we must remind ourselves that throughout the 1850s, Dickens had witnessed a steady decline in his standing with educated reviewers.[4] In their notices for novels like *Little Dorrit,* reviewers had frequently portrayed Dickens as a pathetic figure—vain, pretentious, and totally lacking in the self-discipline necessary for genuine literary achievement. In James Fitzjames Stephen's now-infamous attacks on *Little Dorrit,* for example, Dickens had been dismissed as hopelessly ignorant, a prisoner of his lower middle-class background: "[H]is notions of law," Stephen wrote, "are those of an attorney's clerk. He knows what arrest for debt is, he knows how affidavits are sworn" (128). Stephen's open contempt for Dickens was unusual, but his assessment of Dickens's character was not, and other reviewers, including some reasonably sympathetic to Dickens, followed him in likening Dickens's mind to that of a clerk and in pointing out Dickens's familiarity with "poor furniture" and "pawnbrokers' tickets" (Bagehot 465–66).[5]

Class biases had also shaped critics' attitudes towards Dickens's readers. Writing in *Blackwood's,* E. B. Hamley had repeatedly characterized Dickens's middle-class readers as "ill-judging," "foolish," and "silly" (495, 503). As he had pondered Dickens's "tendency to abandon his strong point as a humorist," Hamley had described the kinds of readers who had distracted Dickens from his true calling: "a booby who aims at being thought a thinker," "a thin young lady of about five-and-thirty, with a pink nose and a blighted heart," and "a kindly, large-hearted detector and extoller of perfection, especially among the lower orders" (495–96). In these descriptions, Hamley had drawn upon the comic stereotypes of Dickens's own fiction, as if to suggest that Dickens should know better than to heed the advice of such ridiculous people. "[D]on't listen to your adulators," Hamley had written, "listen to *us,* your true friend and admirer'' (503); and with that conclusion, he had presented Dickens with a simple choice—the adulation of the masses or the respect and admiration of the elites—implying that it would be impossible, even for Dickens, to enjoy both at once.

The terms in which Hamley framed this choice were the terms in which many critics described the options available to Dickens. Yet unlike Hamley, who expressed guarded optimism about Dickens's future, some reviewers concluded that it was too late. Dickens had already chosen the "applause of the many" over the esteem of the few, Walter Bagehot explained, and his unfortunate choice was now irrevocable:

> Mr. Dickens was too much inclined by natural disposition to lachrymose eloquence and exaggerated caricature. Such was the kind of writing which he wrote most easily. He found likewise that such was the kind of writing that was read most readily; and of course he wrote that kind.   (486)

Bagehot remarks that "no critic is entitled to speak very harshly of such degeneracy,'' yet in his commentary on Dickens's "natural disposition'' he does portray Dickens as a kind of "degenerate,'' describing him as not only lachrymose but effeminate. "Even in his earlier works,'' Bagehot observes,

> it was impossible not to fancy that there was a weakness of fibre unfavorable to the longevity of excellence. This was the effect of his deficiency in those masculine faculties of which we have said so much,—the reasoning understanding and firm far-seeing sagacity. It is these two component elements which stiffen the mind, and give a consistency to the creed and a coherence to its effects,—which enable it to protect itself from the rush of circumstances.

> (486)

Edwin Eigner has cited this passage to show that Victorian critics associated fiction (especially polemical or political fiction) with the "feminine imagination'' and nonfiction with "masculine reason'' (231–34). The context of the passage suggests, however, that Bagehot was concerned not only with the distinction between fiction and nonfiction, but also with the differences between high art and popular culture: "great and enduring works'' are linked with what Bagehot calls the "masculine faculties'' and "inferior productions,'' in which an author simply caters to the demands of the public, with a feminine "weakness of fibre'' (486). For Bagehot, then, it is Dickens's desire for popularity, his readiness to bend where he should remain firm, and not his choice of fiction over nonfiction, that calls his masculinity into question. Bagehot concludes his exploration of Dickens's unmanly "sensibility to circumstances'' by casting Dickens in the role of fallen woman—like Hamley, he mocks popular fiction by turning to images developed in popular novels—implying that if Dickens had relied on the sound advice of "good critics,'' he would not have "succumbed'' to the "temptations'' of writing for the masses (486). Having given in to those temptations, Bagehot implies, Dickens has lost something he can never regain.[6]

Dickens rejected the alternatives forced upon him by critics like Bagehot, and by the end of the 1850s he had begun to search for ways of demonstrating that he need not choose between popular success and lasting literary achievement. In 1857, he oversaw publication of the Library Edition of his works, an edition designed for affluent readers, and in 1858, with his first series of public readings for profit, he reached out to a much wider, less exclusive audience.[7] Crucial to Dickens's search was the founding of *All the Year Round,* the weekly two-penny magazine in which *Great Expectations* first appeared. Like *Great Expectations* itself, *All the Year Round* has been described as "a by-product of Dickens's marital disruption" (Sadrin 11); and in many ways, that description is accurate, since the magazine grew out of a dispute over the personal statement in which Dickens had tried to justify his treatment of his wife.[8] Nevertheless, the magazine was not only an attempt to establish "the validity of his grievances and the rightness of his cause" (Sadrin 13), but also a vehicle for some of his grandest literary ambitions, a way of showing that his critics had badly underestimated both his abilities and his audience.

In November of 1859, as *A Tale of Two Cities* was completing its serial run in *All the Year Round,* Dickens revealed the full extent of his ambitions for the magazine in a brief editorial announcement:

> We purpose always reserving the first place in these pages for a continuous original work of fiction . . . And it is our hope and aim, while we work hard at every other department of our journal, to produce, in this one, some sustained works of imagination that may become a part of English Literature.   (95)

At the time of Dickens's announcement, as John Sutherland has explained, it was not merely audacious but "revolutionary" to suggest that works of permanent value could emerge from a two-penny weekly (168). By making such a suggestion, Dickens had committed himself to a kind of literary experiment: he was betting that the audience for serious fiction was much larger and smarter than anyone else had imagined; and in a few months, his hunches paid off, as the new magazine became an enormous success. Spurred by the immediate popularity of its weekly serials, sales of *All the Year Round* soon trebled those of *Household Words* (Patten, "Sales" 619). More importantly, the new magazine attracted an audience of which Dickens could feel proud. By March of 1860, he was assuring contributors that they could "trust the audience with anything that is good. Though a large one, it is a fine one" (Nonesuch *Letters* 3:152). In assembling this impressive audience, Dickens had reason to feel that he had once again succeeded in ways that others could not even imagine. His critics had assumed that the audience for fiction could be either "large" or "fine," but not both. With each passing week, it seemed, he was proving them wrong.[9]

3.

Dickens's hopes for the new magazine—his pride in its achievements, and his belief in its ability to vindicate himself, his writing, and his readers—serve as a striking backdrop against which to view the emergence of *Great Expectations.* That backdrop is not entirely unfamiliar, of course, since biographers have long recognized that sagging sales of the magazine, brought on by the failure of Charles Lever's serial story, *A Day's Ride,* were the immediate cause of Dickens's decision to publish the novel in weekly installments. Yet even when biographers have acknowledged the importance of Dickens's decision to rescue the magazine, they have not given much attention to the letters in which the decision was announced, justified, and dramatized.[10] As a result, biographers have also overlooked the possibility that Dickens was not only frustrated but excited by his dealings with Lever. In fact, Lever's failure—and the ensuing crisis for *All the Year Round*—were vital sources of energy and inspiration for Dickens; and in the course of responding to that crisis, Dickens crystallized a new image of himself, portraying himself not only as a concerned editor and capable writer, but also as a reluctant, manly hero. It is this image of himself as clear-headed and tough-minded, able to triumph where other men had failed, that he would take into *Great Expectations,* and this image that he would carry through the novel itself.

In Dickens's early letters to Lever, written before the debacle of *A Day's Ride,* Dickens sought not only to flatter Lever but also to reassure himself. He had hoped that George Eliot would agree to appear in *All the Year Round,* and he had been keenly disappointed when he realized that she did not intend to do so. In the wake of this realization, he had been forced to move up the publication date for Lever's story by several months (Sutherland 175), and he was anxious to convince himself that his negotiations with both Eliot and Lever had worked out for the best. On 21 February 1860, he told Lever that

> Adam (or Eve) Bede is terrified by the novel difficulties of serial writing; cannot turn in the space; evidently will not be up to the scratch when Collins's sponge is thrown up.
>
> Consequently, I want to begin your story in July; that is to say, I want to have in type, four weekly Nos. *at the end of June,* and to keep that amount ahead, while the story lasts.   (Nonesuch *Letters* 3:151–52)

Dickens's insistence on having four numbers done by the end of June may have seemed unreasonable, yet instead of pretending that it would be easy for Lever to meet such a deadline, Dickens appealed to Lever's sense of pride, largely by describing serial writing as a kind of masculine proving ground. He revises George Eliot's name from "Adam" to "Eve Bede," as if to suggest that her femininity is the source of her reluctance to take on the "novel difficulties of serial writing"; he then implies that those difficulties are compounded in the case of weekly serialization, where the shortness of individual installments forces a writer to "turn" in a very small "space"; and finally, he likens Wilkie Collins to a prize-fighter, exhausted after having gone the distance against a brutal opponent. For Dickens, then, serial writing is not a feminine pursuit, but a manly art, requiring intelligence, imagination, strength, and endurance. Serial writers need not capitulate to their readers, as critics like Bagehot had implied, but must instead exert an almost physical domination over the audience: indeed, they must lay into their readers from the start, and not let up until the end. Had George Eliot been up to such a challenge, she might have become an "Adam"; by refusing it, she has reverted to being an "Eve."[11]

By October, however, it had become clear that Lever would not be up to the scratch either. *A Day's Ride* has been described as a "disaster," a "dud story," whose defects alienated readers and drove down circulation (Sutherland 176–77); yet as Dickens thought about Lever's failure, he realized that he had been given a perfect opportunity to display his own prowess, to show off his mastery of the conventions of serial fiction. Returning to the notions of manliness that he had employed in his original letter to Lever, Dickens steels himself for the challenges ahead of him; and on October 4, after telling Forster that "the property of All the Year Round was far too valuable, in every way, to be much endangered," he reveals his plans to rescue the ailing magazine with a serial story of his own:

> Last week, I got to work on a new story. I had previously very carefully considered the state and prospects of All the Year Round, and, the more I considered them, the less hope I saw of being able to get back, *now,* to the profit of a separate publication in the old 20 numbers. However, I worked on, knowing that what I was doing would run into another groove. I called a council of war at the office on Tuesday. It was perfectly clear that the one thing to be done was, for me to strike in. I have therefore decided to begin a story, the length of the Tale of Two Cities, on the First of December—begin publishing, that is. I must make the most I can out of the book. When I come down, I will bring you the first two or three weekly parts. The name is, GREAT EXPECTA-TIONS. I think a good name?   (Nonesuch *Letters* 3:182)

By describing the meeting as a "council of war," and by implying that it was "perfectly clear" to everyone present that he should be the one to "strike in," Dickens likens himself to an old soldier, pressed into a battle that only he can win. In keeping with this new identity, he emphasizes his steadfastness in the face of impending disaster, noting that he has continued to work on his story despite ever-increasing doubts about the possibility of "getting back" to "the old 20 numbers." Throughout most of the letter, his tone is brisk, efficient, and decisive. Yet even near the end, when it becomes more playful, he remains utterly convinced of the rightness of his own artistic choices, implying that he not only thinks but knows that Great Expectations is a very "good name" for his new novel.[12]

Two or three days after telling Forster of his decision to "strike in," Dickens sent a "business report" to Lever (Nonesuch *Letters* 3:183). Again assuming the role of a grizzled veteran, Dickens begins by noting that Lever's story had failed to *"take hold"* and goes on to report the consequences of that failure: circulation has become affected and subscribers have started to complain. "I have waited week after week, for these three or four weeks," he says gravely,

> watching for any sign of encouragement. The least sign would have been enough. But all the tokens that appear, are in the other direction; and therefore I have been driven upon the necessity of considering how to act, and of writing to you.
> There is but one thing to be done. I had begun a book which I intended for one of my long twenty number serials. I must abandon that design and forego its profit (a very serious consideration, you may believe), and shape the story for these pages. I must get into these pages, as soon as possible, and must consequently begin my story in the No. for the 1st of December. For as long a time as you continue afterwards, we must go on together.
> (Nonesuch *Letters* 3:184)

Dickens's treatment of Lever has often been described as kindly and gentle (see, for example, Johnson 2:966 and Sutherland 177); and at several points in the letter, Dickens does attempt to comfort Lever, assuring him, for example, that "this might have happened with any writer":

> It was a toss-up with Wilkie Collins, when he began his story, on my leaving off. But he strung it on the needful thread of interest, and made a great success. The difficulties and discouragements of such an undertaking are enormous, and the man who surmounts them today may be beaten by them tomorrow.
> (Nonesuch *Letters* 3:184)

At other points, however, there is an unmistakable sense of exasperation, conveyed largely through Dickens's vigorous rhythms and emphatic diction: "week after week . . . any sign . . . the least sign . . . all the tokens." And in the end, despite the many expressions of concern for Lever, there is also a trace of condescension: Dickens may insist that "this might have happened with any writer," but he clearly does not think it will happen to him. For him, the "toss-up" is not between success and failure, as it has been for Lever and even Collins; rather, it is a toss-up between a successful weekly magazine and a profitable novel in twenty parts.[13]

In subsequent letters to Lever, Dickens continued to send mixed messages, providing reassurance while also suggesting that he was bound to succeed where Lever had failed. On October 15, perhaps in deference to Lever's feelings, Dickens characterized serial writing not as an endurance test, but rather as a game of chance, in which success was the result of sheer luck:

> Surely, my dear Lever, not quite to succeed in such a strange knack, or lottery, is a very different thing from having cause to be struck in one's self-respect and just courage. It was but the other day that Bulwer and Adam Bede were both speaking to me with a kind of scared wavering between temptation and repulsion—and each with a direct personal reference—on this very head.
>
> (Nonesuch *Letters* 3:187)

Back in February, before the failure of *A Day's Ride,* Lever had been set apart from "Eve Bede," but now he is identified with her. To be sure, Dickens makes a point of referring to Eliot as "*Adam* Bede" and of noting that her concerns are shared by Edward Bulwer-Lytton; yet by suggesting that George Eliot is "scared" of serialization, frightened by the demands it would make upon her, Dickens returns to his original rhetoric of fear, courage, and heroic action—even as he attempts to avoid it.

This rhetoric was, of course, entirely consistent with that of his own recent novels. In books like *A Tale of Two Cities,* Dickens had imagined the glories of making gallant sacrifices, and in his letters to Forster and Lever, he would continue to do so, insisting that he must heed the call of duty and suggesting that he was the only man capable of conducting this particular rescue mission. In one of his letters to Forster, however, Dickens acknowledges that the sacrifice of a twenty-number serial is "really and truly made for myself" (Nonesuch *Letters* 3:183). He had never been in this situation before, and may never have had as much at stake. Lever was scattering the audience that he had worked so hard to amass, destroying the evidence of his ability to defy his critics. By rescuing *All the Year Round,* he was protecting his reputation and securing his achievements. He not only realized this, he relished it, immediately grasping the dramatic potential of a moment unprecedented in his long career: "by dashing in now," he told Forster, "I come in when most wanted" (Nonesuch *Letters* 3:183).

4.

Dickens's decision to publish in weekly installments rather than in monthly numbers has frequently been praised, and indeed that decision is often identified as one of the main reasons for the success of *Great Expectations*. Arguing along these lines, David Trotter has said that the novel's "virtues flow from its compactness" (vii), while Margaret Cardwell has observed that "Dickens may have thought of *Great Expectations* as a 'sacrifice' . . . but subsequent readers have greatly appreciated its economy and concentration" (xviii). The triumph of *Great Expectations* can be attributed not only to its compactness and economy, however, but also to its sense of purpose, its relationship to Dickens's own sense of "striking in" and "dashing in," of being wanted and of having the rare ability to satisfy such wants.

Dickens's commanding sense of his own ability is evident throughout the novel. It can be felt, for example, at the ends of his weekly installments, where he asserts his control over the reader and demonstrates his mastery of the serial form. As he manages these endings, Dickens consistently employs what Carol Martin has described as "open-ended closure" (48), wrapping up one installment while also pointing ahead to the next. At the same time, he also achieves a remarkable degree of variety in his endings, relying sometimes on pathos (as when Pip recalls his "strong conviction" that he "should never like Joe's trade" [30]) and sometimes on humor (as when Pip and Herbert Pocket suddenly recognize each other as the "prowling boy" and the "pale young gentleman" [106]).[14] The most portentous and perhaps the most revealing of Dickens's endings, however, the one that seems to tell us the most about his feelings for this novel, appears near the end of the second volume, as Pip anticipates his reunion with Magwitch. Wrapping up the chapter in which he confronts Estella about her relationship with Bentley Drummle, Pip announces the approach of an event that has long "impended over [him]":

> In the Eastern story, the heavy slab that was to fall on the bed of state in the flush of conquest was slowly wrought out of the quarry, the tunnel for the rope to hold it in its place was slowly carried through the leagues of rock, the slab was slowly raised and fitted in the roof, the rope was rove to it and slowly taken through the miles of hollow to the great iron ring. All being made ready with much labour, and the hour come, the sultan was aroused in the dead of night, and the sharpened axe that was to sever the rope from the great iron ring was put into his hand, and he struck with it, and the rope parted and rushed away, and the ceiling fell. So, in my case; all the work, near and afar, that tended to the end, had been accomplished; and in an instant the blow was struck, and the roof of my stronghold dropped upon me.   (309–10)

In this paragraph, Dickens not only invokes but revises the Eastern story—which, as Stanley Friedman explains, originally "[made] no comment about the slowness of the procedure [used to trap the sultan]" (217). By emphasizing the deliberation and care with which the sultan's doom was "wrought," Dickens reminds his eager readers of "all the work, near and afar," that he has invested in *Great Expectations*. Turning the plot against the sultan into a figure for the plot of his own novel, he revels in his own cunning and applauds his own achievement, offering an implicit rebuke to the many critics who had accused him of not knowing how to construct a coherent story (see, for example, Hamley 497).[15]

As the reunion scene unfolds, both the convict and the novelist are flushed with "heat and triumph" (317). Tellingly, Magwitch exults not only in his reunion with the "dear boy" who has treated him nobly, but also in the act of setting and staging the reunion scene. Delighting in the chance to manipulate his audience, Magwitch heightens the suspense with a series of increasingly pointed questions: "Might a mere warmint ask what property? . . . As to the first letter of that lawyer's name now. Would it be J?" (316). These questions bring confusion and pain to poor Pip, yet they are so intensely gleeful, so clever and so pleased with their own cleverness, that readers are soon swept up by their giddy, manic energy. Finally and fittingly, that energy is released in the novel's grandest example of self-assertion, the passage in which Magwitch reveals his secrets and tells his story:

> "Yes, Pip, dear boy, I've made a gentleman on you! It's me wot has done it!
> I swore that time, sure as ever I earned a guinea, that guinea should go to you.
> I swore arterwards, sure as ever I spec'lated and got rich, you should get rich.
> I lived rough, that you should live smooth; I worked hard, that you should be
> above work. What odds, dear boy? Do I tell it, fur you to feel a obligation?
> Not a bit. I tell it, fur you to know as that there hunted dunghill dog wot you
> kep life in, got his head so high that he could make a gentleman—and Pip,
> you're him!"   (317)

To be sure, Dickens does not invest all of his sympathies with Magwitch: he understands what Pip is suffering, and he portrays Pip's agonies with genuine delicacy and tact. Yet although he understands why the convict's return might be mortifying to Pip, Dickens clearly delights in the efficiency and elegance of the trap he has set for his unsuspecting hero. That the complex emotions of the reunion scene should resolve themselves in an exhilarating declaration of authorship—"It's me wot has done it!"—is perhaps the best indication of his hopes for the scene, and indeed for the novel as a whole. He has been determined to take advantage of the opportunity created by Lever's failure, to show that his own powers remain undiminished, and now, like Magwitch, he not only insists on the excellence of what he has done, but demands recognition as the one who has done it.[16]

To grant Dickens this recognition, as I have tried to show throughout this essay, we must not only reread and reinterpret *Great Expectations,* but also reconsider the letters and reviews surrounding it. Too often, such writings are treated as if we already knew all about them, as if they could not possibly yield any new meanings or implications. Yet there is no way of telling in advance what a close study of even the most familiar sources might reveal, no way of knowing what might happen if those sources were treated as texts with compelling literary qualities of their own. In Dickens's case, such an approach reveals the difficulties he was facing, the challenges he was taking on, and the stories he was telling both to himself and his biographer, as he began *Great Expectations.* As I have also tried to suggest, such an approach does not minimize the novel's links to Dickens's boyhood traumas and midlife crises but instead provides us with an opportunity to explore other connections, to see that although the novel is a product of bitter self-knowledge, it is also an opportunity for unapologetic self-assertion.

Prompted by this vision of the novel, we might conclude that the keenest irony in *Great Expectations* is not that Pip's secret benefactor turns out to be a criminal, but that a novel so explicitly critical of ambition is itself so confident and so open about its own ambitions. As Pip struggles towards maturity, he dreams of "London and greatness" (146), only to discover that he has to settle for obscurity and a kind of exile in Egypt. His experience is one of diminishment and defeat, and by the end of the novel, as Peter Brooks has shown, he has been emptied of desire, forced to admit that the future holds nothing for him. By contrast, Dickens refuses to be diminished, and he insists on using this novel to reassert his dream of greatness and regain control of his own future. Far from giving up on plot, as Pip must do, Dickens attempts nothing less than to recast the story of his own career. Against the critics who have charted a steep decline since the glories of *Pickwick* and *Nickleby,* he insists on a steady progression to the pinnacle of *Great Expectations,* thus raising the possibility that even greater achievements might lie ahead of him.

Although the novel was not universally admired, many reviewers agreed that *Great Expectations* was "the creation of a great artist in his prime" (Chorley 44), with E. S. Dallas presenting the book as unmistakable proof that "the weekly form of publication was not incompatible with a very high order of fiction" (6). Dickens could scarcely have been surprised by such praise, since his goal had always been to elicit it. In *Great Expectations,* as in the letters leading up to the novel, he had presented himself as a writer whose gifts were not fading, but only just beginning to emerge. That others found this self-presentation persuasive is evidenced by their representations of Dickens. A few weeks after *Great Expectations* had finished its run in *All the Year Round,* Dickens saw the shop windows filled with a caricature of himself. The drawing showed Dickens at his writing desk, looking out at the viewer rather than down at his manuscript. He points with his left hand at his huge forehead, which is evidently the source of whatever he is putting on the page. Through its articulation of the relation between Dickens and his writing, the caricature makes his work seem effortless and his imagination boundless. The image delighted Dickens, and he told a friend to make a point of seeing it:

> I hope you have seen a large-headed photograph with little legs representing the undersigned, pen in hand, tapping his forehead to knock an idea out. It has just sprung up so abundantly in all the shops, that I am ashamed to go about town looking in at the picture-windows, which is my delight. It seems to me extraordinarily ludicrous, and much more like than the grave portrait done in earnest. It made me laugh when I first came upon it, until I shook again, in open sunlighted Picadilly.   (Nonesuch *Letters* 3:228)

In this letter, Dickens makes a mockery of modesty, claiming that he is embarrassed by the drawing, and then immediately admitting that it is indeed "like" him. The caricature may exaggerate some of his features, but as Dickens implies, it also acknowledges his stature as the public's favorite novelist—the one, as the caption says, "FROM WHOM WE HAVE GREAT EXPECTATIONS."

NOTES

1. As Edgar Johnson once explained, the argument is not that *Great Expectations* in any way reflects the "outward events" of Dickens's life, but rather that it explores "humiliations and griefs" that "he kept buried from all the world" (2:982–83). According to Jack Rawlins, whose "Great Expiations" is notable for its readiness to consider the differences as well as the similarities between Pip and Dickens, "it has been recognized by most critics that Pip is Dickens, in a way that's striking even in terms of Dickens's habitually autobiographical art" (668, n.4). A brief list of recent studies based on the assumption that *Great Expectations* is an autobiographical novel would also include works by U.C. Knoepflmacher, Gail Turley Houston, Margaret Cardwell, and Kate Flint.
2. Dickens's familiarity with the conventions of the Victorian life-and-letters biography dates back to the beginning of his literary career, when he entered into the controversy surrounding John Gibson Lockhart's life of Sir Walter Scott. Dickens's defense of Lockhart, advanced in three separate articles for the *Examiner,* has been linked not only to his admiration for Scott but also to his frustration with his own publisher, Richard Bentley (see Slater 32 and Pilgrim *Letters* 1:428, n.1; for Scott's importance to Dickens, see Kathryn Chittick's *Dickens and the*

1830s, chapter two.) It was in this period that Dickens was also forced to recognize that he had become the subject of a biographer's scrutiny. In February of 1838, a few months before his first article in defense of Lockhart, Dickens picked up a copy of a Durham newspaper and stumbled across an item billing itself as an "Autobiography of Boz" (see Pilgrim *Letters* 1:367). Dickens was outraged by this spurious "autobiography"—not least because it had grossly overestimated his income—and within a week after finding it, he had demanded an apology from the paper's editor and a raise from Bentley, asserting that he was being worked at a rate "beyond Scott himself" (Pilgrim *Letters* 1:370). Pip has a similar experience while eating at the Blue Boar: taking up a "dirty old copy of a local newspaper," he discovers a garbled account of his "romantic rise in fortune," one identifying his "earliest patron, companion, and friend" as a "highly-respected individual not entirely unconnected with the corn and seed trade" (231). Pip becomes resigned to the presence of such events in his life, but his experience of celebrity, though treated humorously, indicates Dickens's keen awareness of its perils. Dickens suggests that celebrities can do little to control their own publicity—he makes it clear that Pip cannot deny the rumors about Uncle Pumblechook's mentoring without making things worse for himself—yet by showing how much Pip has to endure from both the press and public, embodied chiefly in Trabb's Boy, Dickens also points out some of the reasons why celebrities might attempt to exert such control in the first place.

3. Reviews of the most recent volume of the Pilgrim *Letters* offer some indication of how Dickens's letters are usually treated. In his review, Malcolm Andrews presents the letters as intriguing, but unproblematic evidence of Dickens's "contrary and complex personality" (132). For Andrews, the letters are to be read and enjoyed, but since their meanings are obvious, they require little in the way of interpretation or analysis. The value of the letters, even as a source of enjoyment, is itself dismissed by Susan Shatto, who begins her review by noting that they "seem produced by an automaton programmed to write in only two styles: affected high spirits, as used for [Mark] Lemon and Forster; and business-like efficiency, as when writing to [W. H.] Wills or Miss Coutts" (41).

4. The best treatment of Dickens's reception in this period remains that of George Ford, who treats the "splitting of Dickens' public" as a complex phenomenon with multiple causes, including the increasing unpopularity of Dickens's social criticism (100), the emergence—first in Thackeray and the Brontës, and later in George Eliot—of "the first serious literary competition of his career" (111), and the critics' "growing dissatisfaction with serial publication itself" (123). Ford also explains that since critics were especially eager to "encourage new talent," they were "more ready to abandon the successful established artist . . . than [was] the average reader" (110).

5. Of course Dickens's father *had* been arrested for debt, and Dickens himself had visited pawnshops on his family's behalf. Since Dickens had been careful to conceal these facts, he may have wondered how they had ended up in the hands of his critics. Stephen's attacks on Dickens, as is now well-known, were motivated by very bitter feelings—Stephen viewed Tite Barnacle, the head of the Circumlocution Office, as a caricature of his own father (see Ford 105)—but less well-known is the fact that Stephen's father eventually urged him to leave Dickens

alone: "I do not know that he has a right to be angry," Sir James Stephen advised, "but I should doubt the wisdom of exciting him any more. He is rather a formidable enemy to deal with, and you are best without enemies" (qtd. Smith 20). Sir James's warnings, it should be noted, came shortly after Dickens had embarrassed his son with "A Curious Misprint in the Edinburgh Review," a withering response to one of the attacks on *Little Dorrit.*

6. Bagehot's assumptions about the connection between femininity and popular fiction, and between masculinity and "great works," were shared by many critics at mid-century. From the 1850s to the 1870s, as Gaye Tuchman has shown, women writers were increasingly identified with the "popular-culture novel" and men with the "high-culture novel."

7. For further information about the Library Edition, see Patten, *Dickens and His Publishers,* 254–55; for a discussion of the public readings and their connections to Dickens's other professional activities, see Schlicke 226–48. The relations and interrelations of Dickens's projects are also acknowledged by Jennifer Wicke in her analysis of Dickens's efforts to "close the hermeneutic circle of publicity": "old ads for the books became new ads for the readings," Wicke explains, "while the readings were themselves ads for the books, sold outside the reading hall" (52).

8. When Bradbury and Evans, the publishers of *Household Words,* refused to print a copy of the statement in *Punch,* Dickens announced his decision to create and edit an entirely new magazine. Dickens's statement is reprinted in Norman Page's *Dickens Companion,* 341–43, and the controversy surrounding it detailed by Patten in *Charles Dickens and His Publishers,* 260–71.

9. The questions of what a mass audience wanted, what it might be persuaded to want, and what it could handle, are taken up in Wilkie Collins's essay, "The Unknown Public," which appeared in *Household Words* on August 21, 1858. In the essay, Collins announces his "discovery" of the "Unknown Public . . . of the penny-novel Journals" (217), which he views with a mixture of amazement, amusement, and longing. At first, Collins describes the "Unknown Public" in unflattering terms, not unlike those in which E. B. Hamley had once described the members of Dickens's own audience. Later on, however, Collins admits that he is intrigued by this "monster audience of at least three millions" (221)—and excited by the thought that such an audience might soon be available to "regularly-established authors" (221). "An immense public has been discovered," Collins explains, "the next thing to be done is, in a literary sense, to teach that public how to read" (222). Dickens never imagined that *All the Year Round* would attract the kind of "monster audience" that Collins had "discovered," but he did see the founding of his new journal as part of the larger process that Collins imagined: that of teaching the Unknown Public to read.

10. In biographies by Kaplan and Ackroyd, for example, the story of Dickens's decision to save his magazine is surrounded and indeed overwhelmed by comments about the "passion of self-exploration" (Kaplan 433). Ackroyd goes further than Kaplan in acknowledging that the "actual form of *Great Expectations* had much more to do with the troubled state of *All the Year Round* than with Dickens's own creative imperatives" (883), but in speaking of the novel's "actual form"

he is thinking of its appearance in weekly rather than in longer monthly installments. In any case, he dismisses Dickens's concern for the magazine as a purely
"commercial consideration" (883), burying his account of the magazine's trou-
bles in the middle of a long paragraph devoted to a variety of issues, including
Pip's emergence from Dickens's "haunted" past (884).

11. Carol Martin has suggested that "the problems of weekly versus monthly serialization were undoubtedly part of the reason George Eliot was unwilling to publish
with Dickens" (16). For a sense of how Dickens viewed those problems at an
earlier stage in his career—namely, the period in which he wrote *Hard Times*—see
the pioneering work of John Butt and Kathleen Tillotson. For a study that takes
Dickens from this stage up to the period of *Great Expectations,* see K. J. Field-
ding's essay on the weekly serials; and for two more recent studies of Dickens's
attitude towards weekly serialization, see the articles by Ellen Casey and J. Don
Vann. Vann's article is especially relevant to my argument, as it focuses (albeit
for different reasons) on Dickens's dealings with Lever.

12. In letters describing earlier weekly serials, Dickens had not been quite so imaginative, or so taken with the narrative possibilities of the letter form. In telling
Angela Burdett-Coutts of his decision to write the serial story that would become
Hard Times, for example, he had spoken only of "a fixed idea on the part of his
printers and copartners in Household Words, that a story by me, continued from
week to week, would make some unheard-of effect" (Pilgrim *Letters* 7:256),
never implying that his efforts were crucial to the survival of the magazine. About
five years later, when announcing the title of *A Tale of Two Cities,* he had told
Forster that it would "fit the opening to a T" (see Forster 2:280–81), but even
in that case, his self-presentation is relatively simple and unselfconscious: he is
happy, relieved, and excited, but he does not try to suggest that he is readying
himself for a decisive battle and does not attempt to portray himself as a reluctant warrior.

13. Lever's side of this story is full of bitter ironies, some quite painful to imagine.
At one time, as John Sutherland explains, Lever had actually been "groomed"
as a replacement and rival for Dickens (162). In 1845, he had been signed to a
huge contract by Chapman and Hall, who had recently lost Dickens to Bradbury
and Evans. By 1847, however, it had become clear that Lever would not be able
to take advantage of his "great chance" (Sutherland 163). His first big novel for
Chapman and Hall was an enormous disappointment—one, according to Sutherland, from which he never fully recovered (163–5). Fifteen years later, with the
debacle of *A Day's Ride,* Lever was forced to watch as Dickens rushed in to
replace *him,* undoubtedly reminded of earlier failures even as he suffered through
new ones. Lever's relationship with Dickens has also been linked to the eternal
question of the revised ending of *Great Expectations* with Jerome Meckier arguing
that similarities between Dickens's original ending and the ending of Lever's *A
Day's Ride* gave Dickens another motive for revision: Dickens, Meckier insists,
would not have wanted anyone to think that he had "copied a resounding failure" (47).

14. To illustrate the wide range of devices and techniques employed by serial novelists, scholars like Carol Martin and Ellen Casey have distinguished among the

many different ways in which writers ended their installments. Martin speaks not only of "open-ended closure," but also of "self-referential endings", in which the narrator addresses the reader directly (50), and Casey distinguishes among four types of endings: "climax and curtain"; "mid-action," which resembles the familiar cliffhanger; "unresolved situation"; and "look to the future," which is much like Martin's "self-referential ending" (99).
15. For Dickens, the significance of this moment was no doubt compounded by the fact that the Eastern Story had been the source of his first literary composition, a tragedy called "Misnar, Sultan of India," which he had adapted from Ridley's *Tales of the Genii* at the age of ten. With his reference to "Misnar," Dickens brings his writing life full circle, linking *Great Expectations* to the stories he had read and written as a boy.
16. Magwitch is himself a kind of author, as Eiichi Hara points out, since he is responsible for "devising, plotting, and writing Pip's story" (593). I would add that Magwitch's skill as a narrator, his ability not only to devise stories but also to imagine their effect on a variety of audiences, is evident from the start of the novel: he instinctively realizes that the best way to terrify Pip is by creating an imaginary bogeyman with a "secret way" of getting at a boy's heart and liver; he also understands what might happen if Pip were forced to tell the story of their encounters on the marshes, and so—almost as if he shared our privileged readerly knowledge of what Pip would have to suffer at the hands of Mrs. Joe—he makes a special point of providing Pip with a cover story, taking full responsibility for the theft of her liquor and pie.

WORKS CITED

Ackroyd, Peter. *Dickens.* New York: HarperCollins, 1990.

Andrews, Malcolm. Rev. of *The Letters of Charles Dickens* [The Pilgrim Edition], vol. 8. *Dickensian* 92 (1996): 131–33.

[Bagehot, Walter.] "Charles Dickens." *National Review* 7 (Oct. 1858): 458–86.

Bodenheimer, Rosemarie. *The Real Life of Mary Ann Evans: George Eliot, Her Letters and Fiction.* Ithaca: Cornell UP, 1994.

Brooks, Peter. *Reading for the Plot: Design and Intention in Narrative.* New York: Knopf, 1984.

Butt, John and Kathleen Tillotson. *Dickens at Work.* London: Methuen, 1957.

Cardwell, Margaret. Introduction. *Great Expectations.* By Charles Dickens. Ed. Margaret Cardwell. Oxford: Clarendon P, 1993.

Casey, Ellen. " 'That Specially Trying Mode of Publication': Dickens as Editor of the Weekly Serial." *Victorian Periodicals Review* 14 (1981): 93–101.

Chittick, Kathryn. *Dickens and the 1830s*. Cambridge: Cambridge UP, 1990.

[Chorley, H. F.] Rev. of *Great Expectations*. *Athenaeum* 1759 (13 July 1861): 43–45.

Collins, Philip. "A Tale of Two Novels: *A Tale of Two Cities* and *Great Expectations* in Dickens' Career." *Dickens Studies Annual* 2 (1972): 336–51, 378–80.

[Collins, Wilkie.] "The Unknown Public." *Household Words* 18 (21 Aug. 1858): 217–22.

[Dallas, E. S.] Rev. of *Great Expectations*. *Times* (17 Oct. 1861): 6.

Dickens, Charles. *Great Expectations*. Ed. Margaret Cardwell. Oxford: Clarendon P, 1993.

———. *The Letters of Charles Dickens*. Nonesuch Edition. Ed. Walter Dexter. 3 vols. Bloomsbury: Nonesuch, 1938.

———. *The Letters of Charles Dickens*. Pilgrim Edition. Eds. Madeline House and Graham Storey. 8 vols. to date. Oxford: Clarendon P, 1965—.

Eigner, Edwin M. "Dogmatism and Puppyism: The Novelist, the Reviewer, and the Serious Subject: The Case of *Little Dorrit*." *Dickens Studies Annual* 22 (1993): 217–37.

Fielding, K. J. "The Weekly Serialization of Dickens's Novels." *Dickensian* 54 (1958): 134–41.

Flint, Kate. Introduction. *Great Expectations*. By Charles Dickens. Ed. Margaret Cardwell. Oxford: Oxford UP, 1994.

Ford, George H. *Dickens and His Readers: Aspects of Novel-Criticism Since 1836*. Princeton: Princeton UP, 1955.

Forster, John. *The Life of Charles Dickens*. 2 vols. London: J. M. Dent, 1966.

Friedman, Stanley. "Ridley's *Tales of the Genii* and Dickens's *Great Expectations*." *Nineteenth-Century Literature* 44 (Sept. 1989): 215–218.

[Hamley, E. B.] "Remonstrance with Dickens." *Blackwood's Edinburgh Magazine* 81 (April 1857): 490–503.

Hara, Eiichi. "Stories Present and Absent in *Great Expectations*." *ELH* 53 (1986): 593–614.

Houston, Gail Turley. " 'Pip' and 'Property': The (Re)production of the Self in *Great Expectations*." *Studies in the Novel* 24 (1992): 13–25.

Johnson, Edgar. *Charles Dickens: His Tragedy and Triumph*. 2 vols. New York: Simon and Schuster, 1952.

Kaplan, Fred. *Dickens: A Biography*. New York: William Morrow, 1988.

Knoepflmacher, U. C. "From Outrage to Rage: Dickens's Bruised Femininity." *Dickens and Other Victorians: Essays in Honour of Philip Collins.* Ed. Joanne Shattock. New York: St. Martin's P, 1988:75–96.

Martin, Carol. *George Eliot's Serial Fiction.* Columbus: Ohio State UP, 1994.

Meckier, Jerome. "Charles Dickens's *Great Expectations:* A Defense of the Second Ending." *Studies in the Novel* 25 (1993): 28–58.

Nisbet, Ada. "The Autobiographical Matrix of *Great Expectations.*" *Victorian Newsletter* 15 (1959): 10–13.

Page, Norman. *A Dickens Companion.* New York: Schocken, 1984.

Patten, Robert L. *Charles Dickens and His Publishers.* Oxford: Oxford UP, 1978.

———. "The Sales of Dickens's Works." *Dickens: The Critical Heritage.* Ed. Philip Collins. London: Routledge, 1971:617–22.

Rawlins, Jack P. "Great Expiations: Dickens and the Betrayal of the Child." SEL 23 (1983): 667–83.

Rosenberg, Edgar. "Last Words on *Great Expectations:* A Textual Brief on the Six Endings." *Dickens Studies Annual* 9 (1981): 87–115.

Sadrin, Anny. Great Expectations. London: Unwin Hyman, 1988.

Schlicke, Paul. *Dickens and Popular Entertainment.* London: Allen & Unwin, 1985.

Shatto, Susan. Rev. of *The Letters of Charles Dickens* [The Pilgrim Edition], vol. 8. *Dickens Quarterly* 14 (1997): 41–3.

Slater, Michael. Introduction and Notes. *The Amusements of the People and Other Papers, Reports, Essays and Reviews 1834–51.* By Charles Dickens. Columbus: Ohio State UP, 1996.

Smith, K. J. M. *James Fitzjames Stephen: Portrait of a Victorian Rationalist.* Cambridge: Cambridge UP, 1988.

[Stephen, James Fitzjames.] "The License of Modern Novelists." *Edinburgh Review* 106 (July 1857): 124–56.

Sutherland, J. A. *Victorian Novelists and Publishers.* Chicago: U of Chicago P, 1976.

Trotter, David. Introduction. *Great Expectations.* By Charles Dickens. Ed. David Trotter. Harmondsworth: Penguin, 1997.

Tuchman, Gaye, with Nina E. Fortin. *Edging Women Out: Victorian Novelists, Publishers, and Social Change.* New Haven: Yale UP, 1989.

Vann, J. Don. "Dickens, Charles Lever, and Mrs. Gaskell." *Victorian Periodicals Review* 22 (1989): 64–71.

Welsh, Alexander. *From Copyright to Copperfield: The Identity of Dickens.* Cambridge, MA: Harvard UP, 1987.

Wicke, Jennifer. *Advertising Fictions: Literature, Advertising, and Social Reading.* New York: Columbia UP, 1988.

Rushdie's Affiliation with Dickens

Martine Hennard Dutheil

> The Ocean of the Streams of Story was in fact the biggest
> library in the universe. And because the stories were held
> here in fluid form, they retained the ability to change, to
> become new versions of themselves, to join up with other
> stories and so to become yet other stories; so that unlike a
> library of books, the Ocean of the Streams of Story was
> much more than a storeroom of yarns.
> Salman Rushdie, *Haroun and the Sea of Stories*
>
> How stories travel, what mouths they end up in!
> Salman Rushdie, *The Moor's Last Sigh*

In his novelistic tetralogy, Salman Rushdie uses the family as a trope to
investigate the question of individual and collective origins. After the publication of *The Moor's Last Sigh,* he declared that he saw this novel as

> the completion of what I began in *Midnight's Children, Shame* and *The Satanic
> Verses*—the story of myself, where I came from, a story of origins and memory.
> But it's also a public project that forms an arc, my response to an age in history
> that began in 1947. That cycle of novels is now complete. ("The Last Laugh,"
> 21)

Steeped in the complexities of the postcolonial condition, these four novels
challenge the traditional values attached to the family, not only by exposing
the tyranny of families but also by subverting the generative model which
underlies the familial system. *Midnight's Children* and *Shame* thematize the
complex nature of origin by holding in suspense the identity of the heroes'
biological parents. Born illegally across cultures, Saleem Sinai and Omar
Shakil multiply father substitutes. *The Satanic Verses* even more daringly
transgresses the law of the father by breaking down aesthetic, moral, and
cultural distinctions (including the one between sacred and profane texts),
although Saladin Chamcha's last-minute reconciliation with his dying father

Dickens Studies Annual, Volume 27, Copyright © 1998 by AMS Press, Inc. All rights reserved.

expresses a desire for rapprochement with the emblem of authority. Finally, *The Moor's Last Sigh* dramatises the tyranny of parental rule within the context of a family torn apart by strike, division, and violence. Burdened with an extravagant and gifted mother and a big-time crook of a father, Moraes is reduced to insignificance before being abandoned by both.[1] In these novels, the image of the family becomes productive only to the extent that its reproductive structure is called into question. Thus, the vertical, linear, genealogical familial logic gives way to a wide, intricate, and changing network of multiple relationships which open up the familial unit to the outside and the other: the old family tree is felled and transformed into the leaves upon which the transformative action of writing can take place.

Rushdie's treatment of the family is part of a wide-ranging critique of naturalized notions that are most intimately bound up with our sense of self and belonging, and which writing puts into play. In "Imaginary Homelands," Rushdie insists on the necessity of moving away from essentialist conceptions of race, culture, and nation. Similarly, he rejects an exclusive allegiance to native traditions to construct his own "family tree" (*Imaginary Homelands* 20–21). Defining himself as a "literary migrant," Rushdie makes use of the liberty granted the contemporary novelist to draw on a host of literary parents. He is happy to list the various members of his "literary family," thereby creating a tension between the constraining laws of genealogy and the free affiliative nature of writing. As he puts it in "Imaginary Homelands" (1982):

> We are inescapably international writers at a time when the novel has never been a more international form (a writer like Borges speaks of the influence of Robert Louis Stevenson on his work; Heinrich Böll acknowledges the influence of Irish literature; cross-pollination is everywhere); and it is perhaps one of the more pleasant freedoms of the literary migrant to be able to choose his parents. My own—selected half consciously, half not—include Gogol, Cervantes, Kafka, Melville, Machado de Assis; a polyglot family tree against which I measure myself, and to which I would be honoured to belong.
>
> (*Imaginary Homelands* 20–21)

Yet in this piece as in several others, where he addresses the question of his "literary parents", he surprisingly omits to mention Charles Dickens. Apart from an early interview with Victoria Glendinning, where Dickens is cited along with Sterne, Swift, Grass, Joyce, Beckett, Flann O'Brien and Márquez, Rushdie is virtually silent about the great Victorian.[2] I want to suggest, however, that Dickens's fatherly—or indeed fathering—presence is felt at crucial moments in *Midnight's Children, Shame,* and *The Satanic Verses.* More precisely, Dickens's paternity is both acknowledged and ironized, in an ambivalent mode characteristic of most postcolonial writing.[3]

Rushdie's efforts to undermine the fixity of heredity question conventional definitions of origin, since a system of *filiation,* which Edward Said defines as a "linear, biologically grounded process, that which ties children to their parents," gives way to *affiliation,* "that is, those creeds, philosophies, and visions re-assembling the world in new non-familial ways" (*Beginnings* xiii).[4] Family, the earliest and most basic unit of reference in the constitution of identity, is thoroughly defamiliarized in novels whose dense intertextuality complicates the notion of original creation. Indeed, as Linda Hutcheon has observed, the intertextual play "put[s] into question the authority of [...] writing by locating the discourses of both history and fiction within an ever-expanding intertextual network that mocks any notion of either single origin or simple causality" (*A Poetics of Postmodernism,* 129).

In *Midnight's Children* and in *Shame,* the presence of Dickens is, like the identity of Saleem and Omar, held in suspense despite the fact that he haunts their births as literary characters through allusions to *David Copperfield.* In *The Satanic Verses,* straightforward references to *Our Mutual Friend* are scattered in the crucial scene of the party, so that Dickens is shown to attend another, bleaker kind of birth: the birth of evil in Saladin Chamcha. The enigma of influence which motivates the plot of the first two novels and in turn informs *The Satanic Verses* is thus repeated at the textual level. Furthermore, the main intertexts of *Midnight's Children* turn out to be Dickens's all time favorites, *Tristram Shandy* and the *Arabian Nights.*[5]

The *Arabian Nights*: from Dickens to Rushdie

> Taking a handkerchief from his pocket, he rubbed briskly: once, twice, thrice. The lights all went on at once. Zeenat Vakil entered the room.
>
> Salman Rushdie, *The Satanic Verses*

There are several allusions to the *Arabian Nights* in *David Copperfield.* Significantly, the legacy of David's deceased father to his son consists of "a small collection of books" stocked "in a little room upstairs [...] which nobody else in our house ever troubled" (*David Copperfield,* 105).[6] There, David finds relief from his dreary life under the iron rule of Mr. and Mrs. Murdstone, "reading as if for life" (*David Copperfield,* 106) *Tom Jones, Don Quixote* and *Robinson Crusoe,* along with the *Arabian Nights* and the *Tales of the Genii.* Later on, at the prison-like school of Salem House, David cements his ambiguous relationship with Steerforth by telling him the stories he read as a child, thus taking on, as Steerforth himself remarks, the role of Scheherazade.[7] The references to the *Arabian Nights* occur in two scenes that mark important stages in David's growth as a writer. The first passage emphasises the consolatory and life-giving aspect of reading, since David survives the hardships of his youth by escaping into books. The second represents a transitional period of remembering and retelling before David evolves into a fully-fledged author. Dickens seems to suggest that reading, appropriating, and transforming stories ("What ravages I committed on my favourite authors in the course of my interpretation of them, I am not in a condition to say"—*David Copperfield,* 144) play a crucial role in the creative process. Through David, he is thus paying homage to the seminal works which enabled him to "give birth" to his own original character.

At the beginning of *Midnight's Children,* Saleem declares that in order to tell the story of the thousand and one children of midnight, he "must work fast, faster than Scheherazade, if I am to end up meaning—yes, meaning—something" (*Midnight's Children* 9). When he resumes the story "which [he] left yesterday hanging in mid-air", Saleem again draws parallels between his narrative situation and his illustrious predecessor's. "[J]ust as Scheherazade, depending for her very survival on leaving Prince Shahryar eaten up by curiosity, used to do night after night" (*Midnight's Children* 24), he unravels the thread of his story, on which his own life also hangs. Yet Saleem's flattering comparison with Scheherazade is ironic, as it follows Padma's blunt dismissal of his efforts as so much "writing-shiting" (*Midnight's Children* 24).

In *The Satanic Verses,* Rushdie self-consciously rewrites the scene of David's voracious assimilation of his father's literary heritage when Changez Chamchawala brings the wanderings of the *Arabian Nights* to an end by letting its collected tales rot in his library. Saladin Chamcha's father keeps "a ten-volume set of the Richard Burton translation of the *Arabian Nights,* which was being slowly devoured by mildew and bookworm owing to the deep-seated prejudice against books which led Changez to own thousands of the pernicious things in order to humiliate them by leaving them to rot unread" beside "a magic lamp, a brightly polished copper-and-brass avatar of Aladdin's very own genie-container: a lamp begging to be rubbed" (*The Satanic Verses* 36). By keeping books under lock and key, Changez refuses his son access to what Saladin considers his rightful legacy: a treasure of words and the imaginary worlds they conjure up, represented by Aladdin's magic lamp. Read in the light of Dickens's text, Saladin's trajectory implies that his own father must also die to release a rich cultural past so that the imaginative and creative faculties of the son are freed to invent a satisfying life for himself at last.[8] In sum, Rushdie establishes a complex filiation with Dickens by reinscribing his novels along with their original sources, and so bears witness to the constant exchange that took place between the cultures of the East and the West. At the same time, the novelist manifests a profound ambivalence towards the authority figures of both cultures, as he sees them to inhibit *and* nurture the creative process. I want to show how, in *Midnight's Children* and *Shame,* Rushdie's dialogue with *David Copperfield* brings out these tensions.

David Copperfield is Born Again

> Dickens has created creatures who cling to us and tyrannize over us,
> creatures whom we would not forget if we could,
> creatures whom we could not forget if we would,
> creatures who are more actual than the man who made them.
>
> —G. K. Chesterton

In *Culture and Imperialism,* Edward Said has convincingly argued that mainstream Victorian fiction, including the novels of Charles Dickens, contributed to the imagination of Empire even when these works were only marginally concerned with life in the colonies. While the stories replicate the power relation between the metropolitan center and its overseas territories, they also sometimes betray unease about the imperial venture. Said notes that in *Great Expectations* the relation between the idle youth Pip and his benefactor Magwitch, exiled in the penal colony of Australia, is emblematic of the attitude of the metropolitan center towards the immense profit it derived from the colonies. Pip's horror at the discovery of the source of his wealth thus dramatises the ambivalence of the imperial imagination, which projects fantasies marked by either fear or delight onto its overseas territories. Rushdie, like Said, focuses on the rare but telling moments when the colonial relationship is played out in Dickens's text and alters their significance by repeating and displacing them from a postcolonial perspective.

Midnight's Children playfully emulates Dickens's fictional worlds in being a work of capacious imagination and comic power. In particular, Rushdie pays homage to *David Copperfield,* whose presence at the birth of Saleem Sinai is attested, as we shall soon see, by a salute of welcome at the beginning of the novel. Like Dickens, Rushdie enjoys juggling with tones, styles and registers. In Victoria Glendinning's words, he notably claims to adapt Dickens's "comic combination of naturalistic background and surrealist foreground." Similarly, he delights in the invention of characters and in artfully combining social satire, sentimental interests, and reflections on the relation between identity and writing.

What Rushdie most significantly adopts from his literary father, however, is the motif of the child of uncertain origin who needs to replace a traumatic past with his own inventions. A changeling raised in a Bombay bourgeois family, Saleem is ejected from the narrower family circle when the enigma of his origin is revealed. In his subsequent life of wandering, he plays the part of the surrogate son to various parental figures. Saleem thus shares the fate of the rejected children that figure in Dickens's major novels: David Copperfield, Oliver Twist, Little Nell, Florence Dombey, poor Jo, and of

course Pip, with whom David shares the earliest memory of a visit to a cold
tombstone in the nearby churchyard. A "posthumous child", David loses his
beloved and frail mother early in the novel and, after suffering the cruelty of
his stepfather, is eventually "adopted" by one of his father's aunts, Miss
Betsey Trotwood.

The narrator had introduced the character of Betsey Trotwood three pages
into the novel, immediately after describing his actual birth: David informs
us that she was briefly and unhappily married to a handsome but violent man
who left her to try his luck in India "and there, according to a wild legend
in our family, he was once seen riding on an elephant, in company with a
Baboon; but I think it must have been a Baboo—or a Begum" (*David Copperfield* 51). This passing allusion to imperial Britain in the colonial imagery
of elephants, monkeys, servants, and exotic mistresses is a vignette which
neatly captures the phantasmic quality of European projections on India.
Their fictitious character is revealed, however, by the "wild legend" running
in the family as well as through the enigmatic nature of cultural difference;
the unfamiliar context defies naming and identification. Description slips over
elusive signifiers which muddle the veracity of the account of the life of
Betsey's husband in India. Hesitating between baboon, baboo, and begum,
David's imagination is thus let loose in a world of word-play.

India is the place where Dickens "exiles" unpleasant characters.[9] Jack
Maldon, the young Mrs. Strong's "paramour" (or so David wants us to
believe), is expediently sent to India by Mr. Wickfield. While the misrepresentations of India are amusingly discarded in favor of other misrepresentations
by David's friends (who, as it were, promote a reassuringly "tame" version
of its "wilderness"), the child's own oriental fantasies are once again based
on the suggestive power of the *Arabian Nights:*

> I recollect it was settled by general consent that India was quite a misrepresented
> country, and had nothing objectionable in it, but a tiger or two, and a little heat
> in the warm part of the day. For my own part, I looked on Mr. Jack Maldon
> as a modern Sinbad, and pictured him the bosom friend of all the Rajahs in the
> East, sitting under canopies, smoking curly golden pipes—a mile long, if they
> could be straightened out.   (*David Copperfield* 300)

The concluding and almost surreal image of the mile-long hookah pipe neatly
figures the impossibility of putting the reality of India straight.

Much later in the novel, we encounter Betsey Trotwood again when she
rescues David from Mr. and Mrs. Murdstone and enables him to begin a new
life "in a new name, and with everything new about [him]" (*David Copperfield* 271–72). In this reconstituted and most unconventional family composed of a gaunt divorcée and her protégé, the eccentric Mr. Dick, David
finds at last some happiness and a home where he can "make another beginning," as the heading of chapter fifteen explicitly states, under the new name

of Trotwood Copperfield. In this way, David symbolically becomes the son Betsey and her long-gone husband never had, and we may extrapolate that this absent father is one of a line with the British Methwold in *Midnight's Children* and the anonymous "Angrez" in *Shame,* who unwittingly give birth to literary sons.

The first chapter of *David Copperfield* starts with the memorable paragraph where David puts his reader and himself to the test of answering a crucial question:

> Whether I shall turn to be the hero of my own life, or whether that station will be held by anybody else, these pages must show. To begin my life with the beginning of my life, I record that I was born (as I have been informed and believe) on a Friday, at twelve o'clock at night. It was remarked that the clock began to strike, and I began to cry, simultaneously.

In *Midnight's Children,* Saleem first gives a boldly positive answer to this question by taking central responsibility for the history of India before being gradually relegated to its margins. Saleem's parentage turns out to be that of the substituted child of romantic comedy and, like *David Copperfield,* the narrator of *Midnight's Children* begins his narrative—and his life—on the auspicious stroke of midnight before he, like his predecessor, starts "meandering":

> I was born in the city of Bombay . . . once upon a time. No, that won't do, there's no getting away from the date: I was born in Doctor Narlikar's Nursing Home on August 15th, 1947. And the time? The time matters, too.Well then: at night. No, it's important to be more. . . . On the stroke of midnight, as a matter of fact. Clock-hands joined palms in respectful greeting as I came.
> (*Midnight's Children* 9)

Reproducing the typically Dickensian dialogue between the conventions of the fairy-tale and the demands of realist fiction, the inaugural scene provides a key as to how the conflict with origin is to be acted out and originality (and individuality) achieved. If the hybridisation of traditional forms is an essential element of this strategy, the type of intervention performed on the famous opening of Dickens's "favourite child" is equally revealing.[10] By displacing the Dickensian reference in time (August 15th, 1947, India's independence day) and in space (the city of Bombay), Rushdie repeats Dickens's original text from the perspective of cultural difference. The grafting of otherness on the repeated motif of the birth of a novel echoing the birth of its narrator estranges its origin, thereby enabling originality. Thus, the striking of the clocks which heralds David Copperfield's birth is supplemented in Rushdie's version by the wonderful image of the "clock-hands join[ing] palms in respectful greetings" (*Midnight's Children* 9). The dead metaphor of the clock-hands is revived through its analogy with the Asian gesture of benevolent salute. Dickens's paternal influence on Saleem's birth is thus literally welcomed, as it were, from afar.

David Copperfield also happens to be the favorite substitute father of Omar Khayyam Shakil.[11] A few pages into *Shame,* the peripheral hero of this political allegory alludes to the first sentence of *David Copperfield* as an appropriate commentary on his own calamitous existence. "Whether I shall turn out to be the hero of my own life, or whether that station will be held by anybody else, these pages must show" is thus reappropriated by Omar who, like David, is "destined to be unlucky in life" and "privileged to see ghosts and spirits" (*David Copperfield* 49):

> "You see before you," he confided, "a fellow who is not even the hero of his own life; a man born and raised in the condition of being out of things. Heredity counts, dontyoutthinkso?"
> "That is an oppressive notion," Iskander harrapa replied.   (*Shame* 24)

Omar rounds off his (unacknowledged) citation with a remark on the importance of heredity, in order to explain his condition as a marginal figure in history (and in the story). On a metatextual level, Omar's appeal to the constraining laws of genealogy draws attention to his incapacity to exist as an original character, since he can only conceive of his destiny in terms that are borrowed from another. In the larger context of the history of Pakistan, the narrative also oscillates between a belief in the determinism of "heredity" and a rejection of this "oppressive notion": after the partition, Pakistan is indeed "that country divided into two Wings a thousand miles apart, that fantastic bird of a place, two Wings without a body, sundered by the landmass of its greatest foe, joined by nothing but God" (*Shame* 178). Rushdie seems to imply that, split from the moment of its creation, Pakiston is doomed to civil war and fratricidal power plays. A hopeless and helpless witness to the relationship between the Westernised Iskander Harrapa and the Islamic General Raza Hyder, in the course of which the adoptive son betrays his spiritual father and puts him to death, Omar can only submit to the violent logic of "unnatural" acts. In Rushdie's version, the political myth of Pakistan is thus recast as the Oedipal or Shakespearean drama, with the difference that, in Rushdie's harsh opinion, "The Zia-Bhutto relationship is tragic—the protégé becomes the executioner—but the figures haven't the stature you can associate with high tragedy. These are people who don't deserve tragedy" ("Salman Rushdie: A Literary Conversation" 248). The history of Pakistan activates Rushdie's own filial anxieties and his ambivalence towards the figure of the father. As a consequence, *Shame*'s fictional world is appropriately riddled with guilt and haunted by the spectres of angry ghosts seeking revenge on those who have humiliated them. The killing of the father, which Rushdie fantasizes in the political history of Pakistan, is narrated with a mixture of horror and the suspect complacency of the one who, as Sara Suleri has aptly diagnosed, "tells lurid family tales with the zeal of a distant relative" (The Rhetoric of English India 177). If Omar's ventriloquism manifests a desire to evade responsibility, the narrator's grappling with the problematic issue of influence brings out the fear and desire to transgress Freud's original taboo. The related issue of influence and transgression, treated with playful irreverence in *Midnight's Children,* takes on much sinister overtones in *Shame* and culminates in *The Satanic Verses.*

In *Shame,* the context for the quotation from *David Copperfield* not only inscribes circumstantial and cultural difference, as in *Midnight's Children,* but it also ironizes and darkens its significance: while the first mention of David's dilemma occurs in a drinking bout, the second takes place during a questioning when Omar Shakil fails to answer Talvar Ul-Haq's questions and, pathetically ineffectual to the end, confesses to the Chief Martial Law Administrator and Federal Security Force that "Other persons have been the principal actors in my life-story" (*Shame* 283). Incapable of taking responsibility for his deeds as well as for his words, Omar's excuse only precipitates his violent end. The appeal to Dickens is shown to be irrelevant in the immediate context of the questioning ("We are getting nowhere," replies Ul-Haq), and is further dismissed as an inappropriate subtext to the narration of Pakistani history. In this sense, Omar's invocation of *David Copperfield* reverses Saleem's: far from having any life-giving power, it provokes Ul-Haq into shooting him in the heart. This first version of his death is followed by his alternative dispatch at the hands of his retarded wife, which bleakly ends the novel. *Shame* thus symbolically decenters Dickens, along with the character who mimics David: "no longer the hero of Rushdie's novel," Dickens is replaced by the sound and the fury of Jacobean drama, or rather the irreducible difference of historical and political specificity.

Our Mutual Friend revisited

Rushdie deliberately hybridises his Western heritage with the Indian oral narrative tradition, from which he borrows the circumvoluted and reiterative structure of his novels.[12] The influence of *The Arabian Nights* on Dickens already showed that cross-cultural borrowing was a fundamental source of literary creativity. From the collection of tales (of mainly Indo-Persian but also Arabic and Egyptian origin) and the work of the prolific Victorian writer, Rushdie convokes two characters, Scheherazade and David Copperfield, who play the "literary parents" of Saleem Sinai as he is born in the first pages of *Midnight's Children.* In *The Satanic Verses,* another unlikely couple is present at the birth of evil in Saladin Chamcha: Podsnap and Iago.

The Satanic Verses inscribes and displaces the Dickensian and Shakespearean heritage when *Our Mutual Friend* and *Othello* are significantly referred
to at a turning-point in the narrative, if only as decor in a postmodern pastiche.
This scene enacts the purely decorative presence of past forms that is commonly associated with postmodern practice and global culture. Yet, in Rushdie's characteristic manner, the literalization of this decorativeness is itself
suspect: the invocation of Dickens and Shakespeare at a turning-point in the
narrative reinvests these sources of inspiration with significance, albeit a
different one from the original. Saladin Chamcha and Gibreel Farishta meet
again at a party organized by the stammering S. S. Sisodia in the Shepperton
film studios where a "huge re-creation of Dickensian London" is staged for
"a musical adaptation of the great writer's last completed novel, renamed
Friend!" (*The Satanic Verses* 421).[13] Dickens commodified serves as a literal
background to a tragi-comic replay of *Othello* when Saladin takes revenge
on Gibreel for letting him down after the fall:

> What follows is tragedy.—Or, at the least the echo of tragedy, the full-blooded
> original being unavailable to modern men and women, so it's said.—A bur-
> lesque for our degraded, imitative times, in which clowns re-enact what was
> first done by heroes and by kings.   (*The Satanic Verses* 424)

Thus, while the setting itself re-presents a vertiginous *mise-en-abyme* for the
postmodern strategy at work in the entire novel, a fetish of British culture is
recycled as the stage (literal and figurative) on which another canonical text
is to be replayed as burlesque, as the self-conscious and theoretically wise
narrator (who knows that literature, just like history, repeats itself only as
farce) points out.[14] The *trompe-l'oeil* of Dickens's London and the revamping
of *Our Mutual Friend* suggest a fairly complex *mise-en-abyme,* as we recall
that Dickens's last completed novel deals precisely with the recycling of dead
objects and even of dead people. Ironically, the actor playing the role of Jesse
"Gaffer" Hexam, one of the waterside men who makes a living fishing for
drowned bodies and robbing them of their valuables in *Our Mutual Friend,*
rescues Jumpy Joshi—Saladin and Gibreel's "mutual enemy"—knocked
cold by Gibreel in the fake Thames during the party. Gaffer Hexam briefly
reappears in the dramatic context of communalist violence in India, when
Saladin Chamcha reads about a massacre of Muslims in the newspapers:
"their corpses . . . dumped in the water, where they awaited the ministrations
of some twentieth century Gaffer Hexam" (*The Satanic Verses* 518). In this
sense, like the narrator, the film producer Sisodia revives, yet transforms by
updating, a novel that itself adapts the perennial myth of death and rebirth
to nineteenth century London. This theme in turn informs *The Satanic Verses*

which begins with "In order to be born again, first you have to die" and goes on to show how the past survives by transforming itself in the present.

The relevance of *Our Mutual Friend* to the scene depicted in *The Satanic Verses* is also evidently linked to the comedy of social life that counterbalances the dark atmosphere of the river and its scavengers. Dickens anatomises the false glitter of the world of Victorian bourgeois society with the Podsnaps and the nouveaux riches Veneerings, who "have a house out of the Tales of the Genii, and give dinners out of the Arabian Nights" (*Our Mutual Friend* 249) in the words of Lady Tippins. Rushdie similarly makes fun of their late twentieth-century descendants who gravitate to the equally artificial world of the film industry and the media:

> Society grandees, fashion models, film stars, corporation bigwigs, a brace of minor royal Personages, useful politicians and such like riff-raff perspire and mingle in these counterfeit streets with numbers of men and women as sweat-glistened as the "real" guests and as counterfeit as the city.
> (*The Satanic Verses* 422)

Our Mutual Friend transmogrified and renamed by show biz wizards as the exclamatory and ambiguous *Friend!* also provides an appropriately ironic commentary on the relation between Saladin and Gibreel, which evolves towards jealousy and enmity during the party, to the extent that Saladin takes on the role of Iago to destroy his former companion. At the moment when Saladin moves towards Gibreel through the crowd of fashionable people, he "seems to see, *right now,* that same sneer upon Farishta's face, that scorn of an inverted Podsnap, for whom all things English are worthy of derision instead of praise" (*The Satanic Verses* 425–26). What triggers Saladin's hatred is thus the recognition of his own image as Podsnap reflected in the sneer of his inverted double, Gibreel, "For are they not conjoined opposites, these two, each man the other's shadow?—One seeking to be transformed into the foreignness he admires, the other preferring, contemptuously, to transform" (*The Satanic Verses* 426). Saladin's revenge takes the form of anonymous phone calls to Gibreel where he sings doggerel verse implying that Gibreel's girl-friend is unfaithful to him, which finally drives him mad.

On another level, the scene repeats the problematic of faithfulness and betrayal in the context of Rushdie's own use and misuse of the literary authorities of the past. In the words of the singing actors, *"What kind of fellow is Our Mutual Friend? What does he intend? Is he the kind of fellow on whom you may depend? Etc. Etc. Etc."* (*The Satanic Verses* 423). The spokeswoman for Rushdie's answer to his predecessors turns out to be a female guest who, "in an expert parody of the Marine Insurance agent's self-important posture, [. . .] launches into her own version of the scheduled musical Podsnappery". She thus repeats with an ironic distance the lyrics of the next act of the musical, Mr. Podsnap's solo, which only slightly adapt Dickens's text:

> *Ours is a Copious Language,*
> *A Language Trying to Strangers;*
> *Ours is the Favoured Nation,*
> *Blest, and Safe from Dangers . . .   (The Satanic Verses 423)*

In the wonderfully comic scene of the original, the fatuous Podsnap condescends to a Frenchman who is at pains to make sense of the conversation.
Instead of engaging with his questions, Podsnap keeps correcting his pronun-
ciation: "Our language," said Mr. Podsnap, with a gracious consciousness
of always being right, "is Difficult. Ours is a Copious language, and Trying
to Strangers. I will not Pursue my Question" (*Our Mutual Friend* 133).
The rhyme pattern of the lyrics, which equate "strangers" with "dangers,"
exposes further Podsnap's national pride, which translates in a distasteful
and distrustful attitude to foreigners. This is particularly striking when Podsnap cuts the Frenchman short as a way of evading a likely challenge of his
arrogant assertion that the English Constitution "Was Bestowed Upon Us
By Providence".[15] Podsnap's reaction is once again to reassert his authority
by taking advantage of the linguistic difficulties of his interlocutor. In this
instance, however, the "otherness" of the Frenchman is explicitly invoked
to prevent dialogue:

> "And ozer countries?—" the foreign gentleman was beginning, when Mr.
> Podsnap put him right away again. "We do not say Ozer; we say Other."
>
> (*Our Mutual Friend* 133)

If Podsnap is a parody of the self-satisfied English bourgeoisie and a representative member of a society in decline and about to fall, Saladin, the "other"
who desperately tries to be assimilated into English society, is a "second
degree" parody himself. By emulating British ways, adopting their tastes and
mimicking their accents, he has become "more English than" (*The Satanic
Verses* 53). As Steven Connor points out, the Dickens musical reveals to
Saladin that cultural identity is not an essence but an "effect—the projection
outwards for global consumption by the tourist and culture industries of an
Englishness that is in some sense already derived from or dependent upon
the images of self from the outside" (*The English Novel in History* 126).
    It is revealing that, to cover Gibreel's singing of the hit number of *Mr 420*,
"Mera Joota Hai Japani" as they fall towards England at the beginning of
The Satanic Verses, Saladin sings the first stanza of "Rule, Britannia!":

> *When Britain first, at Heaven's command,*
> *Arose from out the azure main,*
> *This was the chapter of the land,*
> *And guardian angels sung this strain—*
> *Rule, Britannia, rule the waves;*
> *Britons never will be slaves.*

The lyrics of the original are quoted in a truncated and comically stressed form as "arooooose from out of aaaazure main" and "and guardian aaaaangels sung the strain" (*The Satanic Verses* 6). Unsurprisingly, and with similar parodic intent, Dickens also has Podsnap quote the national anthem as a conclusive authority to end his dialogue with the Frenchman. The insistent allusions to Podsnap at the party reveal to Saladin that self-hatred results from being "An Indian translated into an English-medium" (*The Satanic Verses* 58). English is indeed "A Language Trying to Strangers" and Gibreel, a master actor himself, sees through Saladin's act, which outdoes what he believes to be "the real thing". Unwilling to "Decline and Fall Off the British Empire" himself (to adapt Silas Wegg's misreading of the title, which he mistakes for the author), Saladin responds by eliminating the one who mocks his alienation by causing an even more destructive mental breakdown in Gibreel. *The Satanic Verse*'s twice removed parodic version of Podsnappery thus reflects on Dickens's critical treatment of "Anglo-centeredness" and foregrounds its more dramatic aspects.

In this sense, *Friend!* crystallizes the ambivalent strategy of appropriation at work in the novel. Do Rushdie and Dickens remain mutual friends in *The Satanic Verses?* If a subversive strategy is evidently at work in Rushdie's appeal to Dickens and Shakespeare, these two icons of British culture also represent the two main aspects of the human theater, which hesitates between comedy and tragedy. While Dickens best captured the vanity fair of "Society" in *Our Mutual Friend,* it was Shakespeare who knew how to interrogate the enigma of evil, "how it's born, why it grows, how it takes unilateral possession of a many-sided human soul" (*The Satanic Verses* 424). As he draws on the great literature of the past, Rushdie searches for new ways of phrasing the same old questions in order to adapt them to the new contexts of a rapidly changing world. The presence of Shakespeare and Dickens attests to their universal relevance, even though they must be submitted to critical and creative rewriting from a different cultural position. "The process of reinscription and negotiation—the insertion of intervention of something that takes on new meaning" therefore combines an homage to Shakespeare and Dickens's insights into human nature with "a contestation of the given symbols of authority" (*The Location of Culture* 193) which enables the production of new forms and meanings.

NOTES

1. In *Haroun and the Sea of Stories,* however, the father-son relationship is treated in the sentimental mode. Haroun embarks on a quest to rescue his father, the

storyteller Rashid Khalifa, and return to him his special gift of storytelling along with his eloped wife. This updated Arabian Nights complete with silly princes, corrupt politicians, and technological conundrums reads like an allegory of Rushdie's own predicament.

2. On the mixed traditions of his novels, see " 'Commonwealth Literature' Does Not Exist" (1983), "Günter Grass" (1984), and "In Good Faith" (1990) in *Imaginary Homelands*. To these incomplete lists of novelistic influences must of course be added the many sources from high and popular culture that Rushdie delights in hybridising, from Ovid to *The Wizard of Oz*, from the Qur'an to the Bombay talkies. The much noted Grass-Rushdie connection is extensively documented by Patricia Merivale, who discusses similarities in narrative technique, structure, tone and themes, among which "ambiguous paternity [which] forms a large part of [their] search for origins" (*Reading Rushdie* p. 84).

3. The language of colonialism extensively used the biological imagery of birth and genealogy to describe the relationship of the imperial center to its colonies as one between parents and children (exemplified, for instance, in Kipling's poetry). The parent metaphor, which naturalizes and thus legitimizes the colonial rule, "stressed age, experience, roots, tradition [. . .]. Above all [parents] are the *origin* and therefore claim the final authority in all questions" (*The Empire Writes Back* p. 16).

4. Said elaborates on the shift from *filiation* (the old paternal authority embodied in family, home, class, country, and traditional beliefs) to *affiliation* in modern fiction and culture at large in *The World, The Text, and the Critic* (esp. 16–24). An alternative model to account for Rushdie's relations to his predecessors would be Harold Bloom's influential "theory of misreading" in *The Anxiety of Influence*, Based on Freud's "family romance", it views creation as a "wrestle [. . .] even to the death" *The Anxiety of Influence* 5) with the strong poets of the past. Among the six revisionary modes identified by Bloom, both *tessera* (a reading of the parent-poem which alters its meaning, and thus entails completion and antithesis) and, in the case of the satanic verses episode, daemonization or the "Counter-Sublime" (which questions the uniqueness of the earlier work and the force of its inspiration) could conceivably be applied to *The Satanic Verses*. However, it seems to me that Rushdie's novels manifest a desire to break away from the genealogical model of influence on which Bloom's theory is premised. Moreover, they involve a cultural translation of the Western heritage which adds a significant socio-political dimension to the process of rewriting which Bloom seems to ignore.

5. Keith Wilson establishes numerous parallels between *Midnight's Children* and *Tristram Shandy*, another of Rushdie's most commented-upon intertexts, including "ill-starred origins [. . .] linked to the striking of a clock" (*Reading Rushdie* 65). In the same volume, Nancy E. Batty discusses the shaping influence of the *Arabian Nights* on *Midnight's Children* as a text which "dramatize[s] the problematic relationship of life to art" (*Reading Rushdie* 69).

6. Dickens is not the only novelist to be fascinated by the *Arabian Nights*. Elleke Boehmer traces the widespread influence of the tales in nineteenth-century works as diverse as Wordsworth's *The Prelude*, Charlotte Brontë's *Jane Eyre*, Anthony

Trollope's *Tales of All Countries* and De Quincey's *The Confessions of an English Opium Eater.* She observes that this particular instance of Orientalist thought interestingly "tak[es] the form of [the East's] own fantasies of a paradisiacal Orient" (*Colonial and Postcolonial Literature* 45).

7. When he learns that David recalls the stories he read as a child, Steerforth suggests the following arrangement in exchange for his protection and friendship: " 'Then I tell you what, young Copperfield,' [. . .] 'you shall tell 'em to me. I can't get to sleep very early at night, and I generally wake rather early in the morning. We'll go over 'em one after another. We'll make some regular Arabian Nights of it.' I felt extremely flattered by this arrangement, and we commenced carrying it into execution that very evening. What ravages I committed in my interpretation of them, I am not in condition to say, and should be very unwilling to know; but I had a profound faith in them, and I had, to the best of my belief, a simple, earnest manner of narrating what I did narrate; and these qualities went a long way" (*David Copperfield* 144–45).

8. This contrasts with Rushdie's description of his father as "a magical parent of young children" in Ian Hamilton's lively pre-fatwa biography. Rushdie's sister Sameen adds: "We never had a 'story a night.' The story never ended. [. . .] One story fell into another story. Some of them were rooted in the 'Arabian Nights,' but he would embellish them and some he would tell straight, probably depending on how imaginative or tired he was feeling. That they never ended is what I remember" ("The First Life of Salman Rushdie," p. 92). Rushdie's loving homage to his story-telling father is of course Rashid Khalifa, Haroun's father in *Haroun and the Sea of Stories,* which he has dedicated to his own son, Zafar.

9. Said notes that "In his new carrier as colonial businessman, Pip is hardly an exceptional figure, since nearly all of Dickens's businessmen, wayward relatives, and frightening outsiders have a fairly normal and secure connection with the empire" (*Culture and Imperialism* xvii). Elleke Boehmer documents this assertion and shows how Australia, like India, "acts to relieve social and sexual embarrassment" in Dickens's novels (*Colonial and Postcolonial Literature* 28). Thus, Mr Micawber believes that "something of an extraordinary nature will turn up on that shore," and fallen Emily is taken to Australia to begin a new life.

10. In the 1869 preface to his novel, Dickens states that, "Of all my books, I like this the best. It will be easily believed that I am a fond parent to every child of my fancy, and that no one can ever love that family as dearly as I love them. But, like many fond parents, I have in my heart of hearts a favourite child. And his name is DAVID COPPERFIELD."

11. Omar Khayyam Shakil is named after a poet whose fate is equally trans-cultural, as the narrator takes pains to point out: "Omar Khayyam's position as a poet is curious. He was never very popular in his native Persia; and he exists in the West in a translation that is really a complete reworking of his verses, in many cases very different from the spirit (to say nothing of the content) of the original. I, too, am a translated man" (*Shame* 29).

12. Rushdie has repeatedly stressed the influence of native oral forms on his novels. Rushdie was notably impressed and inspired by a famous story-teller of Baroda who used to gather huge crowds of listeners: "Listening to this man reminded

me of the shape of the oral narrative. It's not linear. An oral narrative does not go from the beginning to the middle to the end of the story. It goes in great swoops, it goes in spirals or in loops, it every so often reiterates something that happened earlier to remind you, and then takes you off again, sometimes summarises itself, it frequently digresses off into something that the story teller appears just to have thought of, then it comes back to the main thrust of the narrative [. . .]. So that's what *Midnight's Children* was, I think, and I think everything about Laurence Sterne, Garcia Márquez, and all that, comes a long way behind that, and that was the thing that I felt when writing it that I was trying to do" (*"Midnight's Children* and *Shame"* 7–8).

13. Steven Connor suggests an interesting parallel with Dickens's *Bleak House* and *Our Mutual Friend,* where the city of London functions as a metaphor for the imaginary space of the text. In *The Satanic Verses,* London (or, rather, a representation of Dickens's London) is condensed on the film-set which superposes residential and derelict areas, collapses and conflates class barriers, "telescoping together [. . .] centres and margins." Alert to the ambivalence of Rushdie's citation, Connor remarks that "There is both mockery and admiration in [his] enjoyment of the vulgar travesty of the novel being brought about in this adaptation" (*The English Novel in History* 124).

14. In his influential essay "Postmodernism and Consumer Society," Fredric Jameson identifies postmodernism as a reaction against the "dead, stifling, canonical [. . .] reified monuments" (*The Anti-Aesthetic* 112) of the establishment; it notably takes the form of pastiche, a type of "blank parody" which incorporates various texts where traditional distinctions between high culture and mass or popular culture are erased. Although it certainly conflates the "high" and the "low", Rushdie's parody of *Othello* is far from blank. Saladin's reenactment of Iago's destruction of Othello/Gibreel and the beautiful blonde Desdemona/Allie Cone is the ultimate evidence of his alienation to "white" values. Indeed, *Othello* "is an obvious focus for counter-discursive interpretations because it centralises racial issues, presenting miscegenation as not just a metaphorical threat to the white society but as an actualised event" (*Post-Colonial Drama* 24).

15. Elleke Boehmer usefully reminds us that such patriotic rhetoric was widespread in the second half of the nineteenth century. She suggests that "In Britain itself, patriotism, called jingoism in its more rabid forms, was perhaps the most powerful medium through which the belief in the Empire was maintained." Theories of racial and cultural superiority combined with the so-called duty to bring civilisation, prosperity, and Christianity to the "savages," conspired to legitimate imperial rule. Indeed, "the Victorians had a genius for fashioning moral ideals which matched their economic needs" (*Colonial and Postcolonial Literature* 35, 36).

WORKS CITED

Ashcroft, Bill, Gareth Griffiths, and Helen Tiffin, *The Empire Writes Back* (London & New York: Routledge, 1989).

Batty, Nancy E. "The Art of Suspense: Rushdie's 1001 (Mid-)Nights" in *Reading Rushdie: Perspectives on the Fiction of Salman Rushdie,* ed. D. M. Fletcher (Amsterdam: Rodopi, 1994), 69–81.

Bhabha, Homi K. *The Location of Culture* (London & New York: Routledge, 1994).

Bloom, Harold. *The Anxiety of Influence: A Theory of Poetry* (London: Oxford UP, 1975).

Boehmer, Elleke. *Colonial and Postcolonial Literature: Migrant Metaphors* (Oxford: Oxford UP, 1995).

Connor, Steven. *The English Novel in History: 1950–1995* (London: Routledge, 1996).

Dickens, Charles. *David Copperfield* Harmondsworth: Penguin, 1986).

———. *Our Mutual Friend* (Oxford & New York: Oxford UP, 1991).

Gilbert, Helen and Joanne Tompkins. *Post-Colonial Drama: Theory, Practice, Politics* (London: Routledge, 1996).

Glendinning, Victoria. "A Novelist in the Country of the Mind," *Sunday Times* (25 October 1981): 38.

Hamilton, Ian. "The First Life of Salman Rushdie," *New Yorker* (25 December 1995 & 1 January1996): 90–113.

Hutcheon, Linda. *A Poetics of Postmodernism: History, Theory, Fiction* (New York: Routledge, 1988).

Jaggi, Maya. "The Last Laugh," *New Statesman and Society* (8 September 1995): 20–21.

Jameson, Fredric. "Postmodernism and Consumer Society" in *The Anti-Aesthetic: Essays on Postmodern Culture,* ed. Hal Foster (Seattle, Washington: Bay Press, 1991), 111–125.

Merivale, Patricia. "Saleem Fathered by Oskar: Intertextual Strategies in *Midnight's Children* and *The Tin Drum*" in *Reading Rushdie: Perspectives on the Fiction of Salman Rushdie,* ed. D. M. Fletcher (Amsterdam: Rodopi, 1994), 83–96.

"Midnight's Children and Shame," Kunapipi, vol. 7, no. 1 (1985): 1–19.

Rushdie, Salman. *Haroun and the Sea of Stories* (London: Granta & Penguin, 1990).

———. *Imaginary Homelands: Essays and Criticism 1981–1991* (London: Granta & Penguin, 1991).

———. *Midnight's Children* (London: Picador, 1982).

———. *Shame* (London: Picador, 1984).

———. *The Satanic Verses* (London: Viking Penguin, 1988).

Said, Edward. *Culture and Imperialism* (London: Vintage, 1994).

———. *Orientalism: Western Conceptions of the Orient* (Harmondsworth: Penguin, 1991).

———. *The World, The Text, and the Critic* (Cambridge, Mass.: Harvard UP Press. 1983).

Sangari, Kumkum, "Salman Rushdie: A Literary Conversation," *Book Review,* vol. 8, no. 5 (April 1984): 248.

Williams, Patrick and Laura Chrisman. *Colonial and Post-Colonial Theory: A Reader* (New York: Harvester Wheatsheaf, 1994).

Wilson, Keith. "*Midnight's Children* and Reader Responsibility" in *Reading Rushdie: Perspectives on the Fiction of Salman Rushdie,* ed. D. M. Fletcher (Amsterdam: Rodopi, 1994), 55–68.

The Creation of Becky Sharp
in *Vanity Fair*

John P. Frazee

> Rebecca Crawley (formerly Sharp) is the principal person
> in the book, with whom nearly all the others are connected:
> and a very wonderfully drawn picture she is, as a woman
> scheming for self-advancement, without either heart or prin-
> ciple, yet with a constitutional vivacity and a readiness to
> please, that save her from the contempt or disgust she de-
> serves. As a creation or character, we know not where Rebe-
> cca can be matched in pose fiction.
>
> R. S. Rintoul, *Spectator,* 22 July 1848[1]

This perceptive appreciation of Becky Sharp by R. S. Rintoul, an early critic
of *Vanity Fair,* has been echoed by most critics since: Becky's characterization is one of the novel's great triumphs. In what follows, I propose to
consider Becky's characterization afresh. First, I want to examine what I take
to be an important formal relationship between Thackeray's first long fiction,
Catherine, and *Vanity Fair,* a relationship that illuminates Thackeray's decision to make Becky "the principal person in the book." And second, I want
to develop the argument that, in conformity with his artistic purposes in the
novel, Thackeray based his characterization of Becky Sharp on two historical
figures from the Regency period, Mary Anne Clarke and Harriette Wilson.

In his astute "anatomy" of *Vanity Fair,* Ralph Rader has described the
the artistic logic behind Thackeray's decision to structure his novel around
two major characters rather than one: dividing the narrative between two
characters both broadens the focus of the novel and makes it possible to
incorporate more characters—and hence a fuller picture of society—into his
fiction. Having two main characters also allows Thackeray to make clear that
the fate he sees as part of the universal human condition—"Which of us is
happy in this world? Which of us has his wish? or, having it, is satisfied?"—is
not essentially a moral predicament. Both good people and bad pursue vain

Dickens Studies Annual, Volume 27, Copyright © 1998 by AMS Press, Inc. All rights reserved.

goals. Furthermore, the pursuit can be both active and passive. To dramatize this point, Thackeray makes one of his central characters, Amelia, conventionally virtuous but passive and the other, Becky, conventionally bad and unscrupulously ambitious (58–59).[2]

If dividing his story between two focal characters was a technical innovation, Thackeray's decision to make those characters women—and especially to make one of them an unscrupulous and even immoral woman toward to whom the reader nonetheless responds sympathetically—was a remarkably bold step for a Victorian novelist to take.[3] To understand his decision, we need only imagine how we would react to the novel's principal characters were they male. Amelia's passivity would have been repellent in a male, while Becky would have been as disgusting as that scoundrel from Thackeray's previous novel, *Barry Lyndon*. With male central characters, Thackeray would have found it difficult if not impossible to maintain the Olympian sympathy required for his novel to have its intended force.

Thackeray experienced the converse of this formal problem in his first piece of extended fiction, *Catherine*. In that novel, he attempted to create an unsympathetic female protagonist, but he found himself unable to sustain such a response. I believe that his struggles and frustrations with this apprentice piece may have contributed to his later decision to create female protagonists for *Vanity Fair*. Accordingly, I want to sketch the connection between the two novels briefly.

Thackeray originally intended *Catherine* as a parody of popular novels that took thoroughgoing rogues as their heroes. Looking back on the novel, however, Thackeray wrote that it "was a mistake all through—it was not made disgusting enough that is the fact, and the triumph of it would have been to make readers so horribly horrified as to cause them to give up or rather throw up the book and all or it's [*sic*] kind, whereas you see the author had a sneaking kindness for his heroine, and did not like to make her utterly worthless" (*Letters* I: 433).

Thackeray's inconsistent attitude toward the novel's central character can be easily illustrated by comparing two passages from late in the novel. In the first, the narrator merges sympathetically with Catherine's consciousness as she reflects on the beginnings of her relationship with Galgenstein, for whose love she ultimately murders her husband:

> "[Catherine] looked at [her son by Galgenstein] as he marched down the street, a long, long way. Tom was proud and gay in his new costume, and was not unlike his father. As she looked, lo! Oxford Street disappeared, and she saw a green common, and a village, and a little inn. There was a soldier leading a pair of horses about on the green common; and in the inn sat a cavalier, so young, so merry, so beautiful! . . . Was it not an honour to a country lass that such a noble gentleman should look at her for a moment? had he not some

charm about him that she must needs obey when he whispered in her ear, "Come, follow me!" As she walked towards the lane that morning, how well she remembered each spot as she passed it, and the look it wore for the last time! . . . [H]ow well she remembered the sound of the horses' hoofs, as they came quicker, quicker—nearer, nearer! How noble he looked on his great horse! Was he thinking of her, or were they all silly words which he spoke last night, merely to pass away the time and deceive poor girls with? Would he remember them, would he?   (*Catherine,* 126; ch. VIII)

Thackeray's sympathetic—indeed sentimental—treatment of Catherine's affection for the worthless Galgenstein contrasts sharply with his treatment, only two chapters later, of Catherine's reunion with Galgenstein:

The count advanced toward the maiden. They both were mute for a while; and only the beating of her heart interrupted that thrilling and passionate silence. Ah, what years of buried joys and fears, hopes and disappointments, arose from their graves in the far past, and in those brief moments flitted before the united ones! How sad was that delicious retrospect, and oh, how sweet! The tears that rolled down the cheek of each were bubbles from the choked and moss-grown wells of youth; the sigh that heaved each bosom had some lurking odours in it—memories of the fragrance of boyhood, echoes of the hymns of the young heart. Thus it is ever—for these blessed recollections the soul always has a place; and while crime perishes, and sorrow is forgotten, the beautiful alone is eternal.
   "O golden legends, written in the skies!" mused De Galgenstein, "ye shine as ye did in the olden days! *We* change, but *ye* speak ever the same language. Gazing in the abysmal depths, the feeble ratioci—"

Here the fictional editor breaks off with deletion marks and indicates in a note that fully two and three-quarters pages were cut from the passage. He continues, "Instead, however, of all this rant and nonsense, how much finer is the speech that the Count really did make? 'It is a very fine evening—egad it is!' The 'egad' did the whole business: Mrs. Cat was as much in love with him now as she ever had been" (*Catherine* 141–42; ch. X). The parodic style of this passage can scarcely be reconciled with Thackeray's earlier sympathetic treatment of essentially the same material.

   That Thackeray lost control of his creation in places is undeniable. It may be attributed in part to his novice hand, and in part, too, to his sentimental attraction to women. But of greater importance for understanding the formal relationship of *Catherine* to *Vanity Fair* is the fact that, as Ray says, the story "grew to have an intrinsic interest for Thackeray" (*Thackeray* 232). More precisely, Thackeray's historical imagination took fire at the creation of a probable setting for Catherine and her crime. His creation of a picture of eighteenth-century life, in the context of which Catherine's story unfolds, was, as Ray says, a "remarkable achievement." But Thackeray's authentic evocation of Catherine's historical predicament actually undermined his parodic intention, for part of that predicament was that women were not, and could not be, morally autonomous beings. Derek Jarrett describes a woman's place succinctly: "[T]he whole point about a woman was that she was *not* self-sufficient. . . . Englishwomen in search of their paradise, whether in heaven or on earth, were expected to look for it in a place prepared for them by a man" (143).

Thackeray's intuitive awareness of woman's dependent position is apparent throughout *Catherine*, but the following passage, in which he describes the consequences for Catherine of entering into an illicit affair with Galgenstein, demonstrates Thackeray's awareness of the socio-historical determinants of Catherine's plight:

> For a man, remorse under these circumstances is perhaps uncommon. No stigma affixes on *him* for betraying a woman: no bitter pangs of mortified vanity; no insulting looks of superiority from his neighbor, and no sentence of contemptuous banishment is read against him; they fall on the tempted, not on the tempter, who is permitted to go free. The chief thing that a man learns after having successfully practiced on a woman is to despise the poor wretch whom he has won. The game, in fact, and the glory, such as it is, is all his, and the punishment alone falls upon her   (*Catherine* 36–37; ch. II)

Part of Thackeray's "sneaking fondness" for Catherine, then, arose from his intuitive recognition that in her historical circumstances, Catherine would have been less free to act than a man, and that her actions would have had far graver consequences for her as a woman than they would for a man.

Thackeray's awareness of the historical reality of a woman's dependence on men is also reflected in his creation, out of the bare mention of their counterparts in *The Newgate Calendar,* of the characters of Corporal Brock, Ensign MacShane, and of course Count Galgenstein, who, together with her husband and son, largely determine Catherine's fate and to whom Thackeray assigns much of the responsibility for Catherine's downfall. Galgenstein seduces and abandons her, and the malicious Brock and her son goad her about her miserable marriage until she finally acts violently to end it. Ray properly calls Thackeray's creation of Galgenstein, Brock, and Ensign MacShane "the triumph of the book" (232). They are so in part because Thackeray had greater freedom to create male characters whom the reader can cordially despise. But those male characters absorb or deflect much of the disgust that, according to Thackeray's original design, ought to have been directed at Catherine. Thackeray's parody collapses. Constrained by his sense of Catherine's historical circumstances. Thackeray simply could not make Catherine sufficiently unsympathetic to achieve his parodic intention, producing the "failure" Thackeray considered the novel to be.[4]

Catherine failed in part, then, because Thackeray's historical imagination and his parodic intention were in conflict. But implicit in his failure with *Catherine* was a lesson that could serve Thackeray well in writing *Vanity Fair,* where his historical and fictional intuitions were compatible. By the nature of a woman's dependent, restricted position in the world (as true of the early nineteenth as of the eighteenth century) a female character tends to be inherently more sympathetic than a male. So when Thackeray turned, six years after *Catherine,* to the writing of a novel about an ambitious but unscrupulous character who would be guilty of any number of immoral actions but whom he desired to be the object of a certain amount of sympathy and a great deal of understanding nonetheless, he had learned what gender to make that character: female.[5] In *Catherine* Thackeray first discovered the affective power of this historico-formal relationship.

II

Having outlined the structural principles of Becky's character, I want now to turn to its material creation, the fleshing out of the character that makes Becky the vivid and compelling figure critics have long admired. In considering the materials out of which Thackeray may have created Becky's character, one must keep in mind Gordon Ray's judgment "that Becky had no single original but shaped herself in Thackeray's mind from his observation of many women and his reading of many books" (*Letters* I, clvii). If so, a full accounting of Becky's sources may be impossible to achieve. Nevertheless, even a partial account will illuminate Thackeray's methods. Scholars have heretofore looked for Becky's sources either among women he knew or among other fictional characters.[6] However, another important source of material for her characterization may be found not in Thackeray's biography or in his reading of novels but in the history of the Regency period itself. Specifically, I will argue that Thackeray derived important aspects of Becky's character and career from the lives and careers of two well-known Regency courtesans, Mary Anne Clark and Harriette Wilson.

The courtesan was not unique to the Regency, but during the period she rose to special prominence and special public notice, contributing nearly as much to the pungent flavor of the period as did the regent himself. The social prominence that she was able to attain owed a great deal to a certain social fluidity that accompanied the moral decadence of the Regency.[7] In such a decadent atmosphere, the Regency courtesan could attain a social position rivaling women more legitimately associated with the great men of the period. She might have a box at the opera, whence young men of position would make pilgrimages from the universities to receive an introduction (Blanch

7). R. J. White suggests that the boxes were taken by courtesans "as shop-windows for their charms" (79). Courtesans gave a yearly ball (called "The Ball of the Fashionable Impures" or the "Cyprians' Ball") at the Argyle rooms that was attended by the *ton*.[8] And a courtesan with a wealthy protector might have been provided with an establishment of her own in London's most fashionable quarter, Mayfair, which the name Vanity Fair is surely intended to echo. In her independence, in the respect accorded her, and in her public visibility, the Regency courtesan must have seemed to the Victorian reader a characteristic embodiment of a radically different world, an impression Thackeray would exploit in his novel.

The disappearance of old standards of conduct, which opened Regency society to the courtesan, had many causes, but one of the most important must have been the notorious conduct of the regent himself, whose career as a rake in general and whose relationship with Maria Fitzherbert in particular were public scandals of long standing. Mrs. Fitzherbert, it may be argued, was not a courtesan; she went through a marriage ceremony with the prince. Still, this ceremony did not prevent the prince from subsequently marrying Princess Caroline while maintaining his relationship quite openly with Mrs. Fitzherbert. Their relationship at least suggests the confusion about (or indifference to?) moral questions among the *beau monde*. Thackeray himself explicitly connects the character of George IV to the morality of the period in an ironic commentary on Becky's certification of virtue:

> But when we consider, that it was the First Gentleman in Europe in whose high presence Mrs. Rawdon passed her examination, and as it were, took her degree in reputation, it surely must be flat disloyalty to doubt any more about her virtue. I, for my part, look back with love and awe to that Great Character in history. Ah, what a high and noble appreciation of Gentlewomanhood there must have been in Vanity Fair, when that revered and august being was invested, by the universal acclaim of the refined and educated portion of this empire, with the title of Premier Gentilhomme of his Kingdom.   (473–74; ch. 48).

In morals as in manners, the regent and later king set the pace. Of course the prince regent was not the only highly placed Regency figure to become involved in amorous adventures and scandal, and the public nature of the Regency courtesan's relations with high society was partly the result of the willingness of several of the more prominent courtesans of the period to publish accounts of the affairs in which they were engaged. Apart from the scandals surrounding the regent's financial-amorous affairs, two others stand out. The first involved the brother of the Prince of Wales, the duke of York, and his mistress, Mary Anne Clarke. In 1809 a scandal broke involving the sale of military commissions and clerical posts by Mrs. Clarke, using her influence on the duke, who was then commander-in-chief of the Army. W. G. Waters describes the Parliamentary inquiry and the public interest it aroused.

The inquiry lasted for nearly seven weeks, and Mrs. Clarke was constantly called to give evidence. People talked of nothing else. The death of Sir John Moore, the victorious progress of Napoleon, the Berlin decrees, all were thrust into the background. No doubt the nation was in death-grips with the most terrible adversary it had ever been called to meet, but the dandies and fine ladies had no time to think of these things, while the House of Commons was privileged to sit week after week feeding upon the most impertinent banter of the most notorious courtesan of the day.   (308)

Unsatisfied with this exposure, which after all she had not turned to pecuniary account, Mrs. Clarke wrote her version of the events leading to the inquiry, *The Rival Princes* (1809), and later her memories. The latter were suppressed, and, according to Waters, eighteen thousand copies burned. Mrs. Clarke's unfulfilled desire to vindicate her position publicly was solaced by the payment of ten thousand pounds and an annuity. Numerous other accounts of her life and of the scandal appeared independently.

The second most famous courtesan to publish her memories—this time with the frank acknowledgment of her intention to realize a profit from her liaisons—was Harriette Wilson, who, with her sisters (especially Fanny, who was at one time the mistress of Lord Hertford, frequently suggested as a source for Lord Steyne's character) rose high in the ranks of Regency society. In 1825, out of fashion, living in Paris, and pressed for money, Harriette Wilson published her memoirs. Sir Walter Scott records in his journal the scandal that attended their publication: "The gay world has been kept in hot water lately by the impudent publication of the celebrated Harriot [sic] Wilson, who lived with half the gay world at hack and manger, and now obliges such as will not pay hush money with a history of whatever she knows or invents about them" (qtd. in Lockhart 585). How hot the water was may be measured by the fact that thirty-one editions of Harriette's scandalous recollections were printed in the first year (Blanch 68).

Thackeray's knowledge of these two Regency courtesans may be established briefly. He evidently read Harriet Wilson's memoirs, for he refers to them in his highly unfavorable review of Lady Charlotte Bury's *Diary for The Times* of 11 January 1838. There he compares the interest of Bury's *Diary* to that possessed by Harriette Wilson's memoirs, among others:

> It possesses that interest which the scandalous chronicles of Brantome, and Rabutin, and the ingenious Mrs. Harriette Wilson have excited before, and is precisely of a similar class . . . [T]he foul tittle-tattle of the sweepings of the Princess of Wales's bedchamber or dressing-room, her table or anteroom, the reminiscences of industrious eaves-dropping, the careful records of her unguarded moments, and the publication of her confidential correspondence, are the chief foundations for this choice work.   (Thackeray, *Papers* 63)

Thackeray's knowledge of the life of Mary Anne Clarke may be assumed on the basis of the fact that he had in his possession at the time of his death one of the numerous books occasioned by Mrs. Clarke's revelations, *Investigation of the Charges against the Duke of York* (Stonehouse 142). Furthermore, Thackeray refers to her liaison with the Duke of York in chapter 47 of *Vanity Fair*. These two most celebrated courtesans of the Regency provided Thackeray with material which, when added to that he acquired from his first-hand knowledge of women like Becky and from his reading of fiction, would have allowed him to create a character who would evoke something of the flavor of Regency decadence in her character and career. A comparison of the Becky's character and career will illustrate the extent to which Thackeray may have based his fictional character on these two historical figures.

To begin with, we may consider the origins of these women. Becky Sharp, we are told, is the daughter of a dissolute artist father and a mother who was an opera singer. Mrs. Bute Crawley's investigations into Becky's past also suggest that Becky's mother was less than virtuous and that Becky was illegitimate (192; ch. 19). Harriette Wilson's origins were slightly more genteel, but still humble—and tainted by her mother's reputation. She was the daughter of a small shopkeeper in Mayfair. Her mother, according to Lewis Melville, "was a most attractive person, who, it would appear, had, like her daughter after her, some amorous adventures" (208). Elizabeth Taylor, the earliest biographer of Mary Anne Clarke, describes her origins as follows: "Her father's name was Thompson, who resided in Bowl and Pin Alley, near White's Alley, Chancery Lane.... In this neighborhood, the moral atmosphere of which was contaminated by the vices of some of the most abandoned prostitutes upon the *pavé,* Miss Thompson, who was naturally of a sprightly and fascinating character, soon attracted the notice of every passing stranger and, like the lilly [sic] of the desert, exhibited her graces to the greater proportion as they were contrasted with the obscurity of her situation" (7–8). This picture of Mrs. Clarke's thriving in a sordid atmosphere is reminiscent of the picture emerging from Mrs. Bute Crawley's researches: "what a queer little vixen his daughter was; how she kept them all laughing with her fun and mimicry, how she used to fetch the gin from the public-house, and was known in all the studios in the quarter" (192; ch. 19).

In spite of her humble origins, Becky acquires an education that makes it possible for her to begin her climb up the social ladder: through her artist father's connection to the institution, Becky is taken on as a charity pupil at Chiswick Mall, where she earns her tuition by tutoring the other girls in French. How Harriette Wilson acquired her education is unclear, but her memoirs show that she was well read. They are also rather ostentatiously sprinkled with French phrases, which suggests the extent to which a knowledge of French was considered desirable among women moving in high social circles. Becky's command of French sets her apart from her respectable but ignorant rivals. We know more about Mrs. Clarke's education. According to Taylor she, like Becky, obtained an education at a fashionable boarding school; her means of doing so suggests something about the lack of esthetic economy of actual, as opposed to fictional, events:

> Through the influence of her father-in-law Miss Thompson obtained occasionally employment in reading copy to the person employed as corrector of the press, in which situation she soon attracted the notice of the son of the overseer of the same printing office, who wishing at the same time to encourage her merit, and to derive pleasure, and, perhaps, future assistance from the cultivation of her talents, placed this young lady, whom he fondly destined as his future wife, at a genteel boarding-school, at Ham, in the county of Essex.   (Taylor 9)

One of the first uses to which Becky puts her education is to act as the illiterate Sir Pitt Crawley's amanuensis. Becky handles Sir Pitt's affairs so capably that he becomes quite dependent on her. When he proposes to Becky, he is motivated partly by his dependence on her abilities. The irony of Becky's situation—despite her lack of official position she finds herself having charge of the affairs of a powerful man—has a historical analogue in Mrs. Clarke's involvement with the duke of York. Mary Anne Clarke became the duke of York's amanuensis, and according to Captain Gronow, the diarist, the duke so relied on her that he would sign papers she presented to him without reading them (43). It seems clear that the scandal over the sale of military commissions was a direct result of his dependence on her for the conduct of his affairs.

Of course the duke of York was not drawn into an affair with Mary Anne Clarke because of her educational attainments. The prerequisite of her position was not necessarily conventional beauty but an attractiveness that might include beauty but transcended it in some way. Taylor describes Mrs. Clarke's attractiveness in the following way: "Her fascinating manners and the graces of her person, far out-pace the powers of the pen. One glance of her eye would impress them more strongly than any description, were such a description extended to a folio" (11). Harriette Wilson was attractive in a way different from Mrs. Clarke. Sir Walter Scott, who met Harriette in 1825, offered this grudging appraisal: "Far from beautiful, but a smart, saucy girl, with good eyes, and dark hair, and the manners of a wild schoolboy" (Lockhart 585). To these piquant attractions should be added others that Scott did not record: Lesley Blanch, the editor of her memoirs, notes "frequent references to her lovely figure, her small waist, and voluptuous bosom" (30).

Like Harriette Wilson in particular, Becky is no beauty. All the usual advantages of conventional beauty are reserved for Amelia, while Becky is described as "small and slight in person; pale, sandy-haired" (12; ch. 1). Even in her youth, though, there is something "odd, and attractive" about her eyes, "so attractive," we are told, "that the Reverend Mr. Crisp fresh from Oxford . . . fell in love with Miss Sharp; being shot dead by a glance of her eyes" (12; ch. 1). In her maturity she acquires some less ethereal charms, laconically described by Dr. Squills: "Green eyes, fair skin, pretty figure, famous frontal development" (194; ch. 19).

The essence of Becky's personality—and one source of her attractiveness to the reader in spite of her misdeeds—is, as Rintoul says, "a constitutional vivacity and readiness to please." These qualities also account for her success in the fashionable world, as she herself knows. When after her fall from fortune she encounters Lord Steyne and his new mistress, the Countess Bella-donna, at a ball in Florence, Becky observes, "That woman looks stupid and ill-humoured. I am sure she can't amuse him. No, he must be bored by her—he never was by me" (649; ch. 64). Becky's understanding of the source of her power over Lord Steyne reflects a historical reality of the Regency courtesan's relations with her aristocratic patrons: mere physical attrac-tiveness was not enough to secure her position. Lesley Blanch describes this reality with reference to Harriette Wilson, but the description has general force:

> In a society of individualists such as that of Regency England, Harriette Wilson had to match her own personality against those of the distinguished men who were her world. She was no beauty, but she was herself, like no one else, and her immense vitality, her wit and lively interest in many things, combined with her independent, take-me-or-leave-me terms, brought her to the top of her profession and made her the fashion. A merely lovely, compliant creature could not have stayed the course for long; she would have been just one more of the ranks of prostitutes who at that time, we are told, swarmed about the city of London.   (7)

Like Harriette Wilson, Becky is a compelling figure because of traits of character that transcend her obvious moral failings.

Among the particular traits that contribute to Becky's rise (and secure the reader's interest in her) are "wit, cleverness, and flippancy" (373; ch. 37). Instances of these abound in *Vanity Fair,* but one particular manifestation deserves mention: Becky's gift for "fun and mimicry" (192; ch. 19). With her talent for imitating the speech of others, Becky establishes her superiority over Miss Pinkerton, amuses Miss Crawley, and delights Lord Steyne. Thack-eray could have gotten the idea for Becky's mimicry from his reading of Harriette Wilson's memoirs. Sir Walter Scott, for one, was struck by her powers of literary mimicry: "There is [in her memoirs] some good retailing of conversations, in which the style of the speakers, so far as is known to me, is exactly imitated" (qtd. in Lockhart 585).

Wit, flippancy, and cleverness are traits shared by Mary Anne Clarke as well. All are evident in her response to a snide question put to her during the

Parliamentary investigation in 1809. The chairman of the proceedings asked her under whose protection she was now, to which she cooly replied, "At present, sir, I believe I am under *yours*" (Melville 241). There is no direct analogue to this remark in *Vanity Fair,* but one may be able to sense in it something of the spirit that makes Becky's character so formidable.

An even more flippant expression of Mrs. Clarke's spirit is recounted by W. G. Waters:

> [H]er beauty and extravagance had won her a notoriety of a certain sort amongst the "dashing Cyprians" of the Brighton of the Regency. She took her dip in the sea, too, or, as the chronicle expresses it, "she distinguished herself as an excellent swimmer, and occasionally used to float upon the liquid element, to the astonishment and admiration of the spectators." (299)

This contemporary account conveys something of the shock value that attached to a woman displaying her skills (and charms?) in this way, a shock value that also attaches to Becky's suggestion that she might take her own dip in the sea at Brighton in pursuit of a reconciliation with Miss Crawley's companion, Miss Briggs:

> "Do you know what I intend to do one morning?" she said; "I find I can swim beautifully, and some day, when my aunt Crawley's companion—old Briggs, you know—you remember her—that hook-nosed woman, with the long wisps of hair—when Briggs goes out to bathe, I intend to dive under her awning, and insist on a reconciliation in the water. Isn't that a stratagem?" (246; ch. 25)

While their attractiveness, education, wit, talent and audacious spirit assured for Harriette Wilson and Mary Anne Clarke a social position far above their street-walking sisters, the sine qua non of their positions was their sexual availability. I want to dilate upon Becky's relationship to Mrs. Wilson and Mrs. Clarke in this important respect because, at first glance at least, the connection between Becky's sexual availability and her rise in society is ambiguous at best.

Up to the period of her residence in Curzon Street, Mayfair (ch. 36), the question of Becky's fidelity is open, though in her relations with both George Osborne and General Tufto, Becky's willingness to be unfaithful is hardly in doubt. But the onset of the battle of Waterloo in the former case and her husband's presence in the latter prevent the affairs from being consummated. During her residence in Mayfair, Becky's infidelity is only hinted at both in suggestive actions and ambiguous commentary. For example, after she meets Lord Steyne, Becky decides that she needs a companion, a "moral sheep dog," and in the following passage the reader is invited to speculate on Becky's real intent in acquiring a companion and on what Becky finds so amusing about the idea: "A sheep-dog—a companion! Becky Sharp with a companion! Isn't it good fun?" thought Mrs. Crawley to herself. The notion tickled hugely her sense of humour" (381; ch. 37). This passage is about as close a glimpse of Becky's own thoughts on her sexual fidelity as the reader is permitted. And though it does her no credit, the passage leaves the exact nature of her intentions unspecified. Similarly, in direct commentary, the narrator is straightforward only about the vanity of Becky's goals, not about the means she is using to achieve them. The following passage is typical:

> "Was Rebecca guilty or not?" The Behmgericht of the servants' hall had pronounced against her. . . . And so—guiltless very likely—she was writhing and pushing onward towards what they call "a position in society," and the servants were pointing at her as lost and ruined. So you see Molly, the house-maid, of a morning, watching a spider in the door-post lay his thread and laboriously crawl up it, until, tired of the sport, she raises her broom and sweeps away the thread and the artificer.   (445; ch. 44)

Sympathy and judgment are masterfully blended her as elsewhere in Thackeray's handling of the question of Becky's sexual involvements. Even after the great confrontation scene in chapter 53, the narrator concludes with questions that deflect the reader's attention from her adulterous involvement with Steyne to the collapse of her vain desires: "What *had* happened? Was she guilty or not? She said not; but who could tell what was truth which came from those lips; or if that corrupt heart was in this case pure? All her lies and her schemes, all her selfishness and her wiles, all her wit and genius had come to this bankruptcy" (ch. 53, p. 535).

After this crisis and fall from fortune, Becky's sexual availability becomes a measure of her degradation, and Thackeray consequently becomes more explicit about it—and in retrospect about her morals when her fortunes were on the rise. Two passages that occur when her fortunes are at their low ebb are especially unambiguous. The first occurs when Becky, accompanied by the coarse Major Loder, "with whom she happened to be traveling at the time," attends a ball in Florence: "Becky saw a number of old faces, which she remembered in happier days, when she was not innocent, but not found out" (647; ch. 64). The second appears when Becky turns up in Pumpernickel: "How was it that she had come to that little town?. . . Let us skip over the interval in the history of her downward progress. She was not worse now that she had been in the days of her prosperity, only a little down on her luck" (656; ch. 65).

If Becky's morals have not changed at this point in her life, the question to be asked is why her immorality was not explicitly stated or represented earlier. Thackeray offers one explanation at the beginning of chapter 64:

We must pass over a part of Mrs. Rebecca Crawley's biography with that lightness and delicacy which the world demands—the moral world, that has, perhaps, no particular objection to vice, but an insuperable repugnance to hearing vice called by its proper name. There are things we do and know perfectly well in Vanity Fair, though we never speak them . . . and a polite public will no more bear to read an authentic description of vice than a truly-refined English or American female will permit the word breeches to be pronounced in her chaste hearing. And yet, Madam, both are walking the world before our faces every day, without much shocking us. . . . It is only when their naughty names are called out that your modesty has any occasion to show alarm or sense of outrage, and it has been the wish of the present writer, all through this story, deferentially to submit to the fashion at present prevailing, and only to hint at the existence of wickedness in a light, easy, and agreeable manner, so that nobody's fine feelings may be offended.   (ch. 64, p. 637)

The conventional considerations of Victorian propriety, marvelously taken to task here, undeniably conditioned Thackeray's handling of Becky's sexual immorality. At the same time, though, he is also responding to the internal demands of his fiction. As Becky vainly pursues social position, Thackeray never wants the reader to lose sympathy with her, to turn away from her in disgust: a reader disgusted by Becky's immorality would not feel implicated in her fate or acknowledge its general significance. But the sympathy of the reader, especially the Victorian reader whom Thackeray addresses in the passage just quoted, would be difficult to maintain when Becky is successful, if the connection between her early success and the granting of sexual favors were made explicit. So Thackeray hides the monster's tail under water during her rise, emphasizing instead those other traits of character that made Regency courtesans like Mary Anne Clarke and Harriette Wilson such compelling figures.

I have dwelt thus on Thackeray's treatment of Becky's sexual conduct because it helps to account for the fact that previous critics have passed over her relationship to Mrs. Clarke and Mrs. Wilson. Recognizing the constraints placed on Thackeray's representation, one might well see a greater resemblance between Becky and these two Regency courtesans that one would otherwise.

Perhaps the most convincing evidence that Thackeray drew on Harriette Wilson and Mary Anne Clarke for his characterization of Becky are the correspondences between their careers and hers. As we have already noticed, all three women come from humble origins but manage to secure an education. Through the liberal use of their gifts, sexual and otherwise, all three rise to fashionable prominence in the world of Mayfair. The extravagance of life there is well-documented in the case of Mrs. Clarke:

She was served by twenty servants, two of them butlers, and three men cooks. The last named were paid a guinea a day wages. . . . Her service of plate was formerly the property of the Duc de Berri, the pier glasses in her reception room cost five hundred pounds, and she drank out of wineglasses bought at two guineas apiece. (Waters 296)

Becky does not live on so grand a scale, although her spending outstrips her income. Nevertheless she, too, acquires some of the spoils of the French emigré, in particular "a gold enameled snuff-box which had once belonged to Madame du Berri" (527; ch. 55). (One need not suppose that Thackeray borrowed the reference to Du Berri from his knowledge of the life of Mrs. Clarke; it has a force quite independent of, and yet at the same time consistent with, the relationship I am suggesting between Becky and the two Regency courtesans. Madame du Berri, like Harriette Wilson and Mary Anne Clarke, was a courtesan, the mistress of Louis XV. She could be said to have possessed all that Becky would desire, wealth and social position, and yet her having these things, far from bringing her happiness, led to her execution in the Revolution. The reference to Madame du Berri thus extends the significance of Becky's fate by linking it to the fate of yet another historical figure who resembles Becky.)

Living in such luxury was enormously expensive, so it is little wonder that, as Blanch observes, a "constant thread of financial worry runs through Harriette's *Memoirs,* and from time to time . . . there are acute crises" (51). How Harriette Wilson managed is unclear. Perhaps, like Becky, she lived on nothing a year. In the absence of regular support from the duke of York, Mrs. Clarke turned to the occupation that brought about the parliamentary inquiry and her fall from fashion—the sale of military and clerical positions. There is a remarkably close parallel, hitherto unnoticed, to Mrs. Clarke's activities in a passage dealing with the very question of Becky's means of maintaining her extravagant style of life in Mayfair:

> How the Crawleys got the money which was spent upon the entertainments with which they treated the polite world, was a mystery which gave rise to some conversation at the time, and probably added zest to these little festivities. . . . People declared that she got money from various simply disposed persons, under pretense of getting them confidential appointments under government. (506–07; ch. 51)

Although the narrator goes on to deny the allegation, the allusion to Mrs. Clarke's activities is nonetheless established.

As a perhaps inevitable consequence of the means by which they achieve and maintain their position in fashionable society, Becky and her historical counterparts all experience a fall from fashion as the result of a scandal. The scandal that brought about Mary Anne Clarke's downfall has already been discussed. Harriette Wilson faded from fashion after she lost a breach of promise suit filed against the Duke of Beaufort, who had promised her an annuity if she stayed away from his son, the Marquis of Worcester (Blanch 450). Becky, of course, is caught by her husband tête à tête with Lord Steyne, and her fashionable career comes abruptly to an end. It is worth noting here that the legal situation in which Becky, Rawdon, and Lord Steyne are involved is called *criminal conversation,* a misdemeanor apparently so common in the period that the contemporary histories abbreviate it as "crim. con." Under the provision of this law, Rawdon could bring suit against Lord Steyne for damages, and it was apparently a favorite means for an unscrupulous husband and wife to secure substantial sums of money from a wealthy and unwary patron, either by pressing the suit or by accepting a settlement. Clearly Lord Steyne thinks that such a trap has been laid for him when Becky declares her innocence. "You innocent! Damn you,' he screamed out. 'You innocent! Why every trinket you have on your body is paid for by me. I have given you thousands of pounds which this fellow has spent, and for which he has sold you. Innocent, by—!'" (533; ch. 53).

Mary Anne Clarke's life contains a possible hint for the situation that brings about Becky's downfall:

> For some years past the Duke of York had employed a Mr. Adam to manage his affairs as agent. Some time in 1805 it came to Mr. Adam's knowledge that Clarke [Mary Anne Clarke's husband] was threatening an action for *Crim. Con.* against the Duke. The "Authentic Memoirs" note a rumour which points in the same direction; "It is reported, however, but with what truth we know not, that he (Mr. Clarke) once visited Gloucester Place when Mrs. Clarke was in the zenith of her splendour, and on being refused admission began to demolish the windows and commit other acts of violence to the no small alarm of the illustrious visitor, who, then melting in Love's ecstasies, was cradled in those arms which in other days had so often encircled the unfortunate wanderer."
> (Waters, 303; see also Taylor 148–49)

After their respective falls from fashion, Becky, Mrs. Clarke, and Mrs. Wilson all retreat to the Continent, Harriette and Mary Anne stopping in Paris. Becky lands at Boulogne, "that refuge of so much exiled English innocence" (639–40; ch. 64), and thence to Paris. There, as at Boulogne and later at Brussels, Becky maintains a show of respectability: "[Y]ou might fancy yourself for a while in good society. . . . Many people did so fancy: and Becky was for a while one of the most dashing ladies of the Countess's *salons*" (643d; ch. 64). Shabby continental respectability was the lot of Harriette Wilson as well. Blanch relates that Harriette "was not of much consequence in Paris, and we sense with what eagerness she welcomes the few Englishmen she encounters" (Blanch 35). By virtue of her annuity (paid to her, according to rumor, in exchange for destroying letters from the duke of York that she had threatened to publish) Mary Anne Clarke was able to retire to Paris (Waters 310).

Perhaps most remarkable about the careers of all three of the ladies in question, given the scandals that led to their falls from fashion, is the fact that all three finally become respectable. Becky "busies himself in works of piety" and has booths at fancy fairs, anticipating the Victorian lady (689; ch. 67). Mary Anne Clarke lived out her life in Paris, "where she lived a quiet and respectable life" (Waters 310). And according to Lewis Melville, Harriette Wilson "spent her last years in England, leading a quiet, respectable, and religious life" (223). If Thackeray was aware of the turn-abouts of the two most notorious Regency courtesans, he would most certainly have felt the hypocrisy of their conversions. Hypocrisy certainly attaches to Becky in her new life as "Lady" Crawley.

In the overall shapes of their careers, then, as well as in certain details of character and circumstance, Mary Anne Clarke and Harriette Wilson may well have supplied Thackeray with material to make Becky's character appear to arise naturally from the historical circumstances of the period he was dramatizing. By so doing, Thackeray would not have wanted his readers to recognize either historical figure as a model for his fictional character. After all, *Vanity Fair* is not a roman à clef. Rather, his goal would have been to give Becky's character, created in response to the internal demands of his novel, a grounding in the life experience of the period in which he set his fiction. Thackeray's borrowing from the lived life of the Regency period would have helped create a bridge between the represented action in *Vanity Fair,* his readers' own perceptions of their world, and the discovered significance in the latter as dramatized in the former. Thackeray's own contemporaries could thus have experienced Becky's fate as having a significance not so much created in the fiction as, in effect, discovered in life itself.

NOTES

1. Reprinted in Tillotson and Hawes 60.
2. We should note here that Rintoul's description of Becky as the novel's "principal character" accurately reflects most readers' reactions to Becky's active versus Amelia's passive pursuit of vain goals but not the structural principle of *Vanity Fair.*
3. Rader points out that Thackeray's use of the morally differentiated Amelia and Becky as his central characters effectively "neutralized morality as the causal factor differentiating happiness from unhappiness," leading many Victorians to think the novel cynical (59).
4. F. C. Cabot describes the same formal problem in slightly different terms: "Mrs. Hayes seemed clearly to be sufficiently roguish, but she also had to be sufficiently

human, if truth were to be served. However, the more real, human, and historically true she became in the novel, the less she served to teach or preach a moral'' (404).

5. That Becky's gender gains an extra measure of sympathy for her, and that this sympathy is in part historically determined, were suggested by Arnold Kettle:

> What is a young woman of spirit and intelligence to do in a polite but barbarous world of bourgeois society? Only two courses are open to her, the passive one or independent rebellion . . . Becky . . . rebels. She will not submit to perpetual slavery and humiliation within the governess trade. And so she uses consciously and systematically all the men's weapons plus her one material asset, her sex, to storm the men's world. And the consequence is of course morally degrading and she is a bad woman all right. But she gains our sympathy nevertheless—not our approving admiration, but our human fellow feeling . . . and she gains it not in spite of but because of her rebellion (20).

6. Ray himself proposed two possible sources. The first is Theresa Reviss, ''the illegitimate daughter of Charles Buller,'' who, according to Ray, gave Thackeray hints for Becky's character in girlhood (*Thackeray* 502). The second is ''the Pauline of [Thackeray's] surreptitious Paris trip,'' who, according to Ray, ''counted for something in his picture of Becky during her vagabond years'' (*Thackeray* 501–02). The only other significant attempt to locate historical biographical sources for Becky's character is Lionel Stevenson's early essay, *Vanity Fair* and Lady Morgan.'' Like Becky, Lady Morgan came from humble origins, received a good education, became a governess, and eventually married into society. Neither Ray nor Stevenson claimed for their proposed sources anything more than a partial contribution to Becky's characterization.

7. J. B. Priestley describes the social situation in the following way:

> Like most aristocracies either decadent or about to transform themselves, this of the Regency was not really very aristocratic. Many of its haughty peers, perhaps the haughiest, had not come out of ancient landed families but out of dubious eighteenth-century fortunes. . . . Though still making much of their closed ranks, in fact they opened them to almost anybody who had either plenty of money or the wit and impudence to be entertaining. The old standards of conduct had almost vanished: *Noblesse Oblige* had been guillotined. (41)

8. See both the English Spy's caricature, reproduced in Blanch, and Cruikshank's caricature, reproduced in White, p. 80, for a sense of the public nature of the courtesan's calling.

WORKS CITED

Blanch, Lesley, ed. *The Game of Hearts: Harriette Wilson's Memories.* New York: Simon, 1955.

Cabot, F. C. "The Two Voices in Thackeray's *Catherine.*" *Nineteenth Century Fiction* 28 (1973:404–16.

Gronow, Rees Howell. *The Reminiscences and Recollections of Captain Gronow.* Abridged ed. London: Bodley Head, 1964.

Investigation of the Charges against the Duke of York. 2 vols. London, 1809.

Jarrett, Derek. *England in the Age of Hogarth.* London: Hart-Davis, 1974.

Kettle, Arnold. "Vanity Fair," in *An Introduction to the English Novel.* London: Hutchinson and Co., Ltd., 1951. Rpt. in *Twentieth Century Interpretations of Vanity Fair.* Ed M. G. Sundell. Englewood Cliffs, NJ: Prentice, 1969.

Lockhart, J. G. *Memoirs of the Life of Sir Walter Scott.* Edinburgh: Cadell, 1845.

Melville, Lewis (pseud. Lewis Benjamin). *Regency Ladies.* New York: Doran, 1927.

Rader, Ralph. "The Comparative Anatomy of Three 'Baggy Monsters'." *The Journal of Narrative Technique* 19.1 (1989): 49–69.

Ray, Gordon N., ed. *Thackeray's Contributions to the Morning Chronicle.* Urbana, ILL: U. of Illinois P, 1955.

——— *Thackeray: The Uses of Adversity.* New York: McGraw, 1955.

Rintoul, R. S., *Spectator,* 22 July 1848. Rpt. in *Thackeray: The Critical Heritage.* Ed.

Geoffrey Tillotson and Donald Hawes. London: Routledge, 1968. 59–60.

Roughhead, William. *The Seamy Side.* London: Casell, 1938.

Stevenson, Lionel. "*Vanity Fair* and Lady Morgan." *PMLA* 48 (1933): 547–51.

Stonehouse, J. H., ed. *Catalogue of the Library of Charles Dickens [and] W. M. Thackeray.* London: Piccadilly Fountain, 1935.

Taylor, Elizabeth. *Authentic Memoirs of Mrs. Mary Anne Clarke.* London: T. Tegg, 1809.

Thackeray, William Makepeace. *Letters and Private Papers of William Makepeace Thackeray.* Ed. Gordon Ray. 4 vols. Cambridge: Harvard UP, 1945–46.

——— *Vanity Fair.* Ed. Peter Shillingsburg. New York: Norton, 1994.

——— *Catherine.* London: Oxford UP, 1908. Vol. 3 of *The Oxford Thackeray.* Ed. George Saintsbury, 17 vols. 1908.

Waters, W. G. "Mary Anne Clarke." *Twelve Bad Women.* Ed. Arthur Vincent. 2nd ed. London: T. F. Unwin, 1897. 289–312.

White, R. J. *Life in Regency England.* New York: Putnam's, 1963.

Letters of Thackeray to the Ashburtons

Kenneth J. Fielding

At the height of his career in October 1852, Thackeray published his *History of Henry Esmond,* opening with a dedication "To the Right Honourable William Bingham, Lord Ashburton." He explained that it was meant to copy the "manners and language of Queen Anne's time," and because of the Ashburtons' "great kindness and friendship," but not everyone believed in such a "Dedication to a Patron," suspecting that it was Thackeray's way of lifting himself into higher society. Yet, as some of his newly available and unpublished letters show, he had strong personal reasons for thanking the Ashburtons and was already on easy terms with them. Looking at the new letters now, they reveal part of their lives, and they give pleasure in themselves.

Though not published before, these letters have been known about and are among a large collection of Ashburton papers recently acquired by the National Library of Scotland. They are made up of the papers of William Bingham Baring, the second Lord Ashburton (1799–1864), his first wife Lady Harriet Mary Montagu (?1805–57) whom he married in 1825, his second wife Louisa Carolina Stewart Mackenzie (1827–1903), married in 1858, their families, and an enormous range of correspondence.[1] Lady Harriet had brought rank to their marriage as the daughter of the earl of Sandwich, joining it to William Baring's wealth as a partner in Baring's Bank. He had a leading place as a reasonable and moderate Peelite conservative; and together they entertained at their grand houses at the Grange, Bay House, and Bath House, Piccadilly, attracting a wide circle of writers, artists and politicians. Among them, in the 1840s and '50s, were Thomas and Jane Carlyle, John Stuart Mill, Tennyson, Monckton Milnes, Macaulay, Tom Taylor, Samuel Wilberforce, A. H. Clough, the poets Henry Taylor and Aubrey De Vere, and many others.

Thackeray soon became a close friend, introduced by Carlyle's former pupil Charles Buller, the liberal politician, who was close to Lady Harriet. Yet at first he objected to her offhand way with some of her guests, and

Dickens Studies Annual, Volume 27, Copyright © 1998 by AMS Press, Inc. All rights reserved.

spoke of her with dislike, rejecting invitations. But the difference was settled; and, after a while, when he received an invitation card to dinner, he returned it with a sketch on the back showing himself kneeling at her feet with his head in flames from hot coals she was pouring on it from an ornamental brazier (Milnes, 233).

One or two of Thackeray's earlier notes come from 1848, but two or three dealing with Buller are central. One, of 15 November reluctantly turning down an invitation to the Ashburton's great country house, was for a gathering at which Buller was "the life of a large party at the Grange" (Milnes, 256):

13 Young St. Kensington
Novr. 15. 1848

Dear Lady Ashburton Although I don't know when I shall ever be able to accept that very kind invitation w*h*. you gave me, yet lest my grace should be run out, and in happier times it sh*d*. be too late for me to ask leave to avail myself of your kindness may I if you please write a line to say what my present unlucky position is, and how I want to come though I can't. I have 3 different books to launch and all the engraving for all the three to do I have a sprained ankle, and my parents come to stay with me; and I write for a weekly and occasionally for a daily paper; I have a railroad-call to pay in six weeks (on a beautiful Irish line where I have the comfort of knowing that all the capital—it is not very big—w*h*. I am forced to invest will be as bread thrown into the sea that *may* return after many days but I don't think without a miracle will,—and with all these obligations to meet I don't see how I can do otherwise than forego a pleasure w*h*. I have been promising myself for many weeks; at least I am bound to acquaint your ladyship with the pitiable position in w*h*. I stand. Every word of this is true: I never calculated my liabilities before, and indeed I tremble as I see them on paper: but I hope nevertheless to meet them all and pay my creditors twenty shillings in the pound. People who have been there tell me what a magnificent house the Grange is and I know how kind the owners have been to me. The coals of fire that one of them heaped on my head are ashes now and don't burn any more—what I mean is that I have thought over and over again how very kindly and generously you have treated me, and I am disappointed at not being able to accept a little more kindness from you. How good that toffy was! I ate it all myself and cut it up with a yataghan the only weapon I had at hand. What they sell in London is not near so good.

My friend Harry Lorrequer has just been lampooning me in his monthly book: being a caricaturist myself I thought I should mind it very much, but I find I don't care. Has this event made much noise in Hampshire? On the other hand the Editor of the Revue des 2 Mondes writes word that M. Philarète Charles 'se propose de faire une série d'articles sur mes écrits, et de les bien faire connoitre à la France' or a phrase better turned to that effect. Thus we have compensations in life.

I hope you will excuse me for writing, excuse me for not coming, and ask me in happier days: but on my word the main point of this note is contained in page 3, the first two lines.I hope Lord Ashburton is well and am yours dear Lady Ashburton

most faithfully/W M Thackeray

Harry Lorrequer (1839) was a novel by Charles Lever, who had just repaid Thackeray's mild mockery with bitter personal satire in his serial *Roland Cashel*. "Coals of fire" (apart from Romans 12:20) refers back to the occasion already mentioned.

A fortnight after the party at the Grange, Buller had an operation for fistula which killed him at the age of forty-two. His death was felt keenly, especially by Lady Harriet, who begged Thackeray to write to her. He promptly did so, and again four days later. The first letter is already known, but only from an incomplete copy made for his confidante Jane Brookfield (Thackeray 2:470–71). They bring us to the heart of Thackeray's connection with the Ashburtons:

13 Young *St*. Kensington Dec*r* 21 [1848]

Dear Madam I don't know whether I was right either in writing or in burning a long letter w*h*. I wrote to you 10 days since, one night when I c*d*. not sleep and was thinking of a great calamity w*h*. had just befallen. I thought I had no right to intrude upon your grief or to know it. I was putting the case to myself, as I suppose one does most circumstances of life, and it was this that made me feel what I can't but suppose to be your grief the more keenly, for if I were to die tomorrow I think I also should leave two women behind me in whose hearts the tenderest remembrance of me w*d*. live as thank God it deserves to do. Say that I die, and live yet in the love of my survivors, isn't that a warrant of immortality almost? Say that my 2 dearest friends precede me, and enter into God's futurity spotless and angelical, I swear I feel that I have 2 advocates in heaven and that my love penetrates there as it were. It seems to me that Love proves God. By love I believe and I am saved. And I think misgivings (about future happiness & the intentions of the Divine Beneficience towards us) are not better than blasphemy: and that you might as well say 'Hate your neighbour, avenge the wrongs done you by doing evil and inflicting pain on your part', as predicate the same of the Almighty or dare to suppose that his Wisdoms & Authority w*d*. think of revenging themselves by making meaner creature miserable. If you have a fearful consciousness, that you here on earth are ardently and fondly pursuing with your affection a friend in invisible regions beatified, removed from the possibility of ill, taken up to the consummation of truth, and in the midst of that glory & perfection I say *loving you still,* how quickly grief sh*d*. give way—and yet I know that no preaching ever talked one out of tears, and that only time dries them: when grief developes itself into Faith so to speak, and becomes an exquisitely fond and tender religious contemplation.

I don't know whether this kind of writing & thought will appear folly and weakness in your eyes—you who write so haughtily about Slipshod virtue as if Virtue could never trip or tire & have sore feet—& at any rate acknowledge that she was weary & foot-sore. I can't brave Fate and walk so erectly: I doubt even whether it is right to do so, in the Journey, I want friends to accompany me, kind arms to hang on: and the older I get, confess more and more the sense of weakness, & the want of sympathy. I can't understand ambition, the game doesn't seem to me worth the candle. What does it resolve itself into? a column in a newspaper. a vulgar butcher with no brains and a constitutional courage gets ten times as much place in History Books and honour in life as the brightest genius the finest intellect the tenderest heart the most upright soul—you know whom I mean. What does one care about honours and successes, and that Lord John thought he was a clever man? Psha—why are we to be always gauging men by success or failure? These are accidents and of this life temporary, but truth and love are eternal. How was the friend who has left you endowed with these?—a constant charity and sweetness, a stainless honour.—Love and Truth most beautiful. And with these credentials and passports he takes the journey, and presents himself at the throne of God.

You know all this before. One cannot offer consolations only a sympathy. Let me offer you mine dear Lady Ashburton and believe that it is most hearty & sincere. With but remembrances to Lord Ashburton I am most faithfully yours.

W M Thackeray

I write from Brighton whither I am come for a few days with my work. There are some verses in my little Xmas book in w*h*. an allusion is made to this subject, and w*h*. indeed were written through one night as I was thinking of it: w*h*. I often do now, for it has struck me with the most profound awe and compassion.

I wasn't at all displeased about your criticism on Pendennis. I like
people not to like things very often. I like to hear the truth. The 2
women are very different, though in certain points very much alike.
M*rs*. Pendennis is my own mother—

The remark about his mother had already been made to A. H. Clough and
others. The Christmas book was *Dr. Birch and His Young Friends,* which
Thackeray ends by asking, "Why should your mother, Charles, not mine,/
Be weeping at her darling's grave?" We are again reminded of the intense
identification Thackeray made between his life and fiction. It was quickly
followed by a letter of probably 25 December:

Dear Lady Ashburton.
I waited till now for the publishers to send me a copy of the little
Xmas book w*h*. contained some verses w*h*. were written through one
night, under the constant pressure of particular feeling—I have had no
books however sent, and have written to the publishers begging them
to send one to your Ladyship.
I fear lest there be a word in a letter w*h*. I wrote from Brighton that
might appear harsh—'haughty' I mean—Pray pardon me for using it.
You will understand that I did not mean it personally—but ethically so
to speak—as if a person too confident of virtue to admit the possibility
of falling.
Fleming told me he thought you would like me to write. I hope I said
nothing to pain you—when I wrote I was myself suffering under the
keenest mental pain—But it is greatly better—pardon me for speaking
about it at all, and believe me

sincerely yours/W M Thackeray

Lady Ashburton remains an enigmatic figure, but a key to understanding
may lie in her seeming want and need of affection. Until now, the sharpest
light to be thrown on her has been a hostile one, in the critical comments of
Jane Carlyle. Lady Harriet's story is still partly to be unravelled; but, in her
relations with Thackeray, we can see warmth and generosity, a concern for
others, a capacity for being hurt, and a willingness to be amused as well as
exercise her wit. Later this year, Thackeray's illness, when he almost died
from "cholera," drew them closer, and it was she who wanted to help him.
He was nursed for a time by Jane Brookfield, the wife of a preacher and
school inspector, the Rev. W. H. Brookfield, who had been at Cambridge
with Thackeray and Buller. He was saved by the attentions of Dr. John
Elliotson to whom he was to dedicate *Philip* (1862); and by the end of October

he had moved from London to convalesce at Brighton, where he read of the trial of the murderers Mr. and Mrs. Manning which began on 25 October:

63 East Street Brighton [1849]

Dear Lady Ashburton./I have fled thus far in search of strength and am rallying somewhat—enough to go out in a Bath Chair and swallow sea-breezes on the pier, but am still very lank and weak and a great deal too much of an invalid to accept your hospitality at the Grange. Later, d.v., I may come & ask for it: though Elliotson warns me in the most solemn manner that henceforth my life is to be that of an Anchorite: and that the magnificent appetite with w*h*. Nature has endowed me for 38 happy years, is to be hung up in the hall as a thing of no further use to me. What should I do then before the seductions of Chief at the Grange? I sh*d*. burst into tears and leave the table.

I saw a threat of good things to be sent to me hinted in your kind note: but I don't know what good things w*d*. be good for me, who get my small meal with a shilling at the butchers—I beg pardon, here is another note all about eating, and you will fancy I think of nothing else. I find the difference of the breeze of Young Street perfumed as it is on melting days by a very powerful tallow chandler my neighbour and the Brighton air immense—I awake here refreshed and—I declare I was going to speak about that subject again—and strange to say such is human perverseness, I am longing to write Pendennis. We are really coming to the interesting part now. The only thing is that people have been so kind to me during my illness that I don't think I have any bitterness left in me, and shall become a maudlin philanthropist belov-ing all the world. Luckily, 2 of my women servants or rather I should say my 2 women servants to whom I have been uncommonly kind & generous cheated and robbed me outrageously as I was lying helpless in bed, and could neither of them be induced to get up before eight o'clock to make me a cup of tea. These rascals save me from ruinous omnibenevolence: & when even I find myself growing too tender I will invigorate myself by thinking of their ingratitude.

I have read the Trial of M*r*. and M*rs*. Manning today with interest (we get the paper here before we do in London) and with inexpressible grief and sympathy, that my Sovereign has the Chicken Pox.

Goodbye dear Lady Ashburton & believe me
most sincerely always, W M Thackeray

A few earlier notes or letters seem to show Thackeray mainly at the time when their friendship was forming: they give quick answers to occasional invitations, with passing jokes. The second of them below (8 Jan. 1848) says that he is free to come now that he knows that he is not wanted for something by Bradbury and Evans, the *Punch* publishers. The third is a letter of acceptance belonging to spring 1848 after the French revolution; and the fourth is about the last double-number of *Vanity Fair.* A pencilled sixth (June 16) shows Thackeray in an easy chair and nightgown surrounded by four seventeenth century costumed figures dancing, while he kicks over his side-table with its medicines.

A drawing of Punch as a knight on horseback is the first [see Fig. 1]²

---

13 Young St. Kensington.
Jan. 8, 1848

Dear Lady Ashburton

I only knew on Saturday whether I should be able to accept your invitation for the 10*th* by an interview with some patrons of mine who live in Bouverie S*t*. Fleet Street. And yesterday being at dinner with the Honourable Frederick Byng he said he would give me place in his post-chaise to the Grange from the station.

I shall be very glad to come with your permission, and hope to find you better than you have been in this Xmas season.

Most faithfully yours dear Lady Ashburton.
W M Thackeray

---

de Kensington ce Jeudi matin [April/May 1848]

Ah Madame! que de bonté. J'accepte, oui j'accepte, mille fois j'accepte; le premier jour, le second jour, tous les jours je suis de Miladi
le serviteur dévoué/Thackeray Socialiste
l'Eugene-Sue de la Grande Bretagne et Canditat à la Députation Nationale³

[June 1848]

Dear Lady Ashburton

I will come with great pleasure, and am
most faithfully yours / *W M. Thackeray*

I am in a dreadful way with Becky this month I am sorry to say she has taken to drinking as well as gambling and is leading a sad disreputable life on the Continent.

PUNCH HIS TRIUMPH.

Figure 1 Thackeray drawing of Punch as a knight on horseback. (Watermark dating 1847.)

[*Written in extremely tiny handwriting*]

Kensington, Friday. April 20, 1849.

Mr. Thackeray will have very much pleasure in dining with Lord & Lady Ashburton on Monday next: Mr. T has only just returned from a professional visit to the West of England and has been ceaselessly occupied since his return, otherwise no snow nor yet no rain would have prevent him from enquiring at Bath House for the health of Lady Ashburton.

Dear Lady Ashburton
I am so much better, that I hope to be well next week, & to wait upon you on Wednesday 16 June Truly Yours WMT.

A letter from Bristol, 24 December 1849, was written when Thackeray was there for the funeral of the historian Henry Hallam's son, Harry, brother of Tennyson's "A.H.H.":

[Sketch of a signboard for the White Lion Inn]

Dear Lady Ashburton./I am due in Paris with my children immediately on a visit of 2 or 3 weeks to my mother—When I return I will ask if you can take me in. I came down here on Sunday for poor H. Hallam's business. He did the very same thing for me when I was ill, and came, did I tell you?, 120 miles to see if he could be of any service to me. The camels are getting through the eyes of the needles every day. . . .

I am going to Sir John Hobhouse's for the feast of the Nativity, and return to London just for a day or two to carry off the young ones. Tizzy called on me one day saying that she had received no letter from me, and looking unutterably Blanche-amoryfield. I am sorry I shall be out of the way when she pays her visit in my neighbourhood: and bless my stars that I have 2 honest girls at home, who think & mean the truth.

I have brought no pens with me except the gold one w*h*. only does for drawing and writing it is like speaking through a trumpet & walking on skates—you may do it, but not with the natural words and every day manner. And as I never wish to tell your Ladyship any stories, and am confident that what you like best is to be spoken to in the natural way, I won't go on with this abominable pen but wish you a happy Christmas./ever faithfully yours/W M Thackeray.

"Tizzy" was the illegitimate daughter of one of the Buller sons, adopted
by their parents, and the "original" for Blanche Amory in *Pendennis* and
Becky Sharp in *Vanity Fair*.

Renewed invitations brought a continued gossiping response about the
pressures of work, the demands of the "trivial" *Punch*, the introduction of
Alexander Kinglake (author of *Eothen*) whom Lady Harriet was glad to take
up, an early reference to Francis W. Newman's influential book asking for
greater reason and honesty in religion, and high praise for a fellow-novelist
Angus Reach:

[early summer 1850]

Dear Lady Ashburton

I should like of all things to come on Sunday BUT I shall then be in
the very thick of my work, and duty orders me stop at home. I wonder
whether you will be at home tonight? After dining with Lady Eddisbury
it would be very pleasant to take tea at Bath House. And I want to ask
permission bring Kinglake some evening: he is such a fine fellow. My
friend the Inspector of schools is in grief just now: losing a brother to
whom he was much attached, and who is carried off by sudden fever.
He was greatly pleased, I suspect, by your letter and by Lord Ashburton's visit. A friend of mine, a Dr. Pacifico who writes in a trivial
periodical remarks in his No. upon the absurd quasi dignity and suspi-
cion w*h*. distinguishes some folks at the commencement of their intercourse with persons of condition who only mean kindness to them and
of course never think about their silly pretensions. It is good when
persons of condition pardon these errors.

After I've made that fortune in America and can afford myself time
and leisure for rumination, I hope I shall write a book containing not
the portraits of my friends but the results of experience and true description of society such as it appears to a middle-aged calm person, whom
personal conceit or prejudices or foolish passions and preferences for
individuals of your sex, have ceased pretty much to disturb. I write to
you because I ought to be writing Pendennis, only it is so much plea-
santer to leave undone those things w*h*. ought to be done and to confess
that there is no health in us.

I have been reading poor F. Newmans Phases of Faith a most ghastly
and unhappy volume: and I heard a very clever man & poet say that a
new novel called Leonard Lyndsay by A. Reach is one of the cleverest
stories that has been produced since the days of Defoe.

I apologise for garrulity—and am very faithfully yours
                                        Kensington Tuesday

                                Kensington. Thursday. [1850?]

Dear Lady Ashburton

I don't give you this to keep I think I see a series out of it [*last nine words inserted above line*], only to look at. It may serve to beguyle you now Lord Ashburton is away: the contemplation of the Good and Beautiful always does console and improve the mind. I saw something like the above seen at a villa at Putney the other day, where Roguy and Poguy [*Punch* characters] were grumbling *'parcequ'il ny avait pas de damn'* Poguy said.

It is because I am to busy to stir out or do anything but my work that I draw this and write to your Ladyship.

'The Initials' is written by the author of Violet the Danceuse. I swear it. I shall be so pleased if I have made the discovery. I hope you are quite well and that I shall have the pleasure of seeing you on Saturday, & bringing Eothen, believe me meanwhile Yours very faithfully W M Thackeray

---

These were followed by an unforgettable occasion, at a dinner with the poet and dedicatee of *Vanity Fair,* Bryan Walter Procter, when Carlyle encountered Henry Reeve, clerk to the Privy Council: "For an hour or more he pitched him about ripping open his bowels and plunging his muzzle into Reeve's smoking entrails." Reeves, who was blamed for the government's Irish policy, was outwardly good-humoured, but noted in his diary that he never forgave Carlyle. Thackeray enjoyed it and, after news of *Pendennis,* recreated the scene for Lady Harriet (29 December):

Dear Lady Ashburton,

Business pressed upon me so severely this month that I delayed writing any private letters of gratitude and acknowledgment for past (and future) favors until the work was done, and the Printers devil out of the premises. I am just rid of the little monster. (He has the proof sheets in that port folio and 6*d*. in his pocket for an omnibus w*h*. I know he will spend in brandy balls) [See Fig. 2.]

I sit down to thank your Ladyship, for ever so, many hares and pheasants now passed away but remembered with kindness, and for your invitation to the Jeames's ball and your offer of a partner on the

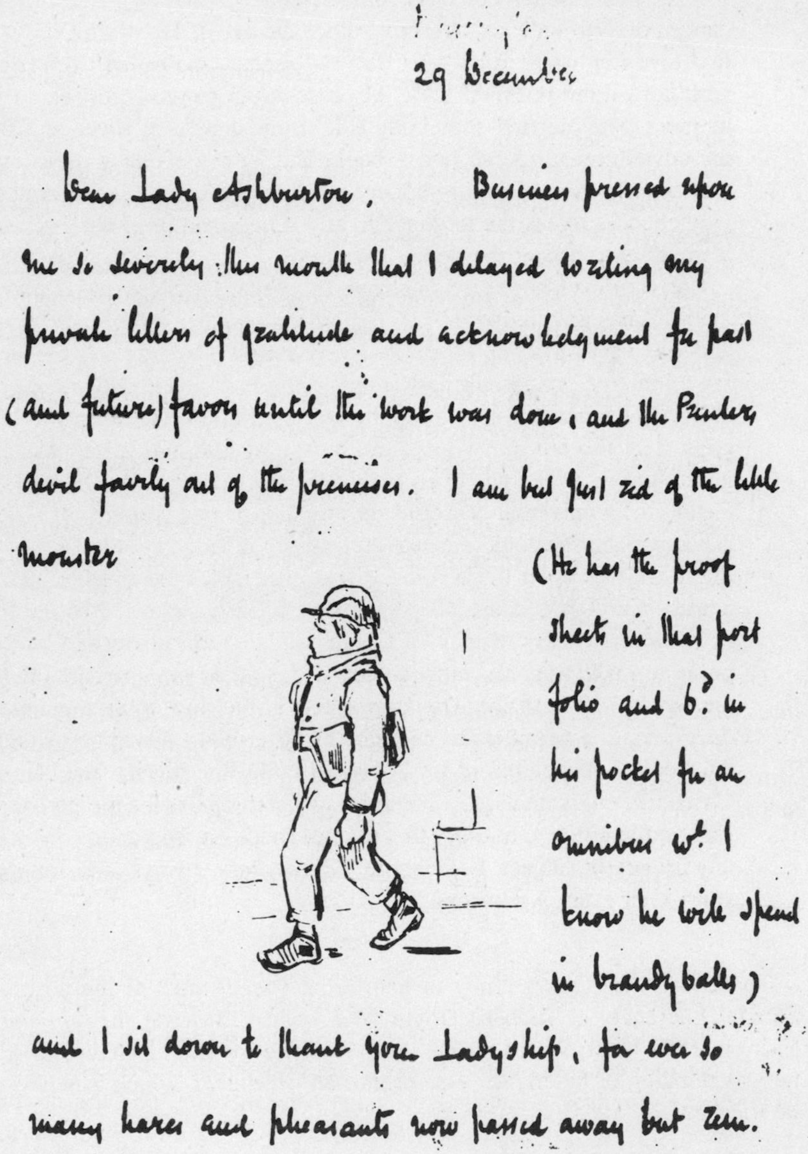

29 December

Dear Lady Ashburton,   Business pressed upon me so severely this month that I delayed writing any private letters of gratitude and acknowledgment for past (and future) favors until the work was done, and the Printer's devil fairly out of the premises. I am but just rid of the little monster

(He has the proof sheets in that port folio and 6d. in his pocket for an omnibus wh. I know he will spend in brandy balls)

and I sit down to thank your Ladyship, for ever so many hares and pheasants now passed away but in.

Figure 2 Printer's devil, 29 December letter

14*th*. I long for that day. If I go to Paris as I am thinking of doing for 1 week had I better not take some lessons in dancing? I never have danced (except with a Governess) since the age of 18, when I upset my first love in a waltz at a Court Ball at Weimar, and rolled over & over with her on the polished floor. My hair began to grow grey from that moment. She married somebody else in the course of time: and I put the adventure of course into a book. But I am steadier now in every way than in those days of slippery youth and if after this warning any lady chooses to ask me to dance in any sober measure, I shall consider it my duty to accept the polite invitation.

Carlyle dined here on Christmas Day (w*h*. I wish your Ladyship a merry Xmas and likewise Lord Ashburton and also a happy new year) and was very mild and kind but it was a great privilege to have him a few nights before assaulting Reeve (of the P. Council Office). He was offended I think and very justly by Reeves white neck cloth w*h*. was a great deal too tall and white, and he ran at him and tossed him and gored him in a way w*h*. everybody admired. At my house he said that Genius was universal & could do anything it had a mind to, when I asked whether he could dance like Taglioni or sing ravishingly or paint like Landseer upon the whole he was rather inclined to think that he could—about w*h*. some people may have their doubts. But the very errors and vagaries of men of Genius are rich and instructive—I was going to make a moral sentence out of this and a neat paradox, but on the whole it is best not. The Carriage is at the door to take me & my daughters to a Milliner for new gowns, after w*h*. I am to be wafted to All Souls College Oxford for 2 days of collegiate revelry and claustral Christmas enjoyments. . . . The errors of men of Genius are perhaps as rich and instructive as—but there is not space on the paper to consider this important subject. Believe me, nevertheless, always most faithfully yours dear Lady Ashburton. . . .

Thackeray was always ready to help artist friends such as the portraitist Samuel Laurence, or Richard Doyle who was to illustrate the *Newcomes*. Early in 1851 he wrote his single surviving letter to Lord Ashburton, when he was thinking of his blank verse drama on Bluebeard, which was never to be finished:

My dear Lord Ashburton You are Israelite indeed and it makes me ashamed of misanthropy and yellow books when I see how good men are, and how kindly, disposed to aid other kind people. Doyle just came here and I couldn't help reading to him a part of your letter—it was so kind you see, I couldn't help it. The commission, I think he is quite willing to undertake, and to do whatever you shall fix—make a drawing or a series, as shall be thought fit.

Why not illustrate some ballads that might afterwards be published, and of w*h.* the copyrights would bring the artist money as well as the design? Tennyson's Lord of Burleigh for instance. One of Milnes's. One by Titmarsh one by any body you think fit. There's a sweet ballad by the latter poet ('The King of Brentford's Testament') w*h.* the young fellow would do beautifully.

I say these because in looking at Doyle's larger drawings they don't seem to me to be so good in quality as his smaller compositions. He has not learned drawing from the life, and his want of education shows itself with the encreazed size of the pictures Witness the drawings in 'Jack & the Giants' just published.

He's a dear good fellow: and as he asked me just now to give him a copy of Pendennis with the kind regards of the author, he [*illustration of two eyes with tears*] almost, like an honest fellow,—full of goodness & kindness simple & grateful.

So you see I conclude that some Camels *do* go through the eyes of needles, and some rich men may have a chance of &c &c.

In spite of all this benevolence, a new play of Bluebeard is forming itself in my mind and will be something diabolically satirical. I wonder whether it will ever be acted at the Grange? it will be so dreadfully clever that it wont do for the public. . .[4]

Probably in June 1851, dated "Kensington, Friday," Thackeray wrote about preparations for a great fancy dress Ball, squeezing the letter into the corner of a pen and ink illustration of a woman in eighteenth century costume:

Dear Lady Ashburton

With this pen with w*h.* I hope to surpass all former efforts, I grieve to be obliged to say that I have no fine waistcoats at all having always cultivated a simple elegance in my costume but I have a scarlet Turkish dress w*h.* is at anybody's service. Shall I bring it on Monday? And if I cannot borrow a gold snuff box (w*h.* is a delicate thing to ask of one's friends) I will go to the play tomorrow and to some fashionable church on Sunday, where I daresay I shall be able to *procure* one. Is your Ladyship going to appear as a Marquise, that you speak of brocade waistcoats & powder? I am sure it is a very pretty dress & Swinton will paint it à raver. I have the honor to be (until Monday)

Kensington. Friday &

Dear Lady Ashburton With this pen with w? I hope to surpass all former efforts, I grieve to be obliged to say that I have no fine waistcoats at all having always cultivated a simple elegance in my costume but I have a Scarlet Turkish dress w? is at any body's service, shall I bring it on Monday? And if I can send boxes & a gold snuff box (w? is a delicate thing to ask of one's friends) I will go to the play tomorrow and to some fashionable church on Sunday, where I daresay I shall be able to procure one. Is your ladyship going to appear as a Marquise, that you speak of brocade waistcoats & powder.? I am sure it is a very pretty dress & Swinton will paint it à ravir. I have the honor to be (until Monday) Your very faithful Sd W M Thackeray

PS. There ought to be patches, I know; but they are so hideous that I can't bear to put them even in a caricature

Figure 3   Letter with sketch of woman in eighteenth-century costume

Your very faithful Serv*t*. / W M Thackeray

PS. There ought to be patches, I know; but they are so hideous that I can't beare to put them even in a caricature

Not all the letters can have been kept. Lady Harriet sometimes liked a clash of temperament, and enjoyed Thackeray's good humoured provocation even if she needed to intervene to protect her fellow-guests. She knew of his insane wife, Isabella, who had lived apart from him since the early years of their married life; and she was aware of his profound affection for Mrs. Brookfield, Hallam's niece. Even this was disrupted by a sharp difference that arose between the novelist and her husband when the Rev. William Brookfield was persuaded of his over-tolerance. At the end of October, the Ashburtons unsuccessfully made every effort to get them all back on the old terms; but all that came from Thackeray's frustration was what he was to recreate in the unhappy marriage of the Castlewoods and the main plot of *Esmond.* It was this affair which gave point to the dedication of the novel.

Few at the Grange knew of these tensions, though it is difficult to think it passed unnoticed. Both families had children to think of. Brookfield pleaded ill-health and set out with his family for Madeira, while Thackeray confided what was left of his feelings to his fiction or *Punch,* and then wrote about November 1851:

Kensington. Wednesday. [Nov. 1851]

Dear Lady Ashburton

The sight of your hand writing was welcome and reproachful—when I was at Vienna and put on my best coat to go dine with a person of quality I found a farewell letter to you in the breast pocket—upon my affidavit this is true: & there was a reason of great hurry of business why I didn't come to Bath House to say goodbye. We had capital tour me and my gals—it was worth not a little to see the pleasure of those honest little people: & to think they will always remember that small holyday.

Thank you very much for asking Miss Anny. She has not her father's beauty but she is a girl made out of pure gold that's the truth a comfort to this venerable writer and I hope and think that some day you will like her and permit her to—to &c—but though large in stature and quite a companion for me she's only fourteen, and I suppose must not come out yet. Thank you for asking her, Sachez Madame que de toutes vos vontés pour moi 'tis that one *wh.* pleases me most. Meanwhile please do not execute your threat regarding the present generation: and let me come down to the Grange on the 31. Almost immediately after

I am going to beat my lecturer drum about the country at Cambridge Edinburgh New York&c—and as I intend. Dg. not to spend a penny of the proceeds but keep the money for the young ones I bid adieu to modesty with the greater readiness.

Of course you have read Sterling's life. It is delightful I think (though Sterling a poor critic speaks very slightingly of somebody whom he met at Madeira and who has I believe 10 times more brains than gentlemen with longer tongues): but I am so glad when I can read and like something writ by the great Master of Craigenputtoch. It feels like a reconciliation: and having admired and believed as a lad, and revolted and doubted as a man, I feel guilty and as it were treacherous towards him. I have written a little notice in the Leader—not about the book but about the feelings with w*h*. one reads it, and recalls the friends of dear Youth. I send my best regards to Lord Ashburton. Poor Brookfield is gone & going to Madeira for 6 months very ill indeed but not so ill as he thinks himself I think—and he takes his wife and daughter with him and I am always sincerely yours dear Lady Ashburton

W M Thackeray

Carlyle's *Life of John Sterling* had just been brutally and hypocritically savaged by Samuel Phillips in the *Times*. He had written anonymously, and Thackeray's daughter Annie, later Lady Ritchie, foolishly made the mistake of claiming the onslaught for her father. It obviously could not have been his: it is contradicted by the *History of the Times*, other letters by Thackeray, and common sense, but it has been accepted on her apparently good authority. For the piece in the *Leader* (8 November 1851) see my account, "Thackeray and 'The Great Master of Craigenputtoch': A New Review and a New Understanding," forthcoming in *Victorian Literature and Culture.*

It is important because of its tribute to Carlyle's writing, good sense and agnosticism; and it shows how of all Thackeray's correspondents he again chose to confide something he meant to be highly confidential to Lady Ashburton.

On his American tour, 1852–53, Thackeray left his daughters behind: there was too much lecturing, socialising, and traveling, duly reported to Lady Harriet. We hear that he was entertained by the historian William Bancroft, whom she had met in England; Francis Meagher, as Thackeray explains, was an Irish rebel of 1848, who had escaped after being transported to Tasmania; and it was Lord Ashburton's cousin, Henry Mildmay, who had introduced him to the Baxter family in New York.

On leaving America he was to ask Sally Baxter to keep him a place in her heart, thinking of her as like Beatrix in *Esmond* and meaning her as a substitute for Mrs. Brookfield, though half reconciled by now and glad for Jane to be "someone" for Lady Harriet to be kind to. He wrote from New York on 14 December 1852:

Dear Lady Ashburton.

I hope you have kept and filed the important letters w*h*. I have sent home. That on the Slave Question and it's probable consequences on the Union; that on American literature and Eloquence as exemplified by the Hon Rufus Choate, the Hon Enoch Scudder &c—that on the Annexation of—well, the truth is that letter writing almost impossible here, and that I see and remark scarcely anything the whole of life being employed in operations apropos of the lectures, the most arduous dinners suppers visits letters & so forth beginning the morning and ending long after midnight. O marvel of Providence that there should be a people so fond of talking and hearing other people talk! Why Anny & Minny will have 200£ a year a piece if I mind what I am about. Indeed I'm thankful and immensely eased in mind by the pretty little turn my fortune is taking: and in a couple of years if called upon to make the Noir trajet shall take my passage par Charon's werry over Styx very much more comfortable than I had thought to do. I have only had one letter from home as yet—Ah mon Dieu what a comfort it will be in a quiet house again, where people don't make speeches to you where men and women say what they think and no more—where the window & curtains aren't damask and gold but where the walls are papered, where the girls don't dress like Mad*lle* Troisétoiles from the Vaudeville, where you have Society and not great thundering routs. It is very curious to watch the 'Upper Ten' as they call themselves and contrast their manners with those of our own beloved phashnabbles! I came across with a very good humoured polyglot old American (who gave me a dinner with 12 dollar wine here the other day) and who is drug broker by trade as everybody here is something. After dinner he took me to a family where I was engaged to tea (Bingham Mildmay introduced me to them such a nice natural handsome sweet mother, such a pretty artless slim nut-brown of a younger sister, and O! O! O! such a bright-eyed bold laughing daring sweet creature of a daughter! O Miss Sally Baxter! O you slim young Pocahontas! O you fiery nymph of Dihanna, your harrows have pearsed this Art in twane!)—Well, my friend Degan knew this family of old, and putting me down at their door says 'My good Sir—will you have the great kindness not to mention that I brought you? The—ah—the Baxters you see are not in ah—the—in the—in *quite* my circle of society in fact,—and—ah—odd as these distinctions may seem to you—they are—ah—in fact you understand.'

It's just like London, only the laws of fashion are different here—The young dandies who have been at the counter all day or plunging about Wall Street, become bucks at night and dance with the beauties of the Upper Ten—In order to be quite at the head of fashion you needn't be able to speak or write English or any other languige, you may sell coals or bones or drugs, but your wife must build a wonderful house must dress in a wonderful way a new gown every night—jackets embroidered with pearls—pounds of grapes in her hair or diamonds feathers or other gimcracks—lace at I don't know how many dollars a yard—give suppers that cost I don't know how many thousands—renew her outrageous Paris furniture every two years & so on—I was never more amused than at a house not *quite* Upper Ten to see two ladies arrive of the most Uppertennest reputation—They came quite late—they looked round quite blandly just for all the world like London—only instead of being introduced to Lady Jasey or the Marchioness of Heydownderry—you are presented to M*rs*. Jones & M*rs*. Haight.

M*rs*. Haight is the Shupreme bong tong—she has a house so wonderful—as wonderful as that Steam-boat I think I wrote you about. It is all sent over from Paris regardless of expense. It is all over lace roco co Cupids Boucher panels—you see the lady's bed room and Haight's bed room—her's is Louis XIV, his is Mauresque—its a curiosity of luxury.—Opposite her lives M*rs*. Parker. M*rs*. Haights is the prettiest house M*rs*. Parkers the handsomest. It is indeed splendid—rich grave and sumptious with tolerable pictures (the only house in N. York where I have seen any) but M*rs*. Parker calls troubadour a trobahder, and hates M*rs*. Haight for having the *other* handsomest housekin in the New world. There is a beautiful M*rs*. Belmont married to a natural son of the noble house of Rothschild—and here there was a ball as splendid as could be, and gorgeosity natural somehow as one is accustomed to the gawdiness of Jews. The Bancrofts live apart from this dancing, supping gorgeous Society—they have handsome parties in a grave European style. They hang English portraits on their walls—Bancroft is very ambitious, of a remarkable ability too and a wondrous fluency. He spoke for an hour the other night as easily as if he had been reading out of a book and a clever book too How he did flatter the New Yorkers! how they all compliment the Empire City the Metropolitan City whose motto is Excelsior and in whose vast hospitality all the nations of the earth find shelter! We dined at a 'Press Club' banquet where 30 speeches were made every one with a great big compliment to your humble servant and Bancroft in the course of his speeches managed to deal out a good card to every single newspaper writer present. He owned that there was one fault in New York—that he was really too happy there (really & without caricature) and vowed so that he wished to end his days in this Elysium that I am convinced we shall hear of him looking out for the Presidential chair.

I have met some of the Irish rebels here; and young Meagher of the sword especially—a most agreeable modest manly young fellow—and have found 1, 2, 3 very pleasant homely families with whom I shall be sorry to part when I go next week to Boston—As for Miss Baxter—O Pocahontas Pocahontas O!

Are you kind to Someone, God bless her?—I know you are and think of you with a constant gratitude for being so good to me when I was so unhappy—Does Carlyle want a couple of thousand pounds?—let him come here. O its a great country for dollars. I send my best remembrances to all who care for them—and am yours and L*d*. Ashburton's always W M Thackeray

---

After returning to England Thackeray wrote mentioning to Sally Baxter's sister, 18 May, that for the first time in the London season he was to meet Lady Ashburton in the "bo mondy."

The end of June 1753 saw him off once more with his daughters on a long continental trip, which, after a winter in Rome writing *The Newcomes* and *The Rose and the Ring,* brought them to Naples by February. In his biography Gordon Ray saw this as a pivotal time for Thackeray, combining distress of body, peace of mind, a happy family life, and a succession of illnesses, with homesickness for London. Thackeray wrote to Lady Ashburton:

> Hotel Vittoria. Naples. March 8, 1854.
> My address is care of Messr. Furse Bankers. Naples

... I wonder how many letters begin with excuses for not writing? This one shall not that is positive. The pen of the letter-writer has dropped out of his aged and labour-worn hand—it is only for the gay the unoccupied and the unhappy—I am not of either of those sorts. In the last 3 months I have written 4 numbers of newcomes and a Xmas book for next year; had 3 illnesses of my own, real illnesses now; and two of Anny and Minny where I am obliged to nurse. They have just had the Scarlatina. Anny is through it and Minny in her fourth day: & the doctor says we must stay at least 3 weeks more at Naples, before I can think of moving them. Such Madam is my simple but touching history. If it bores you to read but a hundredth part as much as me to act—ah how melancholy you will be!—The weather is paradisal since yesterday: the cold was severe before: and Capri out of my window looks like a purple island in a Fairy Tale. Perhaps you don't see the resemblance? Well, it looks of an amethyst colour, and so picturesque and beautiful that happy Princes & Princesses might inhabit in golden palaces that lubly place. When I (on very rare occasions it must be owned) begin to write to you: I fancy you are sitting opposite and going to laugh at me for what I say. That is why I am always explaining and explaining you see. Indeed you are very welcome to laugh. I should like to do as much myself and remain for when if I thought it very pleasant.

I have a queer existence. I must avoid people for fear of giving them the infection and yet I must not tell what is the matter the Dr. says, for fear the Landlord should turn me out of the Hotel. I have to lie, therefore on many occasions, and prevent the ardour of people who want to come and be kind to my girls sit with them & what not. Lady Gainsborough sent me down a kind message to that effect & Lord G: with a view to my personal salvation an odious book called The Eclipse of Faith or a visit to a religious Skipjack Have you read it. On the other side of the hedge sits Mrs Craven and pointing to her mother Church says Even enter into this 'venerable bosom.' I have made acquaintance with a dozen of converts and like, and am interested by, some of them very much. But the old Church. Ah me! He of Chelsea is not farther removed from it than I am (I thought of Him of Chelsea—because I wrote ah me)[5]

I have heard of your being very kind to some friends of mine at the Grange who were much as happy as circumstances would admit under your ladyship's elegant roof. I wish I was under it. It is handsomer and cheaper than this; and there are no mosquitoes to bite every morsel of nose left exposed out of the bed.

Everybody is disposed to be uncommonly kind and hospitable here as at Rome: and from the little peep I have had into Neapolitan Society I should like to see more. There are very frank gay artless-seeming kind women whom I have seen at Mrs. Craven's. But I am the major domo in attendance on two daughters and it is impossible to leave them and go gadding. Isn't it cruel upon a young fellow formed for society? Well, he does his duty pretty well but grumbles and brags a great deal about it.

It gave me rather a comfort to dine at Ld. Hollands the other day, and see that he was not allowed to eat any dinner. The Cravens have also a fine palace and a genteel hospitality—Do. Mr. & Mrs. Lowther. The young Nortons are here. If I were to put one of them in a book people would say that character was impossible. It is very curious to a devotee and—and quite the reverse. The younger boy has married a Caprian peasant and I saw them taking her out for a walk the other day and accustoming her to a bonnet & shawl: just as the colts under my window are broke to a saddle & a trot. He has written some really fine verses. Lady Strahans piety and goodness is the theme of general praise—I have not been to see that Godly woman: nor to the kings ball w*h*. I might have gone there—but a costume—eh! The Academy gives pretty entertainments. There are wondrous young bucks driving in great state for ever and ever over the Chiaja—Costumes in Naples there are no more. The oysters are very excited—I think this is all my news of Naples—and it is not much: not very entertaining is it? But I am anxious to shake hands with you sometimes, remembering old kindnesses: & being always yours very sincerely.

W M Thackeray

Norton says Lord Bath when he was here used perpetually to igsclaim Damn that Thackeray—supposing I had lampooned his Lordship: w*h*. I never did any such thing. I hope your husband is well and send him my regards: and when I come home please will he teach *me* something useful? I wish I had begun this now in the upright hand: you get more into a page you know.
14 March. This has been lying on my table during these days, the eminent writer have been ill in bed a good deal of that time. Now everybody is well—young & old: & I wish we were back again and I were going to drink tea at Bath House this very evening. Please remember me to anybody you think w*d*. like to know about us.

Lord Bath was Lady Harriet's nephew, and it is said that Thackeray openly declared that he was lampooned as Lord Farintosh in *The Newcomes* (Maunsell Field, *Memories,* 132–33). Lord Holland and Lady Caroline Norton, high in London society if low on the fringes of respectability, had helped to raise Thackeray himself. Brinsley Norton married his peasant wife, who became Lady Grantley when he succeeded as fourth Baron in 1875.

———

At the end 1854 he was too ill to visit the Grange. The friendship was there, but long letters were either not written or kept. Challenged again by a critic in the *Revue des Deux Mondes,* he nevertheless replied that he was indebted to the Ashburtons for "the very greatest kindness at a period of the deepest grief and calamity. I have said somewhere that it is the unwritten part of books that would be most interesting" (Thackeray, III: 390–91).
Does that give us the real point of the letters: that they can now tell us more of the unwritten part of Thackeray's life? Perhaps they do, partly: he remains a great figure of his age about whom anything is important. Even an association not central to his life lets us learn more about him. He comments

Figure 4 Thackeray's "social merry-go-round" (see endnote 5)

o his work and others', takes us abroad or closer to friends who are dear to him such as Buller and Jane Brookfield; his letters bring us more closely into the entire web of his major fiction and journalism, humor and illustrative genius. Are there other major Victorians whose relations with their children was so easily loving? They are not easy to think of. Are not such questions at the heart of a right response to Thackeray's ironies, and allowable rather than dismissable? Even more, to help our sense of the tug between his irony and sentiment, is it not good to have an understanding of how our intimacy is aroused by such letters as these, and by his own sense of wanting "friends to accompany," "kind arms to hang on," or others to mock,—with the comfort of seeing Lord Holland disallowed his dinner, or knowing that Thackeray has cheating servants to save him from "omnibenevolence"? He constantly seeks enjoyment and expresses it. The point of even his casual letters is that writing and living go hand in hand.

NOTES

1. Thanks are due to the authorities of the National Library of Scotland for the chance to consult and make use of these Ashburton papers, MSS Acc. 11388; also to Edinburgh University Library Special Collections for patiently facilitating consultation of the MSS, and to Mrs. Belinda Norman Butler for her kind permission to reproduce them. I have made some use of them in "Kind arms to hang on to," *Times Literary Supplement,* 12 Dec. 1997, and in the forthcoming article in *Victorian Literature and Culture* mentioned above, otherwise they have not been published before. They are given almost completely, with slight cuts duly marked with periods; but they do not include two short notes to Louisa Lady Ashburton, and one to Miss Berry. The intention is to give enough annotation for them to be intelligible without over-annotation.
2. The source of the cutting is not traced, nor even the twins referred to. There has never been a Chancellor of the Exchequer named Grey, but perhaps they were wrongly supposed to be born to Lady Grey, who was not called Jane, wife of Henry, third Earl Grey (1802–94), prominent members of the Ashburton circle.
3. Eugène Sue (1804–57), French sensation novelist; after the 1848 revolution he was to sit for Paris as a socialist in the Assembly, 1850 until exile in April 1851; with a reference to the British Chartist Nationalist Convention, 1848.
4. *Bluebeard,* a blank verse drama, was unfinished, see Ray (1945) 2:732, 735n.
5. Thackeray returns to recognizing Lady Ashburton's genuinely affectionate relationship with Carlyle, now being at least partly revealed in *The Collected Letters of Thomas and Jane Welsh Carlyle,* ed. K. J. Fielding, Clyde Ryals, Ian Campbell, Aileen Christianson, and others, 26 vols. ongoing (1970–). One of Thackeray's sketches with these Ashburton letters shows the social merry-go-round of the Ashburton group, including Carlyle in the foreground, saying, "On the whole

this is endurable. It is only round & round, no Gehenna-born shams about progress here,'' while presumably Jane (hiding her head) says "It is the name of 'merry go round' that makes one take to this! Ach Gott, as if there were not whirl enough in life!'' The other illustrations are all NLS: MS 11388, and are clearly referred to in the letters.

WORKS CITED

Milnes, Monckton. *Monographs Personal and Social,* by Lord Houghton. London, 1873.

Thackeray, William Makepeace. *Letters and Private Papers.* 4 vols. Ed. Gordon N. Ray. London, Oxford University Press, 1945.

Maternal Roles and the Production of Name in Wilkie Collins's *No Name*

Debra Morris

Critical treatment of Collins's use of family to signify larger cultural issues, particularly the claustrophobic nature of domesticity, offers a strong departure point for my argument about maternal figures in *No Name*. Helena Michie examines sisterhood in *No Name* as one of Victorian society's "mechanisms for coping with the specter of female difference," and Jenny Bourne Taylor indicates that Magdalen enacts roles that are "exaggerated re-enactments of the world that she has lost" and suggests that "Magdalen's transgression is transformed into adaptation by pushing the codes of moral management through their own limits" when she plays various roles such as " 'a [y]oung lady at home,' " a governess, and an "innocent middle-class girl" (Michie 401, Taylor 137, 138). Both Michie and Taylor explore the family's construction of female identity without showing how fully mothers, and the role culturally assigned them, haunt Collins's novel. Tamar Heller examines the Gothic, a genre which places mothers and daughters at its center, and explores Collins's use of a traditionally female genre. She shows how female sexuality, rebellion, and revolution are linked and suppressed in Collins's major novels, and thus marginalized, mirroring the status of Collins's works in the literary marketplace (introduction). Like Heller, I think Collins's maternal figures are important. They provide a way to assess his sympathy toward women and their effacement in a society that places so much meaning on inheritance and name, the cultural domain assigned to the father. I will argue that a culturally determined narrative which draws strength from a traditional, Western vision of motherhood underlies the actions Collins's strong heroines exhibit as they try to carve out less traditional existences for themselves. I think more emphasis needs to be placed on how maternal power is threatening not only to men but to the women who find themselves trapped in maternal discourse simply by virtue of being daughters themselves.

Dickens Studies Annual, Volume 27, Copyright © 1998 by AMS Press, Inc. All rights reserved.

Offering a more concrete basis for the maternal influence unconsciously realized in *No Name,* Catherine Peters's recent biography of Wilkie Collins' *The King of Inventors* uses his mother's "substantial autobiographical manuscript," a document "until now never identified or discussed by her son's biographers" (4). This document locates Collins's debt to his mother as it "gives a very different picture of [Collins's mother's] background and early life from the publicly accepted one, rapidly sketched in Wilkie Collins's life of his father, and repeated by his own biographers" (4). Importantly for my argument, Peters identifies traces of Collins's own mother in *No Name,* suggesting that "the description of the eighteen-year-old Magdalen, before the family disasters, is very similar to Harriet's (Collins's mother) self-portrait of a giddy girl, witty, lively and attractive, her father's favourite" (250). Peters indicates further that Harriet's passion for acting reveals the ways in which Collins's characterization of Magdalen bears a maternal resemblance (250). Harriet, when "[f]aced with family catastrophe and the need to earn her own living . . . proposed to become an actress. She was persuaded, with great reluctance, to become a governess instead" (250). As Peters suggests, Harriet never tests the Magdalen in her and and instead becomes like the "docile Norah" (250). In "renounc[ing] all personal ambition during marriage," Harriet supported her husband in his career as a painter and "taught the children their early lessons" (31). Harriet's devotion to her role as mother, and the similarities Peters traces between Collins's mother and especially Magdalen suggest that Collins's maternal characters, those silent, enigmatic figures, are worth exploring as keys to his view of the relationship between the sexes, as well as what has been recognized as his sympathy toward women.[1]

I.

No Name (1862) is particularly important to this argument because it shows one strong daughter figure trying to escape the implicit loss of voice embedded in her culture's narrative of motherhood. Before analyzing the trap Magdalen's society imposes on her, let me summarize the novel's plot. In *No Name,* Norah and Magdalen's parents, while legally unmarried, share a household as husband and wife and raise their daughters in the semblance of a legally bound family. Although Mr. Vanstone eventually takes Mrs. Vanstone as his wife when his legally recognized wife dies, he is killed before he has a chance to change the terms of his will and provide for those he can now identify as family. Thus Norah and Magdalen lose their name when their parents die and when they fall victim to a legal system that undermines their moral right to their father's inheritance. I will argue that the substance of *No Name,* detailing Magdalen's quest for revenge, allows her to engage in roles in which she uses her sexuality, making herself a projection of male desire, to ensnare others, and for a purpose other than what society would view as the conventional production of her father's name, the role a woman is traditionally expected to assume. The roles Magdalen takes on indicate her desire to keep herself from becoming one of patriarchy's victims and follow her changing attitude towards the name of the father and all that a relationship to the symbolic embodies. Throughout her adventures Magdalen plays out various maternal narratives before embracing the traditional one, and these narratives fail specifically *because* they allow her to express herself as a sexual subject.

To understand the limitations Magdalen faces as one expected to become a mother, I will be drawing from Kristeva's vision of the myth of motherhood as outlined in her essay "Stabat Mater" since it articulates the loss of voice and sexual self Collins's text explores. Kristeva identifies the Virgin Mary as the "traditional representation of motherhood" (160). In this vision, the mother, "impregat[ed] without sexuality; . . ., preserved from masculine intervention, conceives alone with a 'third party', an non-person, the Spirit," thus denying the mother "the flesh" and insuring that "the symbolic link alone is to last" (164). Sexuality is undermined in that the Virgin "assumes her feminine denial of the other sex (of man) but overcomes him by setting up a third person: I do not conceive with you but with Him" (180). The Virgin Mary then provides no model for intimacy between the sexes and minimizes the integral role a woman's sexuality plays in furthering lineage. Further questioning the components inherent to the myth of motherhood, Nancy Chodorow and Margaret Homans add to my discussion as well by emphasizing a division between a young girl's development and a young boy's, a distinction mirrored by Collins's division between the world of sons and the world of daughters.

II.

In this argument I look at *No Name's* exploration of the trap embodied in motherhood, like the one Kristeva, Chodorow, and Homans uphold. This view of motherhood suggests that the power mothers hold over themselves and others is strikingly limited because that power is contingent on absence. *No Name* emphasizes the distinct effects the maternal and paternal legacies have on Magdalen's search for justice in a society that erases the maternal and limits the forms of its expression to insure a reliance on the paternal, as it is both psychologically and legally defined.

Collins's preface foreshadows the terms of Magdalen's problematic return to the familial when he tells us that the world of this novel holds no long hidden mystery. Its characters do not keep secrets from the audience for a prolonged period of time as happens in *The Woman in White*. The linear quality of Collins's plot in which "all the main events of the story are purposely foreshadowed, before they take place" suggests that Collins's text is constructed like a well-linked chain, a neat uncluttered movement from one event to the next like that which characterizes the paradigmatic relationship between fathers and sons (preface). This departure then is interesting in a novel so preoccupied with inheritance, wills, and the family name. It could be argued then that in presenting *No Name* in this manner, Collins's text reveals a world that sees patriarchy as necessarily defining every aspect of life. The text then impresses upon us that while Magdalen might perceive herself as adventuring outside this paradigm, her maneuverings ultimately only lead her closer to its embrace. This text, constructed like Magdalen's world, manipulates Magdalen and by extension mothers in general, into what is culturally conceived of as their "appropriate" place in Victorian society.

Collins begins his story about the Vanstone daughters with an example of a father and son relationship. Mr. Clare, the Vanstones' neighbor, raises three sons alone after his own wife dies. Here Collins's text provides an extreme example of a family governed by patriarchy. While this family is obviously not to be measured as a model, it would seem to serve as an indicator of how society at large treats women and how it conceives of the "appropriate" place for mothers in general. The mother of this family, figuratively and literally negated, inhabits that space beyond the borders of this predominately male world defined by fathers and sons. This, Kristeva scholar Kelly Oliver would suggest, is an extreme reenactment of the primary separation, the distance that a child creates between himself and that threatening maternal body, a body, that "threatens identity," as it makes the borders between self and other increasingly fragile (57). Preserving this distance, Mr. Clare thinks about his loss in the abstract and remains "philosophically resign[ed]" to it (26). His memory of his wife is secondary to his preoccupation with his library as Mr. Clare "abandoned the entire direction of his household to the slatternly old woman who was his only servant, on the condition that she was never to venture near his books, with a duster in her hand, from one year's end to the other" (26). His wife is kept from language because of her death, but the "slatternly old woman" through Mr. Clare's orders remains distant from the symbolic, the world that seemingly provides access to power in this society.

Mr. Clare's household, with an absent maternal figure, is less than ideal, as is his attitude towards parenting: "As a father, he regarded his family of three sons in the light of a necessary domestic evil, which perpetually threatened the sanctity of his study and the safety of his books" (26). He sees his sons as an immediate threat to the private time he uses to explore the world of language in general. His library "not only filled all the rooms in his modest

little dwelling, but lined the staircases and passages as well'' (26). Chodorow
would argue that Clare is typically masculine in his self-definition as a ''boy
has engaged, and been required to engage, in a more emphatic individuation
and a more defensive firming of experienced ego boundaries'' (166–67).
Unlike a girl's, a boy's sense of self is based neither on his capacity to build
relationships nor on his capacity to provide empathy. The world of language
insulates Clare from sources of connection, the means he has to build relationships within his home. Collins's text then suggests that the very structure
that keeps fathers and sons tied together also ironically keeps them from
substantially assuming the role of caretaker. This sense of self further lets
Clare create both himself and others in very much a ''male'' model: ''His
views of human nature were the views of Diogenes, tempered by Rochefou-
cault'' (26). His views of humanity are derived not by experiencing others,
but through sources which keep him fully removed from them. While Clare
hides behind the symbolic values his culture creates, Collins suggests his
internal emptiness. Books isolate him and keep him from connecting to those
he is meant to love. Through Mr. Clare's character Collins shows how shallow
the ties between these family members are and by extension he criticizes
those connections based on lineage. While the name of the father holds this
family together, the abstract label it depends upon also allows him to place his
dead wife far into the distance and it allows him to '' 'dismiss the unimportant
accident of [his sons'] birth from all consideration' '' (27).

   The child he raises, Francis Clare, the man Magdalen falls in love with, is
both passive and lazy. Appropriately, Magdalen and Frank fall in love under
the spell of the theater and their roles as lovers in the play *The Rivals*. Frank
lets Magdalen lead him, and her power over him makes it clear that she acts
in a way Victorian society would find unnatural, as she manages his opinions
and directs the course of their intimacy. Magdalen's acting allows her to
display her body to others and to fashion herself, expressing what Michie
describes as ''the promiscuous multiplication of . . . identity.''[2] She gives life
to her sexuality and recreates herself on the stage rather than in a culturally
accepted way, in the capacity of a mother like the paradigm Kristeva describes. Although Magdelen on some level preserves her alliance with the
traditional vision of motherhood the Virgin Mary represents by denying the
other sex in her act of reproduction, she too ''inappropriately'' delights in
herself as a sexual subject.

   When Magdalen manipulates the other actors into allowing her to play
both Julia and Lucy, Frank makes clear his passivity in the activities: '' I said
nothing—I only agreed with the ladies' '' (46). Frank compliantly allows
Magdalen to reproduce herself, to use her creative powers for something
other than the furthering of culture as society would define it. In this way
Collins's text suggests that marrying Francis Clare is not an appropriate

choice for Magdalen: Collins's text reveals that when Magdalen manages his opinions, and later when she controls his presentation of self in helping him rehearse for the play, she fails to assume her "appropriate" place in relation to him. However, I would argue that ironically while no one would want Magdalen trapped in marriage to Frances Claire, it would seem that Magdalen expresses herself more freely in this relationship than she does in the one that results in her more "appropriate" marriage, a marriage that ultimately destroys the strong presence that makes her such an interesting heroine.

When Frank passively succumbs to Magdalen's charms and her desire for his participation in the play, it is clear that Magdalen is not yet resigned to her appropriate role in relation to the symbolic:

> When Frank presented himself in the evening, ignorant of the first elements of his part, she took him in hand as a middle-aged school-mistress might have taken in hand a backward little boy. The few attempts he made to vary the sternly practical nature of the evening's occupation by slipping in compliments sidelong, she put away from her with the contemptuous self-possession of a woman of twice her age.   (40–41)

In this scene, as she mediates between the masculine and the feminine, it could be argued that Magdalen actively tries to control Frank's language rather than conceiving herself as the passive bearer of his name or his language, a Madonna figure in its truest sense. The text too, because it describes her as a "middle-aged-school-mistress" characterizes her as spinster-like and thus aligns her to one who has not borne children to further the name of the father in society. By detaching herself from a culturally acceptable maternal discourse, Magdalen attempts to exert the kind of control over another's word she pursues later, a power viewed as inhibiting rather than promoting family.

At this point in the novel it would seem as though the bond between Mr. Vanstone, and his daughter, Magdalen, is the strongest one Collins's text presents. When Magdalen tries to manipulate her father into giving her permission to act, she coyly suggests to him that, " 'there is never any difference of opinion between us' " (33). Even more noteworthy is the final tactic she employs with her father, a tactic that echoes Shakespeare's *Much Ado About Nothing*. Significantly, Magdalen mimics the words Benedick speaks to Beatrice at the play's conclusion: " 'fourthly, because I give him a kiss, which naturally stops his mouth and settles the whole question' " (33). She takes on a man's role, seeing herself in control of stopping rather than bearing her father's words and his impact on society, taking on an active rather than passive role in her relationship to him. More important, her early action reverses the culturally "proper" role she later assumes with Captain Kirke, who stops her mouth with a kiss at the novel's conclusion and controls her flow of words before taking her as his wife.

Magdalen first turns to her father when she discovers her youthful love for Frank and realizes that he is being sent to China. She actively proposes a marriage to Frank, telling her father that " 'There is nobody to speak for us, . . . except me' " (68). Again she speaks of her union with another in an active rather than passive manner, suppressing Frank's voice, his language, with her own as though their voices are one. Mr. Vanstone, in hearing his daughter's words, realizes she is growing. When she expresses her interest in another, Mr. Vanstone begins to dwell on the natural world and in particular on its death. Collins's narrator tells his readers:

> If the summer scene which then spread before Mr. Vanstone's eyes had suddenly changed to a dreary winter view—if the trees had lost all their leaves, and the green fields had turned white with snow in an instant—his face could not have expressed greater amazement . . .   (68)

Collins uses an appropriate metaphor to express Mr. Vanstone's surprise at his daughter's growth. Collins's text, in aligning her budding sexuality with the transformation of summer into winter, represents the way masculine desire constructs its objects, and thus the way in which a mother's sexuality is unconsciously erased. Homans suggests in her discussion of the acquisition of representation language that for a male child "learning representational language (and discovering some of its implications)" can be connected with "a loss that is equivalent to the mother's death," the mother who is often associated with nature (4). Representational language allows a male child to pursue substitutes for his mother's forbidden body, to fulfill with another the desire he feels for her. Collins's text suggests that Mr. Vanstone perceives Magdalen's sexuality in terms of a narrative that distanced him from his mother and her sexuality, foreshadowing the way Magdalen will allow her sexuality to be negated to insure her own survival in this particular culture.

While Magdalen seems to be closely allied with her father, it appears that Norah holds a closer relationship to her mother, and a closer allegiance to the culturally assigned role her mother embodies. Adding to this distinction between sisters, Norah's first love, George Bartram, unlike Magdalen's, is a man whose appearance "presented the likeness [of her father] in his younger days" and thus keeps Norah's narrative confined to the structure of lineage (529). In keeping with this distinction between sisters, Collins's narrator describes the relationship between mother and daughter: "Her eldest child, now descending the stairs by her side, was the mirror in which she could look back, and see again the reflection of her own youth" (6). The mother and daughter are tied by a mirror through which the mother can envision her past. Collins's text also implies that Norah's mother is the mirror in which Norah can envision her own future. This portrait upholds a unity between mother and daughter, so it makes sense that Norah changes little after her mother's

death, for she, within herself, possesses marks of her mother's "identity."
She never wholly loses that sense of herself as a fragmented extension of
others, a mediator for the symbolic realm without a clarified voice of her own.

While the text upholds the distinctions between sisters, it also indicates
how clearly their choices are similarly limited simply because they are daughters. When Magdalen begins the process of revenge, she takes on a disguise.
Initially she disguises herself as Miss Garth, her governess. While referred
to as " 'our second mother,' " Miss Garth is a governess whose children
under her care are importantly not her own (135). This first disguise that
Magdalen adopts is suggestive, as she stays in touch, at least on an artificial
level, with those who are most representative of maternal qualities and yet
distant from the actual process of birth.

While Magdalen takes on the disguise of a governess and fails to achieve
what she desires, Norah literally becomes a governess herself and fails to
show control over the children in her charge (230). She too in her failure
becomes an object of vision and of judgment:

> The people in the street stopped and laughed; some of them jestingly advised
> a little wholesome correction; one woman asked Norah if she was the child's
> mother, another pitied her audibly for being the child's governess.   (221)

Norah as a governess has little impact on the household she is a part of or
the children who are under her charge. Her ineffectiveness, her inability
to shape the children, is made even clearer when Norah defines happiness
for Magdalen:

> "The way to happiness is often very hard to find; harder, I almost think, for
> women than for men. But if we try patiently, and try long enough, we reach it
> at last-in Heaven, if not on earth."   (253)

Although actively seeking happiness, Norah suggests that happiness for a
woman can only be experienced in an invisible, spiritual, and indeed, empty
world like the one her mother now inhabits. Collins's text shows how closely
society has aligned the two sisters, not because their personality would lead
them to follow the same path, but because society has denied them the chance
to explore their individual voices outside the boundaries of the law.

Because Norah accepts the law, she is not defined by the boundaries the
novel uses to define the realm Magdalen attempts to control. Norah's story,
unlike Magdalen's, remains a part of the background in the form of letters.
She is once removed from Magdalen's story, placed in the distance like her
mother, and denied direct access to the main action of the novel. As Oliver
suggests, a daughter, always bound to her mother, "makes her mother abject
in order to reject her," and in the process "also makes herself abject, rejects

herself'' (61). In keeping with this erasure of boundaries defining the self, Norah's tale is relegated to sections of the novel called ''Between the Scenes, Progress of the Story through the Post.'' Collins's text separates Norah's life taking place ''Between the Scenes,'' moving it away from the boundaries and the bodily that is a part of the world Magdalen inhabits, suggesting their differences in terms of the presentation of self. Norah is passive to the extent that even though George Bartram reads her emotions correctly, she ultimately needs another to explain her love and to undo the words she has spoken, indicting their inherent lack of value and thus her allegiance to a narrative that undermines her control over voice and language. In getting George Bartram and Norah back together, Miss Garth does so at the expense of Norah's capacity to act and her capacity to speak in a way reflective of her desires when she tells George to pursue his marriage proposal further: '' 'Don't take No for an answer . . . [Women] act on impulse; and, in nine cases out of ten, they are heartily sorry for it afterward' '' (563). In the economy of the narrative, Norah earns love and money through her passivity and by ultimately embracing Victorian society's traditional vision of motherhood.

Magdalen, unlike Norah, refuses to be passive and tries to maintain control over her presentation of self. When she becomes an actress, creating herself as an object of vision, she plays two different parts. For one of these roles, Magdalen creates a caricature of her sister, one which Michie suggests emphasizes their sexual differences, ''the difference between the fallen and the unfallen, the sexual and the pure woman'' (404). Magdalen goes on to discuss why she performed this particular role '' 'to an audience of strangers' '' (52). Magdalen herself suggests the unity between sisters when she tells Norah: '' 'In your place, I should have felt flattered by the selection' '' (52). Magdalen fictionalizes herself in the image of another, namely Norah, one who is aligned to and comfortable with the maternal as her culture defines it. Magdalen then, it could be argued, superficially assumes the traditional narrative of the maternal without making herself subject to its laws. By empowering herself as a sexual subject, she lingers between the world of the feminine and the world of the masculine as they are culturally delineated, each of which promises her nothing but a living death.

As the secrets of the family are revealed, Collins's text further elaborates on the role of the maternal and the role Magdalen eventually unconsciously assumes. When Magdalen's father dies, her mother becomes tragically ill. Collins's text emphasizes Mrs. Vanstone's dependence on her husband:

> Before another hour had passed, the disclosure of the husband's sudden death was followed by the suspense of the wife's mortal peril. She lay helpless on her widowed bed; her own life, and the life of her unborn child, trembling in the balance. (83)

Yet, as Oliver in her analysis of Kristeva would suggest, the important union here is not the one that connects husband and wife. Rather, the union between mother and child even in death establishes a mother's one area of control, that she is "master" of a life that once born demands her loss of self (Oliver 66). The novel's unsettling account of this union reveals the power mothers have over their children as they bear them and, tragically, the futility of that capacity to control, accompanied as it is by her own death. This "mastery" then affords women a power to be revered because it furthers lineage, but one that has to be concealed because it involves the sexuality that is seen as threatening. Mrs. Vanstone does produce a "frail little life—faint and feeble from the first" which "survived her till the evening was on the wane, and the sunset was dim in the quiet western heaven" (90). This image, I would argue, indicates the trap Magdalen faces. By assuming roles that do not further her role as a mother in the traditional paradigm Kristeva outlines, she actually loses control over those she believes are under her power. Yet in producing life the mother must give up her sense of self and disappear to have any form of power.

After Magdalen's father dies and her mother's death appears imminent, Collins describes each daughter's reaction to her personal tragedy. Miss Garth senses a distinction between Norah's and Magdalen's responses to their loss: "Her least anxiety was for the elder sister. The agony of Norah's grief had forced its way outward to the natural relief of tears. It was not so with Magdalen" (83). Norah, at this point in the novel, produces tears, indicating her natural alignment to cultural perceptions of the feminine and her emotional tie to another. She makes herself vulnerable to others, expressing the emotions she feels. Even at the death of her father, the man to whom she seemed so close, Magdalen remains "tearless" (83). Incredibly, "[n]othing roused, nothing melted her" (83). As she keeps her capacity for empathy hidden from public view, and tries to be a less traditional woman, Magdalen instead takes a culturally traditional masculine pose.

Magdalen's attempt to control the vision she produces for others and her belief in her own separateness surface after the loss of her parents. After running away she seeks to reclaim her inheritance. She meets Captain Wragge, a man for whom "not even the widest stretch of courtesy could have included him at any time in the list of Mrs. Vanstone's relatives" even though he claims to be a distant relation (21). Magdalen decides to place herself under a contract to Captain Wragge when he asks her to " 'Place your departure from York, your dramatic career, and your private inquiries under my care' " and she answers " 'I do' " (181). The relationship between them figuratively relies on the prostitution of her body and provides a bleak measure of the relationship between the sexes. It suggests that even Magdalen's attempt to escape the symbolic places her under contract, binding her to the words of others. I would argue that even more importantly, this marriage does not further her escape as much as she would imagine and indeed foreshadows her marriage to a more socially acceptable Captain, who while clearly more honest, will control her presentation of self even more completely.

When trying on a role for Captain Wragge to show him her capacity for disguise, Magdalen imagines

> Frank came back to her from the sea, and the face of her dead father looked at her with the smile of happy old times. The voices of her mother and her sister talked gently in the fragrant country stillness, and the garden-walks at Combe-Raven opened once more on her view.   (183)

When she hears the disembodied voices of the female members of her family as they are associated with the natural world she makes them less and less corporeal, while she sees her father in terms of his face, the part of the body most fully associated with spoken language. Ironically, however, she gives her mother and her sister a voice and a relational language embodied in a conversation, while her imagination does not associate language with either her lover Frank or her father, whom she places in the far removed distance as "dead" (a designation she does not give her mother even though she is no longer alive). She rescues them from the "milk and tears," the "metaphor of non-speech, of a 'semiotics' that linguistic communication does not account for" that Kristeva sees as associated with the Virgin Mary (174). Magdalen also gives them a voice rather than defining them in her imagination as only the "holder of sound" (Kristeva 173). For as Kristeva suggests, "We are entitled only to the ear of the virginal body, the tears and the breast. With the female sexual organ changed into an innocent shell, holder of sound, there arises a possible tendency to eroticize hearing, voice or even understanding" (172–73). She gives her mother value in death, trying to change the problematic path her society has determined for her, significantly a sexuality embodied in a voice Magdalen herself will be denied in life when she later marries.

When Magdalen meets Captain Wragge's wife, she continues to enact maternal qualities that do not require her to actually become a mother. The gigantic infantilized Mrs. Wragge, as Deidre David states, "feels herself deprived of identity by the incessant discipline of male directions; she becomes, in a sense, somewhat like Magdalen, a woman deprived of her identity as inheriting daughter and disciplined by laws that legislate legitimacy and correct irregularity" (193). Captain Wragge describes his wife as " 'the crookedest woman I ever met with' " (163). She disturbs the kind of linearity one would associate with legacy and with the paradigm that allows for society's continuation although even she in the end becomes contained in a

portrait announcing her husband's words. While around her husband, Mrs.
Wragge complains of a buzzing in her head, a buzzing which begins when
she loses herself in her motherly concerns for others. This is especially apparent when she describes her previous employment to Magdalen: " 'The gentlemen all came together; the gentlemen were all hungry together; the gentlemen
all gave their orders together—' " (164). She becomes confused as she makes
herself available to the demands of anonymous men and conceives herself
as merely a "holder of sound" (Kristeva 173).

While Magdalen also comes to lose herself in the words of others, she
initially uses her sexuality to maintain control over her place in society. Her
adventures outside the traditional paradigm of motherhood lead her to her
cousin Noel Vanstone, the son of the man who has kept her from her rightful
inheritance, and Mrs. Lecount, his housekeeper. Noel upholds the worst values of patriarchy and enacts them to the extreme. He thinks of his father in
terms of the bargains he has brought into the house and thus merely in terms
of the legacy he leaves behind as it is shallowly conceived:

> "All these things are my father's bargains. There is not another house in En-
> gland which has such curiosities as these. . . . Mrs. Lecount is like the curiosi-
> ties, . . . she is one of my father's bargains."   (230)

Despite his preoccupation with money, his name is associated with
birth—ironic in a man so frightened of life itself. In a sense Collins's name
for this character is representative of the ways in which birth has been co-
opted by the male world of legacy that denies the important presence of the
mother. Noel's potential legacy has little to do with heart as Mrs. Lecount
describes his physical weaknesses to Magdalen: " 'There is no positive disease; there is only a chronic feebleness . . . a want of vital power in the organ
[heart] itself' " (227). Lacking the empathy a heart gives life to, Noel cannot
see himself in relation to others and thus only views Magdalen as an object
of desire.

Noel is infatuated with Magdalen and seeks her hand in marriage. He is
"enchanted" when Magdalen coquettishly imitates Mrs. Lecount's "smooth
voice, and Mrs. Lecount's insinuating graces of manner" (364). Magdalen's
choice of Mrs. Lecount as an object to feed Noel Vanstone's desire is suggestive. Mrs. Lecount has taken care of him and "has lived in [Michael Vanstone's] service ever since his wife's death," and as Collins's text tells us
"has acquired a strong influence over both father and son" (197). She even
goes so far as to compose Noel's will, dictating it to him, indicating that her
power, unlike that of the Virgin Mary, is not subsumed by her acknowledgment of the power the world of the symbolic holds over her (465). Like
Magdalen, she has tried to remove herself from the demand that she actually

become a mother. Because Mrs. Lecount's legacy has little to do with further-ing the name of the father, it is defined by death: " 'I had no other legacy. There is the Tank. All the Subjects died but this quiet little fellow—this nice little toad' " (227). By imitating Mrs. Lecount, Magdalen actively controls language and produces it in the guise of one who has become a guardian figure and has replaced Noel Vanstone's mother without producing heirs to bear the father's name, thus allowing her to perpetuate her ambiguous rela-tionship to the maternal discourse her society values.

When Magdalen realizes that she is becoming increasingly compromised, that indeed she has " 'lost something,' " she cries to " 'Mother Earth: The only mother [she has] left' " (273). Her overt despair coincides with the time when Captain Kirke is initially bewitched by her beauty, a man who distinctly makes the point, " 'I'm old enough to be her father' " (284). In making this allusion to their age difference Kirke points to his capacity to renew her association with traditional family. When she laments " 'Mother Earth' " as the only mother she has left, he points to himself as her potential father. Although Captain Kirke indicates the power Magdalen has over him, he also uses words that describe her in an otherworldly manner, creating her as an abstraction. While he is attracted to Magdalen, he at first runs away from any involvement with her. He prefers the sea, telling his sister: " 'The only sweetheart I have any business with at my age is my ship' " and remains in pursuit of the abstract representation of female sexuality which he can control (285).

Captain Kirke does save Magdalen, and as her savior he appropriately links the daughter's narrative to the father's, showing how fully the father's story determines the daughter's. The name Kirke first enters the Vanstone narrative when after making a less than ideal marriage, Mr. Vanstone becomes involved with another woman, Magdalen's mother, a woman who acts the role of wife even though legally she is not his wife. The woman who is legally Mr. Vanstone's wife marries him only for money and is tarnished by her " 'misconduct prior to the ceremony' " (99). A Major Kirke, father of Mag-dalen's future husband, saves Magdalen's father from suicide. While Magda-len is busy setting out her plans for revenge, Captain Kirke recognizes Vanstone as " 'a name my father used often to speak of in his time' " when going over the visitor's list in trying to identify Magdalen and seeing Noel Vanstone's name on it (281). Collins's text emphasizes the name she inherits from her father in defining her and eventually saving her. Thus Magdalen relies on the Kirkes, their lineage, and the narrative this particular father shares with his son for her renewal in society, a renewal that involves mar-riage and the death of her control over language. The text then upholds patriarchy's power to act as nurturing caretaker, while at the same time subversively suggesting that it is this very power that disenfranchises women and thus limits the choices they actually have.

Magdalen begins yielding to the traditional maternal paradigm when Mrs. Lecount discovers the plot against Noel Vanstone and Magdalen is forces to make a quick marriage. At this time Magdalen's passivity is emphasized: "Magdalen passively put on her hat; passively accompanied her companion along the public walk, until they reached its northward extremity" (393). Her passivity finally leads to a suicide attempt. The words she envisions as her last are to Captain Wragge and are those of a caretaker: " 'be kind to your wife for my sake' " (406). She enacts those nurturing manners so important to a mother toward a woman old enough to be her mother, finally becoming a passive woman without control over the vision or language of another.

Further indicating her surrender to the values of her society, Magdalen assumes the role of a maid, at which time her employer changes her name to " 'Lucy' " (513). She has come full circle, as the name is reminiscent, as Taylor observes, of her role in the play *The Rivals,* although this time she has so little social or psychic power that she does not name herself (137). She takes on the identity of Louisa, her maid, a woman who is not married and has her lover's child out of wedlock. Magdalen not only takes on the role of a mother, but one whose circumstances resemble that of her own parents (497). When "[h]er whole nervous system [gives] way," she finally reclaims her role within family (580).

Captain Kirke, symbolic of this traditional family, saves her and nurses her back to health. When she is sick, she connects Captain Kirke to her father:

He stooped, and lifted Magdalen in his arms. Her head rested gently on the sailor's breast; her eyes looked up wonderingly into the sailor's face. . . . Her mind had wandered back to old days at home; and her few broken words showed that she fancied herself a child again in her father's arms.   (576)

During her recovery, she learns to listen as Captain Kirke saves her and becomes her constant caretaker: "Her questions were endless. Every thing that he could tell her of himself and his life she drew form him delicately and insensibly" (593). She no longer is valued for her words, but rather she becomes the passive source that brings his words to life. He becomes an "egoist" in her hands, implying her final loss of identity even before she marries him (593). Having restored a father figure in her life, Magdalen becomes completely passive. She is silenced in the last words of the text, this time with a kiss and thus finally succumbs to her place in society.

In conclusion, Collins's text gives an account of a mother's power in *No Name,* and connects it to the effacement women experience. In her biography, Peters cites Collins's thoughts as they appeared in *The Guilty River, Arrowsmith's Christmas Annual* (1886, 3) about the relationship of parents and children:

Our mothers have the most sacred of all claims on our gratitude and our love. They have nourished us with their blood; they have risked their lives in bringing us into the world; they have preserved and guided our helpless infancy with divine patience and love. What claim equally strong and equally tender does the other parent establish on his offspring? What motive does the instinct of his young children find for preferring their father before any other person who may be a familiar object in their daily lives? They love him—naturally and rightly love him—because he lives in their remembrance (if he is a good man) as the first, the best, the dearest of their friends.   (as cited in Peters 75)

Collins's language describing the distinction between a mother's and a father's hold over a child is suggestive. The mother's is "sacred" and otherworldly while the father remains grounded in the world as an unthreatening "friend" (as cited in Peters 75). The mother "nourishes [a child] with blood" as though in raising a child she moves increasingly closer to death. This language too reveals the immense gap between the worlds of mothers and that of fathers, and shows then why Magdalen fails as she attempts to define herself. For although throughout her journeys Magdalen uses the language more typical of the male realm to escape the effects of the law, to escape the narrative of traditional motherhood, it fails to empower her. Rather, Collins's text reveals that Magdalen has no choice but to embrace her assigned role as her steps outside the law only draw her closer to its terms.

NOTES

1. See, for example, Robert Ashley's *Wilkie Collins* (New York: Roy, 1952), pages 70–80 for a discussion of a Collins's relationships with women.
2. Helena Michie, " 'There is No Friend like a Sister': Sisterhood as Sexual Difference," *ELH,* 56 (Summer 1989), 412. Michie indicates the history behind Collins's use of the theater: "Amateur theatricals are used, of course, from *Mansfield Park* onward, . . . for the expression of inappropriate erotic feelings." Also consider Céline Varens of Jane Eyre and Charlotte Brontë's use of acting in *Villette.*

WORKS CITED

Ashley, Robert. *Wilkie Collins.* New York: Roy, 1952.

Chodorow, Nancy. *The Reproduction of Mothering: Psychoanalysis and the Sociology of Gender.* Berkeley: U. of California P, 1978.

Collins, Wilkie. *No Name.* Ed. Mark Ford. London: Penguin, 1994.

David, Deidre. "Rewriting Male Plot in Wilkie Collins's *No Name:* Captain Wragge Orders an Omelette and Mrs. Wragge Goes into Custody," *Out of Bounds: Male Writers and Gender[ed] Criticism.* Eds. Laura Claridge and Elizabeth Langland. Amherst: U of Massachusetts P, 1990.

Heller, Tamar. *Dead Secrets: Wilkie Collins and The Female Gothic.* New Haven: Yale UP, 1992.

Homans, Margaret. *Bearing the Word: Language and Female Experience in Nineteenth-Century Women's Writing.* Chicago: U of Chicago P, 1986.

Kristeva, Julia. *The Kristeva Reader.* Ed. Toril Moi. Tr. León S. Roudiez. New York: Columbia UP, 1986.

Michie, Helena. " 'There is no Friend like a Sister': Sisterhood as Sexual Difference." *ELH* 56 (Summer 1989): 401–21.

Oliver, Kelly. *Reading Kristeva: Unraveling the Double-bind.* Bloomington: Indiana UP, 1993.

Peters, Catherine. *The King of Inventors: A Life of Wilkie Collins.* New Jersey: Princeton UP, 1991.

Taylor, Jenny Bourne. *In the Secret Theatre of Home: Wilkie Collins, Sensation Narrative and Nineteenth Century Psychology.* New York: Routledge, 1988.

Entangled Genders: Plasticity, Indeterminacy, and Constructs of Sexuality in Darwin and Hardy

David Garlock

Contemporary readers of *On the Origin of Species* readily recognize Charles Darwin's challenging of traditional classificatory systems of species differentiation. (In chapter two, he explicitly repudiates the typological foundations of speciation, referring to the term "species" as "a mere useless abstraction, implying and assuming a separate act of creation" [43]). Less generally acknowledged is Darwin's correlative negation of rigidly-defined models of gender dichotomization. Yet, a careful reading of Darwin's major work yields ample evidence that his anti-essentialist take on biological diversity is frequently applied analogistically to sexual variability as well.

A close reading of passages dealing with sexual identification and classification in Darwin's *Origin of Species* and *Descent of Man* suggests that the current trend toward reexamination of rigidly-defined norms of sexuality owes much to Darwin's demystification of the principle of androgyny in nature. In the world of post-Darwinian biology, the conceptualization of a single primordial hermaphrodite or population of hermaphrodites overthrows the traditional model of two separately-created progenitors of the human race. (In Shaw's wonderfully audacious revision of the Pentateuch in which he reconfigures the Genesis myth bringing it into conformance with evolutionary theory, the primordial mother/father of humanity is portrayed as the prophet/prophetess Lilith.[1]) Darwin's trans-gendered evocation signaled a break with deeply-entrenched typological constructs of sexuality; the implications of this shattering of yet another heretofore inviolate, divinely-appointed template are still resisted in our own time, while the widespread acceptance of Darwin's imaginative model of a world in which the plasticity of all constructs and structures—biological, geological, sexual, social, and psychological—advances apace.

Dickens Studies Annual, Volume 27, Copyright © 1998 by AMS Press, Inc. All rights reserved.

Barely daring to speak its name until recently, the principle of gender-transcendence has also been slighted or completely overlooked in the·works of Thomas Hardy, a late-Victorian whose work frequently lends itself to an explicitly Darwinian reading. That Hardy acknowledged Darwin's role in shaping many aspects of his world view is documented by his major biographers and in *The Life of Thomas Hardy,* Hardy's autobiography written in the third person. The autobiography classifies the young Hardy as "among the earliest acclaimers of *The Origin of Species*" (153).

The world of Hardy's Wessex, like the world of Darwin's *Origin* and *Descent,* repeatedly recurs to models of morphological plasticity, an abandonment of the fixed and immutable models evoked by the natural theologians of Darwin's day. In his *Descent,* Darwin describes the role of variability in relation to development, invoking the plasticity motif: ". . . There can, however, be no doubt that changed conditions induce an almost indefinite amount of fluctuating variability, by which the whole organization is rendered in some degree plastic" (417). Both Darwin and Hardy celebrate the principles of process and fluidity, abandoning essentialist canons of rigidly-structured classificatory demarcations, effectively anticipating our century's focus on population dynamics, or "population thinking" in the phrase popularized by Ernst Mayr.[2] This viewpoint represents a radical departure from venerable cosmological models such as Plato's cave allegory of the visible universe or the Edenic myth of Genesis, traditional models which envisage all extant life forms as degenerated replicas of primeval perfection.

Departing radically from traditional concepts of primordial "types," Darwin's choice of language in the opening chapter of the *Origin* suggests that domestic breeders are like sculptors, as if the raw materials of biological life were a kind of artistic medium: "Breeders habitually speak of an animal's organization as something plastic, which they can model almost as they please" (30). Throughout his work, Darwin suggests analogical parallels between the plasticity of biological forms and other kinds of plasticity represented in the natural world. From his friend and mentor Charles Lyell, Darwin had derived the model of geological plasticity, as evidenced by the fluidity of the planet earth, whose surface folds, bobs, and undulates (albeit slowly, or in fits and starts) over a sea of molten magma. Both Lyell and Darwin also viewed linguistic forms and structures, manifestly derived from extinct forms and structures long abandoned, as an apt representation of the principle of plasticity applied to the sounds and gestures that comprise human utterance. In fact, the plasticity of all systems and structures observable in the sensible world is a recurrent theme throughout the works of both Darwin and Hardy. Rigid typological demarcation is alien to the universe they envisage, whether the subject is the geological foundations of the earth, the biological foundations of life, or the typological foundations of sexuality. Implicit in Darwin and Hardy is the notion of individual sexualities, or of sexual "populations" of individuals who exist independent of foreordained typologically constrictive models.

Conversely, the natural theologians of the nineteenth century, some of whom had been Darwin's respected mentors during his Cambridge years, subscribed to a teleological view of sex and sexuality consistent with their essentialist doctrine of speciational immutability. The gender dimorphism of Genesis ("male and female created he them" 1.27) suggested that every individual born of human parents would be irrefutably classifiable in terms of one of two polar opposites. In chapter fifteen of *Natural Theology,* William Paley cites the distinguishing differences between the sexes as an irrefutable argument for divinely-ordained design:

> But relation perhaps is never so striking, as when it subsists, not between different parts of the same thing, but between different things. The relation between a lock and key is more obvious, than it is between different parts of the lock. A bow was designed for an arrow, and an arrow for a bow; and the design is more evident for their being separate implements.
> Nor do the works of the Deity want this clearest species of relation. The sexes are manifestly made for each other. (191)

The "lock and key" analogy to male and female genitalia, while far from original with Paley, is characteristic of the typological frame of mind. Paley's is a world in which everything fits—or is supposed to fit—according to the patterns conceived by divine Mind. Males and females are constituted as if modeled after some cosmic blueprint, each crafted separately and individually. The divine template leaves little allowance for blurring of sexual boundaries, in contrast with the world of Hardy's fictive imagination in which sexual compatibility—physiological and psychological "fit"—seldom occurs.

Gender differentiation is far from perfectly realized in Hardy. In *A Pair of Blue Eyes,* we learn from the narrator that Henry Knight "was not shaped by Nature for a marrying man" (366), an oblique reference to physical and/ or psychological inadequacy. Elfride Swancourt is unaccountably jealous of the relationship between Stephen Smith and Henry Knight, effectively blurring the distinction between same-sex and opposite-sex relationships:

> "I don't care how good he is; I don't want to know him, because he comes between me and you. You think of him night and day, ever so much more than of anybody else; and when you are thinking of him, I am shut out of your mind." (72)

In *Two on a Tower,* blond and radiant Swithin St. Cleve is described in terms that suggest androgyny: "His features were sufficiently straight in the contours to correct the beholder's first impression that the head was the head of a girl" (9). Lady Constantine, on the other hand, is handsomely dark and mysterious; the youth who fascinates her is blond and "pretty":

> Her hair was black as midnight, her eyes had no less deep a shade, and her complexion showed the richness demanded as a support to these decided features . . . she continued to look at [Swithin's] pretty face before her. . .   (9)

Fracturing the model of sex-role expectations occurs frequently in Hardy. In *Jude,* Sue Bridehead jumps out of a second-story window to avoid physical intimacy with Mr. Phillotson. Nor is her sexual relationship with Jude, whom she loves spiritually if not always carnally, without its enigmatic inconsistencies: "Jude felt much depressed; she seemed to get further and further away from him with her strange ways and curious unconsciousness of gender" (157). The complexity of the relationship between Jude and Sue suggests a spiritualized, quasi-Platonic love undermined by an ambivalence toward physical intimacy. This is clearly not the world of the natural theologian where the sexes are formed, physically and psychologically, for compatible and perfect relationships, "manifestly made for each other" (191).

In contrast with the traditional model of rigidly differentiated sexualities and sexual roles, as the nineteenth century progressed, the developing sciences of embryology and comparative anatomy offered more and more evidence that each individual begins life as a hermaphrodite, and, consequently, embodies both physical and psychological characteristics of both sexes throughout life. The typological construct of an unadulterated individual being who is "all-man" or "all-woman" was, therefore, challenged by observable phenomena. Essentialist dogma could not hold if the constructs of sexuality proved to be a fiction, having no correspondence with observable populations of individuals possessing varying degrees of male and female qualities and traits.

With characteristic imaginative genius for harmonizing the claims of Scripture with the findings of science, distinguished scholars such as William Whewell, Hugh Miller, and David Brewster resisted any hint of blurred lines of demarcation—speciational or sexual. There was a great deal at stake. Like the biblical literalists of our own age, nineteenth-century defenders of divine revelation recognized that allowance for classificatory ambiguities, whether constructs of gender or species, undermines the authoritative purposiveness inherent in a doctrine postulating a Paleyan Designer engaged in creating forms modeled after other-worldly, perfect design.

Ineluctably opposed to the natural theologians' enterprise, the Darwinian/ populationist model is as detrimental to traditional notions of gender typologies as to notions of speciational fixity. In dealing with issues of sexuality and sex determination, the Darwinian revolution implied an upheaval of the traditional constructs of gender differentiation. Inherent in the Darwinian model of sexual classification, as with the model of species determination, is the notion that the lines of demarcation distinguishing males from females—as well as those separating both sexes from hermaphrodites—are not as pronounced or definitive as is commonly supposed. In chapter six of his *Descent,* Darwin suggests that the affinities which unite all existing and extinct species are analogous to the affinities that unite the sexes:

> There is one other point deserving a fuller notice. It has long been known that in the vertebrate kingdom one sex bears rudiments of various accessory parts, appertaining to the reproductive system, which properly belong to the opposite sex; and it has now been ascertained that at a very early embryonic period both sexes possess true male and female glands. Hence some remote progenitor of the whole vertebrate kingdom appears to have been hermaphrodite or androgynous.
>
> (525)

Darwin goes on to point out that among human beings and other mammals "the males possess rudiments of a uterus with the adjacent passage, in their vesiculae prostaticae" (525), a fact difficult to explain according to the creationist/essentialist model. (We can only speculate that Victorian prudery prevented Darwin from adducing the equally anatomically obvious example of the female's possession of a rudimentary penis in the form of the clitoris.)

Among other anatomical obsessions shared by a number of scientific writers of the period was the existence of rudimentary breasts found on human males and other vertebrates of the mammalian class. In a universe designed and ordered by an omniscient and omnipotent deity, what purpose could be assigned to these embarrassingly useless features? In *Of the Plurality of Worlds,* the astronomer William Whewell draws an analogy between the barren surfaces of presumptively lifeless planets in the solar system and the non-nutritive breasts of human males:

> [The planets Mars and Jupiter] look like the terrestrial breasts of Nature: but are they really nursing breasts? . . . Or are they mere images of such breasts? male teats, dry of all nutritive power?   (341)

The supposed analogous relationship between barren planets and nonfunctional "male teats" reveals much about the typological mindset, and also suggests the foundational significance of well-defined sex-role constructs within the canons of essentialist doctrine. The notion of sexual ambiguity—any hint of bisexuality, gender-transcendence or pansexuality—suggests ambiguity of design and purpose to the Christian Platonist, as Saint Paul and a long line of his evangelical successors have long recognized; the threat is clearly perceived by the Apostle, who reserves his most opprobrious language for those who dare to violate traditional sexual boundaries:

> For this cause God gave them up unto vile affections: for even their women did change the natural use into that which is against nature: And likewise also the men, leaving the natural use of the woman, burned in their lust one toward another . . . they which commit such things are worthy of death
>
> (Rom. 1.27–32).

An extreme example of the attempt to reconcile the typological mindset with anatomical features of the human body is Philip Gosse's elaborate exploration of the subject of Adam's navel, a work that purports to explain the logical necessity of believing that Adam was created complete as a sexually-developed adult, with a navel indicative of a birth that never occurred, and with a "thoroughly ossified skeleton" (*Omphalos* 294). Eventually, the proponents of nipple-and-belly-button theology generated more ridicule than allegiance, as their arguments became less and less compatible with the models of plasticity proferred by Darwin and his defenders. The plasticity of all organic structures (demonstrable in the observable plasticity of human anatomy), analogous to the principle of plasticity undergirding Lyell's theory of the earth, became a kind of theoretical linchpin suggesting the plasticity of all organizations—natural, psychological and philosophical.

Meanwhile, the natural theologians held steadfastly to their doctrine of rigid definitions and demarcations. A few pages past his reconciliation of phenomena anatomical and astronomical, Whewell explicitly links his doctrine of planets and pectorals with Platonic idealism:

> The mode in which Plato expressed the doctrine which we are here urging was, that there were in the Divine Mind, before or during the work of creation, certain archetypal Ideas, certain exemplars or patterns of the world and its parts, according to which the work was performed.   (372)

Darwin's treatment of the mysteries of underdeveloped breasts in the male provides yet another example of his progressive abandonment of canons of essentialist tradition. Like Whewell, Darwin finds the phenomenon provocative, and in need of explanation: "The possession by male mammals of functionally imperfect mammary organs is, in some respect, especially curious" (*Descent* 525).

Characteristically, Darwin links humankind with primordial ancestors in his offering an explanation that suggests a closer relationship to hermaphroditism than traditional gender typologies admit. The "imperfect mammary organs" of men may, in fact, be anatomical fossils, relics of androgynous ancestors whose sex roles did not necessarily conform to the norms of modern human society and culture. Darwin points out that the nurturing role is not at all the exclusive lot of females in nature, and suggests that among primordial human ancestors lactation may have occurred in both sexes: "It may be suggested . . . that long after the progenitors of the whole mammalian class had ceased to be androgynous, both sexes yielded milk, and nourished their young" (526).

In the first chapter of his *Descent,* Darwin makes reference to man's hermaphrodite heritage:

> Rudiments, however, may occur in one sex of those parts which are normally present in the other sex; and such rudiments, as we shall hereafter see, have often originated in a way distinct from those here referred to.   (401)

In the following chapter, entitled "The Development of Man from Some Lower Form," Darwin once again strikes the keynote of plasticity—the malleable nature of life itself in all of its various forms, with human morphology not excepted: "There can, however, be no doubt that changed conditions induce an almost indefinite amount of fluctuating variability, by which the whole organization is rendered in some degree plastic" (417).

The notion of an analogous relationship between speciational and sexual plasticity is encountered, embryonically, in Darwin's "Notes and Sketches, 1837–1844" edited by Sir Francis Darwin and published as part of his father's *Autobiography.* One entry, which Sir Francis offers as "of miscellaneous interest," is perhaps of greater interest than either Charles Darwin or his son could immediately perceive, in that it seems to contain the kernel of Darwin's later linkage of sexual and speciational morphology with what came to be the populationist model of sexual and speciational determinants:

> When one sees nipple on man's breast, one does not say some use, but sex not having been determined—so with useless wings under elytra of beetles—born from beetles with wings, and modified—if simple creation merely, would have been born without them.   (123)

The anti-essentialist view of sex and sexual differentiation is also encountered in chapter two of Darwin's *Origin.* The essentialist dichotomization of the sexes is alien to the Darwinian model of sexuality, which allows for multiple sexual classifications:

> Individuals of the same species often present, as is known to every one, great differences of structure, independently of variation, as in the two sexes of various animals, in the two or three castes of sterile females or workers amongst insects, and in the immature and larval states of many of the lower animals. There are, also, cases of dimorphism and trimorphism, both with animals and plants.   (40)

The blurred binary opposites of masculinity and femininity are perceivable in many of Hardy's most memorable characters.[3] The theme of androgyny and/or sexual ambiguity seems less openly apparent in Hardy's later, more mature work, while in the earlier stages of his evolution as a novelist, this theme often surfaces in more readily-recognizable form. Close readings of passages dealing with character delineation, particularly in the earlier works, disclose a tendency to people his fictive world with individuals who are, to some recognizable degree, gender-transcendent. In this essay I have chosen to focus primarily on Hardy's first published novel, *Desperate Remedies,* a generally neglected mid-career novel, *A Laodicean,* and his last novel, *Jude the Obscure.* I have selected these works because they provide the most explicit examples of Hardy's predilection toward inversion and subversion of traditional canons of gender identity. However, traces of gender bending and the challenging of sex-role dichotomization are detectable in much of Hardy's work, as Margaret Higonnet and other recent critics have demonstrated.

The roots of sexual ambiguity in Hardy are perhaps most readily detectable in his career-launching novel of 1871. Not yet bedeviled by Grundyism and Grundy-sensitive editors, Hardy introduces in *Desperate Remedies* a cast of characters remarkably free from rigidly-defined canons of gender identification. Both the physiological and psychological portraiture hint at gender-transcendence. Edward Springrove's physiognomy is an important focus in the novel's early pages. In fact, Cytherea Graye's obsession with his appearance prior to her first encounter with the young man sets the stage for the narrative description of her initial impressions:

> He was rather above her brother's height. Although the upper part of his face and head was handsomely formed, and bounded by lines of sufficiently masculine regularity, his brows were somewhat too softly arched and finely pencilled for one of his sex . . . (30)

We may justifiably attach some significance to Hardy's first handsome hero in his first published novel being introduced as a near-perfect young man whose appearance suggests that he is a composite of both masculine and feminine characteristics. From a purely physiological standpoint, this reminds us of Darwin's recognition of the fact that "[r]udiments . . . may occur in one sex of those parts which are normally present in the other sex" (*Descent* 525).

While both Cytherea Graye and Cytherea Aldclyffe are described as attractively handsome, the novel's great beauty is a male, described in detail by an apparently sexually ambiguous narrator who seems equally appreciative of physical pulchritude in both sexes. The physical attractiveness of the mysterious and sinister Aeneas Manston suggests a teasingly androgynous blend of masculine and feminine characteristics:

He was an extremely handsome man, well-formed. . . . The most striking point in his appearance was the wonderful, almost preternatural, clearness of his complexion. There was not a blemish or speck of any kind to mar the smoothness of its surface or the beauty of its hue. . . . Eyes and forehead both would have expressed keenness of intellect too severely to be pleasing, had their force not been counteracted by the lines and tone of the lips. These were full and luscious to a surprising degree, possessing a womanlike softness of curve, and a ruby redness . . .   (150)

"Full and luscious" lips—a notably rare quality for any male character in English literature—suggests Manston's status as a kind of *homme fatal*. It is partly Manston's blend of masculine and feminine features that makes him so disturbingly attractive, and at the same time sinister, in the mind of Cytherea Graye: "He had faced the window, looking fixedly at the sky with his dark strong eyes. She seemed compelled to do as she was bidden, and looked in the too-delicately beautiful face" (154).

Cytherea Aldclyffe, like Edward Springrove and Aeneas Manston, is introduced to the reader in terms that suggest androgyny:

There was a severity about the lower outlines of the face which gave a masculine cast to this portion of her countenance. Womanly weakness was nowhere visible save in one part—the curve of her forehead and brows; there it was clear and emphatic.   (59)

In the paragraph preceding this description, Hardy's narrator describes the meeting of the elder and younger Cythereas as if the two women were blending into a single personality, a description which seems to prefigure the strange metamorphoses in Hardy's 1897 novel *The Well-Beloved*. The women are described in a passage that seems almost a poetic evocation of morphological plasticity, laced with a hint of autoerotic, narcissistic sensuality, as if the women are mesmerized by the mysterious alchemy of their own mirror images:

Both the women showed off themselves to advantage as they walked forward in the orange light; and each showed too in her face that she had been struck with her companion's appearance. The warm tint added to Cytherea's face a voluptuousness which youth and a simple life had not yet allowed to express itself there ordinarily; whilst in the elder lady's face it reduced the customary expression, which might have been called sternness, if not harshness, to grandeur, and warmed her decaying complexion with much of the youthful richness it plainly had once possessed.   (59)

The Hardyan motif of sex-role reversal makes its first appearance in *Desperate Remedies*. Cytherea Aldclyffe, in many respects a gender-transcendent personality, is placed in the role traditionally played by a male suitor, as she

attempts to seduce Cytherea Graye into physical intimacy and the renuncia-
tion of all rivals. Focusing on whether or not the narrator is describing a
lesbian encounter misses the point, in my opinion. The essentialist-driven
obsession with classificatory labels (lesbian, homosexual, heterosexual, bisex-
ual, asexual, bachelor-girl, etc.) is itself suspect within the context of a Har-
dyan/Darwinian universe, in which all traditional notions of demarcation are
effectively canceled. Hence, it is impossible to determine where motherly
love ends and eroticism begins, since the participants themselves are exploring
the boundaries (in the relationship between the two Cythereas); where friendship ceases and homoerotic attraction begins (as with the intense feelings
generated between Henry Knight and Stephen Smith, whose mutual affection
is transfigured by their subsequent rivalry over Elfride Swancourt); or where
gender identity begins and ends (particularly in the case of Jude and Sue).

Whatever motivations we ascribe to Miss Aldclyffe in *Desperate Remedies,*
her aggressive behavior toward Cytherea Graye places her among Hardy's
long procession of characters who defy gender stereotyping:

> Miss Aldclyffe removed her arms from Cytherea's neck. 'Tis now with you as
> it is always with all girls,' she said, in jealous and gloomy accents. 'You are
> not, after all, the innocent I took you for. No. No.' She then changed her tone
> with fitful rapidity. 'Cytherea, try to love me more than you love him—do. I
> love you more sincerely than any man can . . . and I—an old fool—have been
> sipping at your mouth as if it were honey, because I fancied no wasting lover
> knew the spot.'   (93–4)

In addition to the direct references to personality traits and tendencies
toward androgyny in many of the characters, there is also detectable in *Desperate Remedies* a pervasive sense of unsolved mystery throughout the novel.
On the surface, this is naturally attributable to Hardy's following the generic
format of the "sensation novel" of the period. It is possible, however, to
read the fact that each of the major characters seems continually bedeviled
and controlled by one or more deep and shameful "secrets," as suggestive
of unmentionable sexual secrets. Miss Aldclyffe and Aeneas Manston dread
"discovery" throughout the novel, as, to a lesser degree, do Cytherea Graye
and Edward Springrove.

In the opening passages, when Ambrose Graye asks the young Cytherea
Aldclyffe to be his wife, she is horrified at the proposal:

> She seemed like one just awakened. "Ah—we must part now!" she faltered,
> in a voice of anguish. "I will write to you." She loosened her hand and
> rushed away.
>   In a wild fever Graye went home and watched for the next morning. Who
> shall express his misery and wonder when a note containing these words was
> put into his hand?

"Good-bye; good-bye for ever. As recognized lovers something divides us eternally. Forgive me—I should have told you before; but your love was sweet! Never mention me." (3)

Ostensibly it is Miss Aldclyffe's having given birth to an illegitimate child that forces this first of many desperate remedies. However, the mysterious declaration that "something divides us eternally," and Miss Aldclyffe's bizarre disappearance suggest other, darker levels of deception and ambivalence. Admittedly, this is neither a necessary nor even a likely interpretation of the first Cytherea's motivation for abandoning her innocent lover. But the language of the narrative, nonetheless, invites a certain level of speculative latitude regarding the complexity of Cytherea's motivations. Cytherea Aldclyffe is, in many regards, the model for more fully developed characterizations of sexual ambiguity and irresolution in Hardy's more mature work.

In *Desperate Remedies* Hardy created a kind of plot template, which he continued to recast and remould throughout his literary career, but from which he never completely departed. The sexuality in later novels became less explicit, as Hardy responded to criticism of some of the novel's lurid features. In *The First Mrs. Thomas Hardy,* Denys Kay-Robinson records Hardy's reaction to negative criticism: "Too late he saw that the lesbian scene and other 'daring' aspects of the book damned it at the outset as a candidate for family reading and therefore for the libraries" (64). It is apparent from Denys Kay-Robinson and other biographers that Hardy, who was inordinately sensitive to criticism of any kind, was forced to bowderlize his work, or at least to resort to innuendo when dealing with extra-marital sex or cryptically erotic same-sex relationships.

Hardy leaves open multiple avenues of possible bisexuality in *Desperate Remedies*. It is not outside the realm of possibility that Cytherea Graye must continue to submit to Miss Aldclyffe's caresses (verbal and/or physical) because of her social position and economic dependence. Likewise, Edward Springrove, though sexually attracted to Cytherea, has also known strong attractions to other men (again, whether physical, spiritual, or both is left for the reader to decide). That conventional distinctions separating homosexual from heterosexual impulses are as bogus as other essentialist-driven demarcations is obliquely suggested by a number of Hardy's narrators. Whether the attraction Miss Aldclyffe feels for Cytherea is sexual or if Edward Springrove's emotional and intellectual attraction to other men has a sexual component depends on the degree of sexual plasticity one chooses to apply to the characters described:

An impressionable heart had for years—perhaps as many as six or seven years—been distracting him, by unconsciously setting itself to yearn for somebody wanting, he scarcely knew whom. Echoes of himself, though rarely, he now and then found. Sometimes they were men, sometimes women, his cousin Adelaide being one of these; for in spite of a fashion which pervades the whole community at the present day—the habit of exclaiming that woman is not undeveloped man, but diverse, the fact remains that, after all, women are Mankind, and that in many of the sentiments of life the difference of sex is but a difference of degree.   (201)

This curious passage suggests a level of sexual relativism reminiscent of Darwin's frequent characterization of physiological sexual differences in relativistic terms:

That various accessory parts, proper to each sex, are found in a rudimentary condition in the opposite sex, may be explained by such organs having been gradually acquired by the one sex, and then transmitted in a more or less imperfect state to the other   (*Descent* 525).

In Hardy, the concept of a physiologically contiguous relationship between the two sexes is expanded to suggest a psychologically contiguous relationship, as well. That the theme of sexual relativism is not developed further in Hardy's more popular fiction is perhaps due to the prevailing specter of Mrs. Grundy along with the pressure to produce fiction suitable for serialization in "family magazines" such as Leslie Stephen's *Cornhill.* Although glimpses of sexual ambiguity and androgyny occur in Hardy's later work, they are usually less explicit than in the earlier novels.

In Hardy's mid-career novel of 1881, *A Laodicean,* Paula Power, a sexual as well as a theological Laodicean, is a character who might well have written Cytherea Aldclyffe's tragic lines "something divides us eternally" to any one or all of her lovers, including her female "lover," Charlotte De Stancy. Paula never submits fully to either her deceased father's Baptist faith, nor to her final choice from among her suitors, the young architectural Laodicean, George Somerset. Paula's relationship with Charlotte De Stancy cannot be called explicitly sexual, but her affection for the young woman places her in the role of a suitor. George Somerset overhears the local inn's landlord describing the relationship between Charlotte and Paula:

. . . they are more like lovers than girl and girl. Miss Power is looked up to by little De Stancy as if she were a god-a'mighty, and Miss Power lets her love her to her heart's content. But whether Miss Power loves back again I can't say, for she's as deep as the North Star.   (51)

When Somerset observes Paula's hesitation on the brink of the baptismal pool, he senses her ambivalent state of mind, an indecisiveness that is not explicitly sexual, but which might take on a sexual cast when considered in the context of other kinds of ambivalences presented in the novel:

... enough was shown to assure Somerset that she had had some experience of things far removed from her present circumscribed horizon, and could live, and was even at that moment living a clandestine, stealthy inner life which had very little to do with her present outward one. (17)

The reference to "things far removed from her present circumscribed horizon" and "a clandestine, stealthy inner life" suggests an illicit secretiveness disproportionate to the description of a mere lapse in evangelical enthusiasm. Once again, although the novel's denouement furnishes an antiseptically heterosexualized overlay sufficient to appease, perhaps even deceive, Mrs. Grundy and her serial-consuming hordes, there is perceivable in Paula's character a hint of sexual, as well as ecclesiastical, license—a noncommital openness to experimentation and a resistance to rigidly-structured role assignment. Admittedly, these oblique implications of sexual ambiguity are not developed to the point of controlling the central plot of the novel. Still, the language employed seems deliberately to open up a wide range of sexual options, both within and beyond the novel's narrative scope.

Charlotte De Stancy, Paula Power's live-in companion, is described in terms that suggest degeneracy of type, with a reference to "confusion" consistent with the novel's thematic presentation of many levels of confusion—artistic, theological, and, in my opinion, sexual: "But it was not the De Stancy face with all its original specialties: it was, so to speak, a defective reprint of that face: for the nose tried hard to turn up and deal utter confusion to the family shape" (29).

Somerset's first encounter with Miss De Stancy explores the relationship between Paula and her young protegée. There is a hint of clandestine secretiveness:

Somerset was looking at the homely affectionate face of the little speaker. "You are her good friend, I am sure," he remarked.
She looked into the distant air with tacit admission of the impeachment. "So would you be if you knew her," she said; and a blush slowly rose to her cheek, as if the person spoken of had been a lover rather than a friend. (35)

A few paragraphs beyond this description of the relationship between the two women, George Somerset refers to Paula Power as "a mixed young lady" (37), ostensibly referring to her catholicity of tastes, but also suggesting the wide range of ways in which Paula might be considered a person of "mixed" character and emotions.

The narrator's early descriptions of George Somerset suggest that the young architect himself shares with Aeneas Manston some peculiar traces of androgyny: "Of beard he had but small show, though he was as innocent as a Nazarite of the use of the razor; but he possessed a moustache all-sufficient to hide the subtleties of his mouth, which could thus be tremulous at tender moments without provoking inconvenient criticism'' (8–9).

Somerset's name suggests the end of a season, the demise of summer—in particular the summer of architectural exuberance, a period whose brightness and glory can only be perceived through a retrospective haze. The sharply defined architectural lines of the Gothic cathedrals and the spirit that created them are now faded, corrupted and hopelessly compromised. Archetypal definition and form has degenerated into an indistinguishable morass of conflictive, blurred, and adulterated compromises. Defects of definition in the realms of architecture and faith seem to be reflected in the physical and psychological characteristics of the human populations of modern times. And blurred lines of sexual definition are reflective of abandoned typological models, remnants of a nobler age, whether authentic or imagined.

The revealing scene in which William Dare effectively ''seduces'' Captain De Stancy by allowing him to see Paula Power performing physical exercise is a study in sexual ambiguity. Dare, who is himself sexually ambiguous in his preternatural boyishness, arranges for De Stancy to see Miss Power when she will appear most attractive—when she dresses in athletic clothing for her workout in a gymnasium. Dare describes the advantage of seeing her exercising in the gym: ''Because when she is there she wears such a pretty boy's costume, and is so charming in her movements, that you think she is a lovely youth and not a girl at all'' (169). Captain De Stancy's seeing Paula in the gymnasium has a profound effect: ''The sight of Paula in the gymnasium, which the judicious Dare had so carefully planned, led up to and heightened by subtle accessories, operated on De Stancy's surprised soul with a promptness almost magical'' (178).

It is apparent from this passage that Paula's boyishness arouses more than Captain De Stancy's ''surprised soul.'' The ''promptness almost magical'' suggests sexual awakening of a kind that De Stancy wishes to quell. The bold and brash William Dare is sexually sophisticated enough to comprehend the complexities of human sexuality, and to use them to his own reprehensible ends.

Earlier in the novel Dare ''seduces'' Somerset's architectural competitor, the less-talented mediocrity, Mr. Havill, into stealing a copy of Somerset's architectural plans, and then making the illicit offer to invade Somerset's apartment. Havill and Dare have dinner, get drunk, and are forced to share a double bed because the inn where they are staying is crowded. Hardy sets the scene for this seduction in terms that allow the reader to decide whether or not Dare's Mephistophelian temptation of Havill includes sexual seduction:

> The same evening Havill asked Dare to dine with him. He was just at this time living *en garcon,* his wife and children being away on a visit. After dinner they sat on till their faces were rather flushed. . . .

Havill who had not drunk enough to affect his reasoning, held up his glass to the light and said, "I never can quite make out what you are, or what your age is. Are you sixteen, one-and-twenty, or twenty-seven? (141)

Overcrowded conditions in the inn require some shuffling of accommodations:

. . . If Mr. Dare would give up his room, and share a double-bedded room with Mr. Havill, the thing could be done, but not otherwise.
To this the two companions agreed, and presently went upstairs with as gentlemanly a walk and vertical a candle as they could exhibit under the circumstances. (143)

The language of this encounter at the end of book two, chapter two, with its suggestive "vertical candle" and "double-bedded room," along with the circumstance of Mrs. Havill and the children being conveniently absent, at least hints at the possibility of Dare's seduction extending to a physical level.

At the beginning of chapter three, the narrative skips to Havill's contemplating the sleeping Dare at two o'clock in the morning: "He lay on his back, his arms thrown out; and his well-curved youthful form looked like an unpedestaled Dionysus in the colourless lunar rays" (144).

Within the context of the novel, William Dare suggests adulterations of many kinds. He is irrevocably "mixed," a kind of distorted mirror-image of the Laodicean protagonists Paula Power and George Somerset. An "unpedestaled Dionysus," he suggests the evil seductiveness of Aeneas Manston in *Desperate Remedies.* Dare's physical attractiveness is a corruption of the Greek ideal, a parodistic copy like the offensive concatenation of architectural styles so despised by Somerset. The narrator explicitly links degraded ancestry with dilapidated architecture: "Charlotte was concerned to see her brother's face, and withdrew from the window that he might not question her further. De Stancey went into the hall, and on to the gallery, where Dare was standing as still as a caryatid" (207). Dare's ability to manipulate the plot is based in large part upon the mixed loyalties of the major characters he seeks to control. His "mixed" sexuality is subtly suggested by the narrator's referring to him as a "boy-man" (322), and by his constant pandering. As a classical caryatid, he supports the patchwork Laodicean architecture of the plot complications, many of which he has instigated.

Paula Power's noncommittal theological meanderings seem to suggest confused sexuality, as well. While visiting Amiens, Captain De Stancy and Paula observe the casual irreverence of worshipers in the cathedral anxious to remove flower pots placed in front an honored saint. De Stancy derides Paul's cynicism:

"I perceive you are a harsh Puritan." "No, Captain De Stancy! Why will you speak so? I am far too much otherwise. I have grown to be so much of your way of thinking, that I accuse myself, and am accused by others, of being worldly, and half-and-half, and other dreadful things—though it isn't that at all." (355)

Ostensibly, Paula's "half-and-half" status refers to her theological compromises. Still, frequently embedded in descriptions of Paula's multiple dilemmas is the suggestion of compromised sexuality, as well. The implication that Paula is "half-and-half, and other dreadful things" is certainly applicable to her half-hearted responses to her various suitors, and perhaps to her sexual identity, as well.

Although gender-transcendence recurs as a recognizable motif in much of Hardy's narrative fiction, after *A Laodicean* it does not resurface as a major preoccupation until his last novel, *Jude the Obscure*. Rejection of traditional roles and constructs of sexuality defines the character of the novel's central love triangle (or quadrangle). In defiance of norms of sexuality and propriety, the character exhibiting the most aggressive toughness (i.e, masculinity) in the novel is Arabella Donn. With all of her limitations, only Arabella exhibits psychological resilience and the kind of hard-headed practicality so often admired in traditionally constructed masculine heroes. In fact, she introduces herself to the virginal and demure young dreamer, Jude Fawley, by assaulting him with the disembodied penis of a slaughtered pig. Throughout much of their relationship the penis-wielding Arabella appears as a dominant force, while Jude is frequently portrayed as compliant and passive. Ultimately, Arabella prevails and survives while Jude surrenders to despair and death.

Jude and Sue, on the other hand, seem in many ways to function as mirror-images of one another, frequently changing roles in a manner that suggests exchanged sexual identities, as well. In "Becoming a Man in *Jude the Obscure*," Elizabeth Langland suggests that the exploding of gender stereotypes is a major value in the novel:

Part of the novel's brilliance derives from Hardy's ability to represent Jude's battle with the class and gender self-constructions his culture offers him. His embattlement gives the novel its richness and generates its tragic denouement.
(*The Sense of Sex* 32)

Jude Fawley and Sue Bridehead are, in many respects, two of Hardy's most androgynous creations. A pervasive anxiety in response to the demands of traditional sex-role constructs characterizes Jude and Sue equally, as Michael Millgate has pointed out in *Career*: ". . . it appears from an early stage that [Jude] and Sue have more than their courtship in common" (321).

In the scene where Sue explains her repugnance at having to submit sexually to Richard Phillotson, the anguish consists in great part from her inability to adapt to the sex role imposed upon her:

> "But it is not as you think!—there is nothing wrong except my own wickedness, I suppose you'd call it—a repugnance on my part, for a reason I cannot disclose, and what would not be admitted as one by the world in general! . . . What tortures me so much is the necessity of being responsive to this man whenever he wishes, good as he is morally—the dreadful contract to feel in a particular way in a matter whose essence is its voluntariness!" (224)

For both Jude and Sue, the constructs imposed by society are intolerably incompatible with their own implacable and frustrated cravings for transcendence; it is clear that their longing to transcend the meanness and circumscriptions of time and circumstance extends also to the inherited constrictions of rigidly-delimited sexual expectations and sexual roles. Boundaries and parameters of sex-role identification, like those imposed by genealogical status and demarcations of social class, militate against their own inviolate sense of being. Hardy's exhaltation of the individual specimen over any traditional conception of a representative "type" places his work within the Darwinian populationist mindset. Ernst Mayr considers this elevation of the specimen over any flawed taxonomic system foundational to our understanding of the Darwinian legacy:

> Indeed, the discovery of the importance of the individual became the cornerstone of Darwin's theory of natural selection. It eventually resulted in the replacement of essentialism by population thinking, which emphasized the uniqueness of the individual and the critical role of individuality in evolution. (42)

For Darwin and Hardy, all classificatory systems are illusory; each individual being—shaped by imponderable aeons, circumstances, and accumulated variability—is faithful to no pre-ordained type or model, but, rather, stands alone as a representation of the unrelenting natural processes that have shaped and defined each unique specimen's existence. For Hardy's gender-transcendent protagonists, all classificatory designations are illusory. Sue and Jude *represent* only themselves. They struggle to define themselves within the context of a Hardyan/Darwinian milieu, in which there are no types or species—only unique, separate, and aspiring individuals.

NOTES

1. In *Back to Methuselah,* Bernard Shaw gives the primordial hermaphrodite the last word (cf. 298–300).

2. Ernst Mayr, one of the major architects of the modern evolutionary synthesis, develops this idea at length in *One Long Argument: Charles Darwin and the Genesis of Modern Evolutionary Thought.*

3. I am indebted to Margaret R. Higonnet's introductory chapter to *The Sense of Sex* for this concept, although she does not relate the principle to Hardy's Darwinism. Higonnet points out that Hardy "shows how the binary opposites of masculinity and femininity blur when embodied in the individual" (3).

WORKS CITED

Darwin, Charles. *Autobiography.* 1876. New York: Henry Schuman, 1950.

——— *The Origin of Species by Means of Natural Selection, or the Preservation of Favored Races in the Struggle for Life.* 1872. and *The Descent of Man and Selection in Relation to Sex.* 1871. New York: Modern Library, 1977. (All quotations from the *Origin* and the *Descent* are taken from this one-volume edition, which contains Darwin's sixth and final edition of the *Origin,* with his 1871 edition of the *Descent* appended as a companion piece.)

Bible. Authorized King James Version, 1611. (Biblical references are from this translation.)

Gosse, Philip Henry. *Omphalos: An attempt to Untie the Geological Knot.* London: John Van Voorst, 1857.

Hardy, Florence Emily. *The Life of Thomas Hardy.* 1930. New York: St. Martins, 1962.

Hardy, Thomas. *Desperate Remedies.* 1871. London: Macmillan, 1976.

——— *Jude the Obscure.* 1896. New York: Bantam, 1981.

——— *A Laodicean.* 1881. Oxford: Oxford UP, 1991.

——— *A Pair of Blue Eyes.* 1873. New York: Harper, 1895.

——— *Two on a Tower.* 1882. Oxford: Oxford UP, 1993.

——— *The Well-Beloved.* 1897. Oxford: Oxford UP, 1991.

Higonnet, Margaret. ed. *The Sense of Sex: Feminist Perspectives of Hardy.* Urbana: U of Illinois P, 1992.

Kay-Robinson, Denys. *The First Mrs. Thomas Hardy.* New York: St. Martin's, 1979.

Mayr, Ernst. *One Long Argument, Charles Darwin and the Genesis of Modern Evolutionary Thought.* Cambridge: Harvard U P, 1991.

Millgate, Michael. *Thomas Hardy: His Career as a Novelist.* New York: Random House, 1971.

Paley, William. *Natural Theology: or, Evidences and Attributes of the Deity; Collected from the Appearances of Nature.* 1802. Houston: St. Thomas, 1972.

Whewell, William. *Of the Plurality of Worlds.* London: John W. Parker, 1854.

Recent Dickens Studies: 1996

Trey Philpotts

Enough already! So a weary reviewer is likely to declare after having waded, sometimes slogged, through more than 100 academic books and articles on Dickens this year. The overwhelming volume of material might be seen as testimony to his continuing relevance as we approach the millennium. Of course, it might also be seen as rather tremendous overkill. Quick multiplication would suggest that, at this rate, more than 1000 academic articles have been published on Dickens since 1986. Inevitably, with this many essays published year after year, much is going to be minor or second-rate, and such, alas, was the case in 1996: essays frequently rehashed tired and familiar themes, often without proper acknowledgment; or were under-researched; or long and over-elaborate; or poorly written; or trivial; or some combination of these qualities. It is not that they were especially bad—many were perfectly competent—just that they were dispensable, grist for the publication mills, but little more. And, yet, amid the bland familiarity and trifling nature of so much, a number of pieces stood out. For starters, I would recommend essays by Tim Cribbs, Geoffrey Hemstedt, Hilary Schor, John Jordan, Helen Small, Mary Armstrong, and Kelly Hager. The best critical book of the year is probably Valerie Gager's *Shakespeare and Dickens;* the best editions, Janice Carlisle's *Great Expectations,* and Michael Slater's collection of Dickens' journalism, *Amusements of the People.* George Newlin's topicon, *Every Thing in Dickens* also warrants mention, as does Brian Rosenberg's book on *Little Dorrit* and Robert Patten's biography of George Cruikshank. These books and articles incorporate a wide variety of critical approaches—old and new historicism, deconstructionism, feminism, cultural criticism, and just plain competent scholarship. What sets them apart is the critics' ability to construct arguments both original and credible, and sometimes downright exciting. In such a very crowded field, this is no mean feat.

Overall, no particular critical approach held sway in 1996. About half of the works incorporated recent cultural and gender theory, and about half

Dickens Studies Annual, Volume 27, Copyright © 1998 by AMS Press, Inc. All rights reserved.

were more traditional in nature. Although the heterogeneous nature of most criticism precludes precise accounting, roughly 17 pieces qualify as cultural criticism, 11 as gender criticism (8 feminist, 3 homoerotic), and 5 as strict deconstruction (though deconstruction's insights are drawn on by almost everyone). More empirical background studies accounted for about 25 of the pieces, with 7 of these providing biographical information. There were about 10 "traditional" studies devoted to analyzing Dickens's writing style or discussing characters or genres and 7 influence and comparative studies. Seemingly out of fashion this year were reader response criticism (1 or 2), psychoanalytic criticism (1), typological criticism (1) and Marxism (1 or 2). *Dickens Quarterly* and the *Dickensian* continue to favor the more traditional and "scholarly" approaches, while *Dickens Studies Annual* was more open to theoretical criticism, though it should be noted that most of the pieces on Dickens were published outside the three Dickens periodicals. Continuing a long-term trend, the most frequently discussed works were Dickens's "dark" novels: *Great Expectations* (10 times), *Little Dorrit* (9), *Our Mutual Friend* (9), and *Bleak House* (7). Otherwise, critical attention was evenly dispersed among most of the other works, though *Sketches by Boz* and *The Pickwick Papers* were all but overlooked, with only one article each. In general, the Dickens that emerged in 1996 was fundamentally a political radical, whose highly "unstable" fictions undermined many of the received truths of mid-Victorian culture.

As for the more mundane details of this review article: I have tried to consider every academic book or article that was published on Dickens in 1996, or at least every academic book or article written in English and that I could find; I've also tried to discuss every chapter on Dickens, as well as the biography of one of his closest associates, George Cruikshank. No doubt I have missed some pieces, and for this I apologize to the writers. To save space, I have omitted consideration of chapters first published as articles that have been previously reviewed in *Dickens Studies Annual*. Though no organizational plan is ideal, the reviews are grouped for ease of access, with a large section at the end devoted to books and articles focusing on individual Dickens works. The essays in the collections entitled *Dickens Refigured* and *Victorian Identities* have been treated together, because of their ostensibly unified nature. With this information out of the way, we are free to shove off from shore. The weather is a bit inclement, and the voyage should be rather rocky. But there's plenty of light up ahead.

Editions and Compilations

After thirty-six years, Penguin has finally published a new edition of *Great Expectations*. This new edition, with an introduction by David Trotter and edited and annotated by Charlotte Mitchell, includes fuller and more plentiful notes than its predecessor, a map of Kent in the early nineteenth century (though there is no map of London), "A Dickens Chronology," the obligatory original ending, Dickens's working notes, and a list of "suggested further reading." Trotter's introduction conventionally sees the novel as "a story of moral redemption" brought about by Pip's confrontation with "his own ingratitude" (vii). Predictably, guilt is said to be something that "clings" to Pip, and Orlick and Bentley Drummle are described as his doubles. When Trotter becomes more venturesome and turns to the social and political concerns of the novel, his analysis is sketchy and vague. Dickens may have been a free-trader, as Trotter asserts, but the relevance of free trade to the novel is never made very clear, other than that it has to do very generally with "circulation" and "blockage."

The series of *Case Studies in Contemporary Criticism,* published by St. Martin's Press, seem to be one of the academic marketing successes of recent years. Each edition includes the complete text, along with brief annotations at the bottom of the page, and a selection of pieces representing different theoretical perspectives, as well as clear descriptions of these perspectives, brief summaries of the representative pieces, and selected bibliographies. Especially valuable are the surveys of biographical and historical context and critical histories of each novel. Janice Carlisle's edition of *Great Expectations* is one of the latest, and one of the best, contributions to the series. Carlisle's survey of contexts is informed and well-written and her discussion of the novel's critical history nicely distinguishes the major areas of critical disagreement. Her selection of criticism includes reprinted pieces by Peter Brooks on plotting, Edward W. Said on postcolonialism, and William A. Cohen on masturbation, as well as a fine feminist piece by Hilary Schor and cultural criticism by Jay Clayton (the last two essays are discussed in their proper place in this review). Both the Penguin and St. Martin's Press editions rely on Chapman and Hall's three-volume 1861 text, with Penguin standardizing a few inconsistencies of punctuation and correcting printing errors, and using some of the emendations proposed by Margaret Cardwell in the Clarendon edition of the novel, and St. Martin's collating the Chapman and Hall text with the 1868 Charles Dickens edition.

Graham Law's attractive new edition of *Hard Times,* published by Broadview Literary Texts, contains a generous sampling of contemporary documents on utilitarianism and industrialization, as well as information about the novel's composition, and early reviews. Especially helpful is a section devoted to industrial fiction, with excerpted passages from Harriet Martineau, Frances Trollope, and Benjamin Disraeli, among others. Law sacrifices breadth for depth in his selection—the documents focus exclusively on utilitarianism and industrialization—and in his introduction perhaps overstates the degree to which "early" utilitarianism was a "declining force" by the mid-1850s, but these are relatively small complaints. Of greater concern is Law's choice of copy text, the "Charles Dickens" edition of 1868, which scholars have faulted for being "devoid of specific textual authority" (*Norton Critical Edition* 233), and which Law chooses without any justification.

Michael Slater's Everyman Dickens series has been a bit of a disappointment. The introductions are generally sound, and the annotations reasonably thorough, but the illustrations suffer from poor reproduction, and the odd-sized books themselves are clumsy to hold, and in the thicker volumes, the inner margins are uncomfortably close to the binding. The real advantage to the Everyman series is its inclusion of hard-to-find "minor" Dickens stories and journalism. Ruth Glancy's finely edited collection of Dickens's *Christmas Stories* is thus cause for celebration. As she points out in her informative introduction, Dickens's Christmas stories challenge those who have unjustly derided his short stories as second rate. Certainly, some suffer from excessive sentimentality or insufficient development, but, as Glancy rightly notes, they also include some of his "most personal, introspective and sincere" writing (xxxiii). As is sometimes the problem with the Everyman series, the illustrations are essentially irrelevant to the text, since they were not published with the stories but only included in editions that followed Dickens's death. But Glancy's headnotes helpfully establish the context for the individual stories and provide detailed information about the other contributors to the collaborative efforts.

Thanks to Michael Slater and Ohio State University Press, Dickensians finally have easy access to much of Dickens's journalism. The second volume of the Dent Uniform Edition of Dickens's Journalism—*The Amusements of the People and Other Papers: Reports, Essays, and Reviews, 1834–51*—includes annotated texts of some of Dickens's most important journalism from the *Morning Chronicle, The Examiner,* and the first year of *Household Words.* While a few of the essays are well-known to Dickensians, much of Slater's collection will be unfamiliar, especially the early reviews and journalistic pieces for *The Examiner,* which have never before been collected. Slater has refined his editorial technique with this second volume, seeming to answer the critics of his edition of *Sketches by Boz* who faulted it for failing to explain the selection and treatment of texts. The text of each essay or review in *Amusements of the People* is the text as it originally appeared in the particular newspaper or magazine (the only exception is taken from a galley-proof). Each selection includes a headnote explaining the context for the piece, much more fully than was usual in the first volume, followed by briefly annotated "Literary allusions," another departure from the first volume. Other brief annotations are to be found in the index. This method allows the reader to grasp the background and then read through the text with a minimum of interruption. Slater's page-length headnotes are concise and informative and help to explain articles that have sometimes been puzzling. My only complaint is that there is simply not more of *The Amusements of the People.* No doubt the exigencies of modern academic publishing have forced Slater to trim. Understandably, he does not include pieces with multiple authors (found in Stone's *Uncollected Writings*), but he also omits multiple articles on the same or similar themes and articles that he feels lack "intrinsic inter-est," which of course is always open to debate. None of this, however, explains why the preface to the series promises that it will include "all the journalism that Dickens published in collected form during his lifetime," including *Reprinted Pieces,* when we find that Slater has omitted a "sequence of detective reminiscences . . . later collected in *RP*" (282). Aside from these quibbles (the last, though, is a contradiction of some importance), *The Amuse-ments of the People* is a judicious, meticulously-edited collection, a must purchase for any Dickensian.

The most modest edition of Dickens this year is *Dickens in France,* a selection of Dickens's writing on France and the French, evidently intended for the general reader. Most of the material comes from *Pictures from Italy, The Uncommercial Traveller,* and *Reprinted Pieces,* though a few letters are also included. This slim book is a genuine delight to hold and read, with its attractive print and wide margins, though scholarly helps are altogether lack-ing. Because the book has yet to find a United States publisher, readers in this country must order directly from In Print Publishing, Inc., 9 Beaufort Terrace, Brighton BN2 2SU, UK (£9.95 and £3 airmail postage, "sterling cheques only please").

George Newlin's *Every Thing in Dickens,* the fourth volume in *Windows into® Dickens,* is a concordance of topics culled from the totality of Dickens's writings—his fiction, plays, journalism, speeches, and collaborations, essen-tially everything except his letters. Taken together, the four volumes compile and categorize a massive amount of material: Newlin estimates that of the approximately eight million words that Dickens wrote, about 860,000 are recorded in *Every Thing* and another 1,172,000 in *Every One* (the general title of the first three volumes). With the publication of *Every Thing in Dick-ens,* readers now have access to a compendium of Dickens' thoughts on the body and mind, authorship, humanity, London, nature, travel, and "his own self, as revealed in his writings." In one of the more remarkable sections, "Last Lines of Death," Newlin records all of the death scenes in Dickens. Another section discusses Dickens's views on smells. But, so, too, can the reader find information on ablutions, addiction, apathy, artists and their work, bachelors, bibles, cannibalism, capitalism, China, cruelty, emotions, fraud, gambling, grief, homosexuality, laughter, manners, melancholy, oratory, pre-tension, private transportation, recreation, sanitation, slavery, snobbery, talk, tobacco, traffic, war, water, and much, much more. If most of the passages are one or two paragraphs, Newlin wisely also includes extended excerpts "of particularly marvelous," though not necessarily famous, scenes.

With this much information, any indexing system may well prove inadequate. Despite its array of lists, indexes, and tables, nothing works very comfortably. Probably the best bet is for readers to browse the section entitled, "Captions, and Their Locations in the Topicon," and hope that they find something to match their subject, though this can be slow and frustrating. Nor is the "Indexes of Words and Phrases" at the back much help. I spent considerable time looking in both places for references to such subjects as respectability, propriety, and self-improvement—and found nothing. This qualification aside, *Every Thing* in Dickens is a major achievement, an evident labor of love for Newlin, who styles himself a "devout amateur," but an "amateur" who has spent hundreds of hours typing in every word, punctuation mark, and space. Newlin's hope that *Every Thing in Dickens* will one day come out on CD-ROM—thus allowing Dickensians more complete access to the information—is a hope to be shared by all.

Studies of More than One Work

As Valerie Gager points out in her introduction to her excellent new book, *Shakespeare and Dickens,* critics have either underestimated Shakespeare's influence on Dickens or they have misjudged it, basing their evaluations solely on the written text of his plays or, in one case, on an anonymous article wrongly attributed to him. By her count, Gager has found "nearly one thousand references to Shakespeare's sonnets and thirty-three plays, approximately 800 more than any prior study of Dickens has identified" (20). Even allowing for overzealousness, this is a staggering addition to our knowledge of Dickens. Gager's thorough familiarity with Shakespeare and Dickens, evident on nearly every page, enables her to detect subtle Shakespearean allusions and echoes and persuasively counter mistaken judgments. So, she believes, scholars have consistently overrated the importance of *King Lear,* especially to a novel like *Dombey and Son,* though Dickens actually "alludes to *King Lear* far less frequently than to *Hamlet, Macbeth,* or *Othello,* with references to Hamlet outnumbering those to *King Lear* by almost six to one" (12). And as for *Dombey and Son,* allusions to *King Lear* "are nowhere to be found, while the plot parallels are not striking. A much stronger case might be made for parallels with any one of Shakespeare's late romances, particularly *The Winter's Tale,* which Dickens saw performed by Macready and [Helena] Faucit before seeing *King Lear*" (13).

Gager begins her book by establishing Dickens's immersion in Shakespeare from a young age. Dickens became so steeped in Shakespeare, and his power of recall was so strong, that out of nearly one thousand references to Shakespeare, Gager can only find "four apparent mistakes," and one of these, she speculates, may have resulted from a compositor's error, while the other three are simple misattributions rather than misquotations (53). But Dickens' familiarity with Shakespeare stemmed from far more than the written texts of the plays: professional stage performances were equally important—especially if Macready was the star—but so too were paintings, bulesques, and amateur production. One of the most impressive aspects of the book is Gager's knowledge of all, the manifestations of Shakespeare in the early- and mid-nineteenth century. She explains, for instance, how Macready's batiste handkerchief, which he famously flourished as Hamlet, found an afterlife in *Martin Chuzzlewit, David Copperfield,* and *Great Expectations.* Gager even corrects the editors of the Pilgrim letters, whose annotations have earned high marks, by explaining that Dickens's frequent epistolary adjuration to "Reply, Reply, Reply!" comes not simply from *The Merchant of Venice* with its "Reply, reply" (3.2.66), but more probably from James Robinson Planché's *Fortunio and the Seven Gifted Servants* with its comic transformation of the phrase into a triple refrain, a play which Dickens both acted in and directed, and saw twice performed on stage.

Gager devotes the next chapter, perhaps the least satisfying one, to "an analysis of the infinite variety of ways Dickens uses Shakespeare for his own creative purposes" (18). She begins by finding several passages from Shakespeare which she believes "inspired" Dickens's own "aesthetic principles," principles about which Dickens himself said very little. So she feels that Dickens's "emphasis on magic and transformation" (as in passages from *Nicholas Nickleby,* chapter 48, and *David Copperfield,* chapter 51) is "inspired by" Theseus' definition of the poet's role in *A Midsummer's Night's Dream.* So, too, she finds "at the very least an authoritative precedent for his habitual use of animism as a literary device" in *The Tempest, As You Like It, Henry V,* and *A Midsummer's Night's Dream* (51). And, as well, she traces Dickens's rapid shifts between comedy and tragedy, summarized in the famous "streaky bacon" passage in *Oliver Twist* (chapter 17), to Shakespeare. The potential difficulty is obvious: such general "aesthetic principles" might easily be attributed to a number of sources. If Gager never overcomes fully the reductiveness and over-simplification endemic to this sort of project, she generally manages to convince, in large part owing to her deft and informed weaving of quotations from Shakespeare and Dickens.

In the next chapter, Gager explains her preference for the categories of quotation, allusion, and echo. Although she largely puts aside questions of authorial intention, she feels it "sometimes possible to trace how Dickens's association of ideas may have developed" (172). Her particular judgments about "echo," the most subtle of the categories, depend on the context of the reference both within a given work and within Dickens' corpus as a whole. A word or phrase that on its own might be inconsequential, if placed in the context of other, more definite, allusions to a given play, probably itself also refers to that play, whether the reference is intended or not. Moreover, the way Dickens uses a word or phrase elsewhere in his work may reveal something about his use in a particular context. These distinctions are both liberating and restrictive: they permit Gager to find "echoes" of Shakespeare that others have missed and to disallow echoes that don't have the context to support them.

Gager then explores the "typical functions of Dickens's Shakespearean references" furnishing numerous examples of the way in which Dickens uses Shakespeare to establish authority, to persuade, to evoke sensations, to create irony (especially through partial quotations), to provide verbal resources and multiple perspectives, and "to establish a mood or symbolic atmosphere" (19). Occasionally, Gager's rapid allusions can bewilder one not thoroughly versed in Shakespeare; a little more of her *own* context would have helped to situate her more obscure references.This preliminary information culminates in Gager's sustained analysis of allusions in *Dombey and Son* and *David Copperfield*. A need for brevity limits my summary of Gager's argument to the former of the two works, although her approach in *Dombey and Son* is typical of *David Copperfield* as well (which she believes echoes *Hamlet*). While acknowledging the Cleopatra motif in Dickens's ironic presentation of Mrs. Skewton, Gager believes that *Dombey and Son* draws most profoundly on *Macbeth*. She properly observes that Dickens's description of Mrs. Pipchin as "a bitter old lady" who had been "pumped out dry" of the "waters of gladness and milk of human kindness" recalls Lady Macbeth much more than "an obscure fifteenth-century Fresco," as argued by another critic. But Mrs. Pipchin is also associated with triple images of witches and black magic that recall the three Weird Sisters. The *Macbeth* imagery is picked up in Good Mrs. Brown, who as another Weird Sister with her prophecies of succession, "points with her finger in the direction [Calker] was going, and laughed" (216), her pointing finger recalling the invisible dagger which "marshals [Macbeth] the way that [he] was going." This conflation of the dagger scene and heath scene, Gager explains, "foreshadow[s] the fates of Edith and Calker." Like the dagger, "the sight of the accusing finger pointing the way to Edith's adultery and his own death continues to haunt Calker after the fortune-teller has disappeared" (216). Gager believes that Dickens possibly borrowed the specific image, not so much from the written text, as from Macready's production of *Macbeth*, which "made much of moving backwards and pointing, as each witch repeated the gesture in turn" (216). This allusion-hunting serves as prelude to a discussion of James Calker's meeting with Edith Dombey in Dijon, where the manager and his potential mistress act out the downfall of Macbeth and his wife, with sound effects apparently borrowed from Macready's production. Gager goes on to show how Mr. Dombey's near suicide echoes Lady Macbeth's final moments. "By gradually absorbing the play within the novel," Gager concludes, "Dickens retains the ambience of the play while the novel floats free of the original context and reshapes itself" (222).

Shakespeare and Dickens concludes with a "Catalogue of Dickens's references to Shakespeare" arranged, after an initial list of general allusions to Shakespeare, in alphabetical order by title of the Shakespeare play. She includes not only references to Dickens's novels but to his letters, speeches, journalism, and minor or occasional pieces, a major undertaking which Gager handles well. Each play begins with a list of general references (for example, general references to Mrs. Skewton as "Cleopatra"), followed by "Complex references" when appropriate (interwoven references to more than one scene), and then references to individual passages from Shakespeare, although it makes it more difficult to find the allusions to Shakespeare in a particular Dickens novel; one has to scan the entire catalogue. Gager also provides two helpful appendices: "John Forster's authorship of 'The Restoration of Shakespeare's "Lear" to the Stage' " and a Dickens-Shakespeare chronology. From beginning to end, *Shakespeare and Dickens* is both authoritative and erudite, a pleasure to read and an impressive addition to the "Dickens and" books that proliferate on so many library shelves.

Grahame Smith's *Charles Dickens: A Literary Life,* one volume in the "Literary Lives" series published by St. Martin's Press, claims to be neither a traditional biography nor a work of literary criticism, but rather a "description and analysis of those aspects of Dickens's working life which have a direct bearing on his professional career" (129). *A Literary Life* seems to have been written for undergraduates and might best be thought of as an introduction, though nowhere does Smith himself make this claim. He generally writes with economy, clarity, and an admirable level-headedness about publishers and serialization, Dickens's reading, his journalism, the influence of theater and popular entertainment on his novels and so forth. But readers coming to the book with hopes of fresh insight will be disappointed. Smith's Dickens is mostly a familiar one: "a media personality" (110) with an "unquenchable thirst for self-expression and approbation" (96), and, in politics, "a sentimental radical" (154). Smith perhaps stresses Dickens's intellect more than usual, though conventionally acknowledging that he was not a thinker "who articulated a position with the extended abstractions of a political economist or a philosopher" (141). But even here, Smith only argues with critics as antiquated as Walter Bagehot and F. R. Leavis. Indeed, for all of the obvious bows to contemporary theory, there is a musty second-handedness about the whole book. Although Smith early on emphasizes the influence of material reality over the uniquely "creative" genius—at one point, describing *The Pickwick Papers* as a "growth" from the "seed" of existing conditions (28)—he never develops the idea very much and eventually resorts to discussing Dickens in the vaguely Freudian terms of his "deep psychic need" (123) and his "burning desires" (122). And Smith takes the better part of a chapter to argue that Orlick functions as Pip's double in *Great Expectations* (the one novel accorded close examination), and that Magwich represents the return of "a deeply submerged memory" (174), though nowhere does Smith cite the well-known arguments of Julian Moynihan or Peter Brooks. More commonly, Smith quotes secondary sources, and at length, when a simple paraphrase and citation would have sufficed. His awkward style of documentation (an uncomfortable mix of parenthetical citation and the old "op. cit." and "ibid." method) only contributes to the problem. I found myself constantly consulting the endnotes to determine who said what, and usually discovering that what I thought was a primary source was, in fact, a secondary one.[1]

To counter the tendency of recent criticism to stress Dickens's more authoritarian or "policing" qualities, *Dickens Refigured: Bodies, Desires, and Other Histories* seeks to "explore the gaps that Dickens's writing lays bare within the dominant discourses and structures of Victorian culture"(1). This is, then, a distinctly radical Dickens "refigured" to fit a self-consciously theoretical model. So, for John Schad, the editor of the collection and the author of its leading article, the Dickensian church is not a "stable . . . [feature] of the landscape" but profoundly subversive. Dickens supposedly associates his churches with wildernesses or crypts or graveyards or sewers or insane asylums or prisons or bells tolling revolution or even sexuality itself. Schad's analysis, however, consistently draws on Dickens's statements about Catholic churches in *Pictures from Italy,* to make points about the Church of England. Dickens's well-known antipathy to Catholicism is barely mentioned in Schad's haste to generalize. Does his image of a priest's candle as a "truncheon" really say something about *Anglican* churches? Other examples also fail to convince. Do the church bells that are said to "[ring] pleasantly in many an airy steeple over France" in *A Tale of Two Cities,* really "threaten nothing less than full-bloodied insurrection" (8), as Schad believes? Surely, the point is that such bells are oblivious to their fate as "thundering cannon"? And, when Amy Dorrit and Maggy spend a few hours in St. George's Church, does its registrar's "admiring gaze" really suggest "an unhomely motivation" (i.e., a sexual one)? Schad conveniently leaves out of his quotation of the original passage the explicit statement that the registrar's gaze suggests that Amy is exhausted (16), implying some dark sexual motivation not present in the text itself.

The second essay in the volume, by Timothy Clark, uses the theories of Maurice Blanchot to attack "The current tendency in criticism" to see "Dickens as a defender of a romantic psychology . . . advocating an ideal of psychic wholeness" because of the supposed "flatness" of his characters (27). For Clark, much of Dickens's writing conveys "a world without interiority" or, as Clark says about Blanchot's idea of the image: "a realm of irreducible materiality whose relation to consciousness is one of what Blanchot terms 'fascination' or 'passion for an image' " (26). Thus, Clark writes, "Blanchot's work enables us to trace in the darker aspects of Dickens a latent if pervasive anti-humanist aesthetic at odds with that writer's expressed romanticism" (22). The most successful part of Clark's essay is perhaps its last part, a detailed discussion of Dickens's late essay, "Night Walks," which Clark calls "Dickens's most concentrated and sustained expression of the nightmare of a world without interiority" (34).

The next writer, Nicholas Royle, puts *Our Mutual Friend* through the Derridean grinder with great facility. What emerges, predictably, is "a world without referentiality" (to adapt Clark's conceit), a world that "articulates and disarticulates, figures and disfigures" itself. What matters is the unstable play of signifiers on the page, "the ceaseless instability, the energies or allergies of disenfranchisement, dislocation, metamorphosis" affecting phrases like "Our Mutual Friend," which Royle impressively deconstructs, though it's not always clear to what purpose.

The dangers of the careless handling of a text are evident in Richard Dellamora's examination of the "Pure" Oliver Twist. Dellamora believes that Dickens parodies "male mentorship" in the famous illustrated scene of "Oliver asking for More"(Cruikshank's illustration is included) and reads the boy's wooden spoon as a phallus pointing from Oliver's crotch to the mouth and eyes of Mr. Bumble. Here the reader draws up short, for the "fat, healthy man" who glowers down on Oliver is *not* Mr. Bumble but the workhouse master. Nor is the thin, round-mouthed women in the rear of the picture, Mrs. Mann, as Dellamora asserts, but a nameless woman who ladles the gruel (59). The difference is important because there's nothing to indicate that the workhouse master functions as Oliver's *mentor* in any way, as Dellamora says of Mr. Bumble. Nor could Dickens conceivably be connotating "gender inversion" in the scene, when "Mrs. Mann" (get it?) is simply not present. Following the lead of William Cohen, Dellamora argues elsewhere that "the insertion of foreign objects into the boys' mouths during the scene [in which Charley Bates and the Artful Dodger size up Oliver] suggests the act of fellatio" (72). The only evidence for this wild assertion is the fact that the Artful Dodger "resumed his pipe" and both Charley and the Dodger "smoked." The orality of the scene is in no way lingered over or emphasized by the narrator. With such a low evidentiary threshold, one wonders why

Dellamora didn't make something of "Mr. Dawkins [giving] his hat a ferocious cock" (72). The mistakes and forced interpretations are unfortunate
because Dellamora has much to say about the consumption of resources and
the consumption of sex, the threat of racial contamination, and the "instability" of Oliver's innocence.

Helena Michie's contribution to *Dickens Refigured* is of greater interest.
Beginning with a brief discussion of Scott Turow's *The Burden of Proof* and
its questioning of the "peculiar term" brother-in-law, Michie explores the
"complicated network of familial or quasi-familial relations" in *Nicholas
Nickleby* to show "how 'family' is a social construct infinitely boundup in
the cultural process of naming and . . . how powerful cultural appeals to 'nature' can be in obfuscating the contructedness of social arrangements" (82).
For Michie, family relations in the novel are fundamentally unstable. "Natural" parenting involves legal authority and legal authority involves fiction.
Uncles become lovers, sisters become mothers, and aunts and mothers become sexual rivals. And the true uncles, the Cheeryble brother, are not uncles
at all. "[N]atural feeling," Michie explains, "is separate from and, indeed,
usually opposed to biology" (86). Conversely, "Even the most sacred familial
relations are not free of the erotic and the violent" (88). And even the
"sincerity" of the brother-sister relation of Kate and Nicholas cannot resist
its melodramatic expression. Central to Michie's argument is her belief that
family is constructed in *Nicholas Nickleby* in favor of the man. In a text filled
with fear of the mother, "the sister comes to stand for the mother . . . in a
way which highlights the fantasy of the brother, not the fantasy of the mother"
(90–91). So, too, does Michie detect "the narrator's need to arrange women
according to generation and to a literal biological potential for reproduction,"
and a "foundational gender asymmetry" that sets Nicholas's emotions over
his sister's (92, 97).

If Michie sees the Dickensian family as fundamentally unstable, Patricia
Ingham sees if "as manipulative and destructive" (114). Ingham's piece
begins sanely enough, with a discussion of the many negatives in the text.
Things become a bit rockier when she tries to make Arthur Clennam into a
picaresque hero (primarily, it seems, because he moves from group to group
in a liner manner), but a picaresque hero who "subverts all progress by ruling
it out in advance" (105). Such a self-cancelling argument invites speculation:
if Clennam is a picaresque hero, but not a picaresque hero in the traditional
sense, perhaps he's not a picaresque hero at all. Ingham juxtaposes the supposedly "linear" nature of Clennam's picaresque progress to an alternative
"centrifugal" plot structure that asserts the value of the family over the
individual. Both plot structures—the linear and centrifugal—have their presiding characters and their dark doubles. For the linear plot, Arthur Clennam
is negated by "Nobody," the alternative self whom Pet Meagles could not

possibly love. For the centrifugal plot, Little Dorrit is negated by "Amy Dorrit," the "Godmother of the Dorrit Mafia" who "shows herself as the perfect liar—often by not speaking" (108). It is this Amy who "displays sexual jealousy towards" her father and harbors "a jealous sense of betrayal" when he announces his engagement to Mrs. General (109–10). This is reading against the text with a vengeance. Little Dorrit's desire to absolve her father of the responsibility of "giv[ing] her up lightly now in his prosperity" becomes, by Ingham's reckoning, "a picture too horrible to contemplate of herself supplanted, betrayed, in effect divorced" (110). And the Roman Charity image (of a daughter suckling her imprisoned father), a metaphor which Dickens uses to describe Amy's loving devotion to her father, becomes an incestuous "confusion" that destabilizes the family and contributes to the downfall of Fanny and Tip. To blame Amy for the decline of the Dorrits seems odd indeed. And Ingham unfairly literalizes the metaphoric when she claims that "The eroticism of such an action is evident from the pictorial version of the scene," as if "the pictorial version" (which she includes) were itself part of the novel (111).

Linda M. Shires examines the constructed nature of autobiographical identity at mid-century, primarily in Dickens and *David Copperfield,* but also in Tennyson's *In Memoriam* and Charlotte Brontë's prefaces and notices about herself and her sisters. All three writers, Shires argues, try to gain mastery over a secret "phase of life which is, from a sober, adult perspective, the least reputable, most disturbing and most narcissistic: childhood and adolescent subjectivism" (123). Such originary secrets need to be read not merely as personal revelations but against a backdrop of cultural history, or what Shires refers to as "The problem of the authorial self at mid-century—its desire to remain private and substantial yet its necessary commodification as spectacle" (122). In the case of *David Copperfield,* this attempt "to reconstitute a fragmented bourgeois subjectivity" (128) involves a narrative excising or displacement of passions—whether associated with the corporeal, the economic, or the homoerotic—that appear "to degrade the subject" (131). For Charlotte Brontë, it involves the banishment of her "incestuous" feelings for Branwell and the infantalization of Emily. For Alfred Lord Tennyson, it involves the masking of his "love for the male" (128). The attributing of complex motives and desires to long-dead writers is always a very problematic business. It seems remarkable hubris to suggest, 150 years after the fact, that Charlotte's impressions of her family were clearly duplicitous—"constructed" to ease her own conscience and please mid-Victorian readers—and yet to claim confidently that we today know the Brontës "as they were" (124).

John Lucas's contribution to *Dickens Refigured* is something of an anomaly. Like the other writers in the book, Lucas describes a more radical Dickens, one who in this case is at odds with both Whig and Tory views of history,

yet he does so without recourse to self-conscious theorizing. There's no talk
here of construction, subversion, or instability and no reference to any contemporary theorist. Instead, Lucas prefers to go back to primary sources—Macaulay's *History of England,* or William Howitt's *The Aristocracy of
England*—to establish the social context for Dickens's attack on a class society in *Bleak House.* The Dickens that emerges is an anti-monarchical sympa-
thizer of Wat Tyler, an "essentially *Republican*" writer who, in *Bleak House,*
writes "the historiography of the present" (149).

Lucas's essay, with its burden of historical fact, would probably be anath-
ema to Diane Elam who condemns "historicist 'memorialisation' " as naive.
Her interest lies with "the novel's debt to *everyday* time" (157). A novel
like *Little Dorrit,* she argues, "does not offer us a window on the past, . . . but
competing theories of time, which can help us to understand what makes a
recovery of historical time problematic" (160). Her "competing theories"
comprise clock time ("rooted in abstract rationality"), organic time ("natural
rhythm"), and psychic time ("individual perception") (168). But more important that the anatomization of time per se is the "alienation" that results
from trying to make sense of these conflicting temporalities. "Alienation,"
she explains, "is the effect of the desire to find the point from which these
accounts may be added up" (169) and "memory remains split between a past
that has never been present and a future for which the meaning of the past
has yet to be" (174).

Dickens Refigured induces a certain numbness in the reader. With the
exception of Lucas and Elam, the same critical moves are trotted out, conducted on their weary paces, and then put to rest, to be replaced by more of
the same thing. Instead of complexity, we get bland uniformity in the name
of complexity. Articles that once might have been on the cutting edge of
critical discourse, now seem predictable and stale. John Schad sees the Dickensian church as not "stable" but subversive; Timothy Clark condemns the
idea of "psychic wholeness" in Dickens; Nicholas Royle praises "the ceaseless instability" of the Dickens text; Helena Mitchie believes family relations
are "unstable"; Patrica Ingham images a dark, "sexually jealous" Amy
Dorrit. The late-twentieth century romanticization of the unstable and disorderly—Dickens "constructed" in the image of ourselves—proceeds apace. It
should come as no surprise, then, that the next essay in the collection, Steven
Connor's "Babel unbuilding," finds that "Dickens's novels seem to act out
a more radical and unsettled aesthetic than his more formal statements announce" (180) and that the "fascination" of *Martin Chuzzlewit* "is the curious, collapsing integrity it derives from its ruination of the architectural"
(199). As with many of the other contributions to *Dickens Refigured,* Connor's piece is a mixture of perceptive insight and loose or sometimes forced
argument. He connects "an extensive and proliferated pattern of thematic

and metaphoric exchanges of height and lowness and vice versa'' in *Martin Chuzzlewit* to the ''architectural myth of human overreach'' (181–82). The adjective ''architectural'' is inserted mainly because the ''myth'' recalls the fall of the tower of Babel. He then connects ''This Babelian exchange of high and low'' to the elevated view from Todgers's, explaining that ''The perspective afforded by this view expresses . . . that desire for panoptic percipience and command . . . a desire that lead to a feverish activity of charting, mapping and epistemologically regulating the chaotic and, of course, architecturally transforming city during the 1840s''(182). One senses the strain in such a sentence, as Connor moves rapidly, and not always logically, from high view, to panopticon, to mapping, to regulating, to, finally, building and architecture. The same kind of straining can be detected in his interpretation of the phrase ''the grace of his design'' (''design'' here would surely seem to mean ''intention'') as suggesting an ''architectural motivation'' (182). Connor finds the ''antidote'' to the ''distances, abstract, and formalized'' architectural perspective to be the novel's ''crammed and mobile plentitude of impingements'' of social space (189). In a similar division of good versus bad, Connor believes that ''Where architectural design establishes form through the geometrical division of space . . . [Tom Pinch's music] has an imaginary power to establish form through the permeation of space'' (193)—except by Connor's reading it is not just ''music'' but ''acoustic architecture'' (193).

Dickens Refigured concludes with essays by David Trotter and J. Hillis Miller. Trotter sees virtue in Dickens's ''lazy gentlemen,'' those casual, and often anonymous, characters who saunter aimlessly along the margins of Dickens's stories. In contrast to the *flâneur,* these ''idle gentlemen'' observe vacantly, without purpose or meaning, their idleness constituting ''an implicit reproach to narratives which endorse strenuous self-making'' (204). For Trotter, the observer on Todger's roof is an idle man, one whose prospect is not panopticon-like, but rather ''removed from action of any kind, or representativeness of any kind'' (205) (Trotter rather weakly describes this unnamed character as a ''not notably purposeful observer''—205.) In contrast to the ''lazy gentlemen,'' Dickens increasingly populated his later novels with ''strenuously purposeful'' figures like Inspector Bucket or Pancks who ''do not merely scan a scene . . . but devour it instantly, extract its essence and then move on'' (211).

J. Hillis Miller sees jealousy in *Our Mutual Friend* as ''one way, though by no means the only way, to break through to a confrontation with an impersonal power alien to the ordinary world of everyday life'' (229). The ''underlying reality'' of this mysterious ''otherness'' or ''energy'' (''It cannot be named directly''—231)—which is both creative and destructive—may provide an alternative to the disconnection, bad faith, and rote actions of "everyday life." Some characters in *Our Mutual Friend* are permitted a descent into this "other" world and return transformed. Others descend and return without change. Still others descend without return. But the descent itself, the "extreme event that breaks up petrified class institutions," remains for Dickens the "only chance for even a local change in the bad condition of society," though "No single descent and return will work as a symbolic transformation of the whole society" (233). Sensibly, Miller resists reading "too happy a providential design [in]to that anarchic underlying energy," believing it occasioned by Dickens's own confrontation with the "other" (234).

If the essayists in *Dickens Refigured* sometimes strain to say too much, Rita Lubitz says far too little in her book on *Marital Power in Dickens' Fiction*. She claims to focus on "the role power played" in the many marriages in Dickens, though Lubitz makes no use of Foucault, of contemporary feminist theory, or of much else for that matter, but is content to summarize plots at length, survey critical reading about individual novels and catalogue types of marriages. There are "dominant husbands and submissive wives" or "dominant wives and submissive husbands" or "more dominant wives and submissive husbands" or "mercenary marriages" or "successful marriages" or "concluding marriages." But little else. Lubitz never gets beyond reductive labelling, remaining content to make a few obvious comments and to quote the critical ideas of others. A characteristic observation is that "The loveless matrimonial union of Fanny Dorrit and Edmund Sparkler in *Little Dorrit* is another illustration of a mercenary marriage entered into for all the wrong reasons" (94). A phrase like "another illustration" is not much to base a book on. Whatever insight *Marital Power* possesses comes almost exclusively from the other critics whom Lubitz cites, though she rarely chooses to engage or argue with her sources.

Donald E. Hall accords *Martin Chuzzlewit, Little Dorrit,* and *Great Expectations* extended treatment in *Fixing Patriarchy,* his study of feminism and mid-Victorian male novelists. Hall detects an historical shift from the secure "linear hierarchy" of the eighteenth century, when rules were fixed and gender duties accepted, to the "fluidly horizontal construct" of the mid-nineteenth century, when gender was shaped by binary opposition and exclusion, and male dominance came actively under threat. *Martin Chuzzlewit* assumes a border position between the "linear hierarchy" and "horizontal construct": it contains remnants of the older order—the androgynous Tom Pinch—as well as defiantly transgressive women of the later period—Sairy Gamp and Mrs. Prig. The troubling, aggressive women reappear in *Little Dorrit,* though now with an emphasis on their impolite staring. The novel is full of women who resist conduct manual advice to look at others in a demure and deferential fashion. Mr. F's Aunt, Miss Wade, and Mrs. Clennam are all brazen starers, threatening women whose aggression is contained by the plot's adjuration to "Duty." But if *Little Dorrit* represents an evolution for Dickens—it "reveals many of the motivations behind anti-patriarchal activity" (184)—it finally proposes "a revivified patriarchy" in the marriage of Amy and Arthur that is "only vaguely modified by love and imbued with concern for dependents" (129). Although Hall is careful not to over-simplify the progressive nature of Dickens's treatment of aggressive women, he believes that "there was a new space in Dickens's own discursive matrix that allowed for changes in gender constructions in response to individual needs" (184). So one finds in *Great Expectations* "rich, complex characterizations of transgressive women" and close attention "to changing social circumstances allowing gender roles to metamorphose," though a brutal anti-feminism is also present. Hall writes with lucidity and an impressive directness of the interplay of resistance and accommodation that accompanied the feminist challenge to mid-Victorian patriarchy (185).

Michal Peled Ginsburg begins her chapter on *Bleak House* and *Our Mutual Friend* by using the ideas of Franco Moretti to distinguish between two plot models: what Ginsburg calls restoration and transformation or, more simply, "hoarding" and "recycling." *Bleak House* she believes to have essentially a restorative plot, marked by a conservative return to beginnings, as major characters like Esther Summerson or John Jarndyce free themselves from the events of the narrative to return to a "plotless, simple, and just life" (143). Conversely, *Our Mutual Friend* has a transformative plot, marked by a radical recycling and self-creation, as a character like John Harmon cares less about regaining his rights than transforming his wealth. In the second part of her chapter, Ginsburg complicates what at first might seem reductive, for her claim "is that texts never purely adhere to one formal model," but as in the case of *Our Mutual Friend,* generate "specific choices as a response to the entire field of possibilities defined by the two opposed models" (148). So if Eugene Wrayburn's "near death obeys the logic of conversion" (152), John Harmon's near death is a disguise instead of a conversion. Ginsburg concludes her otherwise acute chapter by somewhat vaguely asserting that "what gets lost by seeing form as historically determined is the relative autonomy of form" (156), a conclusion that does not necessarily seem warranted by the discussion that precedes it (though this judgment might be more relevant in the context of the book's argument as a whole).

Some of the best essays revisit common ideas, infusing them with new energy and complexity. Such is the case with Tim Cribb's "Travelling through Time: Transformation of Narrative from Early to Late Dickens," to my mind the most perceptive and stimulating essay on Dickens in 1996. Cribb is hardly the first scholar to find connections between changes in style and changes in society, but he's one of the most insightful. His method is deceptively simple: he correlates "formal invention in writing with social change" by focusing intensely on three fictional journeys that are said to represent Dickens' early, middle, and late manner: Tom Pinch's journey to London in *Martin Chuzzlewit,* the famous rail journey in chapter seven of *Dombey and Son,* and the much less well known travel descriptions in "Barbox Brothers," one of Dickens's contributions to the extra Christmas number of *All the Year Round* in 1866. For Cribb, the languorously-paced coach ride of the early years of the nineteenth century is reflected in the open, transparent description of travel in *Martin Chuzzlewit,* with each detail concretely realized and the journey's goal energetically pursued. The advent of the steam railway leads to an abstraction of space and a greater detachment of viewpoint, influencing Dickens's depiction of rail travel in *Dombey and Son* and his more detached moral analysis. In the "Barbox Brothers," Dickens's language is radically transformed for a third time. Now the narrative is "controlled by the timetable," and human relations exist within an routinized system "in which time and events as particularities . . . are abolished" (84). In this final stylistic incarnation, Dickens's text "initiates one of the first strategic moves of modernism: it abdicates its mimetic and expressive powers, in a sense admits defeat" (86). Isolating three scenes permits Cribb to elucidate their stylistic subtleties with great precision, though arguably at the expense of the perspective that comes with a fuller engagement with the entire range of Dickens's work. Yet oversimplifications are kept in check by Cribb's sound judgment and his nuanced reading of grammar set in very specific social contexts.

Victorian Identities (ed. Ruth Robbins and Julian Wolfreys), a collection of essays influenced by contemporary theoretical criticism, contains two articles on Dickens. In the first, "Dickensian Architextures or, the City and the Ineffable," Julian Wolfreys deconstructs Dickens's London and shows (any guesses?) that "In writing London, Dickens clearly opens up the fixed, essential and monumental to a questioning and destabilization, invoking techniques which require the use of disparate multiplicity" (203). Wolfreys believes that Dickens's "fragmentary" evocation of London serves "as a non-hierarchical counter-balance to the bureaucratic, ideological architectures" (205). Although he provides a relatively nuanced reading of Dickens's London, his argument hinges on its own dualism—good anarchic London versus bad authoritarian London (Wolfrey's sympathies are clear)—and re-establishes its own hierarchy.

Geoffrey Hemstedt's "Inventing Social Identity: *Sketches by Boz,*" the second article in *Victorian Identities,* also discusses Dickens's London, but less reductively. For Hemstedt, the London of *Sketches by Boz* "is a protean city, offering abrupt juxtapositions and inventories of things for which there seem to be no serviceable taxonomy" (216). But what may sound predictable (would anyone argue these days that Dickens created a *monolithic* London?), is in Hemstedt's hands merely the starting point for a series of fascinating observations on self-creation and improvised social being. "The dynamic of the *Sketches,*" Hemstedt writes, "lies in Boz's sense of different potential meanings of the elements he observes. Commodities litter the text, and fascinate the writer partly because they seem to challenge his ability to discover order where there seems to be only disorder" (222). Hemstedt's own "sense of the different potential meanings" (too various to summarize here), and his ability to relate these meanings to the rest of Dickens's work, make this essay consistently illuminating. For all of this praise, I have one small criticism of *Victorian Identities* as a whole: its annoyingly self-congratulatory tone. Not only do the editors carry the obligatory introduction, where they briefly summarize the articles and lavish general praise on the group of writers as a whole, but another introduction by James R. Kincaid and an afterword by William Baker, both of which are unstinting in their general commendation of the collection. Kincaid's introduction is particularly egregious. "These essays," he writes, "seem to me so sophisticated, so sly that they deserve to be called wonderfully, superbly stupid. No one is writing to sell out to competence; to grind out smugly another good reading, to do a 'fine job' " (xii). I find it hard to imagine a more smug, and embarrassing, condemnation of the "smugness" of others.

Jan B. Gordon's "Dickens and the Political Economy of the Eye" is the lead essay in this year's *Dickens Studies Annual,* and one of the most formidable pieces of criticism on Dickens published in 1996. In this densely deconstructionist piece, Gordon figures "seeing" as a "repressed revisionary activity" that cancels "some first *impression*"(2). For Gordon, looking through such first impressions leads to a "constant devaluing and revaluing" that constitutes an "*economy:* one vision compensat[ing] for the loss of another" (2). Essentially, Gordon is interested in loosening up boundaries. Instead of reading characters or situations separately, he sees them as mutually involved in an "economy of exchange" (16), a complicated interplay of signs and signifiers (he even provides a chart to clarify what he believes are the parasitical relations in *Great Expectations*). As Gordon sees it, for instance, the voyeur is not simply outside looking in, but is inevitably co-opted by the gazing process, "enmeshed within some larger economy of the eye": "any mastery is compromised by its absorption within a ritual which confines the subject of the gaze" (14). Similarly, in the midst of an extended discussion of the porosity of barriers that "create a mediated, negotiable gaze," Gordon conjectures that even prisons might "possibly be a fiction," a rather troubling reductionism, especially in light of Gordon's mistaken assertion that the Marshalea functions "in fact . . . as an 'out-prisoner' prison" (15). Such prison walls "are really but simulated walls" and these simulated walls are like writing itself. But for Gordon it's not just prisons, but social position as well, which is "revealed as largely a rhetorical or simulational procedure" (17). There's no denying Gordon's intelligence, and the stimulating nature of his argument, though I suspect that readers hostile to deconstructionism will find much to irritate them.

John M. L. Drew would have been well-served had he cut by half his two-part piece on Dickens's travelling essays and *The Uncommercial Traveller.* After a promising introduction that argues for the centrality of travel narratives to Dickens's work, Drew has too many quotations and too much dead space. For example, in the first part of his essay, we learn that Dickens travels to specific locations to make his abstract political points more specific or that "References to topical events, newspaper reports, the weather and so forth, also helped to locate his movements in the recent past" (91). Both points are worth making, but not at the length Drew devotes to them, especially since he fails to do much with them. The essay is much better in its second half, in part because Drew begins to use theory to give himself something to say. If Benjamin's idea of the *flâneur* is becoming increasingly shopworn in discussions of Victorian walking, it is still a useful concept and one well-employed by Drew. He also draws revealing correlations between Dickens's "reading" of London and the travel theories of Michel Buton and makes insightful use of Frederic Schwarbach's study of "Terra Incognita." Drew is especially good in pointing out Dickens's use in *The Uncommercial Traveller* of the language of the foreign mission, the very institution that he deplores elsewhere.

Elana Gomel provides a fascinating, if rather daunting, reading of bodily synecdoche in *Dombey and Son, A Tale of Two Cities,* and *Our Mutual Friend.* The body in parts, Gomel believes, represents a coming together of the "discourses" of sexuality, violence, and money, though "the body in parts is also the point where these discourses begin to break down; where the body, burdened with an excessive weight of cultural inscriptions . . . appears to resist this unification" (49). The body in parts, which contemporary theorists associate mainly with women, is in Dickens a characteristic of men as well. Gomel thus argue that when Bradley Headstone's desires for Lizzie Hexam "explode" his coherent identity, reducing him to "a haggard head suspended in the air," "The feminine implications of synecdoche itself add a touch of gender ambiguity to such descriptions" (52). "The male body," Gomel believes, "is 'cancelled' by the force of excessive desire, and what is left—the head—hints at the ultimate feminization of castration" (52–53). For Gomel, such de-stabilization subverts rigidly defined gender roles, and is positive because it is subversive, for "the prevalence of bodily synecdoche in Dickens's descriptions of women may be understood not as a denial of female sexuality but as its covert recognition" (57). This welcome subversion extends to the politics of *A Tale of Two Cities,* in which "Dickens's revolutionary body of parts is not only monstrous and destructive but also vital, and in a sense, immortal" (60). In *Our Mutual Friend,* the synecdoche becomes involved with the economics of capitalism, though again the splitting into parts is connected to a proliferation, which here results from industrial expansion and not sex.

Gomel's theoretically-charged piece, with its large interpretative leaps and scant attention to stylistic detail, would probably annoy Robert Alter, who insists that contemporary literary studies, with their emphasis on politics and ideology, "have lost the essential sense that style has its unique enchantments, and that those enchantments can often be a privileged vehicle of insight" (130). Alter's sensitive readings of passages from *Dombey and Son* and *Our Mutual Friend* make a strong case for style, although "sensitivity" to a text is surely in the eye of the beholder, as more politically-minded critics like Gomel would no doubt argue. K. J. Fielding also urges a return to the text, if text includes not just the novels themselves but the whole Dickens corpus: his journalism, letters, and occasional writing. Too often, he believes, critics have failed to do their homework, speculating airily, and inaccurately, about Dickens's ideas, without first knowing what he actually wrote about those ideas. "[T]here has to be a starting point in what are sometimes dismissed as simple facts" (201), Fielding says simply. His case in point is recent writing about Dickens and science. Fielding's own "simple facts" show that Dickens was not a Darwinian as some contemporary critics have assumed, but rather a Larmarkian. That is, Robert Chambers' anonymous *Vestiges of the Natural History of Creation* (1844), which described "the so-called Lamarckian theory of evolution," had greater influence on Dickens than Darwin's *Origin of Species* (1859), which he never directly mentioned. And to the common argument that *Bleak House* somehow embodies thermodynamics and new discoveries in electricity, Fielding argues that the word "science" (in the modern sense) never occurs in the novel, nor is there any mention of electricity, fields of force, or magnetism, despite Dickens's clear willingness to allude to science when he deemed it appropriate. Casual associations of the heat death of the sun and entropy with Dickens's work also comes under fire by Fielding. Fielding's cautions are salutary for the most part, though the "facts" are not quite as clear as he sometimes implies. Dickens *did,* after all, include three articles on Darwinism in *All the Year Round* in 1861 (Fielding admits as much), at least one of which was pro-Darwin. And perhaps he underestimates the degree to which influence can operate unconsciously, beyond the purview of the individual, and thus not be available for conscious reflection.

Like Alter and Fielding, Julian Markels too is an older scholar grown disenchanted with current critical fads, though his criticisms come from an avowedly Marxist perspective. Arguing for a "reviving in literary criticism," Markels believes that an engagement of contemporary Marxist theory with the 'holistic focus" of the New Criticism of the 1950s would resist the "reifications" of contemporary theories that "deny us each and all the agency that would enable us to think globally and act locally" (198) and would return literature to the nonprofessionals. In particular, Markels praises Stephen Resnick's and Richard Wolff's *Knowledge and Class* (1987), with its ideas of conceptual "points of entry" and relativism, as a theoretical model for the type of criticism he favors, although his brief description of their ideas is too vague to be very persuasive. Seizing on Resnick and Wolff's terminology, Markels argues that only one of Dickens's later novels uses class as "its entry point"—*Little Dorrit.* Despite the evident class conflict in *Hard Times,* Markels believes that it "cops out" in its depiction of the workers and of Stephen Blackpool's emphasis on "muddle," whereas he finds *Little Dorrit's* representation of class to be "coextensive with the entire novel as a patterned and completed fabric" (209). For Markel, this "fabric" weaves together the class similarities of Mr. Merdle and William Dorrit and the "idealization of work, of pristine and productive labor" in the linked figures of Daniel Doyce and Amy Dorrit. Markels's description of the current academic environment is heart-felt and honestly personal, if sometimes a bit overstated and "reifying," a word he uses to bludgeon his opponents. His discussion of *Hard Times* and *Little Dorrit* is often interesting, especially his analysis of the novels' "witness to the incorruptible integrity of labor in the face of capitalist appropriation" (211), though it's hard to see how it represents some new and "reviving" trend in Marxist literary theory.

Helen Small shows how Dickens's public readings incorporated many of the class tensions surrounding the idea of the "common reader." "[U]nder Dickens's active management," Small writes, "the idea of the reading public became the means to a liberal celebration of reading as the forum in which all classes could come together, united in the enjoyment of a common sensibility" (269). Dickens's readings afforded the public a chance to see itself as a discriminating collectivity, as a single, essentially classless, entity under the spell of a master mesmerist. But as Small also points out, this constitution of an ideally unified reading public was wrought with conflict. For the poorest classes, the shilling-priced tickets were an unaffordable luxury. For those who could attend, the line between working and middle classes was never entirely removed: box seating, for example, seems to have remained privileged. And Dickens's own letters reveal how frequently the crowds verged on violent disintegration. All in all, Small offers an exemplary reading of a cultural idea in its original context yet also informed by an awareness of both current reading theory and knowledge of the latest historical interpretations of such complicated issues as class.

In "The Absent Jew in Dickens: Narrators in *Oliver Twist, Our Mutual Friend,* and *A Christmas Carol,*" Jonathan H. Grossman views Dickens's Jewish characters as something more than anti-Semitic stereotypes. "Dickens's constructions of Jews should be understood as meaningful and complex

Jewish silences'' and not ''a failure of representation,'' he argues (52). So Grossman believes Fagin is essentially a cipher in *Oliver Twist*, a vacancy in the midst of ''an entire structure of anti-Semitism'' (52) revealed in the epithet, ''the Jew.'' But the epithet, at least for much of the latter half of *Oliver Twist* and certainly in its 1867 revision, belongs essentially to the middle-class characters who use the epithet, ''the Jew,'' to name Fagin, and not to the narrator or to Dickens (at least in the latter half of the novel and especially in the 1867 revision), and not to the members of the underworld who usually refer to Fagin by his name. Thus, Grossman believes, Dickens ''critically encompasses, rather than identifies with, these middle-class characters'' (42). Because Dickens's Jews are invariably caught up in a world of public display, they are forced to act ''in response to a representation'' of Jews generally, as in the case of Riah in *Our Mutual Friend* who must ''begin performing for what he sees as Christian-prejudiced eyes''(47). Grossman concludes his fine analysis of the ''absent Jew'' with a brief discussion of Scrooge, whom he sees as probably Jewish though ''only under erasure.''

Reviewing over one hundred books and articles in a relatively short span of time almost inevitably forces the reviewer to confront his own limitations. Sooner or later, he's bound to come across something that he simply doesn't understand—at least not with the thoroughness necessary to write an adequate review. I met my Waterloo with Garrett Stewart's two chapters on Dickens in *Dear Reader,* his study of the ''conscripted audience in nineteenth-century British fiction.'' Stewart has established a reputation as a major critic. Unfortunately, his preference for pretentious language, elaborate metaphors, constant interruptions, wordiness, and contorted syntax gives new meaning to the word ''opaque.'' When he talks of ''coasting at times on an undulatory depth of lexical mutations and phonotextual viscosity that may nevertheless sustain (8) a mimed psychodynamic of reciprocal self-construction between storytelling 'voice' and figured reader''—and this is only a very small section of a very, very long sentence—one doesn't know whether to grab the dictionary or the trash can. In general terms, Stewart considers the poor sales of *Master Humphrey's Clock* and *The Old Curiosity Shop* ''in relation to the elaborately implicated reading of Dickens's narrative production—and its continuous repackaging—across both that piecemeal novel and its weekly frame'' (174) and seems particularly interested in the way that the works give birth to a new Victorian reader, one 'inducted . . . through the psychodynamic relays of characterization and narration'' (211). This is the general argument. The details are even less clear. *Dear Reader* may be the major work that Jay Clayton claims for it on the back cover. If so, for the book's own sake, one wishes the general argument were more intelligible and that Stewart, with his sophistication, hadn't so stymied comprehension.

Laurie Kane Lew argues that both Dickens and Ruskin endeavor to broaden the definition of verisimilitude to include the ''poetic'' and the subjective.

Ruskin emphasizes the poetic "reality" of Edwin Landseer's sentimental painting *The Old Shepherd's Chief Mourner,* its faithfulness to an emotional truth, largely ignoring that quality that made it so popular with mid-Victorian audiences: its correspondence to a readily recognizable world. According to Lew, this tendency of Ruskin to heighten "our sense of the emotion of *beholding* the 'real' recalls "the often hallucinatory atmospheres in Dickens" (63) which join "the poetic and the ordinary functions of language in a deliberated but uneasy synthesis" (64). In particular, Lew sees Dickens's description of the scene following Little Nell's death as a "model" behind Ruskin's reading of the Landseer painting; and she believes that, like Dickens and Cruikshank, Ruskin created word-paintings that "unsettle our sense of a stable referential field" (69). The focus of Lew's perceptive essay is almost entirely on Ruskin, with Dickens being used for purposes of comparison and mainly at second hand (her observations on Dickens deriving from such critics as Taylor Stoehr and J. Hillis Miller).

This year's *Dickens Studies Annual* concludes with two excellent review articles. In her survey of "Fifteen Years of Work on Victorian Detective Fiction," Anne Humphreys points out the "obsessive" attention given to "a handful of canonized texts by three male writers—Charles Dickens, Wilkie Collins, and Arthur Conan Doyle" (259), with Sherlock Holmes accounting for a large chunk of this material. The real crime, Humphreys explains, is the lack of attention paid to the enormous amount of detective fiction by more obscure writers, many of whom are women. Barry V. Qualls locates a few bright spots in 1993's batch of Dickens criticism—most notably, Mary Poovey and Miriam Bailin—although most of it he finds derivative and thin, often weighed down by misapplied Foucault, and only rarely engaging "with Dickens as a marvelously exuberant *writer*" (275).

Dickens on Film

Michael Pointer's *Charles Dickens on the Screen* surveys the many film, television, and video adaptations of Dickens works. Unfortunately, the book holds few surprises and is rather sloppily put together. We learn that *A Christmas Carol* and *Oliver Twist* are the most performed Dickens works, that David Lean's *Great Expectations* is perhaps the best Dickens film, that Carol Reed's *Oliver!* is entertaining but unfaithful, and that Anthony Newley's Quilp was an utterly embarrassing failure. Pointer also has kind words for Christine Edzard's *Little Dorrit* (1987), another unremarkable judgment (though I confess to finding the movie six hours of unrelieved tedium). The most valuable parts of the book are probably its discussion of the many silent versions of Dickens (again, *Oliver Twist* and *A Christmas Carol* win out)—though Pointer is necessarily limited in most cases to a sentence or two on each—and, at the back of the book, a chronologically-arranged list of adaptations. The most curious part of the book may well be Pointer's survey of the many television adaptations of *A Christmas Carol,* often as a special Christmas episode of a serial. *Bewitched, My Favorite Martian, Family Ties,* and *The Dukes of Hazzard* all receive the Dickens treatment. And Pointer *does* include some fascinating bits of trivia. We discover, for instance, that Charles Laughton was tested for the role of Mr. Micawber, the part later performed by W. C. Fields in the famous 1935 production of *David Copperfield.* According to Elsa Lanchester, Laughton's wife and herself an actor in the movie, Laughton felt he lacked the "necessary music-hall technique" (56). All that remains of Laughton's aborted foray into Dickens is a marvelous photograph of Laughton in costume, with shaved head and a wonderfully Micawberesque expression on his face (included in Palmer's book), So, too, we learn of David Lean's rage at Carol Reed's *Oliver!* for lifting large chunks from his acclaimed 1948 film. But beyond a few pedestrian observations, Pointer remains satisfied to list actors and pass impressionistic judgments. And although his diligence at tracking down the many filmed versions of Dickens is admirable (even including a pornographic version of *A Christmas Carol*), Pointer's treatment of the information is thoroughly unscholarly. He fails to include citations for his sources, refers to "K. J." or "Ken" Fielding as "Keith" (2), and informs us that *Bleak House* was "Dickens's last completed novel" (97). And he fails to indicate in his catalogue of films which are extant, which are on videotape, which he has actually watched, and where a reader might go to locate the more obscure ones. Pointer even arranges the photographic "stills" from the movies oddly: at first, they seem placed chronologically, but he quickly departs from the scheme for no apparent reason. *Charles Dickens on the Screen* is an interesting, occasionally fascinating, first-step toward a fuller appreciation of the Dickens on film, but much remains to be done.

Graham Petrie begins to meet this need in his examination of early silent adaptations of Dickens's novels, with a specific focus on the four films produced by the Nordisk Company in Denmark from 1921 to 1924. Whereas Pointer often writes about the early silent movies at second hand, Petrie has actually seen *Scrooge, or Marley's Ghost* (1901), *The Boy and the Convict* (1909), and *Little Emily* (1911), which gives his writing a freshness and insight usually absent in Pointer's book. But even when both men have watched the same film, Petrie's analysis is superior. While Pointer is usually content to characterize performers as "well-matched," "really fine," and "suitably fierce and repulsive," Petrie is counting title cards (he gives us the exact number of the four Nordisk films), permitting him to observe "that at least a third of the running time of each film is taken up with title" (191).

Pointer in his much longer book only makes passing mention of one of the film's "excessively wordy intertitles" (43).

Illustrations and Illustrators, Portraits and Painters

In his later years, George Cruikshank had ossified into a great public figure, though fewer and fewer Victorians were willing to buy his works. For some, he seemed the Conservative crank, a self-absorbed extremist given to pugnacious pronouncements and embarrassing exaggerations, with an unfailing capacity to irritate. For others, he was "the venerable George," the knight errant of the Temperance movement, crusading with religious fervor against the dangers of drink and commanding the love and devotion of thousands of serious and sober teetotallers. One of the many virtues of Robert Patten's two-volume biography of George Cruikshank, the second volume of which was published in 1996, is his ability to negotiate the many sides of the great illustrator's personality. For the first time, we have a fair-minded, balanced biography of a man who seemed to have an unerring instinct for landing himself, time and again, in all sorts of scraps. For all of his brilliance as an illustrator and satirist—at the end of the second volume Patten makes convincing claims for the importance of his subject's work—Cruikshank seems to have lived much of his life in muddle and confusion.

Patten is a careful and thorough biographer who serves his subject well. He persuasively argues that Cruikshank's claim to have originated many of the characters and scenes of *Oliver Twist,* was not just the self-serving raving of some crackpot deep into senility, but something that he had repeated for years, and indeed with independent confirmation from others. If finally Patten is left with speculation, the speculation seems moderate and probable, especially given the egos of both illustrator and novelist. "Dickens may have heard Cruikshank out and then taken his own way," Pattern believes. "[B]ut that way was so like the one his artist proposed that each would feel proprietary about the result" (54).

Patten's thoroughness is most evident in his exploration of Cruikshank's business arrangements. With fine precision, Patten teases apart complex contractual negotiations to show points of confusion or disagreement between artist and publisher or artist and committee. Misunderstandings proliferated in Cruikshank's life, often ending in his public embarrassment. If Cruikshank is never quite innocent in such matters, his motives were rarely mean or entirely self-serving, as the press of the day, and many later commentators, have frequently made out. Patten is also strong in his explications of Cruikshank's etchings and paintings, which are both plentiful and beautifully reproduced. He detects a "tug-of-war between the author's sensibility and the artist's" in *Sketches by Boz* that reveals "that the plates are not *representations* of the text, but *responses* to it" (38). Cruikshank's sketch of "Monmouth Street," Pattern writes, "has little to do with a pessimistic view of life, nor does it endorse a Hogarthian connection between idleness and dissipation. The amusements of the people here, and in other plates of the period, tend to be revitalizing, comparatively innocent, and harmless" (41)—much different, in other words, from Dickens' written description. Patten also provides detailed readings of Cruikshank's famous Temperance series, "The Bottle," and of its follow-up, "The Drunkard's Children," both of which are reproduced in toto, and offers a stimulating reading of Cruikshank's very last illustration, "The Rose and the Lily," a haunting depiction of a monster arising from the depths of a pond, an image which Patten believes "resonates with issues central to Cruikshank's whole oeuvre" (503).

Despite its many fine qualities, volume two of *George Cruikshank's Life, Times, and Art* doesn't fully satisfy. Sometimes Cruikshank the man is lost amid the welter of facts, some of which are not very relevant. Information about Dickens's and Ainsworth's contractual problems is necessary to set Cruikshank's difficulties in context, but does Patten need to describe the disgrace of one of the artist's oldest friends, "Mummy" Pettigrew (152), an anecdote which seems to have no direct bearing on Cruikshank? Does he need to include two full paragraphs listing the names and occupations of those guests attending George and Eliza's silver wedding anniversary in 1875? Of course, both might be relevant, and perhaps are in a distant sense, but they impede the narrative flow. An accumulation of facts—and these are just representative of a general problem in the narrative—does not make a man, no matter how well researched and carefully scrutinized. At times, I couldn't help but wonder if Cruikshank really *deserved* two lengthy volumes, especially since the final volume spends so much time recording decline and failure. As Patten himself admits toward the end of his biography, Cruikshank remains an "oddly elusive personality" (497). We know almost nothing about the artist's feelings for his first wife (Patten passes over this in a quick chapter) and very little about his feelings for his second wife. We don't know if Cruikshank kept a mistress, as Patten suspects, or if he had twelve children by the woman. We don't know if Cruikshank was finally a hypocrite, if he kept a private supply of wine, as his final will suggests. Patten accumulates facts almost as a hedge against these perplexing and finally unsolvable mysteries. The facts don't explain the mysteries or in most cases even provide clues; too often, they just sit there, inert. Of course, much of this is inevitable. Biographers necessarily try to gain purchase on what is "elusive" by describing, and describing. But describing is not understanding. Pattern does as well, I suspect, as anyone could have done with Cruikshank, and probably "understands" him better. But I found myself at the end with an oddly disgruntled feeling, as if I still didn't have a grasp on Cruikshank and probably never would, despite what is almost certain to be the definitive biography of the man.

In "Furniss, Dickens and Illustration," Gareth Cordery examines the illustrations of Harry Furniss, who drew 500 plates for the 1910 Library Edition of Dickens's work. The fact that Furniss illustrated Dickens forty years after the master's death does not seem to pose much of a problem for Cordery because "his illustrations reveal fresh insights into his art, and to raise questions about the relation of author to illustrator, of later illustrators to earlier illustrators, and of text to illustration" (35). In reality, Cordery devotes very little space to discussing these "insights"—other than to suggest that Furniss sometimes misses the point of the novels he is illustrating—and says almost nothing about the important epistemological question of "the relation of author to illustrator." Most of the two-part essay, rather, is taken up with a largely empty comparison of Dickens and Furniss as men and as artists. Dickens and Furniss, we learn, both admired Hogarth, were self-taught and spontaneous, though both looked different and came from different social backgrounds. As to why any of this matters, beyond a vague "suitability" of temperament, Cordery never makes very clear. In the end, the reader is left with some knowledge of what a minor artist thought of Dickens long after he was dead, but not much else.

Of more interest is David Parker's discussion of a much greater artist than Furniss, Vincent Van Gogh. Van Gogh was a devoted student of Dickens who avidly read the novelist's works, quoted from them with ease, and even contemplated such minor matters as Dickens's changing attitude toward America and Americans. Parker claims that Van Gogh's debt to Dickens is sometimes "stated" and then says, ambiguously, that Van Gogh "thought of" "The Starlight" chapter of *Hard Times* when he painted *The Starry Night* in 1889. Does this mean that Van Gogh somewhere actually "stated" the influence or is the supposed influence implicitly "stated" because of the similarity of subject and title (surely fairly common)? The difference is important because Parker's evidence for Dickens's influence on Van Gogh is otherwise rather slim. The painter possibly gleaned some of his subjects and techniques (the *chiaroscuro* of *The Potato Eaters,* for instance) from the illustrations of Dickens's later work and perhaps derived the "empty chair" from Luke Fildes's depiction of Dickens's "empty chair" on the day of his death (though Parker admits that the motif has "a long history in European art"). But none of this seems persuasive enough to warrant Parker's conclusion that "Van Gogh learned more about narratives from Dickens, than from anyone else" (175).

In "Can't You See a Hint?": The Mysterious Thirteenth Illustration' to *Edwin Drood*," Don Richard Cox attempts to interpret one of Luke Fildes's preliminary sketches for *The Mystery of Edwin Drood* (preserved in the Gimbel Collection at Yale University). The drawing, labelled H1794, carries an incomplete caption, "Can't You See a H . . . ," which someone has completed as "Can't You See a Hint?" Cox surveys a number of possible, if rather far-fetched, interpretations of the sketch which might lend credence to many different theories about the mystery, but concludes that most likely the sketch is merely an earlier version of "Under the Trees," the final illustration for Chapter 3, and that the captain records Rosa's question to Edwin in the text, "Can't You See a Happy Future?" In other words, the sketch is really not very important, and, unfortunately, neither is this article.

Philip V. Allingham's discussion of the original illustrations for Dickens's *A Holiday Romance* (readily available for the first time in the Everyman Dickens series) also proves disappointing. Allingham believes that the illustrations, which first appeared in the American children's magazine *Our Young Folks* in 1867, "augment and comment upon the original text" and consequently "should not be omitted from a consideration of how this four-part serial by Dickens would have been interpreted by the original readers" (34)—even if Dickens himself had no say in their production. This seems a fair enough point, although Allingham says nothing about how the text and drawings *would* "have been interpreted," other than to explain how the drawings, a rather mediocre bunch at best, "Americanize" the text by changing minor details.

Andrew D. Bean and Catherine Griffey establish that "The Samuel Drummond Portrait of Charles Dickens" is really a picture of the young novelist, a fact contested by an earlier generation of Dickens scholars. A copy of the painting, which Angela Burdett-Coutts believed showed a good likeness of Dickens, has recently (1996) been placed on display at the Dickens House in London. Equally good news is provided by Andrew Xavier who informs us that the original chalk and crayon drawing of Samuel Laurence's well-known portrait of a young Dickens, along with the portrait of Catherine Dickens by Laurence, has been purchased at auction by the Dickens House Museum and are now on display at the museum. The Dickens House has also received a sketch by Luke Fildes of (apparently) Kate Perugrini, Dickens's youngest daughter, dated 13 June 1880. Peter Wells, who donated the piece, suggests that the sketch seems to have been drawn by Fildes from memory or from another likeness since Kate is depicted as a young women and "some architectural discrepancies" exist between the background and the real Gad's Hill (111). Unfortunately, the caption beneath the reprint of the sketch (in *The Dickensian,* vol. 92, p. 110) erroneously dates the picture as 13 June 1860, a mistake which "corrects" the confusion while doubling it in the future.

John Woolford describes some of the stamps issued to commemorate the works of Charles Dickens. In 1993, the British Post Office released five stamps on the 150th anniversary of *A Christmas Carol* and in earlier years has commemorated *David Copperfield, Oliver Twist,* and *The Pickwick Paper.* Dickens stamps have also been issued by St. Helena (*Bleak House*) the Cayman Islands (*Barnaby Rudge, Martin Chuzzlewit*), and the British Virgin Islands (*A Tale of Two Cities, Great Expectations*), some of which Woolford reproduces in his article.

Biographical Background

Sidney and Carolyn Mosses's treatment of "The Charles Dickens-Thomas Powell Vendetta" of the late 1840s might have made a fine monograph, but as a book of 150 pages, the "story in documents" seems inflated and self-indulgent. The tale itself is an interesting one, involving fraud, forgery, libel, journalistic infighting, and, in the words of the Mosses, a Dickensian "vendetta" against Thomas Powell, a one-time friend of Dickens, who stole from his employer and escaped to America, where he attacked Dickens in print. Powell may have been one of the sources for James Carker in *Dombey and Son,* as his employer, Thomas Chapman, was believed by some at the time to be the "original" for Dombey himself (and by the Mosses currently). The book consists of the documents surrounding the controversy—letters, newspaper accounts, legal material—introduced by brief contextual descriptions, and, occasionally, some speculation about motives and intentions. The Mosses seem to include everything they could unearth, even minor notices and, apparently, every letter of Dickens on the subject, though they make little effort to justify their tiresome "documentary" approach. Surely, a briefer survey of the information, with relevant quotations, would have enhanced readability and might have provided just as much information. As it stands, *The Charles Dickens-Thomas Powell Vendetta* will probably remain an antiquarian curiosity.

Scholars continue to be fascinated by Dickens's strangely passionate response to the early death of his sister-in-law, Mary Hogarth. His recurring dreams, his declarations of intense feeling, and, most odd of all, his embarrassing desire to be buried beside her have all sparked numerous theories about the erotically-charged, and quite illicit, relations between the two young people. In "Dickens and the Death of Mary Hogarth," David Parker argues that death itself permits Dickens to appropriate his sister-in-law, to release her "from context into text" (72), and thus make more of her than ever existed in real life. "He constructed an after-life for her, both in order to meet his own emotional needs, and . . . in order to assimilate her into narratives he would make, about himself, and about his imaginary creations" (72). Parker offers an important rebuttal to those critics who too often take Dickens simply at this word, underestimating his tendency to make stories of his life, to invest it with a narrative significance not necessarily present in fact.

Relations between famous writers are almost always of interest and, certainly, Charles Dickens and Henry Wadsworth Longfellow were two of the most celebrated writers of their day. Unfortunately, Edward L. Tucker's "References to Longfellow's *Journals* (1856–1882) to Charles Dickens," which for the first time publishes all 44 of Longfellow's journal entries relating to Dickens, reveals very little about either man. We learn, for example, that Longfellow was disappointed with one chapter of *Little Dorrit,* and that in 1867 Dickens looked ''somewhat older, but as elastic and quick in his movements as ever'' (205), and that his public reading was ''not Reading exactly; but acting, and quite wonderful in its way'' (206). The only very interesting entry is Longfellow's claim in 1861 that *The Pickwick Papers* ''contains all Dickens in embryo, as an Overture does an Opera: themes and motifs just touched upon, which are more elaborately developed in later works'' (205). Longfellow's shock at his friend's sudden death is moving, but hardly surprising (he could not stop thinking of the image of Dickens lying dead at Gad's Hill). In a second short piece, published separately, Tucker uses Longfellow's *Journals* to identify the exact date on which Dickens and Henry James met (November 26, 1867). Of most interest is a quotation from *Notes of a Son and Brother,* in which James described his awestruck meeting with the great novelist, a memory that James, who was 24 at the time, ''always superlatively cherished.''

In ''Charles Dickens's Travelling Medicine Chest,'' David Dickens and the late Norman M. Jacoby, a retired medical publisher and a consultant pediatrician, set out to prove that Dickens suffered from asthma. In the course of their quest, they come across the medicine chest which Dickens carried with him on his 1867 trip to the United States. But the chest turns out to be a dead end, for David Dickens and Jacoby decide that its contents have ''no significance in proving that Dickens suffered from asthma.'' The laudanum and other opiates present in the chest, they admit, ''were as ordinary and as usual as the contents of any other medical chest at the time'' (24), and thus ''The hypothesis about Dickens's asthma remains to be proved, disproved or argued about'' (24)—a rather tremendous anti-climax at the least.

The first public readings of Dickens's novels may be dated to May 1844, when a temporarily out-of-work actor, William Pleater Davidge, began to perform the works of ''Boz'' to positive reviews. Robert Simpson Maclean draws on the recently unearthed lecture notes of Davidge to reconstruct these early readings, which included an introductory lecture on Dickens and brief snippets from his early works, most frequently *Sketches by Boz* and *The Pickwick Papers.* Davidge anticipated modern scholars by recognizing the importance of *Martin Chuzzlewit* and the seriousness of *David Copperfield,* though he had little luck anticipating which passages Dickens himself chose to read.

Giliam West describes Dickens's little house at 11 Selwood Terrace in the summer of 1835, near the home of his fiancée, Catherine Hogarth and provides a photograph of the house and a detail from Greenwood's "Map of Chelsea."

Social and Political Background

After more than a century of Dickens scholarship, and despite much first-rate work on the subject, a vast amount still remains to be learned about his political and social views. And much that we do know is often not sufficiently contextualized, but is simply described in isolation, apart from any contemporary discourse of events. Certainly, no single effort has unearthed so much fresh information in recent years as the wonderfully detailed annotations of the Pilgrim edition of Dickens's letters, but even these are limited to a few lines. The publication of further *Companion* volumes to Dickens' novels promises to add further information. But how much context is enough? *Household Words* and *All the Year Round* still remain virtually unplumbed, with the exception of a relatively few, oft-mentioned, pieces written by Dickens himself. Only a handful of social context pieces were published this year (several are discussed under the appropriate novel), and with mixed results, some providing genuine insights and discovering new information, others rehashing. M. Gabriella Caponi-Doherty's description of Dickens's sympathy for Italian nationalism and his acquaintance with several exiled Italian patriots does a bit of both. She does a pretty good job of setting Dickens's attitudes in the broader context of English views about Italians and Italian nationalism, although overall the article seems under-researched and too reliant on secondary sources, especially William J. Carlton's "Dickens Studies Italian" (*Dickensian* 61.101–08), H. W. Rudman's *Italian Nationalism and English Letters* (1940), and E. Morelli's *Mazzini in Inghilterra* (1940). She fails to draw at all on *Household Words* and *All the Year Round* and does not even mention Dickens's fiction. I found the piece quite helpful in its discussion of *The Uncommercial Traveller* essay, "The Italian Prisoner" (13 October 1860), but otherwise far from definitive.

Murray Roston's discussion of "Commodity Culture in Dickens," in a book about *Victorian Contexts,* is over-long and insufficient. Arguing against Dorothy Van Ghent's well-known observation that in Dickens material reality overwhelms people, Roston believes more positively that people overwhelm material reality, that the Victorians transformed objects through self-projection. As Roston explains, this animation of objects reflects "the proprietary mode of a thriving society which proudly regarded the articles it had created or had acquired as projections of personality, absorbing their owner's tastes, traits, and quirks'' (113). The problem with Roston's broader cultural analysis is that it doesn't explain very much. Roston finds great significance in a change in furniture styles during the Victorian period, believing that the increased individuation of designs influenced Dickens's elaborate descriptions (though Roston doesn't say ''influenced'' but the much weaker ''cannot be unconnected with''). He then brings in Victorian architecture, with its ''hybrid combination of styles'' and Victorian economics, with its wider selection of goods, all to say what? That there are broad similarities between Victorian furniture, architecture, and literature? In a general sense, at least, this is obvious. The Victorian Web devotes a page to just this conjunction. But Roston only uses this general point to make a few uninspiring comments about Dickens, such as that the Dickensian character often gives life to his or her surroundings—a reversal of Van Ghent perhaps, but how current is Van Ghent? Roston never engages with more recent, and arguably more sophisticated, examinations of the relations of people and objects, other than for a brief mention of J. Hillis Miller.

Influence Studies

Stephen Jacobi finds similarities in emotion and temperament between Dickens and Angus Wilson, the British novelist and critic, although not specific borrowings in his literary works. ''The influence must be of the more impressionistic, less consciously appropriated kind,'' Jacobi observes (123). Both writers are said to favor ''the untidy and the unexpected,'' to be fond of the overarching symbol, and to be responsive to social concerns, although ''the best evidence of any psychological correspondence . . . is probably their shared restlessness'' (123). Jacobi recognizes that ''Many of these points of contact could be easily applied to a number of novelists writing in the same broad tradition'' (123), although he generally convinces that ''Dickens remained the presiding builder'' (124) for the imagination of his devoted reader and biographer. Rodney Stenning Edgecombe, in a brief note, finds two points of contact between Patrick White and Charles Dickens: their use of conditional formulations and the similar codas to White's *Riders in the Chariot* and Dickens's *Our Mutual Friend.*

The Pickwick Papers

Marisa Sestito believes that Dickens's complex and ambiguous ''dark'' novels are anticipated by the interpolated stories found in *The Pickwick Papers,* with their conflicting voices and narrative experimentation. Unfortunately, Sestito's argument stays at the level of generality, a fact borne out by her catch-all title, "Divided Dickens," and such commonplace observations as that *A Tale of Two Cities* and *Great Expectations* make use of doubles; that the interpolations in *Pickwick* "act as strategic shocks, as a negative relief within the comic predictability" (39); that Dickens uses *Pickwick* "as an amazing frame containing coexisting and intermingling opposites" (39); and that Sam Weller and Alfred Jingle both "stand out because of the peculiarity of their language" (39).

Oliver Twist

In "Dickens, Bakhtin, and the Neopastoral Shepherd in *Oliver Twist*," David Wilkes views the criminal den at Saffron Hill as "a neopastoral community" (67) with Fagin as bad shepherd. In Dickens's hands, this retreat is not an idyllic bower but "a parodic place where the need for human warmth and stability are met" (67). Wilkes' evidence of the den's essential pastoralism sometimes rests on very shaky grounds. Is Fagin's toasting fork really a shepherd's crook or is the card-playing of the young thieves really a "neopastoral contest" (70)?

The criminal den receives very different treatment from Larry Wolff, who emphasizes the homoerotic nature of Fagin's world. Wolff discovers a "radical indeterminacy" in the text toward criminality, an indeterminacy that recognizes "the possibility that the boys [in Fagin's den] maybe sold for sex" (228). Predictably, this "indeterminacy . . . exposes . . . a failure of ideological alignment, revealing the suppressed inconsistencies in the ordering of crucial binary oppositions" like "male and female, heterosexuality and homosexuality" and so forth (228–29). Such "indeterminacy," of course, is always easy to locate. Wolff finds it in Nancy's description of Oliver's future criminality: "He's a thief, a liar, a devil: all that's bad, from this night forth." According to Wolff, this list moves from specificity to the "breakdown" of descriptive expression in the culminating phrase "all that's bad," which Wolff reads as homosexuality. He seems to miss the fact that "all that's bad" is not a culmination of the series but rather, as the placement of the colon suggests, a summation of it. In other words, the statement is not a "progression" of crimes toward some troubling indeterminacy, but a static description of Oliver's evident criminality (for Wolff's "progression" to hold, "a liar" would have to be clearly worse than "a thief"). Wolff makes a great fuss over the "all that's bad" phrase because he has relatively little in the novel on which to hang his strained argument. In a similar vein, he argues that Fagin's "banking on Oliver's looks . . . suggests the possibility of sexual commerce in boys'' (233), but fails to mention the obvious point that Oliver's innocent looks would be of tremendous importance to a pickpocket. Wolff even sees a homoerotic competition between Mr. Brownlow and Fagin for the possession of Oliver. By Wolff's reckoning, Dickens seems to have been aware of all of this but policed his text in order to make it palatable to a mid-Victorian reader. This kind of article moves between truism and absurdity. Of course, given the prevailing attitudes toward homosexuality, Dickens, Mayhew, Acton, and others were likely to suppress the reality of male prostitution and, to this degree, ''gender'' crime (male pickpockets, female prostitutes). But does this make Oliver ''into pornographic bait for readers'' who fail to recognize ''the possibility of his sexual exploitation'' (247)? Does this mean Dickens deliberately mislead the reader as to the true nature of Oliver's crimes (as Wolff at times suggests, although he is never very clear on this score)?

For Jeremy Tambling, *Oliver Twist* provides a model of the author re-reading his work as he writes it and changing its shape accordingly. Dickens's progressive revisions of the novel twice remove the word ''digression,'' reflecting his attempt ''to centre the events of the text'' (49) in accord with nineteenth-century ideas of unity and coherence. But ultimately, Tambling believes, the best reading of *Oliver Twist* appreciates the novel's montage-like plurality, its ''excess, its unconscious, and its series of shocks mediated through the hardness of separate objects'' (51), which connects the novel both to the eighteenth-century digressions of Henry Fielding and the twentieth-century experimentations of a filmmaker like Serge Eisenstein.

Nicholas Nickleby

The parodic elements of *Nicholas Nickleby* make the melodrama more digestible for Tore Rem. The novel's melodramatic scenes never stand alone, he believes, but are balanced by comic counterparts. So Nicholas's serious pursuit of Madelaine Bray is parodied by his mistaken chasing after Cecilia Bobster or by the mad neighbor's quixotic love for Mrs. Nickleby. And the many sentimental farewells receive their comic comeuppance at the Crummles' public farewell of Nicholas. Rem's article is a useful corrective to those critics who deride the ''cheap melodrama'' of *Nicholas Nickleby,* though some of what he says seems obvious. One would have liked more on the ''continuous struggle'' between parody and melodrama, which Rem merely states as a given. John Bowen also argues for a more complex reading of *Nicholas Nickleby,* for ''the peculiarly ambivalent transformational energies of Dickens's writing undercut the domestic ideology of early Victorian capitalism through the frankness of economic forces beneath it'' (154–55). Families are not ''the 'counter-image' of the modern marketplace,'' as Nancy

Armstrong would have it, but are rather permeated with economic strains. It's the family again which provides the "most richly comic and symbolically ambivalent spaces and structures in the book" (164), a sort of carnivalesque transgression.

The Old Curiosity Shop

Modern readers are prone to see Dickens's sentimentality as a flaw in artistry, a concession to popular taste and to his own Victorian propensity to wallow in tears and good feelings. But in "The Old Curiosity Shop and the New: Dickens and the Age of Machinery," Norris Pope shows that Dickens's sentimentality was a decidedly political act, "a powerful 'sentimental' critique of the 'iron laws' of political economy" (149. If much of Pope's article is unremarkable—his discussion of political economy is pretty basic stuff—its contextualizing of sentiment is a useful corrective to those who too casually deride Dickens's embrace of feeling. Jerome H. Buckley's "Little Nell's Curious Grandfather" finds Nell's grandfather to be the most enigmatic character in *The old Curiosity Shop* and "the most complex psychologically," "an intricate intruder upon the simpler allegorical elements of Nell's story" (87).

American Notes

American Notes receives extended treatment in volume 23 of *Nineteenth Century Prose,* which includes four essays on Dickens's travel narrative first presented as papers at an MLA annual meeting, and an introductory essay by Patrick J. McCarthy. McCarthy, who provides background information and summarizes the essays that follow, mainly focuses on the "truth claims" of *American Notes,* which he believes were influenced by "the pressure of time and money and the need to be entertaining"(4), as well as a growing disappointment that the United States was not "a renewed version of the Old World with its best features retained" (9). The other essays in the volume generally betray their initial status as conference papers: they tend to be short and under-researched and can be quickly summarized. William Sharpe believes that in *American Notes* Dickens satirizes the tradition of the strolling urban spectator by representing him as a "solitary swine" detached from human involvement or compassion, a characterization that reflects Dickens's own disenchantment with the *flâneur* persona he had used in *Sketches by Boz,* though Sharpe's evidence for this is somewhat slight. Laurie Carlson attributes contemporary attacks on *American Notes* to its anomalous, genre-busting mix of fiction and fact and speculates that the frankly subjective nature of Dickens's book anticipates the "New Journalism" of the late twentieth century, an argument that would have been a lot more convincing had she first set the book in the context of the 1840s (a few quotations from contemporary reviewers are not sufficient). Patricia M. Ard prefers Dickens's epistolary descriptions of his American trip to his published version in *American Notes,* concluding unremarkably that Dickens modulates his writing to his audience, and that therefore his letters to his friends in England were more emotional and direct than the somewhat watered down account that reached the public. David Stevens also emphasizes the shaping of *American Notes,* in his case the way travel narratives say more about the writer's own culture than the culture actually being described. Writing as a Southerner, Stevens is particularly sensitive to Dickens's disparagement of the South, which Stevens partly attributes to a "European" view of nature, with its stress "on order and inter-connection rather than difference and antagonism" (45). Once Dickens is "confronted by a land where the demarcations of country and city are anything but clear," Stevens believes, he "revolts at the way he sees the landscape encroaching on every aspect of American life" (44). Stevens's discussion of the "Framing of America" is probably the most stimulating and completely conceived of the four essays in this volume.

A Christmas Carol

Joseph D. Cusumano's attempt to turn "The Christmas Carol" into a self-help handbook, or a "New Age Classic," is surely the oddest work of the year, and probably of most years. For Cusumano, "The Christmas Carol"is a primer in self-transformation: through a process of gradual spiritual enlightenment, Scrooge's "wounded inner child' becomes a happy, fully functioning adult. Pop psychology, New Age mumbo-jumbo, chakras, the *kundalini* syndrome, alien abductions, and near-death experiences—all are brought to bear on a Scrooge for whom one begins to feel rather sorry. The fact that Dickens provides very little information about Scrooge's "wounded inner child" poses no obstacle to Cusumano, who wonders if he were not the victim of an alcoholic family or of physical or sexual abuse. He wonders too if Dickens knew about Hindu chakras (spiritual centers) and if he wrote "The Christmas Carol" to a Hindu plan. But what's most unsettling about the book is the way Cusumano mixes pop psychology with the language and ideas of contemporary theoretical criticism, mirroring some of our own obsessions back to us. So à la New Historicism, he prides himself on fashioning a Dickens for the late twentieth century; and, recalling structuralism, he divides the story into a zillion categories; and he speculates wildly about everything, including sex, our latter-day critical obsession. My favorite moment is in a section entitled, "Scrooge's Functional Power Chakra," in which Cusumano admits that "the energy release in Scrooge's Sex Chakra did not manifest itself" obviously, though he believes that the bells that greet the reformed Scrooge on his awakening are "not-so-veiled linguistic references to Belle, the object of his youthful sexual desire, and to the awakening of his raw sexual energy," an association which he feels is "obviously implied" (90). One might scream "Bah! Humbug!" and throw the book aside if it were not for the fact that at least Cusumano takes Dickens's story seriously—he sincerely believes it to be a guide to "spiritual reawakening," and who are we to laugh? After 150 years, Dickens might have been quite pleased that his "New Age Classic" still had the power to change people.

In "The Incorporation of *A Christmas Carol:* A Tale of Seasonal Screening," Caroline McCracken-Flesher shows how Dickens's most popular work has regularly been used by corporate culture to stimulate consumerism. Commercial interests have transformed Dickens's message of charity into a command to buy more and more merchandise. "In its telling," McCracken-Flesher explains, "the tale has no function other than to generate corporate sales" (99). Even a latter-day film like Bill Murray's *Scrooged,* which on a first viewing may seem to attack television's excess, only underwrites it more subtlety. The real charm to McCracken-Flesher's piece—and there are many charms—is its hilarious and disturbing description of a television production of Dickens's tale for the Chrysler "Shower of Stars" series, shown on CBS in the mid-1950s. "[W]hat better way to combine the time for joyful giving, the way to joyful living," the host intones during a commercial break, "than a gift of one of these superb new station-wagons of The Forward Look '56? For here, truly, is the gift that keeps giving in year round driving pleasure" (107).

According to Toru Sasaki, the Japanese have a love affair with *A Christmas Carol,* which they see as "one of the most famous works of English literature, possibly in the same league with *Hamlet*" (188). Sasaki leaves aside the question of *why* the Japanese would be so remarkably fascinated with *A Christmas Carol* (to the tune of about 30 translations) to discuss the distinction in Japanese ghost stories between "Yu-rei" (haunting humans) and "Yo-kwai" (strange creatures). Sasaki argues that a corresponding distinction exists in Dickens's tale between Marley and the three Christmas spirits, though he doesn't make much of this distinction other than to "find Dickens's creative engagement with Marley rather feeble" (193).

Dombey and Son

Mary Armstrong's study of female homoerotic desire in *Dombey and Son* is one of the more significant pieces on Dickens published this year, and likely to be one of the most debated. Following the lead of Jane Tompkins in *Sensational Design,* Armstrong argues for a gendered understanding of sentimentality, though one that also embraces "intra-female eroticism" (298). The "ideological flawlessness of female sentimentality," Armstrong observes, "renders [the nineteenth-century sentimental] heroine supremely available for the (highly melodramatic) psychological, sexual and social dramas of other women who labor under, but do not meet, the same standards of perfection" (283). In the case of *Dombey and Son,* Florence's perfection occasions Susan Nipper's transgressive, melodramatic tirades, "her language of critique" that is displaced "onto her body/self" (291), though the homoeroticism of the relationship is ultimately defused by Susan's return to heterosexual womanhood (she marries Mr. Toots), as well as by the comic exaggeration of Susan's character. Edith Dombey represents a much "darker threat of female refusal and desire" (293), Armstrong believes. She is a bought woman whose hope for a "lost innocence" is "eroticized in the controllable space of Florence's bedroom, where Edith lingers over Florence's body with obsessive interest" (294). But as with Susan, Edith desires to settle Florence "happily into male circulation and restore normalcy" (295). Female homoerotics, in other words, eventually operate in service of an essentially conservative, and masculine, ideology—this despite the disruption of the plot. Women cannot, by this reading, "save the day" (296). The subtlety and intelligence of Armstrong's argument are impressive, though readers' reactions will inevitably depend on whether she has persuaded them of the homoerotic nature of Florence's female relationships. On this score, I'm not so sure. Much of the contact between the women seems "innocent" in context and less "physically intense" than Armstrong would suggest.

Margaret Wiley describes the class tension inherent in wet-nursing and points out its effect on Dickens's depiction of Polly Toodles in *Dombey and Son.* Wealthy women, reluctant to lose their figure or wear themselves out, would frequently hire working-class wet-nurses to provide breast milk for their babies. But these working-class women commonly suckled wealthy children at the expense of their own, who were forced to rely on cow's milk, beer, and tea, and who often died as a result. High mortality rates for these "dry-nursed" infants, and the possible spread of syphilitic infection occasioned by wet-nursing, led medical men to question the fairness and safety of the practice. In *Dombey and Son,* though, Dickens treats wet-nursing in a comical way. Miss Tox is a figure of fun in the novel, as is Polly Toodles, with her healthy, happy, and notably clean home. "It is fascinating," Wiley writes, "that Dickens, ever the astute social commentator, makes no effort to discuss the harsh social realities surrounding wet-nursing" (223). She attributes this silence to Dickens's own guilt over his wife's use of wet-nurses. Unfortunately, Wiley fails to provide any evidence for this guilt, other than to establish that some Victorians felt guilty, and to say that therefore Dickens *must* also have felt so. The last two pages of the essay hinge almost entirely on her speculation and are filled with phrases like "I suspect," "If we can trust Mary Hogarth's assessment," "If this is true," "If he and Catherine hired ten wet-nurses" (for which there is no solid evidence). Indeed, Wiley includes only one quotation from Dickens on the subject, and this suggests his entire indifference. Dickens's silence, of course, *could* imply guilt, but it could as easily imply disinterest.

David Copperfield

Michael Hollington's book-length introduction of *David Copperfield* is intended to help French graduate students with their exams. Perhaps the least satisfying part of the book is the quick survey of the textual editions of *David Copperfield,* its backgrounds, and the points of comparison with other works. A three-page discussion of "social, cultural, and literary background," may be adequate for graduate students, perhaps, but it is little more. And altogether absent is any discussion of the major critical perspectives on *David Copperfield* (the kind of thing Janice Carlisle does so wonderfully in the St. Martin's edition of *Great Expectations*). The core of the book though, is not introduction, but analysis. And here Hollington is on much firmer ground. He sees the novel as fundamentally a *Bildungsroman,* but one where self-development is rendered both complex and problematic. If Hollington's local insights are sometimes better than the overarching argument—which gets obscured in a rather bewildering number of chapters, sections, and subsections—his reading of individual scenes and textual details is first-rate. I found myself particularly fascinated by his discussions of physiognomy, horizon imagery, and the ambiguous nature of striving in the novel.

Kelly Hager perceptively instances David Copperfield as an example of a novel of divorce—thus reading against or "estranging" the novel from the many interpretations which see it as a novel of marriage. Hager discovers refreshing complexity in several key women characters. She finds Dora Copperfield aware of her inadequacies and believes she "seeks to compensate for them by asserting them all the more strenuously" (998), playing the role of the "child-wife" as a way to avoid blame for failure. And Hager reads Emma Micawber's recurrent suggestion that she will "never desert" her husband as "a pathetic, repetitive, bleat or despair," a recognition that she *can* never desert Micawber. And Betsey Trotwood, the one character actually to leave her husband, is all the happier for her decision. The fact that Betsey "looks quite traditional" in the end is explained, Hager feels, by Dickens's nervousness about his attack on the institution of marriage itself. This nervousness is further evinced in Dickens's use of the Annie Strong *faux* adultery plot to distract the reader from the genuinely failed marriages of the Micawbers and Copperfields. Although Hager believes that "to call Dickens or his work feminist would be anachronistic and misinformed," she argues that a reader alert "to the silences and gaps" in his texts, may detect a "competing text," one feminist in "its effect to educate readers about the woeful state of the law respecting women and marriage" (1016). Hager's impressive dismantling of the text's surface meaning—her "estranging" of it—to reveal its underlying cultural conflicts is one of the finest pieces of the year.

Mark Cronin finds "major points of textual relations" between *David Copperfield* and Thackeray's *Pendennis.* According to Cronin, both novels depict "gentlemen rakes" caught in similar maternal/romance triangles; both offer competing views of the artist; and both use August von Kotzebue's melodrama, *The Stranger,* for ironic purposes. Cronin does not simply list similarities, but demonstrates how *David Copperfield* responds to *Pendennis,* which began serialization a step ahead of Dickens's novel. Unfortunately, Cronin ends rather abruptly. Some summing up and reflection on the larger meaning of the differences would have been helpful.

Bleak House

The *Bleak House* article to be reckoned with in 1996 is undoubtedly Jan B. Gordon's massively long " 'In all Manner of Places, All at Wunst,' " an 81-page chapter from his book, *Gossip and Subversion in Nineteenth-Century British Fiction.* Those critics most sympathetic to the aims of deconstructist theory, and probably many others as well, will find Gordon's essay to be something of a tour de force, a virtuostic deconstruction of *Bleak House* that examines with great, and even obsessive, detail the self-cancelling nature of the novel (among many other ideas). Not surprisingly, given his theoretical orientation, Gordon finds *Bleak House* to be a novel that resists "totalization" at every level, even as it is "permeated with 'fallen' vestiges of allegory" that suggest some unitary scheme (1963). Because semiotic "slippages" always accompany the reproduction of signs, "the novel seems incessantly to remind us of its provisionality, as if it too existed as a copy of something else" (165). The provisional nature of the novel extends to its serialization, which Gordon reads as "a sequence of overlapping 'installments' which impede possession of some 'whole story,' even as it whets a reader's appetite for some totalization" (210). Gordon has much more to say on *Bleak House* than this—at 81 pages he'd better have—though some of it seems pretty predictable after about twenty pages (I must confess to some judicious skimming myself). Of course, as is often true of a deconstructionist like Gordan who ostensibly resists "totalization," he himself engages in the most totalizing of arguments—that everything is ultimately a play of signs without meaning beyond itself. And as is also sometimes the case, the closer one looks at the examples, the less convincing the grand generalizations become. Is the "little voice" of the "large advocate with great whiskers" in chapter 1 of *Bleak House*—which Gordon immediately translates as "the still, small voice of ad*vo*cacy"—really "shut out" by the advocate's "interminable brief" (thus privileging writing over speech), as Gordon claims, or are they just placed in parallel, as seems more likely?

Kenneth Fielding's"*Bleak House* and Dickens' Originals: 'The Romantic Side of Familiar Things' " argues for the importance of "real-life" models to Dickens's imagination, judging that "so far as readers were aware of originals, they helped to place the characters and their context in the contemporary scene" (130), and "because they could be associated with underlying themes" (126). Perhaps the most celebrated of all of the "originals" was Leigh Hunt, the source for Harold Skimpole, one of Dickens's most distasteful creations. Adam Roberts shows how in *Bleak House* Dickens effectively "inverts" Hunt's writings, distorting their meaning and even implying the very opposite of what Hunt originally intended. "Skimpole," Roberts writes, "is not a mimetically reproduced Hunt, but an ironic anti-Hunt; a character defined by inverting the original" (184). Or, as Dickens himself claimed in his "Remonstrance" to Hunt's son, he preserved the surface reality while inventing his fictional character's "imaginary vices."

Lisa Jadwin sees *Bleak House* as a "revision" of *Jane Eyre,* "a subtle nineteenth-century *Shamela* possibly designed to refute the radical form and ideology" of Charlotte Brontë's novel (111). The qualifier, "possibly," is one of the few times in her tendentious article that she shows any hesitation. She reads Dickens's failure ever to refer to *Jane Eyre* as a "feigned ignorance" occasioned by his refusal to question "male hegemony," his resentment over a woman's narrative too much like his own, and his inability "to confront the feminized nature of" his early experiences (113), though when it suits her argument, Jadwin asserts that "Dickens avoided both his major female contemporaries and their works" (George Eliot and Elizabeth Gaskell apparently do not count) and "arguably never read Brontë" (116). The connection between *Bleak House* and *Jane Eyre* is hardly new—as a footnote acknowledges—although Jadwin makes no attempt to rebut directly Anny Sadrin's defense of Esther Summerson in "Charlotte Dickens" (*Dickens Quarterly* 9.47–57), merely according it a passing mention in a footnote. Nor does Jadwin come to grips with feminist criticisms of *Jane Eyre*. But consistently she's willing to attribute the darkest motivations to Dickens, even ascribing to him the desire to have his sister serve in Warren's blacking warehouse in his stead, a bit of biographical whimsy for which no evidence exists (Dickens's envy of his sister's opportunities notwithstanding).

Laura Fasick shows how Dickens's emphasis on suffering as an opportunity for spiritual growth minimizes material conditions, deflecting *Bleak House*'s "initial impulse toward large-scale social criticism" (143). Even Jo, ostensibly one of the novel's most "physical" characters, becomes disembodied on his sickbed, transformed into an icon of personal sympathy, and not of social restucturing. Although discussions of the inadequacy of Dickens's social analysis are legion, Fasick brings considerable insight into the specific evasions surrounding disease.

Hard Times

Leona Toker reads *Hard Times* as a critique of utopian ideals and thus as a precursor of later utopian/dystopian novels such as H. G. Well's *A Modern Utopia,* Aldous Huxley's *Brave New World,* and Vladimir Nabokov's *Bend Sinister.* At times, the article suffers from the typical problem of typological studies, the squeezing of resistant fictional material into pre-established categories at the cost of historical specificity, though generally her categories are more liberating than restrictive. Reading *Hard Times* in the context of later utopian novels helps salvage it from the past, making its attacks on the Gradgrind school seem part of a larger confrontation with totalitarianism, censorship, and the "totalizing tendencies of the modern age" (226). This kind of approach can be horribly anachronistic, of course, although by and large Toker steers clear of overstatement and remains sensitive to the ambiguities of the text.

Jatindra Nayak and Himansu Mohapatra argue that Fakir Mohan Senapatri's late nineteenth-century novel, *Chha Mana Atha Guntha,* offers "a more incisive critique of the utilitarian order" than does Dickens's *Hard Times.* Nayak and Mohapatra make a persuasive case that India suffered enormously from utilitarian dogma and argue well for the percipience of Senapatri's novel, though many Dickensians will probably bristle at the suggestion that *Hard Times* "colludes with utilitarianism insofar as it articulates no criticism of the use of the colonies as a test site and a safety value on the part of the master society" (81). Dickensians are likely to bristle for a different reason at Richard A. Currie's comments on repressed anger in *Hard Times.* Currie's big point—one that he makes for six long pages—is that the Gradgrind family repress anger. And that's it. The entire article consists of long plot summary, tediously long clauses ("A variation in the technique of object protection known as the narcissistic defense that Dickens explored in what Paul Schlicke calls the King Lear novels, Louisa . . ."), tangled syntax ("Louisa's protection assumes the form of a martyr"), one horrid misspelling ("scarcasticaly"), and a total absence of original argument. Currie's comments—"discussion" is too grandiose a word—culminate in such nuggets as "Dickens employs this device [fire] to suggest the repressed nature of

Louisa's feelings'' (148) and "Louisa's conversation with her father when she abruptly presents herself to him after leaving Bounderby provides further evidence that Louisa's suppression of her angry and passionate feelings is ending" (149).

Little Dorrit

One of the better books of the year is Brian Rosenberg's *Little Dorrit's Shadows: Character and Contradiction in Dickens*. An examination of character in a single novel may sound unpromising in these days of wide-ranging cultural studies, but in Rosenberg's hands such tightness of focus is anything but restrictive. He uses *Little Dorrit* to elucidate character issues throughout Dickens's oeuvre and to serve as a touchstone for broad speculations about realism itself. Rosenberg sensibly situates his argument between those theorists who challenge representation altogether and those essentialist critics who believe character corresponds to a reality outside of the text.While acknowledging that "The basic premises upon which each position is founded . . . are irreconcilable" (11), Rosenberg argues for a criticism which "attends both to the dissimilarities between text and world . . . and to the habits of characters to inspire . . . speculation that carries the reader beyond the confines of language" (11). In the case of Dickens, such criticism shows how his dense descriptive passages—with their many qualifiers, hesitancies, and contradictions—actually prevent seeing and stand in the way of simple representation, and how his vivid personalities actually embody doubts about the coherence of personality. "[T]he brilliant creator," Rosenberg explains, "is locked in perpetual conflict with his own doubts about the nature and truth of his creations" (24). Dickens reproduces, that is, the very tensions at the heart of the modern debate about character. Rosenberg writes with clarity and persuasiveness, though *Little Dorrit's Shadows* loses steam towards its end—its chapters growing shorter and some of its ideas more commonplace (Rosenberg says of Dickens's novels, for example, that "personality itself [is] distributed among a collection of fragmented and fragmentary characters"—112).

Arlene Young explores the conventional representation of the lower middle class in the early and mid-Victorian period and then shows how Dickens manipulated those conventions "to expose the hypocrisy and venality of the Victorian bourgeoisie" (484). Young does a good job of defining the characteristics associated with the lower middle class—small size, shabby appearance, small-mindedness, and inferiority—but then falsely expands on those characteristics, distorting and confusing them, when she begins to analyze Dickens's texts. Are the Meagles to be identified with the lower middle class, as she argues, because they live in a "temperate insular, dull but comfortable domesticity" (503)? Or because they fail to give grand dinner parties? Or because of their social pretensions? Does Arthur Clennam and Amy Dorrit's "modest life of usefulness and happiness" really betoken lower middleclassness? Nothing in her initial discussion of the lower middle class warrants such grand generalizations.

Rodney Stenning Edgecombe believes that archaeological allusions in *Little Dorrit* satirize the cultural and social pretensions of early and mid-Victorian England, thereby "alienating the ordinary" and establishing its similarity to older, superseded civilizations (66). In broad terms, Edgecombe is surely correct, although much of his argument is essentially a rehash of Nancy Aycock Metz's 1990 essay, "Little Dorrit's London: Babylon Revisited" (*VS* 33.465–86), a more sustained examination of the novel's archeological imagery. Edgecombe, whose intelligence and sensitivity shines through much that he writes (four pieces on Dickens this year), is sometimes his own worst enemy: his showy use of foreign phrases (*per impossibile, species aeternitatis*) and obscure words (apotropaic, deictic) often detract from the cogency of his arguments.

In a facile reading, Robert Sirabian accords Flora Finching a self-consistent personality that seems at odds with the ambiguity of her dense and complex voice. For Sirabian, Flora is a fully conscious role-player, with "the freedom to explore other selves that social convention and day-to-day duties prohibit" (217). Role-playing is supposedly Flora's "creative means of self-discovery, of challenging her fixed identity"(217). Sounding like the successful acolyte of some self-help guru, Flora plays "for her own enjoyment" and "to create a new self" (218). Her tippling and the dark shades of her verbal fecundity seem altogether to have eluded Sirabian.

A Tale of Two Cities

A Tale of Two Cities receives separate treatment only once this year, testifying to its current lack of fashion among contemporary critics, though whether the novel is really less prominent in the classroom, as Richard M. Myers asserts, is more open to question. Myers's essay has no evident reason for being, other than that it marks one of a number of "Literary Alternatives to Postmodern Politics," in a volume written almost entirely by people other than professors of literature (Myers is a professor of Political Science). Myers fails to cite any critic later than the mid-1960s and has nothing original to say about *A Tale of Two Cities*. Instead, he passes a few impressionistic judgments and makes points that are either very loose—"it would be silly to fault Dickens for a lack of historical rigor, for he is not writing history" (66) or exceedingly obvious—"The title he actually chose makes much more sense because it suggest a duality or contrast" (69).

Great Expectations

John O. Jordan's "Partings Welded Together: Self-Fashioning in *Great Expectations* and *Jane Eyre*" uses Joe Gargery's observation that "life is made of ever so many partings welded together" as the basis for a fascinating meditation on the significance of partings in the two well-known novels. Partings are gaps and goodbyes, which themselves are anticipations of the "great final parting" of death. But they "are also . . . bits of knowledge, of language, as well as bits of human experience that make up the self" and, as well, "connectors, links in a chain that can bind things and people together" (31). Jordan uses these multiple connotations to show, among many valuable insights, that "goodbyes in *Great Expectations* do not mark the ending of a narrative sequence, as they tend to do in *Jane Eyre*" (27), which leads him to conclude that Dickens "is the great novelist of goodbyes" and Charlotte Brontë "the novelist of muted or understated farewells" (32).

In her fine feminist reading, Hilary Schor tries to extricate Estella from her role in Pip's story of suffering and victimization. For Schor, Pip "remains insufferable to the end of the story" (541), a monomaniac who subsumes Estella into his own masculine narrative, denying her any choice or individuality apart from his own masochistic need for her. As Schor herself observes, this reading is validated by the text itself, for "it is Estella who most often critiques Pip's vision, who points out to him the folly of his obsession . . . " (549). Accordingly, Schor prefers the second ending to the novel because "it gives Estella back her voice," as she asks for a friendship and a separate existence (556).

A very different reading, but equally successful, is Jay Clayton's study of the postmodern incarnations of the "Great Expectations" story. From an Elvis Love Train with "Great Expectations" specials to a *Saturday Night Live* skit called "Great Expectorations" to a hockey show about Wayne Gretzky called "Gretz Expectations," Dickens has been alluded to, parodied, commercialized, and remade. The pastiche and contradiction inherent in such treatments cause Clayton to wonder if Dickens "is perhaps the most postmodern nineteenth-century writer" (611). Especially illuminating is Clayton's comparison between a 1947 comic book version of *Great Expectations*—invested with the *machismo* and grim earnestness of the post-war years—and a self-reflexive and parodic comic book version from 1990. But the postmodernism of the novel is not, Clayton believes, simply a late-twentieth-century invention, for *Great Expectations* "mixes cultural signs from different periods as pervasively and as incongruously as any postmodern text" (621).

Elizabeth Campbell argues that Dickens draws upon early nineteenth-century chapbooks for "the language of fortune" which she finds in *Great Expectations*. So the famous opening scene showing Pip upended by Magwich in the graveyard recalls "The World Turned Upside Down,' a motif traditionally associated with fools' days," but which in the early nineteenth century could be found in such popular works as *The World Turned Upside Down or the Folly of Man Exemplified in Twelve Comical Relations Upon Uncommon Subjects* (154). Campbell's argument is generally persuasive, although perhaps she stretches her point a bit to find a significant correspondence between Pip's accession to wealth and *The History of Fortunatus*. The idea of renewable fortune seems sufficiently general—at least as Campbell presents it—to raise questions about the close parallels between *Great Expectations* and this particular chapbook.

Martine Hennard Dutheil also focuses on language in *Great Expectations,* but from a more theoretically sophisticated point of view. According to Dutheil, Pip learns in the course of his story that words, which as a child he takes "literally at their face value" (168), are elusive and "irreducible to his control" (172). The "difficulties of the interpretive act"—the slippage between signifier and signified—open up opportunities for the reader to play in an "interpretive playground . . . midway between blindness and insight" (172). Although her basic thesis that *Great Expectations* is fundamentally about words—here the reading of words—seems stale at this point, Dutheil's close readings of several passages are sensitive to the nuances of Dickens's prose, and in one instance (Pip's "struggle" through the alphabet in chapter seven), she engages in one of the most insightful "deconstructions" of the year.

Patrice Hannon complains that critics who read *Great Expectations* for plot (she cites Peter Brooks as a notable example) miss out on the humor of style, which often works against plot development. For Hannon, Pip's imaginative rendering of a scene, told by way of circumlocutions and metaphoric repetitions, takes precedent over what is actually present in the scene. Pip "continually imagines alternative realities," Hannon writes, and "spins stories alongside the autobiographical reportage in a voice that is not only charming but indispensably unique in its cadences and its imaginings" (99). The elaborate and fantastic nature of Pip's language is generally lost, she believes, as the story moves forward to its conclusion, a loss which accounts for "a large part of the extraordinary melancholy" of the final scenes (105). Hannon's close attention to the "cadences and . . . imaginings" of Pip's language is welcome indeed, although she never distinguishes Pip's language from the language of that other first-person narrator, David Copperfield, or of Dickens's third-person narrators more generally. One is left wondering, in other words, how "indispensably unique" Pip's language actually is.

Hugh Crago sets himself an imposing task: to draw conclusions based on a study of the ten-year period when, as a boy over forty years ago, he first read *Great Expectations*. Rather predictably, he finds that his reading of other, simpler novels and his own life and family experiences (even unconscious ones) were "crucial" to his understanding of the novel. The major problem is Crago's tendency to speak in reductive terms of cause and effect while at the same time (apparently) eschewing it. "Re-reading renders linear concepts of 'sources and influences' of 'cause and effect,' simplistic," he writes (688). Yet, in practice, he doesn't allow for the complexity of the reading and remembering experience and entertains few doubts about his boyhood reception of *Great Expectations*. Hugh Loftig's *The Voyages of Doctor Dolittle*, he confidently asserts, "linked the themes of feeling 'different' and set apart . . . with the concept of hidden knowledge; [Enid] Blyton's *Five Go to Smuggler's Top* tied the theme of hidden knowledge to the darker family secrets more typical of my mother's line" (6919.

One is left wondering, in a different way, why Michael Tatham's discussion of "The Role of Millwood in *Great Expectations*" was ever published. Tatham finds it "more than a little incredible that a reclusive and half-crazed old woman should apparently have no difficulty in persuading her adopted daughter to forget her natural inclinations and play out an avenging role in her relationships with men" (107). His explanation for this almost "total nonsense"? Miss Havisham and Estella are derived from Millwood, the heartless prostitute of George Lillo's play, *George Barnwell, The History of, or The London Merchant* (1731). Tatham writes as if he were making some entirely original argument, and without any apparent awareness of William Axton's *Circle of Fire* (1966), which long ago explored the connection between *The London Merchant* and *Great Expectations* in much greater detail and with more authority. And Tatham fails altogether to consider any other influences. Worse, when Miss Havisham and Estella refuse to play by his rules, he accuses Dickens of concocting "sheer nonsense" and imagines Lillo's Millwood of laughing at the absurdity. He then blithely advises us of how the plot "should" have developed and confidently asserts in an endnote that "There is no doubt in my mind" that the original ending would have been much better than the one Dickens actually chose (109). There is no doubt in my mind, that Tathum would be well-advised to find someone else to write about for a while.

Our Mutual Friend

Henry James famously complained of the "exhaustion" of Dickens's last complete novel, of its artificial, "intensely written" nature. With a fine ear for linguistic subtleties, Rodney Stenning Edgecombe argues that such "exhaustion" is really a "wholly controlled' technique, consciously employed by Dickens, to reveal the empty phrases and tired formulas underlying mid-Victorian orthodoxies. If Edgecombe's pretentiousness becomes tiresome, his recognition of allusions is impressive, especially since he actually *uses* those allusions to reveal something significant about the deliberately subversive language of Dickens. All too often in Dickens studies, recognition of allusions is either forced or ends where it begins—with the recognition. Symptomatic of this latter problem is Edgecombe's other piece on *Our Mutual Friend*. Having "never found a gloss" for the description of Veneering as "a kind of sufficiently well-looking veiled-prophet" (chapter 2), Edgecombe supplies a very improbable one: Archbishop Whately's characterization of the Tractarians in 1838 as "Veiled Prophets" (from Ezekial 13.17–18 and 21), a name he never used publicly. A much more likely source is Thomas Moore's popular narrative poem, *Lalla Rookh* (1817), in which the evil Mokanna, "The Veiled Prophet of Khorassan," deceives his followers (see Michael Cotsell's *Companion to Our Mutual Friend*).

Mystery of Edwin Drood

Speculation about "the mystery" of Edwin Drood is inevitably a loser's game, although great fun to play notwithstanding. The latest participant is David Parker, the curator of the Dickens House Museum in London, who believes that simple aesthetic considerations demand that Edwin survive Dickens's narrative. To murder Edwin would be to cut off his developing character unnaturally. Both his unacknowledged love for Helena Landless and his youthful folly, Parker believes, would seem to require development and completion. Parker's knowingly unfashionable argument—he draws on Aristotelian concepts of causality and closure—is certainly plausible, although hedged with so many inevitable "ifs" that the Drood game is still on. Gerhard Joseph, more fashionably, shifts the focus from the mystery's solution to the open-ended nature of the narrative and the reader's desire for closure. Joseph, following the lead of such critics as Peter Brooks and Frank Kermode, believes that narrative furnishes a conclusiveness absent in actual life. To fulfill his own desire for conclusion, Joseph reads *Edwin Drood* as if it were complete and as if were, as in fact it was, the last chapter in Dickens's life. For Joseph, "the novel comes to a satisfactory close" since it begins with Jasper's opium dream of compulsiveness in a chapter entitled, "The Dawn," and ends with another opium dream of compulsiveness in a chapter entitled, "The Dawn Again." The ending satisfies in another way as well: Jasper's dream provides "a kind of retrospective allegory on the repetitive nature of Dickens's art and life," for his "career is precisely a series of repetitive acts that mark an aesthetic journey, of doing the same 'fanciful' thing over and over again . . ." (170, 173).

NOTES

1. Nor is Smith entirely accurate. In his chapter on "Dickens and Social Institutions," he evidently confuses administrative reform of 1865 with franchise reform of 1867, two very different types of radicalism. The book also has its share of minor errors, some undoubtedly typographical. So Humphry House becomes "Humphrey," the Reform Association meets in June 1885 not 1855, "Stone" is said to have written *A Dickens Chronology,* and, in the endnotes, *Dickens and Popular Entertainment* seems to lack a writer.

WORKS CITED

Alligham, Philip V. "The Original Illustrations for Dickens's *A Holiday Romance* by John Gilbert, Sol Eytinge and G. G. White, as these appeared in *Our Young Folks, An Illustrated Magazine for Boys and Girls,* Vol. IV." *The Dickensian.* 92 (Spring 1996): 31–43.

Alter, Robert. "Reading Style in Dickens." *Philosophy and Literature* 20 (May 1996): 130–37.

Ard, Patricia M. "Charles Dickens' Stormy Crossing: The Rhetorical Voyage from Letters to *American Notes. Nineteenth Century Prose* 23 (1996): 34–41.

Armstrong, Mary. "Pursuing Perfection: *Dombey and Son,* Female Homoerotic Desire, and the Sentimental Heroine." *Studies in the Novel* 28 (Fall 1996):281–301.

Bean, Andrew D., and Catherine Griffey. "The Samuel Drummond Portrait of Charles Dickens." *The Dickensian* 92 (Spring 1996): 25–30.

Bowen, John. "Performing Business, Training Ghosts: Transcoding *Nickleby. ELH* 63 (1996): 153–75.

Buckley, Jerome H. "Little Nell's Curious Grandfather." *Dickens Studies Annual* 24:81–91.

Campbell, Elizabeth. "*Great Expectations:* Dickens and the Language of Fortune." *Dickens Studies Annual* 24:153–65).

Caponi-Doherty, M. Gabriella. "Charles Dickens and the Italian Risorgimento." *Dickens Quarterly* 13 (September 1996): 151–63).

Carlson, Laurie. "Categorizing *American Notes:* Dickens as New Journalist." *Nineteenth Century Prose* 23 (1996): 25–32.

Clark, Timothy. "Dickens through Blanchot: the nightmare fascination of a world without interiority." *Dickens Refigured: Bodies, desires and other histories.*" Ed. John Schad. Manchester: Manchester UP: 22–38.

Clayton, Jay. "Is Pip Postmodern? Or, Dickens at the End of the Twentieth Century." *Great Expectations.* Ed. Janice Carlisle. Case Studies in Contemporary Criticism. Boston and New York: Bedford Books of St. Martin's Press, 1996.

Connor, Steven. "Babel unbuilding: the anti-archi-rhetoric of *Martin Chuzzlewit.*" *Dickens Refigured: Bodies, desire, and other histories.*" Ed. John Schad. Manchester: Manchester UP:178–99).

Cordery, Gareth. "Furniss, Dickens and Illustrations." *Dickens Quarterly.* Two parts. 13 (March 1996): 34–41 and 13 (June 1996): 98–110.

Cox, Don Richard. " 'Can't You See a Hint?': The Mysterious 'Thirteenth Illustration' to *Edwin Drood.*" *The Dickensian* 92 (Spring 1996): 5–18.

Crago, Hugh. "Prior Expectations of *Great Expectations:* How One Child Learned to Read a Classic." *College English* 58 (October 1996): 676–92.

Cribb, Tim. "Travelling through Time: Transformations of Narrative from Early to Late Dickens." *The Yearbook of English Studies.* 26 (1996): 73–88).

Cronin, Mark. "The Rake, The Writer, and *The Stranger:* Textual Relations between *Pendennis* and *David Copperfield.*" *Dickens Studies Annual* 24:215–40.

Currie, Richard A. "Repressed anger in a family context: Dickens's *Hard Times* as psychological text." Proceedings of the 12th International Conference on Literature and Psychoanalysis: 145–51.

Cusumano, Joseph D. *Transforming Scrooge: Dickens' Blueprints for a Spiritual Awakening.* St. Paul, Minnesota: Llewellyn, 1996.

Dellamora, Richard. "Pure Oliver: or, Representation without agency." *Dickens Refigured: Bodies, desires and other histories.*" Ed. John Schad. Manchester: Manchester UP: 55–79.

Dickens, Charles. *The Amusements of the People and Other Papers: Reports, Essays and Reviews, 1834–51. The Dent Uniform Edition of Dickens' Journalism.* Ed. Michael Slater. Columbus: Ohio State UP.

——— *The Christmas Stories.* Ed. Ruth Glancy. London: Dent. 1996.

——— *Dickens in France: Selected Pieces by Charles Dickens on France and the French.* Brighton: In Print, 1996.

——— *Every Thing in Dickens: Ideas and Subjects discussed by Charles Dickens in His Complete Works. A Topicon.* Compiled and edited by George Newlin. Westport, Connecticut and London: Greenwood, 1996.

——— *Great Expectations.* Ed. Janice Carlisle. Case Studies in Contemporary Criticism series. Boston and New York: Bedford Books of St. Martin's Press, 1996.

——— *Great Expectations.* Ed. Charlotte Mitchell, with introduction by David Trotter. London: Penguin, 1996.

——— *Hard Times.* Ed. Graham Law. Ontario, Canada: Broadview, 1996.

Dickens, David, and Norman M. Jacoby, MD, FRCP. "Charles Dickens's Travelling Medicine Chest." *The Dickensian* 92 (Spring 1996): 19–24.

Drew, John M. L. "Voyages Extraordinaires: Dickens's 'travelling essays' and *The Uncommercial Traveller*" (in two parts). *Dickens Quarterly* 13 (June 1996): 76–96.

Dutheil, Martine Hennard. "*Great Expectations* as reading Lesson." *Dickens Quarterly* 13 (September 1996): 164–74.

Edgecombe, Rodney Stenning, "Patrick White and Dickens: Two Points of Contact." *The Journal of Commonwealth Literature* 31 (1996): 111–14.

——— "Reading through the Past: 'Archaeological' Conceits and Procedures in *Little Dorrit.*" *The Yearbook of English Studies.* Modern Humanities Research Association. 26 (1996): 65–72.

——— " 'The Ring of Cant' " Formuliac Elements in *Our Mutual Friend.*" *Dickens Studies Annual* 24:167–84.

——— "The 'Veiled-prophet' in *Our Mutual Friend.*" *The Dickensian* 92 (Winter 1996): 208–209.

Elam, Diane. " 'Another day done and I'm deeper in debt': *Little Dorrit* and the debt of the everyday." *Dickens Refigured: Bodies, desires and other histories.* Ed. John Schad. Manchester: Manchester UP: 157–77.

Fielding, Kenneth. "*Bleak House* and Dickens' Originals: 'The Romantic Side of Familiar Things.' " *Dickens Studies Annual* 24:119–34.

——— (K. J.). "Dickens and Science?" *Dickens Quarterly* 13 (December 1996): 200–16.

Fasick, Laura. "Dickens and the Diseased Body in *Bleak House.*" *Dickens Studies Annual* 24:135–51.

Gager, Valerie L. *Shakespeare and Dickens: The Dynamics of Influence.* Cambridge: Cambridge UP, 1996.

Ginsburg, Michal Peled. ''The Case Against Plot in 'Bleak House' and 'Our Mutual Friend.' *Economies of Change: Form and Transformation in the Nineteenth-Century Novel.* Stanford: Stanford UP, 1996.

Gomel, Elana. ''The Body of Parts: Dickens and the Poetics of Synecdoche.'' *The Journal of Narrative Techniques* 26 (1996): 48–74.

Gordon, Jan B. ''Dickens and the Political Economy of the Eye.'' *Dickens Studies Annual* 24 (1996): 1–35.

————— '' 'In All Manner of Places, All at Wunst': Writing, Gossip, and the *State* of Information in *Bleak House.'' Gossip and Subversion in Nineteenth-Century British Fiction: Echo's Economies.* Houndsmills: Macmillan Press: New York: St. Martin's Press, 1996.

Grossman, Jonathan H. ''The Absent Jew in Dickens: Narrators in *Oliver Twist, Our Mutual Friend* and *A Christmas Carol.'' Dickens Studies Annual.* 24:37–57.

Hager, Kelly. ''Estranging David Copperfield: Reading the Novel of Divorce.'' *ELH* 63 (1996): 989–1019.

Hall, Donald E. *Fixing Patriarchy: Feminism and Mid-Victorian Novelists.* New York: New York UP, 1996.

Hannon, Patrice. ''The Aesthetics of Humour in *Great Expectations.'' The Dickensian* 92 (Summer 1996): 91–105.

Hemstedt, Geoffrey. ''Inventing Social Identity: *Sketches by Boz.'' Victorian Identities: Social and Cultural Formations in Nineteenth-Century Literature.* Ed. Ruth Robbins and Julian Wolfreys. London: Macmillan Press: New York: St. Martin's Press, 1996. 215–29.

Hollington, Michael *David Copperfield.* Didier Érudition CNED, 1996.

Humphreys, Anne. ''Who's Doing It? Fifteen Years of Work on Victorian Detective Fiction.'' *Dickens Studies Annual* 24:259–74.

Ingham, Patricia. ''Nobody's fault: the scope of the negative in *Little Dorrit.'' Dickens Refigured: Bodies, desires and other histories.* Ed. John Schad. Manchester: Manchester UP: 98–116.

Jacobi, Stephen. ''Influence and Anxiety: Angus Wilson and Charles Dickens.'' *The Dickensian* 92 (Summer 1996): 115–25.

Jadwin, Lisa. '' 'Caricatured, not faithfully rendered': *Bleak House* as a Revision of *Jane Eyre.'' Modern Language Studies* 26 (Spring and Summer 1996): 111–33.

Jordan, John. ''Partings Welded Together: Self-fashioning in *Great Expectations* and *Jane Eyre.'' Dickens Quarterly* 13 (March 1996):19–33.

Joseph, Gerhard. "Who Cares Who Killed Edwin Drood? Or, On the Whole, I'd Rather Be in Philadelphia." *Nineteenth-Century Literature* 51 (September 1996): 161–75.

Lew, Laurie Kane. "Writing Modern Pictures: Illustrating the Real in Ruskin and Dickens." *Studies in the Literary Imagination* 29 (1996): 55–72.

Lubitz, Rita. *Marital Power in Dickens' Fiction.* New York: Peter Lang, 1996.

Lucas, John. "Past and present: *Bleak House* and *A Child's History of England. Dickens Refigured: Bodies, desires and other histories.* Ed. John Schad. Manchester: Manchester UP: 136–56.

Maclean, Robert Simpson. "William Pleater Davidge presents an 'Evening with Charles Dickens': Some Newly Discovered Manuscripts of the First Dickens Reader." *The Dickensian* 92 (Winter 1996): 195–207.

Markels, Julian. "Toward a Marxian Reentry to the Novel." *Narrative* 4 (October 1996): 197–217.

McCarthy, Patrick J. "Claiming Truth: Dickens and *American Notes.*" *Nineteenth-Century Prose* 23 (1996): 1–11.

McCracken-Flesher, Caroline. "The Incorporation of a *Christmas Carol:* A Tale of Seasonal Screening." *Dickens Studies Annual* 24:93–118.

Michie, Helena. "The avuncular and beyond: family (melo) drama in *Nicholas Nickleby.*" *Dickens Refigured: Bodies, desires and other histories.* Ed. John Schad. Manchester: Manchester UP: 80–97.

Miller, J. Hillis. "The topography of jealousy in *Our Mutual Friend.*" *Dickens Refigured: Bodies, desires and other histories.* Ed. John Schad. Manchester: Manchester UP: 218–35.

Moss, Sidney P., and Carolyn J. Moss. *The Charles Dickens-Thomas Powell Vendetta: The Story in Documents.* Troy, N.Y.: Whitson, 1996.

Myers, Richard M. "Politics of Hatred in *A Tale of Two Cities.*" *Poets, Princes, and Private Citizens: Literary Allusions to Postmodern Politics.* Ed. Joseph M. Knippenberg and Peter Augustine Lawler. Lanham, Maryland: Rowman and Littlefield, 1996.

Nayak, Jatindra, and Himansu Mohapatra. "A Comparative Study of Charles Dickens's *Hard Times* and Fakir Mohan Senapati's *Chha Mana Atha Guntha.*" *The International Fiction Review* 22 (1995): 80–88.

Parker, David. "Dickens and the Death of Mary Hogarth." *Dickens Quarterly* 13 (June 1995): 67–75.

————. "Dickens and Van Gogh." *The Dickensian* 92 (Winter 1996): 165–76.

———— "Drood Redux: Mystery and the Art of Fiction." *Dickens Studies Annual* 24:185–95.

Patten, Robert L. *George Cruikshank's Life, Time, and Art: Volume 2:1835–1878.* New Brunswick, New Jersey: Rutgers UP, 1996.

Petrie, Graham. "Dickens in Denmark: four Danish versions of his novels." *Journal of European Studies* 26 (June 1996): 185–93.

Pointer, Michael. *Charles Dickens on Screen: The Film, Television, and Video Adaptations.* The Scarecrow Press: Lanham, MD., and London: 1996.

Pope, Norris. "The Old Curiosity Shop and the New: Dickens and the Age of Machinery." *Dickens Quarterly* 13 (March 1996): 3–18.

Qualls, Barry V. "Recent Dickens Criticism: 1993." *Dickens Studies Annual* 24:275–91.

Rem, Tore. "Melodrama and Parody: A Reading that *Nicholas Nickleby* Requires." *English Studies* 77 (May 1996): 240–54.

Roberts, Adam. "Skimpole, Leigh Hunt, and Dickens's 'Remonstrance'." *The Dickensian* 92 (Winter 1996): 177–86.

Rosenberg, Brian. *Little Dorrit's Shadows: Character and Contradiction in Dickens.* Columbia: University of Missouri Press, 1996.

Roston, Murray. *Victorian Contexts: Literature and the Visual Arts.* New York: New York University Press, 1996.

Royle, Nicholas. "Our Mutual Friend." *Dickens Refigured: Bodies, desires and other histories.* Ed. John Schad. Manchester: Manchester UP: 39–54.

Sasaki, Toru. "Ghosts in *A Christmas Carol:* A Japanese View." *The Dickensian* 92 (Winter 1996): 187–94.

Schad, John. "Dickens's cryptic Church: drawing on *Pictures from Italy.*" *Dickens Refigured: Bodies, desires and other histories.* Ed. John Schad. Manchester: Manchester UP:5–21.

Schor, Hilary. " 'If He Should Turn and Beat Her': Violence, Desire, and the Woman's Story in *Great Expectations.*" *Great Expectations.* Ed. Janice Carlisle. Case Studies in Contemporary Criticism series. Boston and New York: Bedford Books of St. Martin's Press: 541–57.

Sestito, Marisa. "Divided Dickens." *The Yearbook of English Studies* 26 (1996): 34–42.

Sharpe, William. "A Pig Upon the Town: Charles Dickens in New York." *Nineteenth Century Prose* 23 (1996): 12–24.

Shires, Linda M. "Literary careers, death, and the body politics of *David Copperfield.*" *Dickens Refigured: Bodies, desires and other histories.* Ed. John Schad. Manchester: Manchester UP: 117–35.

Sirabian, Robert. "Dickens's Little Dorrit." *The Explicator* 54 (Summer 1996): 216–19.

Small, Helen. "A Pulse of 124: Charles Dickens and a pathology of the mid-Victorian reading public." *The Practice and Representation of Reading in England.* Ed. James Raven, Helen Small, and Naomi Tadmor. Cambridge: Cambridge UP, 1996.

Stevens, David. "Dickens in Eden: The Framing of America in *American Notes.*" *Nineteenth Century Prose* 23 (1996): 43–52.

Tambling, Jeremy. "Dangerous Crossings: Dickens, Digression, and Montage." *The Yearbook of English Studies* 26 (1996): 43–53.

Tatham, Michael. "The Curious Connection: The Role of Millwood in *Great Expectations.*" *The Dickensian* 92 (Summer 1996): 106–09.

Toker, Leona. "*Hard Times* and a Critique of Utopia: A Typological Study." *Narrative* 4 (October 1996): 218–34.

Trotter, David. "Dickens's idle men." *Dickens Refigured: Bodies, desires and other histories.* Ed. John Schad. Manchester: Manchester UP: 200–217.

Tucker, Edward L. "James and Charles Dickens." *The Henry James Review.* 17 (1996): 208–09.

———. "References in Longfellow's *Journals* (1856–1882) to Charles Dickens." *Dickens Studies Annual* 24:197–214.

Wells, Peter. "Kate Perugini: Some Observations Arising from a Drawing by Sir Luke Fildes, R. A." *The Dickensian* 92 (Summer 1996): 111–14.

West, Gilian. "Selwood Terrace: A Note." *The Dickensian* 92 (Winter 1996): 210–11.

Wiley, Margaret. "Mother's Milk and Dombey's Son." *Dickens Quarterly* 13 (December 1996): 217–228.

Wilkes, David. "Dickens, Bakhtin, and the Neopastoral Shepherd in *Oliver Twist.*" *Dickens Studies Annual* 24:59–79.

Wolff, Larry. " 'The Boys are Pickpockets, and the Girl is a Prostitute' ": Gender and Juvenile Criminality in Early Victorian England from *Oliver Twist* to *London Labour.*" *New Literary History* 27 (1996): 227–49.

Wolfreys, Julian. "Dickensian Architextures or, the City and the Ineffable." *Victorian Identities: Social and Cultural Formations in Nineteenth-Century Literature.* Ed. Ruth Robbins and Julian Wolfreys. London: Macmillan Press; New York: St. Martin's Press, 199–214.

Woolford, John. "The Mysteries of Charles Dickens." *Scott Stamp Monthly* 14 (July 1996): 24–25.

Young, Arlene. "Virtue Domesticated: Dickens and the Lower Middle Class." *Victorian Studies* 39 (Summer 1996): 483–511.

Xavier, Andrew. "Charles and Catherine Dickens: Two Fine Portraits by Samuel Laurence." *The Dickensian* 92 (Summer 1996): 85–90.

Index